E-COMMERCE I
BUSINESS MA

C000025715

E-COMMERCE LAW FOR BUSINESS MANAGERS

C Chatterjee LL.M (Cambridge)
LL.M.PL.D (London) Barrister

FINANCIAL
WORLD
Publishing

Financial World Publishing
4–9 Burgate Lane
Canterbury
Kent
CT1 2XJ
United Kingdom

T   01227 812012
F   01227 479641
E   editorial@ifslearning.com

Financial World Publishing publications are published by The Chartered Institute of Bankers, a non-profit making registered educational charity.

Typeset by J&L Composition, Filey, North Yorkshire, YO14 9AH
Printed by Antony Rowe Ltd

© The Chartered Institute of Bankers 2002

ISBN 0-85297-564-3

Contents

Chapter 1

Basic concepts

Chapter 2

International action for the promotion of trade and services by electronic means

Chapter 3

Electronic Communications Act, 2000

Chapter 4

Digital signatures, digital cost payment and the legal status of electronic money

Chapter 5

Concluding contracts over the Internet

Chapter 12

Electronic commerce and some general tax issues

Chapter 13

Jurisdiction

Table of Statutes

European Union Law

87/95/EEC   Council Decision of 22 December 1986 on Standardization in the field of Information Technology and Telecommunications *Official Journal* L 36, 7 February 1987, *Official Journal* L 036, 07/02/1987 at pp. 0031–0037

92/295/EEC   Commission Recommendation of 7 April 1992 on Codes of Practice for the Protection of Consumers in respect of Contracts Negotiated at a Distance (Distance Selling), *Official Journal* L 156, 10/06/1992 at pp 0021–0022

91/250/EEC   Council Directive on the Legal Protection of Computer Programmes, L. 122 of 14 May 1991, *Official Journal* L 122, 17/05/1991 at pp 0042–0046

93/13/EEC   Council Directive of 5 April 1993 on Unfair Terms In Consumer Contracts, *Official Journal* L 95 21 April 1993, *Official Journal* L 095, 21/04/1993 at pp 0029–0034

1994   Council Regulation (EC) No 3381/94 of 19 December 1994 setting up a Community Regime for the Control of Exports of Dual-use Goods, *Official Journal* L 367, 31/12/1994 at pp 0001–0007

95/46/EC   Directive of the European Parliament and of the Council of 24 October 1995 on the Protection of Individuals with regard to the Processing of Personal Data and on the Free Movement of such Data, *Official Journal* L 281, 23/11/1995 at pp 0031–0050

97/7/EC   Directive of the European Parliament and of the Council of 20 May 1997 on the Protection of Consumers in respect of Distant Contracts, *Official Journal* L 144 04/06/1997 at pp 0019–0027

97/13/EC   Directive on a Common Framework for General Authorisations and Individual Licences in the field of Telecommunications Services of 10 April 1997, *Official Journal* L 117, 07/05/1997 at pp 0015–0027

98/34/EC   Directive of the European Parliament and of the Council of 22 June 1998 laying down a Procedure for the Provision of Information in the field of Technical Standards and Regulations, *Official Journal* L 204, 21/07/1998 at pp 0037–0048

1999/93/EC	Community Framework for Electronic Signatures Directive of 13 December 1999, *Official Journal* L 013, 19/01/2000, at pp 0012–0020
2000/31/EC	Directive of the European Parliament and of the Council of 8 June 2000 on Certain Legal Aspects of Information Society Services, in particular Electronic Commerce, in the Internal Market ('Directive on Electronic Commerce'), *Official Journal* L 178, 17/07/2000, at pp 0001–0016
	Directive of the European Parliament and of the Council concerning the Processing of Personal Data and the Protection of Privacy in the Electronic Communications Sector, COM(2000) 385 Final; 2000/0189 (COD) dated 12 July 2000

International Declarations, Conventions, Guidelines and Treaties

1968   Brussels Convention Jurisdiction and Enforcement of Judgments in Civil and Commercial Matters

1973   European Convention

Convention on the Grant of European Patents (European Patent Convention) 5 October 1973

1980   Rome Convention on Contractual Obligations, 1980

1996   WTO Declaration on Trade in Information Technology Products

UNCITRAL Digital Signatures, Certification Authorities

UNCITRAL Model Law for Electronic Commerce

WIPO Copyright Treaty

WIPO Performance and Phonograms Treaty

1997   WTO Agreement on Basic Telecommunications Services

1980   OECD Guidelines on the Protection of Privacy and Transborder Flows of Personal Data

1985   OECD Declaration on Transborder Data Flows

1988   Lugano Convention Jurisdiction and Enforcement of Judgments in Civil and Commercial Matters

1997   OECD Guidelines for the Security of Information Systems, 1992: Review of Implementation, 1997

1999   OECD Consumer Protection Guidelines

Treaty of Amsterdam

Vienna Convention on Contracts for the International Sale of Goods

Treaty on European Union

2000   OECD Model Tax Convention

2001   OECD published its Report entitled 'Tax Treaty Characterisation Issues arising from E-Commerce'

OECD Double Taxation Convention

Table of Cases

Adams v Lindsell [1818] 1 B & Ald 681
A.C. Buildings & Sons Ltd v Rider [1858] A.C. 240
Aikwright v Newbold (1881) 17 Ch. D. at 318
Allied Marine Transport Ltd v Vall do Rio Etc (The Leonidas D) [1985] 1 W.L.R. 925
Amherst v James Walker Goldsmith and Silversmith Ltd [1983] Ch. 305
Amin Rasheed Corporation v Kuwait Insurance Co [1984] A.C. 50
Andrews v Hopkinson [1957] 1 Q.B. 229
Anns v Merton London Borough Council [1978] A.C. 728
Associated Japanese Bank International Ltd v Crédit du Nord SA [1989] 1 W.L.R. 255
Attwood (Inspector of Taxes) v Anduff Car Wash Ltd [1997] S.T.C. 1167
Avnet Inc v Inoact Limited [1998] F.S.R. 16

Banque Keyser Ullman S.A. v Skandia (UK) Insurance Co Ltd [1990] 1 Q.B. 665
Barnes v Irwell Valley Water Board [1939] 1 K.B. 21
Barrow v Scammell (1881) 19 Ch. D. 175
Blacker v Lake and Elliott Ltd (1912) 106 L.T. 533
Beckett v Cohen [1972] 1 W.L.R. 1593
Beckett v Newalls Insulation Co Ltd [1955] 1 W.L.R. 8
Bell v Lever Brothers Ltd [1932] A.C. 161
Beloff v Pressdam Ltd [1973] 1 All E.R. 241
Bennett v Chemical Construction (G.B.) Ltd [1971] 1 W.L.R. 1575
Bigg v Boyd Gibbons Ltd [1971] 1 W.L.R. 913
Blackpool and Fylde Acro Club Ltd v Blackpool B C [1990] 1 W.L.R. 25
Bookmakers Afternoon Greyhound Services Ltd v Wilf Gilbert (Staffordshire) Ltd [1994] F.S.R. 723
Bowerman v Association of British Travel Agents Ltd 1995 N.L.J. 1815
Box v Midland Bank Ltd [1979] 2 Lloyd's Rep 391
Bradley v London Electricity plc [1996] S.T.C. 1054
Briess v Woodley [1954] A.C. 333
Brinkibon Ltd v Stahag Stahl und Stahlwarenhandelsgeselleschaft mbH [1983] 2 A.C. 34
Bristol Tramways Co Ltd v Fiat Motors Ltd [1910] 2 K.B. 841
British Airways Board v Taylor [1976] 1 W.L.R. 13
British Broadcasting Corporation v Talbot Motor Co Ltd [1981] F.S.R. 228
British Insulated and Helsby Cables Limited v Atherton [1926] A.C. 205
British Leyland Motor Corporation Ltd v Armstrong Patents co Ltd [1986] 2 W.L.R. 400
British Medical Association v Marsh (1931) 48 R.P.C. 565
British Oxygen Co Ltd v Liquid Air Ltd (1925) Ch. 383
B R S v Arthur Crutchley Ltd [1968] All E.R. 811
Burroughs v Abbott [1922] Ch. 86
Butler Machine Tool Co Ltd v Ex-Cell-O Corporation (England) Ltd [1979] 1 W.L.R. 401

Other Primary Sources

Benchmarking the Digital Economy www.cabinetoffice.gov.uk/innovation

General Usage for International Digitally Ensured Commerce, the ICC

Guide to Enactment of the UNCITRAL Model Law on Electronic Commerce (1996)

HM Customs and Excise Notice No 703

HM VAT Imports and Warehoused Goods Notice No 702

Inland Revenue's Guidance Manual, entitled 'Capital Allowances', (Machinery and Plant)

Inland Revenue Guidance Manual entitled 'Company Taxation'

Inland Revenue Guidance Manual entitled 'Double Taxation Relief'

Inland Revenue Statement of Practice, SP/90 (9 January 1990)

'Licensing of Trusted Third Parties for the Provision of Encryption Services' (1997)

Law Commission Working PaperNo 110 entitled *Computer Misuse* published in 1988

Law Commission Paper, entitled *Computer Misuse*, Report No 186, cmnd 819 (1989)

OEDC Policy Brief No. 1 (1997), www.oecd.org.publications/Pol.brief/9701–Pol. Htm>

OECD publication entitled 'Dismantling the Barriers to Global Electronic Commerce', 16 October 1997, at p. 3, see http://www.oecd.org

OECD, 'Electronic Commerce: Opportunities and Challenges for Government', Paris (1977)

Official Records of the General Assembly, Fortieth Session, Supplement NO. 17 (A/40/17), Chapter VI, Section B.

Recommendations of the OECD Council concerning:

> Guidelines for the Security of Information Systems dated 26–27 November, 1992, Doc. C(42) 188/Final

Guidelines Governing the Protection of Privacy and Transborder Flows of Personal Data dated 23 September, 1980, Doc. C(80) 58/Final

Guidelines on Cryptography Policy dated 27 March, 1997, Doc. C(97) 62/Final

Ministerial Declaration on Authentication for Electronic Commerce dated 8–9 October, 1998, Doc. C(98) 177 (Annex 3)

Ministerial Declaration on Consumer Protection in the context of Electronic Commerce dated 8–9 October, 1998, Doc. C(98) 177 (Annex 2)

Ministerial Declaration on the Protection of Privacy on Global Networks dated 8–9 October, 1998, Doc. C(98) 177 (Annex 1)

'Promoting Electronic Commerce' (cm 4417), the Department of Trade and Industry, London, The Stationery Office (1999)

Rules for Uniform Domain Name Dispute Resolution Policy adopted by ICANN on 26 August 1991, 39 *International Legal Materials* (2000) 952

Scottish Law Commission, entitled *Report on Computer Crime,* Scot. Law Com. No 106 (cm 174)

'Secure Electronic Commerce Statement', (1998)

'Transfer Pricing Guidelines for Multinational Enterprises and Tax Administrations', Paris, OECD (July, 1995)

UK Government paper entitled 'Electronic Commerce – The UK's Taxation Agenda' HM Treasury Release 173/99 and 175/99

White Paper entitled 'Modernising Government'

White Paper, 'Our Competitive Future: Building the Knowledge Driven Economy', September (1999)

Published Works and Books

Arora, A — *Electronic Banking and the Law* (1993)

Beatson, J — *Anson's Law of Contract* (27th ed, Oxford, Oxford University Press, 1998)

Brindle and Cox (eds) — *Law of Bank Payments* (1999)

Chatterjee, C — *Legal Aspects of Transnational Marketing and Marketing*, (London, Cavendish 1996)

Cheshire, Fifoot and Furmston — *Law of Contract* (13th ed)

Common Law Library — *Chitty on Contracts* (London, Sweet & Maxwell, 1999)

Davies, Paterson and Wilson — *UK GAAP* (London, Macmillan, 1998)

Hickey, J B et al — *E-Commerce: Law, Business and Tax Planning* (Bristol, Jordans, 2000)

Honnold — *Uniform Law for International Sales* (1988)

Murray, Andrew D — 'Entering into Contract Electronically: The Real WWW' in *Law & the Internet: A Framework for Electronic Commerce*, L Edwards & C Waelde (Eds), Oxford, Hart Publishing (2000)

North P M and Fawcett, J J — *Cheshire and North's Private International Law* (London, Buttherworths, 1999)

Oppenheim, L — *International Law*, vol. I (Lauterpacht Ed)

Perry & Ryder — *Thompson's Dictionary of Banking* (London, Pitman) at 333

Reed, C — *Computer Law* (London, Blackstone Press, 1996)

Simon's Direct Tax Service (London, Butterworths) (This is a loose leaf publication)

Articles

Atiyah	(1976) 39 *Modern Law Review* 335
Adams	(1977) 40 *Modern Law Review* 227
Chatterjee, C	'OECD Guidelines for Consumer Protection in the Context of Electronic Commerce', *Financial Crime Review* (2000) at 62
Chatterjee, C and Lefcovitch, A	'Best Efforts may not be Good Enough', *Construction Law,* vol. 11, Issue 3 at 27–29 and vol. 11, Issue 4 at 14–18
Chatterjee, S K	*Legal Aspects of Transnational Marketing and Marketing*, London, Cavendish, (1996) at 58
Chissick and Kelman	*Electronic Commercial Law and Practice* (1999) at 130–131
De Moor, A	'Intention in the Law of Contract: Elusive or Illusory?', 106 *The Law Quarterly Review* (1990) *LQR* 632–655
Finlayson-Brown	'Mondex: Structure of a New Payment System,' (1997) 12 *Journal of International Banking Law*, 362
MacCormick, N	'Beyond Sovereign State', 56 *Modern Law Review* 1–18 (1993)
MacQueen	'Third Party Rights in Contract: English Reform and Scottish Contracts', 1 *ELR* (1997) at 488
Saul Miller	'Payment is an On-line World' in Law and the Internet: A frame work for Electronic Commerce, L Edwards and C Waelde (Eds), Oxford, Hart Publishing (2000).
Vorster, J P	'A Comment on the Meaning of Objectivity in Contract,' 103 *The Law Quarterly Review* (1987) 274–287
Winfield, P	'The History of Negligence in the Law of Torts,' 42 *The Law Quarterly Review* (1926) 184–201

Introduction

Business through electronic means is not a completely new phenomenon; banks in particular have been engaged in electronic transmission of funds, whether within their national boundaries or internationally, for some years. However, recently, the entire business community has become involved in e-Commerce, and its ramifications can now be more clearly perceived than ever before; in fact, they are not only far reaching but some are also disturbing.

E-Commerce has its advantages and disadvantages; whereas its advantages become obvious in carrying out business and transactions, the business community needs to take precautionary measures against its misuse and abuse in order to ensure that the disadvantages of e-Commerce do not outweigh its advantages.

This work aims at familiarizing the reader with the basic issues pertaining to e-Commerce, ranging from contracting to issues relating to tax and intellectual property. The government of the United Kingdom has shown its determination to promote e-Commerce by developing a policy for the near future which has been embodied in its publication entitled Modernising Government.

The European Union has already taken a commendable initiative in promoting e-Commerce and at the same time highlighting the possibilities of abuse and misuse of the use of e-Commerce. Consumer protection has received priority on the EU's agenda on e-Commerce and of course, legislation has been developed in the UK for the protection of consumer interests.

E-Commerce is a branch of business activity, the study of which entails acquiring knowledge in a variety of disciplines, namely business in general, technology and the law. It is not possible to explain in detail all aspects of e-Commerce-related issues in one work. Attempts have therefore been made in this work to identify and analyse some of the important issues relating to e-Commerce. The purpose is not to produce a specialist work, but to familiarize the reader with the general and business issues relating to e-Commerce.

The reader is reminded however that with the advancement of science and technology and as more uses of e-Commerce become manifest, the business community will encounter more abuse of the system. International co-operation for keeping the abuse of e-Commerce under control is essential.

I. Basic concepts

I.I Introduction

Although the use of the Internet is well-established and users are familiar with most of the technical terms related to the use of the Internet and e-Commerce, it is nevertheless found appropriate to define certain basic concepts for avoidance of doubt. Furthermore, unless the basic concepts have been clarified, the legal issue emanating from the use of the Internet and e-Commerce will not be sufficiently clear to the reader.

It is the purpose of this chapter to define these basic concepts hoping that the reader will find them useful: the caveat must be entered, however, that not all technical terms will be included.

I.2 Certain basic concepts

I.2.I What is e-Commerce?

E-Commerce simply stands for commercial transactions or business activities which are conducted by electronic means. Therefore, it may involve the exchange of goods or services, including advice rendered relating to the exchange of goods or services, financial or otherwise, between two or more individuals or legal entities using electronic means.

E-Commerce transactions include acquiring products, goods and services through a website catalogue or downloading computer software by accessing the appropriate website.

The business implications of e-Commerce are profound. According to the Organisation for Economic Co-operation and Development (OECD), E-Commerce will have:

'far-reaching economic and social implications. Current ways of doing business will be profoundly modified.'[1]

When the term 'commerce' is broadly defined under e-Commerce, it may encompass many types of business, whether commercial or otherwise. Thus, on-line service provisions may be brought under this system. In effect, it is for the initiator to determine whether the services it wishes to provide should be on the Internet and once it is on the Internet, e-Commerce is initiated.

E-Commerce does not, therefore, know any geographical bounds. In fact, this is one of its important characteristics. However, trading or introduction of services over the Internet may raise a large number of legal issues, and the most important ones pertaining to e-Commerce have been explained in this work.

1.2.2   The internet

The word Internet stands for inter-working of networks, that is, access to or acquisition of information from other networks with permission to do so. Information cannot be accessed to or transferred from a network unless it has been placed on a website. The Internet cannot, therefore, become functional unless 'input' of information has taken place on a chosen website by the provider of information. In order for the Internet to work the following elements are essential:

- networks;
- choice of website;
- supply of information.

Thus, the more the networks, the better will be the use of the Internet system.

In order to make the system even more sophisticated, national, regional and international networks are being continuously developed and improved so that more information can be accessed to or transferred from one type of network to another—provided compatibility of networks exist.

The capacity to store information on a particular network (the technical term of which is megabytes) becomes an important issue: in other words, the higher the megabytes, the larger is the storage capacity of information. Hence, the fight amongst manufacturers to develop more sophisticated equipment and technology with higher megabytes, and the capacity to store and acquire information as quickly as possible. Once an item of information has been obtained, then that information may be transmitted electronically—e-communication or e-mail.

---

[1] OECD Policy Brief No. 1 (1997), www.oecd.org.publications/Pol.brief/9701–Pol. Htm>

There is no need to explore the historical origins of the Internet but it is safe to say that in the world of defence the use of transmission of information through networks has become popular, particularly since the 1980s.

Although computers on different networks can communicate with each other, it is to be emphasized that each network is separable and separate: hence the legal issue of accessing networks without prior permission remains important. This issue has been further developed in a subsequent chapter. Thus, ownership and control vests in individual computers and networks separately: hence the issue of copyright of information becomes relevant.

1.2.3   Electronic mail (e-mail)

Electronic mail (e-mail) stands for the mailing of information by electronic means. E-mail is simply a way of transmitting the information, whether obtained through the Internet networks or not; but in practice users tend to use both routes in order to save time and money. Furthermore, until another new invention takes over, perhaps in the commercial world e-mail provides the fastest method of providing information from one corner of the world to the other. To a user, e-mail simply involves developing a message, say, in the form of a letter or a report and then transmitting it electronically through computers and networks. Of course, transmission by e-mail cannot take place unless both the sender and the recipient of the message have e-mail facility and an e-mail address.

Although information can be transmitted speedily by e-mail, there is no guarantee that the recipient will read the message promptly.
There are certain disadvantages of transmitting by e-mail:

- if the message is not successfully transmitted owing to mechanical fault, the intended recipient may not be able to contact the sender of the message unless the e-mail address became apparent to the intended recipient;
- by contrast with the system of transmitting messages by facsimile, unless the recipient opens up his computer, he will not be aware that an urgent message is awaiting him.

Of course, these problems should not arise in responsible business houses, as they should be checking their equipment on a regular basis, if not continuously. Therefore, unless notified beforehand, an intended recipient of a message transmitted by e-mail may not be aware of the message instantaneously. The advantages of transmitting messages by e-mail, however, outweigh its disadvantages.

1.2.4   Usenet

Usenet is a facility that provides users with a means of posting information or requesting information in defined areas, that is, defined news or information groups. Usenet is, therefore, a direction to users to use the net—hence the title: but the use of this device is limited to designated computers or news servers. In other words, users may obtain (download) the information, including data from certain designated programmes (usually known as new readers) to access or transmit (post) information, even in the form of digital data. News groups can cover any topic, which may not otherwise be available to the members of the public. Through usenet many closed user groupsmay obtain services from private news servers. This is where legal problems arise: if a news group's activities are considered to be unacceptable, whether for social reasons or otherwise, access to that group may be prohibited, but the new group may contest the censorship or prohibition on the principle of freedom of expression, and currently, under the Human Rights Act 1998.

1.2.5   The world wide web (WWW)

The world wide web is not a network: it represents a descriptive identity code by which a user may be contacted. The world wide web is, therefore, allowed to be chosen by the user itself and an information-seeker may contact the intended information provider through the latter's website. It is through www that businesses may expand worldwide by specifying the goods and services they can supply and at what price or fee. The hypertext transfer protocol (HTTP) is used to access and transfer documents. The same protocol may be used to transfer files in the way similar to the file transfer protocol (FTP). HTTP requires a connection while transmitting data, thus, in transmitting data it needs fewer network resources than many other protocols. HTTP has its inherent advantages, namely, it is small and allows access to HTML pages (Hyper Text Markup Language),[2] in addition to accessing information provided by other protocols, such as FTP and WAIS (the Wide Area Information Services—a document delivery service based on indices of document collections).

Many legal issues may arise from the www system, including whether access to information was gained legally or not. One of the more important issues is whether a provider of information has misrepresented facts or provided information which may be regarded as contrary to the public policy or public morality of the jurisdiction(s) concerned.

1.2.6   Servers and clients

Computers connected to the Internet are often described as servers or clients. A server stands for a programme: the purpose of which is to provide a service to another programme—that is, provide data or information and thus, a computer may be capable of running programmes as servers.

---

[2] It is not a protocol. The client programme, which is popularly known as the browser accesses the server which in turn transmits data. Browsers can read documents in HTML format.

A client, on the other hand, is a programme which accesses and uses a service provided by a server. A client, therefore, obtains, uses or even interacts with a service, but a computer can run both clients and servers. The distinction between a server and a client may be explained in the following way: whereas a programme acts as a server, when it provides a service, a client uses or accesses a service when it provides a service. However, always to be remembered is that a computer can run both servers and clients.

1.2.7   File transfer protocol (FTP)

This is a protocol that provides the facility to transfer data from one computer to another, by a connection between the computers. Any file that is electronically storable may be transferred by using this protocol. Users use an FTP client to access an FTP server, and thereafter the required files. Users can also transfer files to the computer on which the server runs, but they must do so only with the prior permission of the FTP server concerned.

1.2.8   Domain names

Internet Assigned Numbers Authority (IANA) allocates addresses to regional IP (Interact Protocol) registers, and eventually to Internet Service Providers. These IP numbers are in numerical form for each computer linked to the Internet. It is difficult to remember a host of numbers so the idea of creating domain names was developed and names are assigned for each address.

The domain name system is hierarchical. The Top Level Domain Names are of a generic nature or they may be Country Code Level Domain Names. There also exist Second Level Domain Names. Examples of registration under the Generic Domain Name system would be: '.com' (for commercial organisations); '.org' (for non-profit-making organisations); '.net' (for network service providers). As it tends to cover the world/domain of a specific type of business or activity, they are called 'domain names'.

The rules for domain name registration vary from country to country. Whereas some have residency requirement, others register on a 'first come, first served' basis, but restrictions may be imposed by each jurisdiction. Residency requirement is not a condition for registration of a domain name in the UK.

The domain name system may give rise to a variety of legal issues: for example, in making an application for registration, the applicant is required to confirm that the domain name applied for does not affect the rights of a third party, and/or that it is not seeking a domain name for an unlawful purpose. In other words, any application made in bad faith and with misrepresentation of facts will attract legal problems. Furthermore, the owner of a registered trade mark may challenge the choice of a domain name on the ground that the name should not be made available as an identical trademark which already exists.

1.2.9   Linking

'Linking' stands for the facility for navigating the Internet. Currently, there are two types of 'linking': the first is 'hypertext reference linking'; and the second, 'inline linking'. In respect of the first type of linking, a user, when transmitted to another site is retrieved by the user's web browser and a copy of the linked document is displayed on the user's screen. In the case of 'inline linking', images originating at another source come within the viewer's website; thus a command in one document achieves an automatic retrieval of the image.

Although linking seems to be a simple device, it may give rise to legal problems. This device may allow jumping over another site's home page by-passing the site owner's advertising, resulting in a reduction in the potential value of the site,[3] which gives rise to legal issues.

1.2.10   Framing

In 'framing', a framed segment of a third party's site is transmitted (imported) into a local website, in order to allow viewers to look through one site into another. Frames may be used by website owners in order to incorporate the entire websites created by others, and to camouflage them with their own advertising. The purpose is to gain increased exposure for their business.

The legal problems that may arise with regard to framing is that it is often difficult to confirm whether the contents may be attributed to the framed site or to a third party. This problem will relate to unfair competition and/or misappropriation especially because the viewer remains unaware of the source of the material (that it comes from a framed site). He may assume that the material was provided by the owners of the displayed site, in which case an action on the ground of unfair competition may arise. Furthermore, trade marks-related disputes may arise if trade marks on the framed site appear beside the contents of the displayed site.

1.2.11   Metatags

This is a term used by website owners enabling Internet search engines to match a website in order to carry out a search query. This device enables site owners to maximize visits to their sites by using a variety of variables or terms; on the other hand, it also allows users to take undue advantage of others' business. The legal issue remains whether the use of metatags constitutes any infringement of trade marks.[4] One way of avoiding this problem would be to prohibit the use of trade names or trade marks as metatags.

---

[3] See further the US case, *Ticketmaster Corporation v Microsoft Corporation*, No. 97–3055 DDP, C.D. Cal. 12 April 1977 located at www.ljx.com/LJXfiles/ticketmaster.
[4] See the US case, *Playboy Enterprises Inc v Calvin Designer Label*, 44 U.S.P.Q. 2nd 1156 (N.D. Cal 1997).

1.2.12   Cryptography

Cryptography is the science of making/keeping a secret message unintelligible to third parties. It renders two important functions: (a) it maintains confidentiality by keeping the substance of a message secret; and (b) it ensures the authenticity of the sender of a message. The two dimensions to cryptography present a dilemma: whereas the maintenance of confidentiality in sending secret messages is necessary, confidentiality may not be maintained in respect of authenticity; furthermore, these two dimensions of cryptography are not necessarily separable and separate. The system of digital signatures, which entails a complex mathematical procedure, is based on asymmetric cryptography. The principal difference between symmetric and asymmetric cryptography is that in respect of the former, the same key is used to both encrypt and decrypt a message. Asymmetric cryptography has become popular since the 1970s. The importance of asymmetric cryptography in transmitting information may be briefly described in the following way: when the parties on each end are unknown to each other, but are communicating over a network, such as the Internet, they may be unable to share confidential information, such as a key, as a third party may intercept during the transmission of that information. Asymmetric cryptography allows the use of separate keys for encryption and decryption, and each user (the recipient and the sender) creates its own key (a long string of numbers) usually known as a 'private key' and 'public key'. Whereas the private key must remain/be kept strictly confidential and remain known only to the user, the public key may be shared with others without sacrificing security.

In this context, the use of digital signatures should be briefly discussed: the data are created in digital form and signed. A mathematical value (commonly known as 'hash value') is created by the computer. This is, in effect, a 'fingerprint' of the message. If the data changes, the hash value will not function and an 'error message' is created. The signer then encrypts the hash value by using his private key, which is added to the data to be transmitted. After transmission of the data over the Internet, the recipient of the data uses the sender's public key in order to create the hash value and the digital signature, and then compares the latter to the digital signature added to the message. If the result is identical, then the recipient becomes certain that nobody has intercepted the data since it was transmitted. The legal aspects of digital signatures have been discussed in a separate section of this work.

1.3   The scenario

There is no need to emphasize that with the aid of electronic means, business can be global; it is as obvious as it is inevitable. It is only a matter of time until it will be truly global, and with the advance of science, it will have even more manifestations. What is more important is to prepare and take advantage of its various uses, and at the sametime learn how to guard against probable abuses emanating from the mechanism. Preparedness for its appropriate use for progress in business, in whatever form: companies; manufacturing industries;

banks; insurance services etc, will entail learning on the part of users and consumers. As for protecting oneself from its abuses: governmental legislation and ethics in business are vitally important.

Furthermore, protection from abuses of technology on a global scale is a matter for which international co-operation is essential. Implementation of the outcome of such-co-operation is another matter of concern, as it will require;

- the use of appropriate technology;
- dissemination of information;
- keeping users and consumers informed of the latest development in e-Commerce;
- the protection of abuse of e-Commerce by legislation;
- making all concerned more aware of business ethics.

The OECD maintains, however, that:

'Care must be exercised not to over-regulate electronic commerce. In its present embryonic state, overly restrictive regulations could stifle innovation and retard growth. At the same time, measures to promote confidence are needed'.[5]

This view is particularly important for allowing everybody access to the Internet and e-Commerce. Income should not be a factor for allowing or disallowing access to information. Restrictive regulations would, therefore, be a hindrance to the free flow of information and keeping business competitive, thus not serving consumers in a competitive fashion. Furthermore, governments should encourage the development of generic networks, rather than maintaining the 'local loop' system[6] that is part of the public switched telecommunication network (PSTN). Any speedier application of e-Commerce in the current circumstances depends upon how speedily local loops may be utilized and the network capacity increased.

A growing information culture is needed; awareness of the need for information needs to be created and developed. In order to serve an informed society, a new infrastructure is necessary, and this may be achieved largely by a pro-active participation of governments, both in the form of encouragement and as pro e-Commerce legislation. Additionally, investment in the public sector, and, in appropriate cases, in the private sector would be highly desirable.

---

[5] OECD publications entitled 'Dismantling the Barriers to Global Electronic Commerce', dated 16 October 1997, at p 3, see http://www.oecd.org.
[6] Currently, most household or business customers are connected to communication networks via copper wires called the 'local loop'.

One of the crucial components of the Internet routing system is the domain name system (DNS) which creates the root of Internet addresses (.com, .org, .net). The current system allows a de facto monopoly to certain designated DNS registrars but the DNS registrars should be much more liberal, and placed on a *de jure* basis. The World Trade Organisation (WTO) has produced some work and provided certain suggestions on the issue of DNS, which has received attention in a separate chapter of this work.

As stated earlier, business or communication through e-Commerce has its advantages and disadvantages. In order to make e-Commerce popular, consumer trust must be developed through honesty, good faith, ethics and the assurance of remedies in the event of any losses. In other words, the vulnerability of the e-Commerce system must be conquered, and consumer trust in it must be developed. According to the OECD:

> 'This vulnerability can erode trust in electronic transactions. The information infrastructure is an attractive target for thieves, terrorists and pranksters, because when to-day's information systems are compromised, extensive damage can be done in a short time, while the open distributed nature of networks makes it difficult to find the culprits. Moreover, the global interconnection of computer systems has increasingly made security an international problem'.[7]

Furthermore, confidentiality and the integrity of data must be maintained. Encryption raises concerns about undetected criminal activities. Governments are not yet unanimous on the issue of how the problem of crime emanating from encryption may be resolved. There does exist a view that access by third parties to private cryptographic keys might compromize security and erode trust in the system.[8] The security issue also centres around the variety of users of cryptographic keys. Whereas some wish to see only the highest level of security, others would prefer to have what is known as a 'latch' rather than a 'lock' system, and allow a 'spare key' to be preserved in a safe place.[9]

According to the OECD, secure technology, such as cryptography, and a predictable regulatory environment for their operation will form the basis for building business and consumer trust in electronic transactions.[10] Digital signatures and electronic representations for the purpose of linking individuals and entities would be less meaningful if not accompanied by a certification mechanism whereby information about transactions and transacting parties would be independently verified. In order to implement this mechanism, the OECD recommended the setting up of a certification authority, which would act

---

[7] op cit, at 5.
[8] op cit, at 6; see also OECD, *Electronic Commerce: Opportunities and Challenges for Government*, Paris (197
[9] ibid.
[10] ibid.

independently in determining the factual information as to a transacting party. The OECD further maintains that different kinds of transactions may require verification of all kinds of information.[11] Of course, in establishing a certification, the responsibilities and liabilities of entities which certify information should be clarified, in addition to making provisions for or taking measures against protection of privacy. In fact, assurances about protection of consumer privacy are important for building consumer confidence. Undue intrusion of privacy may be counter-productive in building consumer confidence in e-Commerce. Therefore, the issue of how to strike a balance between protection of privacy and deriving benefits from e-Commerce becomes an important issue. Not much research has yet been done on this issue. According to OECD, a dialogue between the public and private sectors would be useful to determine which businesses must have on-line privacy, to educate the public about these issues, and to develop technological societies.[12] A degree of self-regulation is necessary.

Commerce/business by electronic means is extremely attractive to customers and business entities and both parties need protection from abuse of technology—the consequential effects of which may be far-reaching. The OECD recommendations on consumer protection have already received attention in a separate section of this work.[13] However, it is to be emphasized that the protection of businesses is also an equally important issue, and this issue may only be tackled by two means: legislation and business ethics. Governments should develop legislation which will have two principal dimensions: promotion of e-Commerce with the help of legislation; and prevention of illicit business or abuse of e-Commerce. The third important dimension of e-Commerce legislation is the provision for the training of legitimate businessmen and consumers to protect themselves from abuse of the mechanism. It is important to emphasize that the effect of abuse of this mechanism does not outweigh the advantages that it may bring to the world of industry and commerce.

Attempts at unduly influencing the decision-making process of customers may be made by dishonest business people through e-mail or the Internet using the mechanism of what is known as the mail shot. This practice may have two important dimensions: (a) unsolicited mail shots may provide many alternatives to prospective buyers; and (b) dishonest business people may misrepresent their products and services with a view to unduly influencing the decision-making process of customers. The OECD recommends that uncertainty as to regulatory measures should be minimized in order to allow businesses and individuals to know in certain terms what type(s) of action, regulatory or otherwise, may be taken by governments. In other words, governments are required to take appropriate and effective measures, regulatory or otherwise, in advance, in order to inform businesses and consumers of what protective measures they should take and what remedies may be made available to them and in what circumstances.

[11] ibid.
[12] op cit, at 8.
[13] Chapter 9.

Although the OECD recommended issuance of certificates by certification authorities as a preventative measure against abuse (whereby a certification authority would inform the seller and the buyer of the jurisdiction applicable to that transaction) it also had reservations about the effectiveness of this system. According to the OECD:

> 'While potentially feasible, there is some question about the practicality of such solutions. They could place a large administrative burden on merchants to calculate, collect and transfer taxes on what often are low-value, high volume products'.[14]

Intellectual property rights are crucial to the development of electronic commerce because information has intellectual contents; thus such rights need to be protected.[15] Duplication of means or similar technology has become a common phenomenon, and such acts breach intellectual property rights. Through TRIPS (Trade Related Aspects of Intellectual Property Rights) and the recent WTO agreements on intellectual property rights and in view of the continuing scientific advancement, governments are required to adopt appropriate and effective legislation promptly. In addition to taking such measures, the OECD rightly pointed out that:

> 'Electronic commerce calls for an evaluation and updating of the commercial codes that govern business transactions. Unless these codes incorporate the digital world, e-commerce will be hampered. The situation is complicated by the inconsistency of codes among countries, many of which are a reflection of culture norms. International harmonisation of these laws will require drafting a model law for commercial practices at international level which can serve as a common framework'.[16]

According to the OECD, the issues which should be addressed at a minimum are:

- legal recognition of electronic signatures;
- acceptance of electronic documents for paper filing requirements;
- the formation, validity and enforcement of contracts;
- the harmonization of rules that govern commercial communications (eg advertising, direct marketing)
- commercial pricing practices.[17]

The responsibility of each participant in the chain-service providers, software developers, intermediaries, consumers etc should be clearly defined.

---

[14] OECD, op cit, at 11.
[15] The intellectual contents of information are often referred to as GII-GIS—Global Information Infrastructure-Global Information Society.
[16] OECD, op cit, at 12.
[17] ibid.

Logistical problems relating to payment and delivery must be overcome. As the OECD suggests, prompt and low-cost distribution channels are needed for delivery of goods, just as they are needed in respect of electronic payments. The OECD summed up the importance of this issue in the following passage:

> 'given the embryonic state of the market and the experimentation now taking place, a cautious approach to government intervention appears appropriate among other things to ensure that any *de facto* standard that emerges is open so that interoperability is achieved and digital anarchy avoided'.[18]

The cost of international parcel delivery is significantly high and time-consuming primarily because of administrative formalities that governments are required to satisfy, including customs clearance procedures. The OECD suggests a 'one-stop shopping' procedure whereby a merchant will collect all taxes, duties and delivery charges from the consumer when the goods are ordered and periodically pay them directly to the importing country concerned. The OECD maintains that:

> 'Such a system (one-stop shopping combined with pre clearance of shipments and the replacement of all paperwork by electronic data interchange (EDI), can make borders effectively transparent and greatly reduce the costs, delays and frustrations currently associated with international parcel delivery'.[19]

In view of the varying degrees of capabilities and resources, no uniform practice in regard to the proposals put forward by the OECD may be anticipated in the near future, although it must be maintained that the proposal is a workable one.

Nevertheless, it must be pointed out that many countries may not welcome the idea of reducing customs duties on imported goods. Of course, the proposal for reduction of customs duties has no relevance to the Members of the European Union. The other issues are of course how best parcel industry costs can be reduced, and how customs duties should be collected on intangible products delivered by electronic means. By the same token, it may be stated that e-Commerce is still in its infancy given that much scientific advancement is clearly anticipated in this area of technology based trade and commerce. Whereas early development of legislation would seem to be helpful in order to regulate e-Commerce, on the other hand, many countries may not be able to amend their legislation speedily enough to cope with the advancement of science and technology. In other words, disparate capacity will remain responsible for a non-uniform participation of states in trade and commerce operated by electronic means.

---

[18] op cit, at 13.
[19] ibid.

It is also considered whether the business of e-Commerce should be entrusted to the private sector in all economies, as in developing countries a significant level of governmental control over this type of business, at least initially, seems to be inevitable. The self-regulatory mechanism may not necessarily be an effective way to protect consumers from the abuses of e-Commerce. What is most obviously needed is a truly international convention regulating the conduct of individuals and business entities at both domestic and transnational levels.

In this connection, mention should be made of the instruments and model laws that various international and inter-governmental bodies have already adopted in relation to e-Commerce:

1. WTO Declaration on Trade in Information Technology Products, 1996.
2. UNCITRAL Digital Signatures, Certification Authorities, 1996. UNCITRAL Model Law for Electronic Commerce, 1996.
3. WIPO Copyright Treaty, 1996.
4. WIPO Performance and Phonograms Treaty, 1996.
5. WTO Agreement on Basic Telecommunications Services, 1997.
6. OECD Guidelines on the Protection of Privacy and Transborder Flows of Personal Data, 1980.
7. OECD Declaration on Transborder Data Flows, 1985.
8. OECD Guidelines for the Security of Information Systems, 1992: Review of Implementation, 1997.
9. OECD Consumer Protection Guidelines, 1999.

OECD's guidelines and recommendations are primarily addressed to its own members—developed countries—, whereas the guidelines and recommendations adopted by the UN organization are addressed to all its member states, be they developed or developing countries. This is unless any particular resolution, declaration or guidelines need to be specifically addressed to a particular class of countries. As stated earlier, although the development of guidelines and conventions is essential, technical assistance is often necessary to ensure their implementation, particularly in developing countries.

1.4   The role of third parties in electronic commerce

The uses and the potential of e-Commerce in business have already been identified. While technology based e-Commerce can be regarded as a remarkable means of communication by the commercial community, its abuses may be phenomenal. In the process of abuse all the basic elements and items may be used: cryptographic keys, digital signatures, digital certificates, and the users.

As explained above, a public key cryptosystem is one in which messages encrypted with one key can be decrypted with a second key and vice versa. In this mechanism, although anybody may use the public key for sending messages, it is only the private key owner who can read them. A private key may only be used by the owner for sending messages. By using a public key cryptograph it is possible that a secure line of communication may be established with anyone who may be using a compatible decryption programme or any similar device. So, an individual wishing to communicate to a stranger can exchange the text of their public keys.

It is to be pointed out that those two users can encrypt their outgoing messages with the other's public key and decrypt the messages they receive with their secret private key. Of course, there will be no security if the private key belonging to either of them is transmitted to a third party. In this process nobody can assure the parties that the e-mail message was not sent to a party by a third party who had access to the number. Thus, in the absence of any independent confirmation, the receiver of a message is in no position to know whether the message really came from the genuine remitter unless a mutually known clue is provided. In order to avoid any abuse in this process, a third party registry of public keys may be useful, provided of course a fool-proof system of accuracy/authorization is adopted. The world wide web system may not provide any remedy in this situation either, as web pages and web addresses may be hacked, and messages intercepted and replaced by an attacker's messages. Unless an advanced scientific device is introduced to tackle this problem of how the genuineness of messages and senders' and receivers' identities may be confirmed, abuse of cryptographic keys will remain unabated.

In so far as digital signatures are concerned it has been explained that a digital signature encrypted with a private key identifies the sender of a message and connects it to the exact message; the precise time at which the message was sent may also be recorded. The user's public key can verify the signature. Under this system, if the message is altered in the slightest way, the signature will not decrypt properly, indicating that the message was intercepted or altered during transit or that the signature was forged by copying it from a different message. Herein lies the insecurity about digital signatures. Acquisition of public keys from third parties or access to such keys by illicit means defeats the purpose of using digital signatures.

Digital Certificates
A digital certificate, which is a computer-based record, should ideally be signed by a central authority (or a certification authority), a neutral third party, which may be a public or private body, confirming certain information, such as whether a key actually belongs to a person who has used it. There is no reason why there may not be more than one confirming authority in a country provided they operate on the same basis and follow the same procedures and standards. When business is technology based, the business world needs to take precautionary measures against fraudsters or those who may abuse technology for illicit gains. These are the days of technology on technology. There may not be any certain method of preventing fraudsters from abusing the e-Commerce

system; one is, therefore, required to take as many precautions as possible to protect one's own position.

1.5   Conclusions

As stated earlier, it is not possible, nor advisable to attempt an exhaustive list of all technical terms relevant to e-Commerce. The terms which have been explained in this chapter are regarded as the most important ones for the purpose of understanding the legal issues relative to them. Other terms have been explained in the form of footnotes, where relevant.

Lawyers and students need to consider the legal aspects of e-Commerce through the use of the Internet. One should not be solely concerned with the adverse effect of e-Commerce, as through the use of the Internet businesses may attract significant benefits, while on the other hand, all businesses will be subject to severe competition. The e-mail system can save costs and time, and product and service publicity can be distributed worldwide within a short period of time. Lawyers and students of law can particularly benefit from the use of the Internet in obtaining the most up-to-date information on cases and legislation. In the UK since 1996, House of Lords judgments, new statutes and statutory instruments have been made available free of charge on the Internet. Because of the vast scope for the use of the Internet, business through e-Commerce has unlimited expansion possibilities, provided of course business houses seize the opportunity and enrich their resources—human, technological or otherwise.

2. International action for the promotion of trade and services by electronic means

2.1 Introduction

International action for the promotion of trade and commerce, including services, took a concrete form during the 1980s. The advancement of technology, particularly in the field of computing, prompted the international community to promote international business in all its forms by electronic means. To this end, various fora, truly international (the UN), inter-governmental (OECD), and the International Chamber of Commerce (ICC), in particular, were utilized. Each of these institutions has developed its ideas and guidelines in respect of e-Commerce. However, each of these institutions has also identified the scope of abuses of e-Commerce in international trade and commerce. Whereas the business community is primarily interested in globalising business and commerce and related services by technological means, it fell primarily on these organizations to highlight the uses and abuses of doing business and trading through electronic means.

It is the purpose of this chapter to examine the guidelines and recommendations which have been developed by these institutions, and to evaluate their contribution to promoting business and commerce by electronic means.

2.2 UNCITRAL Model Law on electronic commerce[1]

As long ago as 1985, the UN General Assembly called upon governments and international organizations[2] to take action for ensuring legal security in relation to the use of automated data processing in international trade. In 1996, UNCITRAL (the UN Commission on International Trade Law) drafted the Model Law on Electronic Commerce in the belief that the adoption of this law would

---

[1] This Model Law was adopted by the UN General Assembly Resolution NO. 15/162 on 16 December 1996.
[2] See *Official Records of the General Assembly*, Fortieth Session, Supplement NO. 17 (A/40/17), Chapter VI, Section B.

assist all States, are primarily the member states of the United Nations, when they may enact or revise their laws. In order to assist the member states, a guide has also been developed by UNCITRAL.

It is to be pointed out however that the Model Law is not binding—it is recommendatory. Although its contents are, in principle, acceptable, the State concerned must have the resources to implement it.

2.2.1   An analysis of the model law

The Model Law has been developed in two parts: Part I relates to electronic commerce in general; Part II deals with electronic commerce in specific areas. Four chapters are included in Part I: chapter I: General Provisions; chapter II: Application of Legal Requirements to Data Messages; and chapter III: Communication of Data Messages. Part II is devoted primarily to transportation and documentation in regard to international carriage of goods. The principal aspects of these provisions are now discussed.

2.2.1.1   General provisions

Under General Provisions the following have been included: Article I (sphere of application); Article 2 (definitions); Article 3 (interpretations); and Article 4 (variation by agreement). The sphere of application under Model Law is wide. This law applies to any kind of information in the form of a data message in commercial activity. The Model Law maintains that the term 'commercial' should be given a wide interpretation in order 'to cover matters arising from all relationships of a commercial nature, whether contractual or not'.[3] The term 'relationships of a commercial nature' includes any transaction of a commercial nature, be it supply or exchange of goods or services, distribution agreement, licensing, franchising, construction of works, leasing etc.

Article 2 provides definitions of the following terms in the context of the Model Law: data, message, electronic data interchange, originator, addressee, intermediary, and information system. According to the Model Law, 'data message' should not be limited to electronic data interchange (EDI), electronic mail, telegram or telex, but would also stand for 'information generated, sent, received or stored by electronic, optical or similar means'.[4] Therefore, in order for a message to qualify as a 'data message' it need not to be transmitted—it is the means of creating such a message that matters. Electronic data interchange (EDI) means the electronic transfer of information from computer to computer using an agreed standard 'originator' of data means 'a person by whom or on whose behalf the data message purports to have been sent or generated prior to storage', but it excludes persons acting as intermediaries for the purpose; an

---

[3] See the definition provided by the Model Law.
[4] Art 2.

'addressee' of a data message stands for a person 'who is intended by the originator to receive the data message', but excludes intermediaries; an 'intermediary' with regard to a particular data message means' a person who, on behalf of
another person sends, receives or stores that data message or provides other
services with respect to that data message'; 'information system' means 'a system for generating, sending, receiving, storing or otherwise processing data messages' These are standard definitions of such terms, and are clear in their
meaning.

In the light of its purposes, the Model Law clearly states in Article 3 that in
interpreting this Law, regard must be paid to its international origin and the
need to promote uniformity in its application. Furthermore, this Law is to be
interpreted in good faith. The Model Law also provides that:

> 'Questions concerning matters governed by this Law which are not
> expressly settled in it are to be settled in conformity with the general prin-
> ciples on which this Law is based'.

It should be mentioned that the Model Law has not defined the 'general principles' but it is perceived that it refers to its objectives. Article 4 provides that
the provisions of chapter III (communication of data messages) may be varied by agreement: this is because the mechanism of communication between
parties may be arranged or settled by the parties themselves. From a legal
standpoint, if communication by electronic means is to be regarded as a bilateral or multilateral activity, then there is no reason to assume that parties
may not vary the provisions of a contractual arrangement between themselves provided the principle of *ad idem* (two minds have met) has been satisfied. The provisions of chapter II are mandatory, that is, they set the
minimum requirements for a party to observe, unless otherwise agreed to by
themselves.

2.2.1.2   Application of legal requirements to data messages

Chapter II of the Model Law entitled Application of Legal Requirements to
Data Messages consists of the following articles: Article 5 (legal recognition of
data messages); Article 5 bis (incorporation by reference); Article 6 (writing);
Article 7 (signature); Article 8 (original); Article 9 (admissibility and evidential
weight of data messages); and Article 10 (retention of data messages). The
Model Law expressly states in Article 5 that no information shall be denied legal
effect on the grounds that it is in the form of a data message. In other words,
Article 5 confers a legal status on information produced in the form of a data
message. The effect of Article 5 bis, legal or otherwise, has been explained in a
separate chapter of this work.

According to Article 6 of the Model Law, a data message meets the requirements in law for information to be in writing so as to be usable for subsequent
references. The requirement of a signature under a legal system in relation to a
data message is met if the identity of that person is confirmed by approved

methods, and that person has approved the information contained in the data message; and that the method is reliable and appropriate for the purpose for which the data message was generated or communicated.[5]

It is provided by UNCITRAL Model Law that if a jurisdiction requires information to be presented or retained in its original form, that requirement will be met by the data message if: (a) the genuineness of the information is assumed since it was first generated in its final form; and (b) that the information is capable of being displayed to the person concerned. Of course, the criteria for assessing the integrity of a data message would be whether it has remained unaltered unless changes were necessitated by endorsement or storage, and 'the standard of reliability required shall be assessed in the light of the purpose for which the information was generated'.[6]

Admissibility of a data message as evidence in any legal proceedings may not be denied. Of course, in assessing the evidential weight of a data message, regard shall be had to 'the reliability of the manner in which the data message was generated, stored or communicated',[7] and to the reliability of the manner in which, in particular, the integrity of the information was maintained, or to the manner in which its originator was identified.

The legal requirements for the retention of data messages may be satisfied if:

- the information obtained therein is accessible and usable for subsequent references;
- the data message is retained in its original format;
- such information is retained in a way which enables identification of its origin, and its destination, including the date and time when it was sent or received. UNCITRAL Model Law maintains that:

'An obligation to retain documents, records or information in accordance with paragraph 1[8] does not extend to any information the sole purpose of which is to enable the message to be sent or received'.[9]

2.2.1.3 Communication of data messages

Chapter III of the Model Law, entitled 'Communication of Data Messages' consists of seven Articles: Article 11 (formation and validity of contracts); Article 12 (recognition by parties of data messages); Article 13 (attribution of data messages); Article 14 (acknowledgement of receipt); Article 15 (time and place of dispatch and receipt of data messages); Article 16 (articles related to

---

[5] Art 7.
[6] Art 8(3).
[7] Art 9(2).
[8] This provision has already been discussed above.
[9] Art 10(2).

contracts of carriage of goods); and Article 17 (transport documents). These Articles will now be analysed.

Under UNCITRAL Model Law, unless otherwise agreed by the parties, two important elements of a contract, offer and acceptance, may be expressed by means of data messages, and where a data message is used in the formation of a contract, that contract may not be denied any validity or enforceability, if it is otherwise valid or enforceable (Art 11). The phrase 'unless otherwise agreed by the parties' maintains the party autonomy rule in the law of contract, which is a universally recognized rule. UNCITRAL Model Law allows parties to specify the circumstances in which the provisions of Article 11 may not apply.

In order to achieve mutual recognition, UNCITRAL Model Law suggests that there should be a declaration of will or other statement between the originator and the addressee of a data message, stating the legal effect, validity or enforceability of a data message. A party may, under the Model Law, limit or restrict the application of the provisions of this Article to whatever circumstance it may determine.

As regards attribution of data messages (Art 13) the Model Law states that a data message must be attributed to the originator of the message if it was sent by such. A data message is deemed to be that of the originator if it was sent: (a) by a person duly authorized on behalf of the originator; and (b) by an information system programmed by or on behalf of the originator.

An addressee is entitled to regard a data message as being that of the originator, and may act on that assumption if: (a) the addressee appropriately applied a process previously agreed to by the originator, for the purpose of ascertaining whether the data message was that of the originator; or (b) the receipt of the data message by the addressee resulted from the actions of a person whose relationship with the originator or his agent enabled that person to gain access to a method used by the originator for the purposes of identifying the origins of the data message. However, this provision does not apply: (a) as of the time when the addressee received the notice from the originator to the effect that the data message is not that of the originator; or (b) at any time when the addressee knew or that the data message was not that of the originator.

When a data message is or is deemed to be that of an originator, or the addressee is entitled to act on that assumption, then the addressee is entitled to regard the data message as one which was intended to be sent by the originator, and to act on that assumption. The addressee is entitled to regard each data message as a separate one, and to act on that assumption unless a data message is a duplicate.

The issue of whether any acknowledgement should be given in any particular form or by any particular method is a matter between the originator and the addressee. Otherwise, an acknowledgement may be given by a communication, automated or otherwise by the addressee or by any conduct of the addressee which would be sufficient to indicate to the originator that the data message has been received. Where however, sending of a data message is conditional upon receipt of an acknowledgement, that condition must be satisfied, otherwise the assumption will remain that the data message was never sent.

Where the originator has not indicated that the data message is conditional upon receipt of the acknowledgement, and no acknowledgement has been received by the originator by the stipulated time, if such time was agreed, and if not, within a reasonable period of time, the originator: (a) may give notice to the addressee confirming that no acknowledgement must be received; and (b) if the acknowledgement is still not received, may, upon notice to the addressee, treat the data message as one which was never sent or exercise any other rights it may have. It is not clear however what 'other rights' the originator may exercise in this respect; presumably, a warning that the data message must not be exploited in any way. Where, in acknowledging the data message, an addressee merely states that it met technical requirements, it may be presumed that the applicable standards have been met.

Article 15 (time and place of dispatch and receipt of message) offers an extremely important guideline as to the time and place of dispatch and receipt of data messages. Paragraph 1 of this Article provides that:

'Unless otherwise agreed between the originator and the addressee, the dispatch of a data message occurs when it enters an information system outside the control of the originator or of the person who sent the data message on behalf of the originator'.

The crucial phrase is 'outside the control of the originator or of the person who sent the data message'. Again, the party autonomy rule has been maintained by using the phrase 'unless otherwise agreed between the originator and the addressee'. UNCITRAL Model Law offers the following guidelines as to the time of receipt of a data message—unless otherwise agreed between the originator and the addressee:

    (a)   if the addressee designates an information system for the purpose of receiving data messages, receipt occurs:
        (i)   'at the time when the data message enters the designated information system;
        (ii) if the data message is sent to an information system of the addressee that is not the designated system, at the time when the data message is retrieved by the addressee; and
    (b)   if the addressee has not designated an information system, receipt occurs when the data message enters an information system of the addressee.'[10]

---

[10] Art 15(2).

These provisions apply even if the place where the information system is located is different from the place where the data message is deemed to have been received. Paragraph 4 of Article 15 clarifies the position: a data message is deemed to be dispatched at the place where the originator has its place of business, and is deemed to be received 'at the place where the addressee has its place of business'.[11] If the originator has more than one place of business, then 'the place of business is that which has the closest relationship to the underlying transaction or where there is no underlying transaction, the principal place of business'.[12] Reference is to be made to the habitual residence, where the originator or the addressee does not have a place of business. Under the Model Law, parties have the right to indicate to what matters these provisions may not apply. The provisions of Article 15 seem to be extremely logical.

Part II of chapter II deals with two specific issues: actions relating to contracts of carriage of goods (Art 16); and transport documents (Art 17). These provisions are now discussed. Article 16 applies to any action arising under a contract of carriage of goods, including but not limited to:

(a) (i)   furnishing the marks, number, quantity or weight of goods;
    (ii) stating or declaring the nature or value of goods;
    (iii) issuing a receipt for goods;
    (iv) confirming that goods have been loaded;
(b) (i)   notifying a person of terms and conditions of the contract;
    (ii) giving instructions to a carrier;
(c) (i)   claiming delivery of goods;
    (ii) authorizing release of goods;
    (iii) giving notice of loss of, or damage to, goods;
(d) giving any other notice or statement in connection with the performance of the contract;
(e) undertaking to deliver goods to a named person or a person authorized to claim delivery;
(f) granting, acquiring, renouncing, surrendering, transferring or negotiating rights in goods;
(g) acquiring or transferring rights and obligations under the contract.' (Art 16)

Where the law requires that any matter referred to in Article 16 be carried out in writing or by using a paper document, that requirement may be met by using data messages, and the legal consequences for failure to use a paper document may be applied to failure to use data messages, where the latter has replaced the former. By the same token, legal obligation emanating from transmission of paper documents in respect of transportation of goods across boundaries will be attributed to the transferor when the means of transfer is data messages. On

---

[11] Art 15(4).
[12] Art 15(4)(a).

the other hand, where the mode of transfer, whether by document or by data messages, must be arranged by the parties beforehand, 'replacement of data messages by paper documents shall not affect the rights and obligations of parties involved' (Art 17(5)). Paragraph 6 of Article 17 provides that:

'If a rule of law is compulsorily applicable to a contract of goods which is in, or is evidenced by, a paper document, that rule shall not be inapplicable to such a contract of carriage of goods which is evidenced by one or more data messages by reason of the fact that the contract is evidenced by such data message or messages instead of by a paper document'.

It is for the contracting parties to determine matters to which the provisions of Article 17 shall not apply.

2.3 Recommendations of the OECD Council concerning guidelines for protection in the context of electronic commerce[13]

2.3.1 Introduction

According to the OECD a global approach to consumer protection is necessary, and disparate national policies may hinder the growth of electronic commerce; thus consumer protection issues may be addressed through international consultation and co-operation.

In April 1998, the OECD Committee on Consumer Policy initiated the development of general guidelines to protect consumers participating in electronic commerce. The purpose of the guidelines was to provide a framework and a set of guiding principles to assist:

(a) governments belonging to OECD in reviewing, formulating and implementing policies and law for effective consumer protection in relation to electronic commerce;

(b) consumer groups and business associations by providing guidance as to what is required for effective consumer protection, and the views of which should be considered in reviewing, formulating and implementing self-regulatory schemes in the context of electronic commerce; and

(c) to provide clear guidance to businesses and consumers engaged in electronic commerce as to the core characteristics of fair business practice, including the need for disclosure of information.

It is to be noted that the primary emphasis in this recommendation is on consumer protection which has two dimensions: (a) to make consumers aware of

---

[13] The text of the recommendations has been published in 39 *International Legal Materials* (2000) 504.

the kind of protection they need; and (b) to make business enterprises aware of what they are not supposed to do, in order to protect the interests of consumers.

OECD aims at implementing the Guidelines:

> 'in a manner that encourages the development of new business models and technology applications that benefit consumers and encourage consumers to take advantage of all tools available to strengthen their position as buyers.'[14]

In this respect UNCITRAL Model Law and the OECD Guidelines share common objectives.

2.3.2   Background to the guidelines

The electronic commerce system assists buyers and sellers respectively to buy and sell goods from a variety of sources at a competitive price. Sale by electronic means is primarily what is known in law as sale by description, which process must satisfy certain criteria to protect consumers from misleading description of goods or non-disclosure of the quality and characteristics of goods. In this respect the OECD Guidelines for Consumer Protection in the context of electronic commerce is significant and timely. The Guidelines are based on the belief that the electronic marketplace will require a global approach to consumer protection, as individual countries may not have the appropriate resources and capacity to cope with the challenges of the global network environment.[15] In view of the disparate national policies as to the reception of the e-Commerce mechanism and the capacity to take preventative measures against abuse of e-Commerce, an internationally agreed approach to deal with e-Commerce related issue is essential. The OECD member countries are required to review their existing consumer protection laws and practices to take account of the aspects of electronic commerce, and derive benefits from each other's experience.

It was in April 1998 that the OECD Committee on Consumer Policy took the initiative to develop a set of guidelines to protect consumers participating in electronic commerce, which provide a framework and a set of principles to assist:

'(i)   Governments in reviewing, formulating and implementing consumer and law enforcement policies, practices and regulations if necessary for effective consumer protection in the context of electronic commerce;

---

[14] The text of the recommendations, op cit, at 506.
[15] See further C Chatterjee, 'OECD Guidelines for Consumer Protection in the Context of Electronic Commerce', *Financial Crime Review* (2000) at 62.

(ii)   Business associations, consumer groups and self-regulatory bodies, by providing guidance as to the core characteristics of effective consumer protection that should be considered in reviewing, formulating and implementing self-regulatory schemes in the context of electronic commerce; and

(iii)   Individual businesses and consumers engaged in electronic commerce, by providing clear guidance as to the core characteristics of information and fair business practices that business should provide and consumers should expect in the context of electronic commerce.'[16]

The OECD Council also adopted the following and referred to them in developing the Guidelines:

1.   Recommendation of the Council concerning Guidelines Governing the Protection of Privacy and Transborder Flows of Personal Data dated 23 September 1980[17];

2.   Recommendation of the Council concerning Guidelines for the Security of Information Systems dated 26–27 November 1992[18];

3.   OECD Recommendation concerning Guidelines on Cryptography Policy dated 27 March 1997[19];

4.   Ministerial Declaration on Consumer Protection in the context of Electronic Commerce dated 8–9 October 1998[20];

5.   Ministerial Declaration on the Protection of Privacy on Global Networks dated 8–9 October 1998[21]; and

6.   Ministerial Declaration on Authentication for Electronic Commerce dated 8–9 October 1998.[22]

One of the reasons for the OECD taking initiative in developing the Guidelines was its awareness of the fact that consumers, in general, will not be familiar with the technicalities and risks involved in speedy cross-border electronic commerce-based transactions; furthermore, both the business community and consumers should be aware of their rights and obligations in the electronic market place. The OECD Council also maintained that electronic commerce should be open and accessible to all consumers, and that governments, business community and consumers, including their representatives, should pay special attention to the development of effective cross-border remedial systems.

OECD aims at disseminating the Guidelines to all relevant government agencies and business sectors involved in electronic commerce, educational institutions

---

[16]   op cit, at 2.
[17]   Doc C(80) 58/Final.
[18]   Doc C(42) 188/Final.
[19]   Doc C(97) 62/Final.
[20]   Doc C(98) 177 (Annex 2).
[21]   Doc C(98) 177 (Annex 1).
[22]   Doc C(98) 177 (Annex 3).

and the relevant public interest groups. According to the OECD Council, the member countries should invite non-member countries to facilitate the sharing of information between themselves. OECD further maintains that in implementing the Guidelines, development of new business models, and application of technology should be encouraged which would benefit consumers.[23]

2.3.3   An analysis of the OECD guidelines

The OECD Guidelines have been developed in four parts: Part I—Scope; Part II—General Principles; Part III—Implementation; and Part IV—Global Co-operation. The main elements of each of these parts are now discussed.

2.3.4   The scope of the guidelines

The scope of these Guidelines (Part I) is limited to business-to-consumer electronic commerce and does not exhaust business-to-business transactions. This is because the Guidelines are concerned with the protection of consumers. Whereas UNCITRAL Guidelines are aimed at promoting international trade and business generally through electronic means and include the issue of consumer protection among others, the OECD Guidelines are addressed exclusively to one issue—consumer protection and related matters.

2.3.4.1   The general principles

The General Principles (Part II) have been developed under various sub-headings:

2.3.4.2   Transport and effective protection

According to the Guidelines, consumers who participate in electronic commerce should be allowed transparent and effective consumer protection which should not be less than what may be made available from other forms of commerce. In order to provide effective protection to consumers, the OECD Guidelines recommended that governments, business, consumers and their representatives should work together so that better means of protection may be devised, and changes to address special circumstances related to electronic commerce may be determined.

2.3.4.3   Fair business, advertising and marketing practices

Consumers' interest must be the primary concern in operating business by electronic means. The Guidelines maintain that businesses engaged in electronic commerce should pay due attention to fair business, fair advertising (that is, no misrepresentation of facts) and marketing practices. 'Fair business' is also concerned with ethics in business; although, in theory, fair business practice is achievable, one should also consider whether it runs counter to 'profit maximization' which is the primary aim of most businesses. 'Fair business' in this

---

[23] See further C Chatterjee, op cit, at 64.

context would also stand for transparency of information in order to allow consumers to make their choices as informed consumers.

The Guidelines offer certain criteria which should be satisfied in order to claim fairness in business. Businesses should not make any representation or omission which is likely to be 'deceptive, misleading, fraudulent or unfair'.[24] The term 'likely to be' means that businesses should be aware of the likely effect of their representations and/or omissions—they should advise consumers with prudence and skill. By the same token, selling and/or promotion of goods or services must not be carried out in a way that might cause unreasonable risk of harm to consumers. All business information available to businesses should be presented in a clear, conspicuous, accurate and easily accessible manner. The global nature of electronic commerce should not violate the regulatory measures operational in the markets they target. Businesses should not use unfair contract terms. Advertising and marketing of products and services should be clearly identifiable, and the names of parties disclosed—this is another aspect of transparency. Consumers should be allowed easy-to-use procedures in order to enable them to choose whether or not they wish to receive unsolicited commercial e-mail messages, and their wish not to receive such messages should be respected. Special care should be taken in advertising or marketing products or services targeted at children, the elderly, the seriously ill, and others who may lack the capacity to 'fully understand the information with which they are presented'.[25]

2.3.4.4   Online disclosures

This issue has been developed under several headings: (i) information about the business; (ii) information about the goods or services; (iii) information about the transaction. According to the Guidelines, businesses engaged in electronic commerce with consumers should provide accurate, clear and easily accessible information about themselves in order to allow consumers to identify the business to their satisfaction. Consumers should be provided with an opportunity to check the membership of businesses with various organizations, and their certification bodies.

In relation to information about the goods or services, the Guidelines provide that:

'Businesses engaged in electronic commerce with consumers should provide accurate and easily accessible information describing the goods or services offered, sufficient to enable consumers to make an informed decision about whether to enter into the transaction and in a manner that makes it possible for consumers to maintain an adequate record of such information'.[26]

---

[24] On this issue one may like to refer to the decision of the court in *Hedley Byrne & Co Ltd v Heller & Partners Ltd* [1964] A.C. 465.
[25] The Guidelines, op cit, at 507.
[26] The Guidelines, op cit, at 508.

In order to allow a consumer to determine whether or not to enter into a transaction, businesses engaged in electronic commerce should provide him/her information clearly and accurately about the terms, conditions and costs associated with a transaction. Information should be as detailed as possible, including, where appropriate, itemized costs, terms of delivery or performance, method(s) of payment, restrictions, limitations or conditions of purchase, safety and health care warnings, after-sales service, policies as to withdrawal, cancellation and refund and warranties.

2.3.4.5   Confirmation process
A consumer should be allowed an opportunity to confirm whether he actually intends to make a purchase, which process, incidentally, is evidence in the insurance market in England, as well as an opportunity to modify an order and to retain a complete an accurate record of the transaction. The legal aspects of the confirmation process by electronic means have been discussed in the chapter on contract by electronic means.[27]

2.3.4.6   Payment
The Guidelines recommend that consumers should be provided an easy-to-use, secure payment mechanism; this provision is meant for preventing any fraudulent use of payment systems. The Guidelines recommend the charge-back mechanism as a means of enhancing consumer confidence in the context of electronic commerce.

2.3.4.7   Dispute resolution and redress
OECD's Guidelines maintain that electronic commerce poses challenges to the existing framework, however, it is not clear what the existing framework on applicable law and jurisdiction is. The determination of the jurisdiction and the governing law, in the absence of a clear choice made by the contracting parties, has always presented legal difficulty. It is for this reason that Article 4 of the Rome Convention on Contractual Obligations 1980 was brought into effect in England by the Contracts (Applicable Law) Act 1990 which provides for the real intention and close connection theories and on this latter issue judicial guidance in England is abundant.[28] The OECD Guidelines recommend that consideration should be given to whether the existing framework for applicable law and jurisdiction needs modification, by paying attention to the issue of providing fairness to consumers and businesses. According to the Guidelines, dispute resolution systems should be such that consumers will have meaningful access to fair and timely resolution of disputes and redress without undue cost or burden. To this end, the Guidelines also recommended the use of the alternative dispute resolution (ADR) mechanism, with special attention to cross-border transactions.

---

[27] chapter 5.
[28] See for example, *Amin Rasheed Corporation v Kuwait Insurance Co* [1984] A.C. 50; and *Coast Lines Ltd v Hudig and Veder Chartering* [1972] 2 Q.B. 34.

The issue of the protection of the consumer from the abuse of electronic commerce has received attention in the Guidelines. In order to respond to consumer complaints, the Guidelines maintain that business and consumer representatives should establish fair, effective and transparent internal mechanisms which will not subject consumers to undue cost or burden. They should also establish co-operative self-regulatory programmes for the purposes of settling disputes. In implementing the ADR mechanism, businesses, consumer representatives and governments should 'employ information technologies innovatively and use them to enhance consumer awareness and freedom of choice'.[29]

2.3.4.8   Privacy
According to the Guidelines, in order to provide effective protection to consumers, business-to-consumer commerce should be conducted in accordance with the privacy principles set out in the OECD Guidelines Governing the Protection of Privacy and Transfer Flow of Personal Data 1980, and take into account the OECD Ministerial Declaration on the Protection of Privacy on Global Networks 1988.

2.3.4.9   Education and awareness
In order to foster informed decision-making by consumers participating in electronic commerce, and also with a view to increasing awareness for businesses and consumers, the Guidelines recommend that governments, businesses and consumer representatives work together to educate consumers about electronic commerce. This aspect of the Guidelines is based on the assumption that effective business and consumer fora exist in all jurisdictions and that governments will necessarily participate in such projects. However, the recommendation, in theory, is a valid one.

2.3.4.10   Implementation (Part III)
As a means of implementing the recommendations in the Guidelines it is stated that the Member countries should at the national and international levels—and in co-operation with businesses, consumers and their representatives—review and, if necessary, promote self-regulatory practices or adopt and adapt to the laws and practices applicable to electronic commerce. The Guidelines further recommended that private sector leadership should be encouraged to participate in consumer affairs and the development of effective self-regulatory mechanisms, in addition to developing technology as a tool to protect and empower consumers.

2.3.4.11   Global co-operation (Part IV)
Under this part, the Guidelines recommended facilitation of communication, and co-operation internationally. Joint action should be taken to combat cross-border fraudulent, misleading and unfair conduct. Bilateral and multilateral agreements may be concluded with a view to achieving global co-operation.

---

[29] The Guidelines, op cit, at 510.

Mutual recognition and enforcement of judgements should be part of global co-operation. Within the European Union, this latter issue may not present, at least in theory, much legal difficulty, but between the EU and third countries, this problem may only be solved either by means of bilateral or multilateral agreements.

2.4   The EU Directive 2000/31/EC of the European Parliament and of the Council of 8 June 2000

2.4.1   Introduction
The following are the primary background reasons for this Directive:

(a)   to seek to forge ever closer links between the States and peoples of Europe, to ensure economic and social progress; to ensure the development of information society services[30] within the internal market which knows no frontiers;

(b)   the development of electronic commerce within the information society which would offer significant employment opportunities particularly in small and medium-sized enterprises;

(c)   to ensure that electronic commerce could fully benefit from the internal market;

(d)   to ensure legal certainty and consumer confidence, the Directive aims at laying down a clear and general framework to cover certain legal aspects of electronic commerce in the internal market;

(e)   'the objective of the Directive is to create a legal framework to ensure the free movement of information society services between the Member States and not to harmonize the field of criminal law as such.'

(f)   'this Directive complements Community law and national law relating to regulated professions maintaining a coherent set of applicable rules in this field.'

(g)   'Member States' obligation to remove obstacles to the use of electronic contracts is to be implemented in conformity with legal requirements for contracts enshrined in Community law.'

(h)   'Co-operation with third countries should be strengthened in the area of electronic commerce, in particular with applicant countries, the developing countries and the European Union's other trading partners.'[31]

---

[30] For the definitions of information society services, see the Directive 98/34/EC of the European Parliament and of the Council of 22 June 1998.

[31] This Directive entered into force on the day on which it was published in the *Official Journal of the European Communities* (17 July 2000).

2.4.2   An Analysis of the Directive

This Directive consists of the following chapters:

> Chapter I: General Provisions (Arts 1–3)
> Chapter II: Principles (Arts 4–15)
> Chapter III: Implementation (Arts 16–20)
> Chapter IV: Final Provisions (Arts 21–24)

There is also an Annex to this Directive, which lists the issues about which derogations from Article 3 are permissible.[32] These provisions are now briefly discussed.

Chapter 1: (general provisions)

The objective and scope of the Directive have been identified in chapter 1. The Directive aims at contributing to the proper functioning of the internal market 'by ensuring the free movement of information-society services between the Member States' (Art 1, para 1). According to paragraph 3 of Article 1:

'This Directive complements Community law applicable to information society services without prejudice to the level of protection for, in particular, public health and consumer interests, as established by Community acts and national legislation implementing them in so far as this does not restrict the freedom to provide information society services'.

This Directive does not apply to taxation issues; agreements of practices governed by cartel law, certain activities of information society services, namely the activities of notaries or equivalent professions 'to the extent that they involve a direct and specific connection with the exercise of public authority'; the representation of a claimant or a defendant of his interests before the courts; and gambling activities, generally.

Article 2 of the Directive provides definitions of various terms: service providers, established service providers, recipient of the service, consumer, commercial communication, regulated profession, and co-ordinated field. Of these terms the definition of 'commercial communication' should be highlighted. According to the Directive, 'commercial communication' stands for:

'any form of communication designed to promote, directly or indirectly, the goods, services or image of a company, organisation or person pursuing a commercial, industrial or craft activity or exercising a regulated profession.'

Information allowing direct access to the activity of a legal entity or a person, in particular a domain name or an electronic mail address or communications

---

[32] The title of Art 3 is Internal Market.

relating to the goods, services or image of a legal entity or a person compiled in an independent manner, do not constitute commercial communications.[33]

Each member is required to ensure that the information society services provided by a service provider set up on its territory 'complies with the national provisions applicable in the Member States which fall within the co-ordinated field'[34] (Art 3(1)). Member states may not restrict the freedom to provide information society services from another member state by invoking the argument of 'co-ordinated field', save on the grounds of public policy,[35] the protection of public health, public security, and the protection of consumer including investors, and in the case of urgency occasioned by the failure of a member state to adequate measures in relation to a criminal investigation.

Chapter II (Principles)
The following are, in brief, the principles under this chapter of the Directive: (1) the first principle is entitled Establishment and Information Requirements. The following sub-principles come under the first principle: (a) the principle excluding prior authorization—this is a sub-principle according to which the taking up and pursuit of the activity of an information society service provider may not be subject to prior authorization or any other requirement having equivalent effect; (b) the sub-principle that the general information must be provided— whereby the service provider shall be allowed to introduce its services, including, its name, address, details of the service it may render, the trade register in which its name is entered, where the service provider is registered in such registers; the relevant supervisory authority where the service provider's activity is subject to an authorization scheme; any professional body with which it is registered; its professional title; and its VAT number; (2) the second principle is the principle of Commercial Communications—under this principle have been included the following sub-principles: (a) information to be provided; (b) unsolicited commercial communication; and (c) regulated professions. The member states are required to ensure that an information society complies at least with the following conditions:

[33] Art 2(f).
[34] 'Co-ordinated field' stands for 'requirements laid down in Member States' legal systems applicable to information society service providers or information society services, regardless of whether they are of a general nature or specifically designed for them' (Art 2(g)). In relation to the co-ordinated field, the service provider is required to comply with the requirements concerning qualifications, authorization or notification pertaining to the taking up of the activity of an information society service, including the behaviour of the service provider, the quality or content of the service and the requirements concerning its liability.
[35] As matters of public policy are included, the prevention, investigation, detection and prosecution of criminal offences, including the protection of minors and the fight against any incitement to hatred on grounds of race, sex, religion or nationality and violations of human dignity concerning individual persons.' (Art 3(4)(a)(i)). The circumstances in which derogations from Art 3 are permissible have been indicated in the Annex to the Directive.

(i)   the commercial communication shall be clearly identifiable;
(ii) the entity on whose behalf the commercial communication is made shall be clearly identifiable;
(iii) if a member state permits promotional offers, such as discounts, premiums and gifts, the details of which must be clearly identified, and the conditions which are to be satisfied to qualify for them;
(iv) promotional competitions or games, where permitted in a member state in which the service provider is established, shall be clearly identifiable, and information on them shall be accessible.

In regard to unsolicited commercial communication, the Directive provides that the member states which permit unsolicited commercial communication by electronic mail shall ensure that such communication by a service provider located in that member state's territory, shall be clearly identifiable. The member states are also required to ensure that natural persons not wishing to receive unsolicited commercial communications from service providers are allowed to include their names in the opt-out registers and that the service providers consult the registers regularly and respect the wish of the registered persons (Art 7).

As regards regulated professions, Article 8(1) of the Directive provides that:

'Member States shall ensure that the use of commercial communications which are part of or constitute an information society service provider by a member of a regulated profession is permitted subject to compliance with the professional rules regarding, in particular, the independence, dignity and honour of the profession, professional secrecy and fairness towards clients and other members of the profession.'

The member states and the Commission shall encourage professional associations and bodies to develop codes of conduct at the Community level, in order to determine the types of information that may be transmitted for the purposes of commercial communication.

The member states are required to ensure that conclusion of contracts by electronic means is permissible under the legal systems, and that the legal requirements are not so onerous as to create obstacles for the use of electronic contracts nor must they be regarded as contracts void of legal effectiveness. These general conditions shall not apply to contracts falling into one of the following categories:

(a)   contracts that create or transfer rights in real estate (but not rental rights);
(b)   contracts required by law the involvement of courts, public authorities or professions exercising public authority;
(c)   suretyship contracts and contracts of collateral securities provided by persons acting for purposes outside their trade, business or profession; and

(d)   contracts governed by family law or by the law of succession.

The member states are required to indicate to the Commission the types of contract to which paragraph 1 shall not apply, and are obliged to submit to the Commission every five years a report on the application of paragraph 2 explaining their reasons thereof.

In addition to other information requirements established by Community law, it is for the member states to ensure that at least the following information is given by a service provider in a clear, comprehensive and unambiguous manner prior to an order being placed by a recipient of the service:

(a)   the technical steps to follow in concluding a contract;
(b)   whether the contract will be filed by the service provider and whether it will be accessible;
(c)   the technical means for identifying and correcting errors prior to the placing of the order; and
(d)   the lawyers who will be used for contracting.[36]

In all member states, service providers are required to indicate the relevant codes of conduct to which it subscribes and information on how those codes can be consulted electronically.[37] These provisions shall not apply to contracts concluded exclusively by exchange of electronic mail or by equivalent means of communications.[38] The following principles shall apply where a recipient of the service places his order through technological means:

- the service provider must acknowledge receipt of a recipient's order promptly and by electronic means; and
- the order and the acknowledgement of receipt are deemed to be received when the addressee is able to access them.[39]

member states shall ensure that service providers make available to recipients of the service, appropriate, effective and accessible technical means allowing them to identify and correct input errors, prior to placement of an order. Again, this provision does not apply to contracts concluded exclusively by exchange of electronic mail or by equivalent means of communication.

The Directive also provides for liabilities of intermediary service providers (Arts 12–14), which have been described under three nomenclatures: 'mere conduit', 'caching' and 'osting'. As regards 'mere conduit' (Art 12) the Directive states that where an information society service consists: (a) of the transmission in a communication network of information provided by a recipient of the service;

[36] Art 10(1).
[37] Art 10(2).
[38] Art 10(4).
[39] Art 11(1).

or (b) of access to a communication network, member states shall ensure that the service provider is not liable for the information transmitted, if the service provider:

    (i)   does not initiate the transmission;
    (ii) does not select the receiver of the transmission; and
    (iii) does not select or modify the information contained in the transmission.

'Transmission' and 'access' in this context would include 'the automatic, intermediate and transient storage of the information transmitted if it takes place for the sole purpose of carrying out the transmission in the communication network, and also provided that the information is not stored for any period longer than is reasonably necessary for the transmission' (Art 12).

The courts and administrative authorities in the member state concerned will have the right to require the service provider to terminate or prevent an infringement.

As regards 'caching' (Art 13) the Directive states that where an information society service consists of the transmission in a communication network of information provided by a recipient of the service, member states shall ensure that the service provider is not liable for 'the automatic, immediate and temporary storage of that information, performed for the sole purpose of making more efficient the information's onward transmission to other recipients of the service upon their request'[40] on the following conditions:

    (a) that the provider does not modify the information;
    (b) that the provider complies with conditions upon access to the information;
    (c) that the provider complies with the rules pertaining to the system of updating of the information by the industry;
    (d) that the provider does not interfere with the lawful use of technology used by industry to obtain data on the use of the information; and
    (e) that the provider acts expeditiously to disallow access to the stored information at the initial source of transmission has been removed from or disabled at the network or that a court or an administrative authority has ordered removal or disablement of such information.

Of course, a service provider may be required to terminate or prevent any infringement by a court of an administrative authority in a member state, in accordance with its law.

Article 14 of the Directive which deals with 'hosting' provides that where an information society service consists of the storage of information provided by a

---

[40] Art 13.

recipient of the service, member states shall ensure that the service provider is not held liable for the information stored at the request of a recipient of the service. This provision shall not apply to the following circumstances:

(a) if the provider has no actual knowledge of illegal activity or information, nor was it aware of facts of circumstances from which the illegal activity or information was apparent; or

(b) that the provider, having such knowledge or awareness of illegal activity or information failed to act expeditiously to remove or disable access to the information; or

(c) when the recipient of the service acted under the authority or control of the provider.

A court or an administrative authority in a member state will have the power in appropriate circumstances to require a service provider to terminate or prevent an infringement. Article 14 does not prevent the member states from establishing procedures governing the removal or disabling access to information.

Member states shall not impose any general obligation to monitor the information transmitted by providers when they are providing services under Article 12 ('mere conduit') or Article 13 ('caching') or Article 14 ('hosting'). However, member states may require information society service providers to inform the competent public authorities of alleged illegal activities undertaken or information provided by recipients of their service.

2.5   International chamber of commerce

2.5.1   General usage for international digitally ensured commerce (GUIDEC)[41]

The document entitled General Usage for International Digitally Ensured Commerce was drafted by the International Chamber of Commerce under the auspices of its Electronic Commerce Project, the objective of which is to develop a multi-disciplinary study to promote and facilitate the emerging global trading system.

This is a Guideline that was initially drafted under the name of the Uniform International Authentication and Certification Practices, but eventually, after the consultation period, it was decided to add the word 'Ensured' to the title.[42]

---

[41] This document was obtained from the Internet, the reference to which is www.iccwbo.org. The author wishes to take this opportunity to make it clear that in certain instances certain passages have been quoted *in toto*, as otherwise, any translated version of those passages would distort the meanings of the ideas and terms maintained by the ICC. The author had no intention to breach the copyright of the ICC.

[42] The term 'Ensure' is used to describe what is usually known as a 'digital signature' or 'authentication'.

The primary aim of this Guideline is to consider the fundamental elements involved in electronic commerce, and the consequences of altering the function of a signatory, and the precautionary measures that should be taken for using the medium (technology) by a third party. It also aims at establishing a general framework for the ensuring and certification of digital messages in different legal systems, through cryptographic techniques. Allocation of risks and liability between transacting parties, and a clear description of the rights and duties of subscribers, certifiers and reliant parties come under its primary policies. The Guidelines have also developed certain underlying policies for the following:

- to ensure the ability of the international business community in relation to the examination of secure digital transactions;
- to promote trustworthy and reliable digital ensuring and certification practices by establishing relevant legal principles;
- to encourage the development of trustworthy ensuring and certification systems;
- to protect users of the digital infrastructure from fraud and errors;
- to adapt ensuring and certification technologies to the existing policies, laws, customs and practices[43];
- to define and clarify the duties of participants in the ensuring and certification system; and
- to foster global awareness in ensuring and certification technology.[44]

GUIDEC does not attempt to define rights and duties of consumers pertaining to transactions in which they may be involved. In developing GUIDEC, attention has been paid to the study developed by the UN Model Law on Electronic Commerce (UNCITRAL Model Law).

2.5.2 An analysis of GUIDEC

GUIDEC has been developed in eight chapters:

 I.   Background

 II.   The Advent of Commercial Electronic Transactions

 III.   Electronic Transactions and Information Security

 IV.   Existing Law and Electronic Transactions

 V.   International Legal Approaches

---

[43] The ICC document includes the aim 'to balance ensuring and certification technologies'; it is not clear how it may be possible to achieve this target.
[44] The underlying policies could have been regarded as part of the objectives of GUIDEC.

These chapters are now briefly discussed.

2.5.2.1   An examination of the principal provisions of GUIDEC
The background, scope objectives and underlying policies of GUIDEC have already been explained. In this section, the principal parts of the document are examined.

2.5.2.1.1 The advent of commercial electronic transactions
This part of the document discusses the following:

- the emerging global electronic trading system;
- EDI and closed networks;
- EDI and efficiencies derived from electronic forms;
- EDI trading agreements; and
- transition from closed systems to open systems and the Internet.

The bases for the emerging electronic trading system have been identified as the rapid evolution of digital communications technologies and expansion of computer networks. Electronic data interchange (EDI) is considered to hold unlimited possibility for creating new channels for distribution, sales and related services. In other words, the application of digital technology to business communications can be a means of expanding international trade and commerce, including service industries, and creating new businesses and commercial opportunities. In contrast with *closed networks communication system* whereby communications are conducted according to written and approved procedures, *closed network technology*, such as EDI, enables computer-to-computer transmission of information, commercial or otherwise, thus reducing delay and the need for paper to pass information from one point to another.

The EDI method requires standardization of formats and forms, and agreement, in advance, between parties, as to what form, format and standards would be used by contracting parties. This method is fast, clean, cheap, accurate and safe—if properly used. Of course, both the sender and receiver of messages must be using the same technology.

ICC maintains that EDI trading agreements, otherwise known as 'interchange agreements' have also served an important function in facilitating and promoting the electronic trading system.[45] It is interesting to note that the use of EDI

---

[45] op cit, at 6.

trading agreements evolved through private agreements, however, in practice, trading partners used contractual terms to minimize risk, through proper arrangements for the use of EDI technology and adopting their own safety arrangements, primarily through a system of confidentiality of data. These private agreements contain flexibility, and parties are at liberty to establish their own specific procedures and conditions that would govern their rights and obligations. Eventually, the Uniform Rules of Conduct for Interchange of Trade Data by Teletransmission (UN-CID) was developed, which served as the basis for many model or standard trading agreements. According to ICC, 'the development of model trading agreements established the foundation for a contractually based legal structure for electronic commerce'.

2.5.2.1.2 Electronic transactions and information security

In so far as electronic transactions and information are concerned, the International Chamber of Commerce pointed out that open networks may also increase the incidence of fraud, particularly due to not having a single locus of responsibility. Whereas 'Intranet' provides assurances of the identity and authority of transactions parties, in open networks, the legal security of transactions is not adequate, as unauthorized access, fraud or other risks may intervene and vitiate transactions. Under this title have been included five items:

- open networks;
- information security;
- public key cryptography and digital signatures;
- ensuring and certification authorization; and
- biometric technology.

As contractual means may not be the most effective method of dealing with security issues effectively, ICC finds the need for a more generally applicable legal approach. ICC maintains that the General Usage in International Digitally Ensure Commerce will enhance 'legal predictability by adopting a system of commercial ensuring' and certifying practices.

ICC recognizes that there exists the need for a stronger system of security for operating open networks; 'ensuring', it maintains the opportunity for higher security in electronic commerce transactions, thereby raising the level of trust which would be placed by users in the global communications infrastructure; that digital signature may provide security to a certain extent. It is to be pointed out however that legislation alone may not provide a fool-proof security system; mutual trust among the parties concerned is essential, although it is not certain how this may be achieved.

The issue of public key cryptography and digital signatures has already been discussed in a separate chapter.

ICC places emphasis on the system of ensuring and certification. Implicit in the ensuring and certification system is the condition that a trusted third party holds a public key. GUIDEC describes this third party as a certifier, who would form the basis for trust in all commercial and non-commercial transactions taking place over open networks. It is the function of certifiers to identify the public key holder, publish and identify and update public keys—the process of which is known as 'certificate issuance'. The certifier should be trustworthy, and the certification authority itself must be an institution trusted by all parties relying on its information. A hierarchy of certification authorities may also be established to reinforce trust.

Biometric technology is concerned with the use of a template on which the signatory physically reproduces his/her signature which will then be related to a previously identified signature, 'specimen', and if it conforms then it would serve the purpose of certification. In other words, this should provide a means of gaining security against fraud.

2.5.2.1.3 Existing law and electronic transactions

ICC maintains that the vitality of the emerging global electronic trading system is dependent upon the capacity and willingness of states to adopt both domestic law and international law to the changing networked infrastructure. Ideally, there should be uniform laws and procedures rather than conflicting legislative efforts made at the domestic level, as there should be an international legal infrastructure to match the needs and demands of an international network for communication by electronic means, in addition to establishing a unified regulatory system for information security, including ensuring and certifying messages.

ICC also points out that under both common law and civil law systems, a digital signature presents a number of legal issues, stemming primarily from the concept and understanding of what constitutes a 'signature' in the prescribed legal manner to validate documents.[46] But of course, it is to be emphasized that unless legal requirements are done away with by official means, in so far as English law is concerned, the requirements for signatures under the Statute of Fraud must be satisfied. In civil law countries, specific formalities in regard to conclusion of contracts are often required to be completed, and such formalities may not be satisfied by electronic means.

Part V of the document briefly explains international legal approaches to digital signatures with particular references to UNCITRAL Model Law on electronic commerce. This Model Law has already been discussed in a separate section of this work. According to ICC however, GUIDEC intends to build on and extend the Model Law's treatment through the concept of ensuring a message.[47] It also maintains that GUIDEC treats the issues relating to intermediaries and non-intermediary third parties more fully than the Model Law.

---

[46] This aspect of the problem has been discussed in a separate chapter of this work.
[47] op cit, at 11.

Part VI of GUIDEC provides a glossary of terms: ensure; certificate; certification provider; statement; certifier; repository; digital signature; hold a private key; human readable form; issue a certificate; notice; person; public key certificate; revoke a public key certificate; subscriber; suspend a public key certificate; technologically reliable; trustworthy; valid certificate; and verify a digital signature.

There is no need to reproduce these definitions, furthermore, certain of these terms have already been defined in this work. The reader may like to consult the ICC document—GUIDEC. Some of these terms are self-explanatory. However, 'repository', according to GUIDEC is a 'computer–based system for storing and retrieving certificates and other messages relevant to ensuring a message'.[48] In defining 'technologically reliable', GUIDEC identifies its objectives as: confidentiality, integrity, availability and legitimate use. 'Availability' stands for securing access to information in order to ensure that legitimate users are not unduly denied information.

GUIDEC places much emphasis on 'trustworthiness' of parties, which is appropriate, however, in defining 'trustworthiness' it includes qualities such as capabilities, competence, performance of one's legal duties and unbiased action. It is to be wondered whether these qualities represent 'trustworthiness' or whether 'trustworthiness' in the context of GUIDEC stands for competence and skill of a person.

Under the broad title of 'Best Practices' GUIDEC includes two sub-titles: 'ensuring a message' and 'certification'. These are now briefly explained.

(a)   Ensuring a message

According to GUIDEC, a message is ensured, as a factual matter, if evidence indicates the identity of the ensurer and that the message has not been altered since it has been ensured. 'As a factual matter' means that it must be factually ascertained who ensured what—there is no room for any law in it. 'A person must attribute an ensured message to the person who actually ensured the message'.[49] 'Attribute' according to GUIDEC means that the person receiving the ensured message must be taken as being associated the ensurer in a significant way, which is usually confirmed by an accompanying expression, or by trade usage. According to GUIDEC it is essential that the person having the ensured message acts in good faith. Messages may be ensured by an authorized agent. However, the role and the capacity of agent remains a legal issue which is considered differently by different legal systems. However, GUIDEC provides that an ensurer must ensure a message according to the appropriate practices for ensuring a message. 'Appropriate' in this context would mean 'appropriate under the circumstances', that is, it reasonably fits the context of the transaction. In

---

[48] op cit, at 15.
[49] op cit, at 23.

the case of bilateral agreements or multilateral agreements, 'appropriateness' should be determined by the parties concerned. In determining what is reasonable under the circumstances, the recipient should consider the following:

(a)   the facts of which the recipient is aware or of which the recipient has notice, including the facts listed in the certificate;
(b)   the value or importance of the ensured message;
(c)   the course of performance between the relying person and the subscriber and the available evidence of reliability or unreliability corroborating the ensured message;
(d)   the same criterion as at (c) in respect of prior transaction; and
(e)   trade usage operated by technologically reliable information systems.[50]

GUIDEC maintains that it is for the creator of an ensured message to clearly indicate in a precise manner what is being ensured, that is, the primary contents of the message. Included in this process are delimitation of the message by the spatial limits of paper, formatting and signing at the end of the message. Parties should agree to these conditions, including delineation of messages in advance; such prior arrangements and agreement should help receivers identify discrepancies and unauthorized use of the device. Furthermore, the reasonable care which is expected of a prudent person is essential for safeguarding an ensuring device.

(b)   Certification

GUIDEC rightly states that a subscriber is required to accurately submit to a certifier all facts material to the certificate. Of course, the person who may be relying on a certificate will have no notice of the fact that the person concerned did not disclose all relevant facts. In most legal systems however, remedies are available for losses sustained as a consequence of misrepresentation or non-disclosure of material facts. Under the UNIDROIT (International Institute for the Unification of Private Law), Principles of International Commercial Contracts (Art 1.9 (1994)), a 'notice' includes a declaration, demand, request or any other communication of intention.

ICC points out that a certificate should be regarded as simply a document which evidences facts, but reliability of facts is a matter for the certificates—the trustworthiness of certificates is a crucial factor. An effective operation of the certification system is dependent upon the certifier's acting in good faith and without negligence. However, whether a certificate will be regarded as admissible evidence or not in judicial or arbitral proceedings depends upon the rule of the jurisdiction. The question remains of the extent of the responsibility of a certifier as to the availability of the information provided. Unless a receiving party is assured of the availability of the certification process, the receiving party will run risks.

---

[50] op cit, at 26.

In dealing with the issue of the trustworthiness of a certifier, ICC maintains that a certifier:

(a)   must use only those information systems which are technologically reliable, and those of the personnel who are trustworthy in issuing a certificate;

(b)   must not have any conflict of interest which would make the certifier untrustworthy in issuing, suspending and revoking a certificate;

(c)   must not be an accomplice to a breach of duty by the subscriber;

(d)   must not participate in a contribution to any act or omission which would 'significantly impair reasonable and foreseeable reliance on a valid certificate'[51]; and

(e)   act in a trustworthy manner towards a subscriber.

According to GUIDEC, a certifier must make reasonable efforts to screen, train and manage the certification process. A certifier must not have any involvement in a transaction, GUIDEC emphasizes that the trustworthiness of a certifier is central to the concept of certification. A certifier has an obligation, under GUIDEC, to make reasonable efforts to notify a person who may be foreseen to be affected by an fact material to the reliability of a certificate which has already been issued.

GUIDEC also places importance on the financial resources of a certifier so that it is able to conduct its business and bear the reasonable risks resulting from the certificates it may issue. 'Reasonable risks' in this context would mean the foreseeable and likely risks. A certifier would be required to keep records of all facts material to a certificate, that is, the facts which may be supported by evidence.

In terminating its business, a certifier must act in a manner which would cause minimal disruption to subscribers and person relying on certificates already issued, and transfer its records to a qualified successor, namely, a professional association or a regulatory agency. Such a successor need not issue new certificates, but must carry on with suspension, revocation and retrieval services. Where no successor is available, all existing certificates may have to be revoked.

According to GUIDEC, a request for the suspension of a public key certificate by a subscriber, or his agent, employee, business associate or a member of the immediate family of the subscriber on the grounds that the security of the subscriber's private key would be compromised, would be enough for the suspension of a public key certificate. The availability of the system of suspending public key certificates should be viewed as a mechanism for managing risks in this regard. By the

---

[51] op cit, at 34. The term 'significantly' may present legal difficulty in that it may not be quantified, and may be based on circumstantial evidence.

same token, in the event of receiving a request for revocation by a subscriber or his appropriately authorized agent, revocation of the certificate must take place, the consequence of which is obvious, that is, the certificate may not be reviewed. The following would be the principal grounds for revocation:

(a) that the certifier confirms that a material fact in the certificate was untrue; and

(b) that the certifier confirmed that trustworthiness of the certifier's information system was so compromised as to materially affect the certificate's reliability.

If, in an otherwise sustainable situation, a certificate is not suspended or revoked, the certifier concerned may incur liability for consequential losses. The circumstances in which a certificate would be suspended or revoked without consent would be identified by the contract between a certifier and its subscriber. In the event of a suspension or revocation, appropriate notices must be issued by the certifier to persons who are likely to be significantly affected by the suspension or revocation of a public key certificate.

In respect of a certificate published in a digital certificate repository, the certifier should publish notice of suspension or revocation in accordance with the standard procedure adopted by the repository concerned, and if the certificate was one which was unpublished, notice should be given to persons who are likely to rely on the certificate and the person requesting the suspension or revocation. In the event of a certifier having failed to give notice, it may be held liable in breach of the contract with the subscriber.

2.6   Conclusions

GUIDEC is intended to serve as a 'foundation document' in the application of digitally ensured electronic commerce.[52] It maintains that in view of the evolving nature of electronic commerce, concepts and definitions will also evolve; thus no document on this subject, at least during its evolutionary period, may be complete. However, the current version of GUIDEC identifies most of the important issues relating to the general usage of international digitally ensured commerce. As stated earlier, unless appropriate technological and legal mechanisms are adopted universally, the most efficient performance of digitally ensured commerce remains to be seen.

---

[52] op cit, at 33.

3. Electronic communications act 2000

3.1 Introduction

'Cryptography' has already been defined in chapter 1 of this work. The Electronic Communications Act is primarily concerned with the facilitation of the use of electronic communications and electronic data storage. The regulation of the providers of cryptographic support services and of data storage forms the basis for achieving the objectives of this Act.

Section 6 of the Act defines 'cryptographic support service' as:

> 'any service which is provided to the senders or recipients of electronic communications, or to those storing electronic data'

'Any service' in this context would mean any service in the context of cryptography support service. The purpose of such service however is to familiarize the use of cryptographic techniques for the purpose of:

'(a) securing that such communications or data can be accessed, or can be put into an intelligible form, only by certain persons; or

(b) securing that the authenticity or integrity of such communications or data is capable of being ascertained.'[1]

The latter part of section 6 (1) aims at limiting the access to data and communication to designated persons under the control of senders and recipients, who may also be authorized to put it into an intelligible form; securing the authenticity or integrity of communication or data is important for ensuring that no communication or data has been transmitted by dishonest or illegal means. However, the Act does not state how the authenticity or integrity of

---

[1] s 6(1)(a) and (b).

communication or data may be confirmed—presumably, this is left for the parties to decide.

The Act has two primary aspects: promotion and facilitation of electronic commerce, data storage etc and the protection of the consumer from abuse of cryptography services. To this end, the Act has been developed in three parts: Part I—Cryptography service providers (ss 1–6); Part II—Facilitation of Electronic Commerce, Data Storage, etc (ss 7–10); and Part III—Miscellaneous and Supplemental (ss 11–16).

The primary purposes of this Act are to build confidence in e-Commerce, prevent the abuse that may occur from the use of technology, including the abuse of confidentiality to secure the legal recognition of electronic signatories and the process under which they should be verified, and to remove obstacles in other legislation to the use of e-Commerce and storage of data in the place of paper documentation.[2]

It is the purpose of this chapter to explain and examine the provisions of the Electronic Communications Act 2000.

3.2   An examination of the Electronic Communications Act 2000

3.2.1   Register of approved providers

The regulatory aspect of the Act needs to be explained. As a first step towards it, the Act in Part I (entitled Cryptography Service Providers) makes provision for establishing and maintaining a register of approved providers of cryptography support services by the Secretary of State, and which shall contain particulars of every person who is approved under any arrangements in force under section 2. Section 1(3) identifies the particulars that must be recorded in the register relating to an approved person:

(a)   the name and address of the person concerned;
(b)   the services in respect of which that person is approved; and
(c)   the conditions of the approval.

Members of the public will have the right to inspect the contents of the register, and in the event of any withdrawal or modification of an approval, the attention of the person likely to be interested in it must be drawn. The register is voluntary—no provider is obliged to make an application for approval.

---

[2] See further *Explanatory Notes to the Act* published by HMSO, London (2000) at 3.

3.2.2   *Arrangements for the grant of approval*

Section 2 of the Act deals with the arrangement for the grant of approvals, which represents an important aspect of the legislation. Approvals may be granted to those who are already established providers of cryptography support services or are proposing to become so, whether in the UK or elsewhere.

The Secretary of State may grant approval to all the services in respect of which approval is sought or in respect of some of them, or grant conditional approval or refuse the application for a grant of approval. The following are the conditions which must be satisfied for obtaining a grant of approval:

(a)   that in providing the services in respect of which approval is granted, the person concerned will comply with 'such technical and other requirements as may be prescribed'[3];

(b)   that the person concerned will continue satisfying the requirements which have been prescribed;

(c)   that the person concerned is and will continue to 'able and willing to comply with any requirements that the Secretary of State is proposing to impose by means of conditions of the approval'[4]; and

(d)   that the person concerned is a fit and proper person for the grant of an approval.

In making regulations under section 2(3)(a) or (b), the Secretary of State shall consult such persons or representatives of persons who, in his opinion, are likely to be affected by those regulations.

It is obvious that the onus of proving the ability to comply with the requirements for the grant of an approval is on the applicant, however, the criteria for the grant of an approval do suggest that only persons of recognisable ability may be allowed approval.

The requirements referred to in subsection (3) of section 2 include the following:

(a)   to provide information 'to such persons, in such form, at such times and in response to such request as may be specified in or determined under the terms of the condition'[5];

(b)   that continuing obligations must be imposed notwithstanding the withdrawal of the approval, whether in whole or in part; and

(c)   that the requirements are framed by reference to 'the opinion or directions of a person specified in or chosen in accordance with the provisions contained in the conditions'.[6]

---

[3] s 2(3)(a).
[4] s 2(3)(c).
[5] s 2(5)(a).
[6] s 2(5)(c).

The requirement to provide information, if not satisfied by the person concerned, shall be enforceable at the discretion of the Secretary of State. Under section 3, the Secretary of State may delegate his functions to another person.

3.2.3   Restrictions on disclosure of information

Section 4 provides that certain information obtained under Part I need not be disclosed—namely that relating to the private affairs of any individual or to any particular business 'during the lifetime of that individual or so long as that business continues to be carried on' without the consent of that individual or so long as the business remains functional, without the consent of that individual or the person carrying on the business. However, this restriction does not apply to any disclosure of information which is made in the following instances:

(a)   to facilitate the carrying out of any functions under Part I of this Act, or any prescribed functions of the Secretary of State or a person to whom he has delegated powers under section 3;

(b)   to facilitate the carrying out of any functions of a local weights and measures authority in the UN;

(c)   to facilitate the carrying out of a prescribed[7] public function[8] of any person;

(d)   in connection with the investigation of a criminal offence or for the purpose of any criminal proceedings;

(e)   for the purpose of any civil proceedings relating to cryptography support services or which are proceedings to which an approved person is a party; and

(f)   in fulfilment of a Community obligation.[9]

The primary objective of section 4 is to safeguard the privacy of the individual and commercially confidential information, unless disclosure of information is deemed justifiable. To provide safeguards either to the individual or a business entity, subsection 6 makes disclosure in contravention of section 4 a punishable offence.

3.2.4   Facilitation of electronic commerce, data storage etc

Whereas Part I of the Act (ss 1–6) is primarily concerned with the methods of regulating cryptography service providers. The facilitation of electronic commerce, data storage and other related matters are the subject matter of Part II (ss 7–10). The first stage of facilitation of e-Commerce is to accord a legal status

---

[7] Prescribed' in this context means prescribed by regulations made by the Secretary of State, or 'determined' in such manner as may be provided for in any such regulation'.
[8] 'Public functions' includes 'any function conferred by or in accordance with any provision contained in or made under any enactment or Community legislation' s 4(4).
[9] s 4(2).

to an electronic signature, and to this end, section 7 of the Act states the circumstances in which an electronic signature may be treated as admissible evidence. Section 7(1) provides that in any legal proceedings:

'(a)   an electronic signature incorporated into or logically associated with a particular electronic communication or particular electronic data, and

(b)   the certification by any person of such a signature,

shall each be admissible in evidence in relation to any question as to the authenticity of the communication or data or as to the integrity of the communication or data.'

An electronic signature is to be either incorporated into or logically associated with any electronic communication or electronic data with a view to establishing the authenticity of the communication or data, the integrity of the communication or data or both. Such an electronic signature is to be regarded as certified by a person if that person, whether before or after making the communication makes a statement confirming that the signature, a means of producing, communicating or verifying the signature or a procedure applied to the signature is either alone or in combination with other factors 'a valid means of establishing the authenticity of the communication or data, the integrity of the communication or data or both'.[10]

'Authenticity' and 'integrity' have been defined in section 15(2) of the Act. The authenticity of any communication or data is to be determined by referring to the following:

(a)   whether the source of the communication or data is a particular person or other source;

(b)   whether the communication or data is accurately timed and dated; and/or

(c)   whether it is intended to have a legal effect.

'Integrity' is to be determined by referring to whether there has been 'any tampering with or other modification of the communication or data'.[11]

The appropriate Minister may, by order made by a statutory instrument, modify the provisions of any enactment or subordinate legislation or any scheme, licence, authorization or approval issued or granted by or under any enactment or subordinate legislation in such manner as he may deem appropriate for the purpose of authorising or facilitating the use of electronic communications or

[10]   s 7(3).
[11]   s 15(2)(b).

electronic storage for any of the purposes specified in sub-paragraph (2) of section 8.[12]

The appropriate Minister[13] shall not make an order authorising the use of electronic communications or electronic storage for any purpose unless he considers that 'authorisation is such that the extent (if any) to which records of things done for that purpose will be available will be no less satisfactory in cased where use is made of electronic communications or electronic storage than in other cases'.[14]

The appropriate Minister may exercise a variety of powers under section 8(4) of the Act, primarily for the purpose of maintaining control over cryptographic service providers. An order may contain provision as to the electronic form to be taken by any electronic communications or electronic storage the use of which is authorized; or as to making the use of electronic communications or electronic storage subject to conditions; or ordering what must be done by a user if it has failed to satisfy the conditions to which the use was subject; or other similar provisions, including provisions as to refusal of acceptance of something in electronic form or the circumstances in which intermediaries may be used or in regard to the keeping of records in connection with any use of electronic communications or electronic storage or in relation to any criminal or other liabilities that may arise in connection with the use of electronic communications or electronic storage. Under section 8(4) orders of the appropriate Minister must be addressed to authorized users.

With the advancement of technology, the techniques of using electronic communications and storage of data may change, hence the need for modification of legislation. The power of the appropriate Minister under section 8(4)(g) includes the power to make an order in relation to cases in which 'the use of electronic communications or electronic storage is so authorized, for the determination of

---

[12] s 8 (2):
'Those purposes are-
  (a) the doing of anything which under any such provisions is required to be or may be done or evidenced in writing or otherwise using a document, notice or instrument;
  (b) the doing of anything which under any such provisions is required to be or may be done by post or other specified means of delivery;
  (c) the doing of anything which under any such provisions is required to be or may be authorised by a person's signature or seal, or is required to be delivered as a deed or witnessed;
  (d) the making of any statement or declaration which under any such provisions is required to be made under oath or to be contained in a statutory declaration;
  (e) the keeping, maintenance or preservation, for the purposes or in pursuance of any such provisions, of any account, record, notice, instrument or other document;
  (f) the provision, production or publication under any such provisions of any information or other matter;
  (g) the making of any payment that is required to be or may be made under any such provisions.'
[13] For the definition of an 'appropriate Minister' see s 9(1).
[14] s 8(3).

any of the matters mentioned in sub-section (5), or as to the manner in which they may be proved in legal proceedings'. Subsection 5 provides that the matters referred to in subsection 4(g) are:

'(a)   whether a thing has been done using an electronic communication or electronic storage;

(b)   the time at which, or date on which, a thing done using any such communication or storage was done;

(c)   the place where a thing done using such communication or storage was done;

(d)   the person by whom such a thing was done; and

(e)   the contents, authenticity or integrity of any electronic data.'

These matters are matters which relate to preventative and curative measures by the government in order to ensure that the appropriate use of electronic communication or electronic storage. The term 'appropriate Minister' is relevant in that more than one government department may be the appropriate department to deal with a particular matter, and the Minister attached to the department concerned will be empowered to make an order. The provisions made be a Ministerial order may include:

'(a)   different provision for different cases;

(b)   such exceptions and exclusions as the person making the order may think fit; and

(c)   any such incidental, supplemental, consequential and transitional provision as he may think fit.'[15]

The Act also provides for modification in relation to Welsh matters[16] and Scottish matters.[17]

3.2.5   Modification of matters

Part III of the Act entitled 'Miscellaneous and Supplemental' deals with various issues, notably modification of licences by the Director-General of Telecommunications, and appeal against modifications of licence conditions. This is an important issue which should be discussed in this connection. Licensing under the EC Telecommunications Services Licensing Directive (97/13/EC) must be non-discriminatory. But section 12 of the Telecommunications Act 1984 requires the Director-General of Telecommunications to obtain the written consent of individual licences if they wish to proceed with modifications without reference to the Competition Commission. Under section 11 of the Electronic Communications Act, the Director-General of Telecommunications may proceed with

---

[15] s 9(6).
[16] s 10.
[17] s 9(7).

licence modifications without making any reference to the Competition Commission provided that he has not received any objections from any licence holder whose licence is to be modified. This section also enables the Director-General of Telecommunications to proceed with a licence modification without reference to the Competition Commission in cases 'where he may consider the licence modification to be deregulatory according to specified criteria'.[18]

In relation to effecting modifications, a new subsection 4A is inserted to replace subsection 3 of section 12 of the Telecommunications Act 1984. Modification of conditions will apply to 'every relevant licensee', instead of 'that person' under the Telecommunications Act. According to section 4A, in the case of a licence granted to all persons or to all persons of a particular class, the Director-General of Telecommunications shall not make any modifications unless: (a) every representation made to him in regard to the modification has been considered by him; and (b) that person running a telecommunication system under the authority of a licence has entered any objection to the making of the modification. In the case of a licence granted to a particular person, the Director-General shall not make any modification unless: (a) he has considered every representation made to him in regard the modification or any modification 'in the same or similar terms' that he is at the same time proposing to make in the case of other licences; and (b) that the requirements of section 12A are satisfied. All modifications must be justified by reasons. Where the Director-General has given notice of a proposal to modify the conditions of a licence, he may, where deemed appropriate, publish the identities of all or all of the persons who objected to the making of the modification unless confidentiality of information is claimed by the person making representations of objections. Representations or objections must be made within the time limit prescribed by the Director-General.

Subsection 4 of section 11 inserts a new section 12A into the Telecommunications Act 1984, which sets out the criteria for effecting any modifications. In fact, an element of progression may be found in the modification procedure. This is now explained. The following procedure is based on the assumption that (a) the Director-General of Telecommunications (DGT) proposed a licence modification and provided the modification (s 12(2) and (3)); and (b) that the Secretary of State has not objected to the proposed modification.

---

[18] *Explanatory Notes*, op cit, at para 61.

Stage 5	Refers to modification to the Competition Commission for its consideration whether the modification is requisite. If the answer is in the affirmative, modification goes ahead.

↑

Stage 4	DGT considers whether the modification is deregulatory (s 12A(3) and (7)[19]. If after consideration, he wishes to proceed with the modification, Stage 5 is activated.

Stage 3	DGT ascertains whether any relevant licensee has made any objection to the making of the proposed modification. If the answer is in the negative, the modification proceeds, and Stage 4 is activated.

↑

Stage 2	DGT considers all representations and objections, if any, (s 12(4B)(a)). If he then decides not to proceed, then modification procedure is abandoned, and no reference is required to be made to the Competition Commission. If he should decide to proceed, then Stage 3 is activated.

↑

Stage 1	Reminders must be issued (s 12A(5) and (6). A reminder must be contained in a notice given by the DGT and draw the attention of the licensees to the contents of the notice, pointing out that he will take modifications if no relevant licensee objects by the specific time (which is usually seven days). Reminders need not be sent to a licensee who has consented to the modification in question.

[19] Section 12A(7):
'For the purposes of this section a modification is deregulatory if:
   (a) the effect of the conditions to be modified is to impose a burden affecting the holder of the licence in which those conditions are included;
   (b) the modifications would remove or reduce the burden without removing any necessary protection;
   (c) the modification is such that no person holding a licence granted under section 7 above to a particular person would be unduly disadvantaged by the modification in competing with the holder of the licence in which those conditions are included.'

One of the most important issues in the modification procedure is to ensure that the licensees have been provided with a reasonable opportunity to state whether they wanted to object to the proposed modification. Furthermore, DGT must satisfy the provisions at section 12A(7)—that is, whether the modification is deregulatory.

Subsection (1) of section 14B of the Telecommunications Act 1984 provides for licensees' opportunities to appeal modifications of licence conditions; but section 2 of the Electronic Communications Act 2000 inserts a new paragraph '(da)' after paragraph (d) of subsection (1) of section 46B of the 1984 Act:

'(da) a decision with regard to the modification under Section 12 of a condition of a licence granted under Section 7 above to a particular person.'

There is no requirement on any person to deposit a key for electronic data with another person[20]; however, this does not prohibit the imposition by an order under section 8 of a requirement to deposit a key[21] for electronic data with the intended recipient of electronic communications comprising the data[22]; nor does it prohibit the making of alternative arrangements for key-storage with a view to preventing the loss of data or the ability to decode it.

3.3   Conclusions

The Preamble to the Act states that the purpose of this legislation is 'to familiarise the use of electronic communications and electronic data storage', in addition to making provision for the modification of licences granted under the Telecommunications Act 1984. The Act does not make provision to achieve these purposes; however, in view of the continuing advancement of science and technology, it may be pointed out that the current legislation may have to pass through an evolutionary process—thus modification of legislation may prove to be inevitable. However, the legislation certainly confirms that the government has a policy whereby e-Commerce will be facilitated.[23]

[20] s 14(1).
[21] 'Key' means 'any code, password, algorithm, key or other data the use of which (with or without other keys) (a) allows access to the electronic data; (b) facilitates the putting of the electronic data into an intelligible form.' s 14(3).
[22] s 14(2)(a).
[23] *Explanatory Notes to the Act* state that the government has also set itself 'targets for making Government services available electronically: all schools and libraries to be connected to the Internet by 2002, with 100% of a government services to be deliverable online by 2005. The Government has also set a target for 90% of its routine procurement of goods to be done electronically by 2000'. op cit, at 1.

4. Digital signatures, digital cash payment and the legal status of electronic money

4.1 Introduction

Digital signatures provide a method whereby authenticity and integrity over open networks are ensured. These signatures are based on a very complex mathematical procedure. It is part of cryptography, which is the service of rendering a secret message to third parties. The principle of digital signatures is based on confidentiality, and its aim is achieving authenticity and integrity. Digital signatures are adopted for security purposes; security being assured by confirmation from the recipient that communications over the Internet have been sent from whom they were supposed to be sent. In this process, a message is encrypted and then decrypted.

It should be emphasized that the special legal aspects of the digital signatures system operate successfully when two parties (the sender and the receiver of the message) know each other and can communicate over a certain or secure channel to share a secret message.

If the parties are unknown to each other and the secret message is sent over an open Internet, then the confidentiality which is the secret of digital signatures may not be maintained as the message may be intercepted over the Internet by an unauthorized third party.

This chapter explains the special legal aspects of digital signatures, digital cash payment and the legal status of electronic money.

4.2 The mechanism of digital signature

The basic mechanism has already been explained in chapter 1 of this work. The data that is to be signed must be created in digital form. A 'hash value' (which represents a mathematical value) is created by the computer, that is in effect a 'fingerprint' of the message. The signer encrypts the hash value with his private key. This process creates a digital signature which is known only to the desired parties. After the data is sent and received over the Internet, the recipient uses the sender's key to activate the hash value and the digital signature. It then compares the digital signature which is appended to the message. If the result is identical, the recipient becomes assured that the data was sent by the real sender, and that no alteration to it has taken place since transmission.

This mechanism also involves the use of 'private key' and 'public key' as explained in chapter 1 of this work. The digital signature mechanism requires that the data that is to be signed must be created in digital form. The value (a mathematical value) which is, in effect, a fingerprint of the message is created. One of the means of ensuring the security of the mechanism is that if the data is changed, the hash value will not correspond to it. A digital signature is unique to both the data and the private key used. After the data is received over the Internet, the recipient uses the sender's public key to reactivate the hash value and the digital signature in order to compare the digital signature appended to the message. If the result is identical, then the recipient can be assured that the signature has not been forged. Thus, the creation of a 'hash value', the encryption of the 'hash value' with a private key, and the confirmation of the data with the correct identification are the essential criteria to be satisfied in operating the digital signature system.

The digital signature system may be applicable to various types of business, including consumers' transactions, through the Microsoft Explorer and Netscape Communicator, and a public key system. This mechanism is adopted to maintain confidentiality of messages transmitted from the sender to the recipient. It must be emphasized however that in writing this work it has been decided not to go into the details of the technical aspects of digital signatures. The purpose is to identify the basic elements in order to allow the reader to understand the legal aspects of such signatures.

4.3 International action taken in regard to digital signatures

The system of digital signatures has drawn the attention of international, intergovernmental and non-governmental organizations. In this section an attempt is made to explain the nature of action taken by each type of organization discussed.

4.3.1 UNCITRAL—Model Law on electronic commerce

The UNCITRAL Model Law on Electronic Commerce was adopted by the UN General Assembly, Resolution No. 51/162 of 16 December 1996. An additional Article 5 bis was adopted in 1998. Article 7 of this Model Law is concerned with 'signature' and, according to this Article, where the law requires a signature of a person, that requirement will be satisfied in relation to a data message provided that:

(a)   a method for identifying that person is used and for indicating that person's approval of the information contained in the data message; and

(b)   in the light of all the circumstances, the method was appropriate for the purpose for which the data message was generated or communicated.

According to the Model Law, the above provisions apply irrespective of whether the requirement is in the form of an obligation. Under the Model Law, a state can specify the circumstances in which the provisions of this Article shall not apply.

The primary objective of Article 7 is to establish a basic standard of authentication for data messages that might be exchanged in the absence of a prior contractual relationship. It also provides guidance as to what might constitute an appropriate substitute for a signature in the event of the parties using electronic communications under a communication agreement.[1] The purpose of the Model Law in this context is to provide useful guidance where under a national law the question of authentication of data messages would be left to the discretion of the parties, and also in those circumstances in which requirements for signature which may be governed by the mandatory provisions of national law, should not be made subject to alteration by agreement of the parties.[2] Furthermore, Article 7 does not make any distinction between 'the situation in which users of electronic commerce are linked by a communication agreement and the situation in which parties had no prior contractual relationship regarding the use of electronic commerce'.[3]

In developing the Model Law, the following aspects of a signature were considered: (a) identification of a person; (b) certainty as to the personal involvement of the person in the act of signing; and (c) to associate that person with the context of a document.

The UNCITRAL Guide pointed out that depending on the nature of the document that was signed, a signature may also perform a variety of functions. In order to avoid abuse of electronic signatures, the Guidelines recommend that an authorization of signature system along the lines still followed by various national systems in respect of attestation of signatures on documents would be appropriate. The purpose of Article 7 is to adopt a comprehensive approach; it establishes the general conditions under which 'data messages would be regarded as authenticated with sufficient credibility and would be enforceable in the fact of signature requirements which currently present barriers to electronic commerce'.[4] UNCITRAL Model Law refers to two basic functions of a

---

[1] See the *Guide to Enactment of the UNCITRAL Model Law on Electronic Commerce* (1996), para 59.

[2] ibid.

[3] ibid.

[4] op cit, at para 56.

signature: (a) to identify the author of a document; and (b) to confirm that the author approved the contents of that document. It is important that under this system of signatures, the originator of a data message is identified, and a confirmation is received to the effect that the originator approved the contents of that data message. In activating this, legal, technical and commercial factors may be taken into account, which would include the following: (a) the level of sophistication of the equipment used by each party; (b) the nature of commercial activity; (c) the frequency at which commercial transactions take place; (d) the nature and volume of transactions; (e) the requirements of a valid signature in a given legal environment; (f) capacity/capability of the communication system; (g) the nature of the authentication procedures set by intermediaries and compliance thereto; (h) the range of authentication procedures made available by an intermediary; (i) compliance with trade usage; (j) the range of insurance cover that may be available for remedies against unauthorized messages; (k) the value, monetary or otherwise, contained in the data message; (l) the availability of alternative methods of identification and the costs of implementation; (m) the degree of acceptance or non-acceptance of method(s) of identification in a particular industry; and (n) any other relevant factor.[5]

On the other hand, as to the issue of security, a flexible and reliable approach is recommended by UNCITRAL, which would be in conformity with the purpose for which a data message is created and communicated. This may be done by means of agreements between the parties concerned. Not only should there be 'trading partner agreements',[6] but third-party service agreements, including intermediaries, should be concluded. The Model Law suggests that 'system rules' may be included in agreements that may be concluded between users of networks and electronic commerce. These rules are administrative and technical rules and procedures which are to be applied when communicating data messages. The Model Law points out that:

> 'the mere signing of a data message by means of a functional equivalent of a handwritten signature is not intended, in and of itself, to confer validity on the data message. Whether a data message that fulfilled the requirement of a signature has legal validity is to be settled under the law applicable outside the Model Law.'[7]

The issue of the validity of a data message that satisfied the requirement of a signature must be dealt with by referring to the appropriate local law.

---

[5] op cit, at para 58.
[6] These agreements are otherwise known as 'communication agreements' or 'interchange agreements'.
[7] op cit, at para 61.

4.3.2   The european union

The most important Directive issued by the European Parliament and the Council of Ministers on the issue of electronic signatures is the Directive entitled a Community Framework for Electronic Signatures.[8] Of course, the EC considered generally the issue of e-Commerce. On 8 October 1997, the Commission presented to the European Parliament, the Council, the Economic and Social Committee and the Committee of Regions a communication ensuring security and trust in electronic communication for a European framework for digital signatures and encryption. It was in December 1997 that the Council invited the Commission to submit a proposal for a Directive of the European Parliament and of the Council, on digital signatures. Both the European Parliament and the Council recognized that electronic communication and commerce necessitate 'electronic signatures' for the purpose of data authentication, as without it the purposes of e-Commerce might be defeated. Both institutions also recognized that for a full implementation of the principle of the free movement of goods, in the fastest possible manner, the importance of the appropriate use of electronic signatures could not be over-emphasized, and that a degree of trust in the customers must be developed for the proper functioning of this system, without prejudice to the Council Regulation (EC) No 3381/94 of 19 December 1994 setting up a Community regime for the control of dual use of goods. This was regarded as particularly important in view of the rapid technological development and the global character of the Internet.

The logic behind the promotion of electronic signatures is that it contributes to the ethos of the principle of the free movement of goods, which is meant for enhancing trade within the European Economic Area (EEA) without any barriers and in the fastest possible manner. The Directive implies that electronic signatures can be a vehicle for increasing business opportunities within the EEA. The Directive, therefore, states that:

> 'Electronic signatures will be used in a large variety of circumstances and applications, resulting in a wide range of new services and products related to or using electronic signatures; the definition of such products and services should not be limited to the issuance and management of certificates, but should also encompass any other service and product using, or ancillary to, electronic signatures, such as registration services, time-stamping services, directory services, computing services or consultancy services related to electronic signatures.'[9]

Harmonized criteria pertaining to the legal effects of electronic signatures, the Directive maintained, will preserve a coherent legal framework across the Community; although different requirements for the legal validity of handwritten signatures are available in national legal system, certificates may be used

---

[8] Directive 1999/93/EC of 13 December 1999; *Official Journal* L 013, 19/01/2000.
[9] op cit, at para 9.

to confirm that identity of the person signing electronically; the Community, therefore, aims at developing advanced electronic signatures based on qualified certificates ensuring a higher level of security. The Directive maintains that electronic signatures may be used in evidence in legal proceedings in the member states, and that:

> 'the legal recognition of electronic signatures should be based on objective criteria and not to be linked to authorisation of the certification- service provider involved.'[10]

In order to develop international electronic commerce transnationally, with third countries, the Directive proposes agreements on multilateral rules with third countries on mutual recognition of certification. According to the Directive, use of pseudonyms in certificates should not prevent member states from requiring identification of persons pursuant to Community or national law.[11]

4.3.2.1   The EU directive entitled a community framework on electronic signatures

4.3.2.1.1 The scope of the directive
It is not the aim of the Directive to harmonize the provision with regard to the confidentiality of information if they are already covered by national provisions. This Directive gives however legal recognition of electronic signatures within the Community, but it maintains that:

> 'a regulatory framework is not needed for electronic signatures exclusively used within systems, which are based on voluntary agreements under private law between a specific number of participants; the freedom of parties to agree among themselves the terms and conditions under which they accept electronically signed data should be respected to the extent allowed by national law; the legal effectiveness of electronic signatures used in such systems and their admissibility as evidence in legal proceedings should be recognised.'[12]

Any step towards harmonization of national rules of contract law is outside the remit of this Directive— in particular, the formation and performance of contracts, or other formalities of a non-contractual nature concerning signatures. Certification services to the public are subject to national rules regarding liability. According to the Directive, electronic signatures will be used in the public sector within national and Community administrations and 'in communications between such administrations and with citizens and economic operators, for example, in the public procurement, taxation, social security, health and justice systems.'[13]

---

[10] op cit, at para 21.
[11] op cit, at para 25.
[12] op cit, at para 16.
[13] op cit, at para 19.

National law will govern the legal spheres in which electronic documents and electronic signatures may be used. Certification services to the public are subject to national rules regarding liability, including data protection legislation and individual privacy, and this Directive does not affect national rules in relation to unlimited judicial consideration of evidence.

This Directive will be reviewed two years after it has been implemented in order to ensure that the advancement of technology or changes in the legal environment do not present any unforeseen difficulty for businesses engaged in this field of activity.

4.3.2.1.2 An analysis of the directive
The Directive consists of 15 Articles under the following heads: Scope (Art 1); Definitions (Art 2); Market Access (Art 3); Internal Market Principles (Art 4); Legal Effects of Electronic Signatures (Art 5); Liability (Art 6); International Aspects (Art 7); Data Protection (Art 8); Committee (Art 9); Tasks of Committee (Art 10); Notification (Art 11); Review (Art 12); Implementation (Art 13); Entry into Force (Art 14); and Addresses (Art 15). It also has four Annexes: Annex I (Requirements for qualified certificates); Annex II (Requirements for certification-service providers issuing qualified certificates); Annex III (Requirements for secure signature-creation devices); and Annex IV (Recommendation for secure signature verification).

In determining its scope, it is stated that the purpose of this Directive is to 'facilitate the use of electronic signatures and to contribute to their legal recognition' (Art 1). In other words, this Directive forms the basis for asking the member states to recognize electronic signatures. In order to ensure proper functioning of the internal market with electronic signatures the Directive establishes certification services.[14]

Issues relating to the conclusion and validity of contracts or other legal obligations prescribed by national or community law or any of these laws governing the use of documents do not come under the purview of this Directive.

Article 2 of the Directive provides definitions of certain key terms which are essential for the understanding of the mechanics of the use of electronic signatures. The text of this Directive has been appended to this work.

The provision for 'market access' (Art 3) should be read with the scope of this Directive in that one of its objectives is to ensure the proper functioning of the internal market. According to this Article, certification services must not be

---

[14] 'Certificate' means 'an electronic attestation which links signature-verification data to a person and confirm the identity of that person', and a 'certification-service provider' means 'an entity or a legal or natural person who issues certificates or provides other services related to electronic signatures'. (Art 2, paras 9 and 11).

subject to prior authorization.[15] The Directive encourages the member states to introduce or maintain voluntary accreditation schemes, which would entail seeking permission, by certification-service providers from public or private bodies at the national level; entrusted with the supervision of compliance with the rights and obligations emanating from the grant of such permission.[16] These schemes must be implemented in a non-discriminatory fashion and with transparency. There should not be any limit to the number of such certification service providers in a member state. It is for each member state to set up what would be deemed as the most appropriate certification system by it, as it is for each member state to ensure that the requirements for secure signature-creation devices (Annex III) are met by the entities concerned, and a determination of conformity with these requirements made by public or private bodies in a member state shall be recognized by all member states.[17] An 'Electronic Signature Committee' is to be set up by the Commission, and the latter shall also establish criteria for member states to determine the criteria that a public or private body in a member state must satisfy for its being designated with the Electronic Signature Committee. The Commission may also establish and publish reference numbers of generally recognized standards for electronic-signature products in the Official Journal of the European Communities. In order to promote the development and use of signature-verification devices in the light of the recommendations for secure signature verification (Annex IV), as well as to protect the interests of consumers, member states and the Commission shall work together.

It is for the member states to decide whether they would make use of electronic signatures in the public sector. In conformity with the provision for 'market access', the 'internal market principles' (Art 4) provide that each member state shall apply its own national provisions to certification-service providers established in its jurisdiction, and that a member state 'may not restrict the provision of certification-services originating in another Member State' (Art 4). Thus, paragraph 2 of Article 4 states that:

> 'Member States shall ensure that electronic signature products which comply with this Directive are permitted to circulate freely in the internal market.'

A qualified certification system should not be the sole criterion for recognition of electronic signatures. In referring to the legal effect of electronic signatures, the Directive provides that it is the duty of the member states to ensure that advanced electronic signatures which are based on a qualified certificate and which are created by a secret signature-creation device satisfy the legal requirements of a signature in electronic form, and that such signatures are admissible as evidence in legal proceedings. The member states are also required to ensure that electronic signatures are not denied legal effectiveness or that they

---

[15] For the various aspects of the certification services, see Annexes I, II, III and IV.
[16] See para 13 of Art 2.
[17] Art 3, para 4.

are not based upon a qualified certificate or that they are not based on a qualified certificate issued by an accredited certification service provider or that they are not created by a secure signature-creation device.[18]

Under the Directive, a certification-service provider is to be held liable for damage caused to any entity or legal or natural person, if damage was caused by virtue of reasonably relying on that certificate. The term 'reasonably' will provoke controversy, but it has to be determined in the context of each case.[19] However, each member state must ensure that in order to hold a certificate-service-provider liable, an entity or legal or natural person has reasonably relied on that certificate in respect of any of the following:

(a) accuracy of information at the time the qualified certificate was issued;
(b) the assurance that at the time the certificate was issued, the signatory identified in the qualified certificate 'held the signature-creation data corresponding to the signature-verification data given or certified in the certificate' (Art 6(b));
(c) the assurance that the signature-creation data and the signature-verification data had a complementary use where the certification-service-provider generated both of them and had not acted negligently.[20]

Member states shall ensure that a certification-service-provider may indicate in a qualified certificate the limits to which it is subject, provided that these limits are recognisable to third parties. However, the certification-service-provider may not be held liable for damages which arise from the use of a qualified certificate and which exceed the limitations placed on it (Art 6(3)). A certification-service-provider may indicate in the qualified certificate a limit on the value of transactions for which the certificate can be used, but the limit must be recognisable to third parties. It is to be noted however that the provisions of Article 6 (Liability) shall be without prejudice to the Council Directive 93/13/EEC of 5 April 1993 on unfair terms in consumer contracts.[21]

In regard to reciprocal recognition of certificates internationally, the Directive, in Article 7, provides that certificates which are issued as qualified certificates to the public in a third country are recognized as legally equivalent to certificates issued by a certification-service-provider established within the Community if one of the following conditions is satisfied:

(a) that the certification-service-provider in a third country has satisfied the requirements laid down in this Directive and that it has been accredited

---

[18] Art 5.
[19] Art 6.
[20] Art 6(1).
[21] O.J. L 95/21 April 1993 at 29.

under a voluntary accreditation scheme established in a Member State[22]; or

(b)   that a Community certification-service-provider which satisfied the requirements of this Directive guarantees the certificate; or

(c)   that the 'certification or the certification-service-provider is recognised under a bilateral or multilateral agreement between the Community and third countries or international organisations'.[23]

In order to develop cross-border certification services with third countries, the Commission will ensure that appropriate standards are adopted by such countries, and shall submit proposals to the Council for appropriate mandates for negotiation of bilateral and multilateral agreements with third countries and international organizations.[24]

It is anticipated that such agreements will obviously be concluded with countries that already have attained high standards in this regard. Where difficulties may be encountered by Community undertakings with regard to market access in third countries, the Commission may submit proposals to the Council for an appropriate mandate for negotiation of comparable rights for Community undertakings in third countries. Article 7(3) provides, inter alia, that:

'Measures taken pursuant to this paragraph shall be without prejudice to the obligations of the Community and of the Member States under relevant international agreements.'

The issue of data protection has received much attention in this Directive. Under Article 8 of the Directive, the member states are required to ensure that certification-service-provider and national institutions for accreditation or supervision comply with the requirement of the European Parliament and Council Directive 95/46/EC on the Protection of Personal Data and on the Free Movement of such Data.[25] Certification-service-providers may collect personal data only directly from the data subject, and data may not be collected or processed for any other purposes without the clear consent of the data subject.

A member state is required to notify the Commission and the other member states of the following:

(a)   information on national voluntary accreditation schemes[26];

(b)   identity (name and address) of the national body responsible for accreditation and supervision[27]; and

---

[22] Art 7(1)(a).
[23] Art 7(1)(c).
[24] Art 7(2).
[25] O.J. L 281 of 23 November 1995 at 31.
[26] See also Art 3(7).
[27] See also Art 3(4).

(c)   the names and addresses of all accredited national certification-service-providers.

The Commission shall review this Directive to determine whether its scope should be modified taking into account technological, market and legal developments, and the review along with legislative proposals shall be submitted to the European Parliament and the Council by 19 July 2003. Member states are required to communicate to the Commission the text of the main provisions of their domestic law which may be adopted in compliance with this Directive.

Compliance with the four Annexes by the member states is extremely important for the implementation of this Directive. The texts of the Annexes are appended to this work.

4.3.3   The International Chamber of Commerce

The proposal for developing international guidelines for international digital commerce was initiated by the International Chamber of Commerce in 1995 in relation to its work on the legal aspects of electronic commerce and the role of certification authorities. Initially, the ICC discussed it under the name of the Uniform International Authentication and Certification Practices (UIACP), but during the consultation period the title was changed to the General Usage for International Digitally Ensured Commerce (GUIDEC).

Chapter III of the document entitled Electronic Transactions and Information Security. The issue of public key cryptography and digital signatures has been discussed. The document maintains that in regard to commercial actors two issues are assured by public key encryption: (a) security of message; and (b) authenticity of transacting parties. The mechanics suggested or described by the ICC are not significantly different from the standard mechanism whereby two keys—a public key and a private key will be used—one of which is never shared with anybody, and the other is shared with everybody generally. This mechanism has already been discussed in chapter 1 of this work. The ICC maintains however that an ensured message is difficult to forge, its use binds the signatory. According to the ICC:

'Digital signature technology also forms the basis for forming legally binding contracts in the course of electronic commercial transactions since it can provide electronically the same forensic effect a signed paper message provides.'[28]

ICC's definition of 'digital signature' is in conformity with the standard definition of the term.

---

[28]   Internet file: //A.Guidec.asp.htn at 8.

4.4   Legal aspects of digital signatures

In the absence of any universally agreed meaning of the term 'digital signature' it proves to be difficult to discuss legal aspects of these signatures in their entirety. However, this term is often used to mean asymmetric cryptography, hence this discussion primarily refers to this terminology. Legal issues pertaining to this form of signature should be dealt with by reference to the relevant law in the most appropriate jurisdiction. However, there exists certain common legal aspects of digital signatures in most jurisdictions:

(a)   The definition of a signature may present a legal problem between foreign jurisdictions, particularly between common law and civil law systems. One of the means of avoiding this problem might be to determine a mutually agreed definition for transactions between parties, providing of course that the definition of 'signature'will not be governed by the law of any chosen jurisdiction. It is to be considered whether a universally acceptable definition of 'signature' may not be adopted and incorporated in national laws. Furthermore, the communication network being truly global in structure, a uniform digital certificate or digital signature system should be adopted for verification purposes. International passports, for example, have been made uniform.

(b)   Attention should also be paid to whether a 'certificate practice statement' which sets out its standard terms and conditions of business, may not be incorporated by reference electronically into its certificates, rather than maintaining the system of 'incorporation by reference' which means that a document referred to in another document may be regarded as incorporated into it. In other words, the practice about incorporation by reference should be uniform.

(c)   The consumer protection issue is of paramount importance, including issues of privacy that will remain important in the future. How liability should be determined in the event of secret information being divulged, and on what basis damages should be quantified, remain thorny legal problems.

Incidentally, Article 5 bis of UNCITRAL Model Law, which deals with incorporation by reference provides that:

'Information shall not be denied legal effect, validity or enforceability solely on the grounds that it is not contained in the data message purporting to give rise to such legal effect but is merely referred to in that data message.'

Article 5 bis was adopted by UNCITRAL in June 1998 and its primary purpose was to provide guidance as to how to deal with the situation where certain terms and conditions, although not stated in full but merely referred to in a data message, might have to be accepted as having the same legal effect as if they had been fully stated in the text of that data message.[29] It is also stated that 'incorporation by reference', the system practised by certain states, stands for a means of stating that certain provisions are detailed in an incorporated document.

Incorporation by reference is commonly followed for the use of electronic data interchange (EDI), e-mail, digital certificates and other forms of e-Commerce. The idea is that the basic messages may be communicated by any of the above mentioned means, and detailed information may be accessible elsewhere. Thus, abbreviations or codes are often used in transmitting messages by the above mentioned means. Furthermore, users and transmitters, in practice, prefer abbreviated and brief versions of messages when one thinks of the diverse trade practices and ranging legal environments in the world. Thus, uniform standards for incorporating data messages prove to be essential. UNCITRAL Model Law, therefore, maintains that:

> 'The establishment of standards for incorporating data messages by reference into other data messages is critical to the growth of a computer-based trade infrastructure. Without the legal certainty fostered by such standards, there might be a significant risk that the application of traditional tests for determining the enforceability of terms that seek to be incorporated by reference might be ineffective when applied to corresponding electronic commerce terms because of the differences between traditional and electronic commerce mechanisms.'[30]

UNCITRAL also maintains that the accessibility of the full text of the information being referred to may be significantly improved by the use of electronic communications by identifying a key word associated with a URL (Uniform Resource Locator).[31]

Article 5 bis intends to facilitate incorporation by reference by removing the uncertainty prevailing in many jurisdictions as to whether the system of traditional incorporation by reference may be applicable to incorporation by reference in an electronic environment, without more restrictive requirements than are applicable to paper-based trade. In determining the scope of Article 5 bis the UNCITRAL Model Law states, *inter alia*, that:

> 'Article 5 bis is not to be interpreted as creating a specific legal regime for incorporation by reference in an electronic environment. Rather, by establishing a principle of non-discrimination, it is to be construed as making the domestic rules applicable to incorporate ... for the purposes of electronic commerce'[32]

---

[29] op cit, at para 46–1.
[30] op cit, at para 46–4.
[31] op cit, at para 46–5.
[32] op cit, at para 46–7.

As an example, it cites that in a number of jurisdictions, existing rules of mandatory law only validate incorporation by reference provided the following conditions are satisfied:

(a) the reference clause is to be inserted in the data message;
(b) the document referred to, should actually be known to the party against whom the reference document might be relied upon; and
(c) that in addition to being known, the reference document should be accepted by that third party.

It is to be emphasized that a varied practice has been developed by various jurisdictions in regard to 'incorporation by reference', which may hinder the intended swift and safe communication system. UNCITRAL felt it necessary to include special provisions in the principal document in the form of Article 5 bis.

4.5   The UK position

The UK position is now reflected in the Electronic Communications Act 2000, which has been examined in chapter 2 of this work. However, there exist judicial guidelines as to what constitutes a 'signature', and this issue has received attention in this section.

4.5.1   Judicial guidelines developed by the english courts

The issue of what constitutes a 'signature' has received the attention of the English courts in a number of cases—the most important of which are:

(a) *Jenkins v Gaisford & Thring*[33]
(b) *R v Cowper*[34]
(c) *McLean v Weaver*[35]
(d) *Re Blücher (Prince), ex p Debtor*[36]
(e) *Goodman v J Eban Ltd*[37]

In *Jenkins*, the deceased, John Jenkins, who had difficulty writing or signing his name, had an engraving made of his usual signature a few months prior to his death, in order that it might be used to stamp or impress his signature to letters and other documents. The engraved signature was put on his will which was duly signed by witnesses. The court initially refused to grant probate on the grounds that the testator's engraved signature did not constitute a signature under section 9 of the Wills Act 1837. However, it was pleaded on behalf of the

[33] 164 E.R. 1208.
[34] 24 Q.B.D. 533.
[35] (1924) T.L.R. 47.
[36] [1931] 2 C.L. 70.
[37] [1954] 1 All E.R. 763.

beneficiaries that in his case 'signed' should be regarded as equivalent to 'marked'. Sir C Creswell held that it would be immaterial whether a mark was made by a pen or by some other instrument. 'The mark made by the instrument or stamp used was intended to stand for and represent the signature of the testator.'[38]

In *Cowper*, the issue was whether a lithographed indorsement could be regarded as a signature for the purpose of filing a plaint by a solicitor. The Court of Appeal (Lord Esher, MR) stated that:

> 'The whole object of the rule[39] seems to me to get the document authenti-cated as coming from a solicitor's office, and if the solicitor has authorised the issue of the lithograph that object is attained. He means it to be his sig-nature and send it forth as his, and that seems to be sufficient compliance with the Act.'[40]

In matters of procedure, therefore, a lithograph indorsement may satisfy the requirements for a signature; furthermore, the intentions of the person con-cerned, that he intended to sign the document, become relevant. Fry, LJ how-ever differed, and placed emphasis upon the 'signed by a solicitor', which was a requirement in this case. According to him:

> 'The registrar may fairly act on what appears at the foot of the particulars as the signature of the solicitor or firm of solicitors, while it is plain that a mere lithograph form, the blanks in which may be filled up at any time, offers no guarantee that it has come under the personal cognizance of the solicitor, or any person authorized to act on his behalf.'[41]

This opinion is of great significance in the case of digital signatures—the personal cognizance of the signatory is crucially important. In the case of e-Commerce no equivalent of signature should do.

McLean v Weaver raised an interesting legal issue, whether a signature on a for-warding letter enclosing a bill, which has not been signed, makes a valid bill. The court answered this question in the affirmative. Banks, LJ maintained that the fact that the name of the firm appeared on the face of the bill of costs did not make it a bad bill; it was a good bill because the letter was signed by Grant McLean (the claimant) who had done the work.[42]

In the case of digital signatures, the issue is important particularly with refer-ence to incorporation by reference; the supplementary documents must also be appropriately authenticated.[43]

---

[38] op cit, at 1209.
[39] Referred to r 10 (Ord 21) of the County Court Rules 1889.
[40] op cit, at 535.
[41] See UNCITRAL Model Law, Art 5 bis.
[42] op cit, at 47.
[43] See UNCITRAL Model Law, Art 5 bis.

In *Re Prince Blücher*, the Court of Appeal took a rigid view of the meaning of the term 'signed by him'. In this case, under the Bankruptcy Act 1914, a debtor who intended to make a proposal for a scheme of composition in satisfaction of his debts, was required to lodge with the Official Receiver 'a proposal in writing signed by him' containing the terms of the scheme of composition. The debtor in this case was so seriously ill that it was impossible for him to sign the proposal, so his solicitors signed the proposal on his behalf. In rejecting the validity of the composition, the Court of Appeal held that:

> 'the words 'signed by him' were explicit; and that there was no ground for altering the words of the statute or giving to the statute a judicial interpretation which would in effect be an amendment or alteration of its plain terms.'[44]

In fact, in the case of e-Commerce by means of digital signatures, for the sake of security, such a rigid view in regard to acceptable signatures would be extremely relevant. Where it is to be signed by a specific person, it must be done so—his agents will not do.

Goodman was again concerned with the meaning of the term 'signed by a solicitor'. In this case, a practising solicitor, under the name of a firm, delivered to the defendants a bill of costs accompanied by a covering letter at the end of which a facsimile of his signature in the name of the firm was endorsed. In an action for the recovery of the costs the defendants maintained that the letter was not 'signed' as required by the Solicitors Act 1932, section 65(2)(ii). The Court of Appeal held that:

> 'the signature on the letter having been shown to have been placed on it by means of the stamp by the plaintiff himself, the letter must be taken to be signed by him within the meaning of s 65(2)(i) of the Act of 1932.'

The Master of the Rolls (Sir Raymond Evershed) said however that such a method of signing did not carry with it 'the same clear authenticity or warrant of responsibility as a signature in the ordinary way'.[45] The signature was to be the writing of his own proper name and not the name of the business which as a solicitor he conducted.[46] Denning, LJ (as he then was) however brought out the legal significance of an actual signature by the prescribed person, when he stated that:

> 'The virtue of a signature lies in the fact that no two persons write exactly alike, and so it carried on the face of it a guarantee that that person who

---

[44] op cit, at 71.
[45] op cit, at 763.
[46] op cit, at 768.

signs has given his personal attention to the document. A rubber stamp carries with it no such guarantee, because it can be affixed by anyone.'[47]

This opinion highlights the importance of personalized signatures in the case of e-Commerce for the purpose of maintaining security. Incidentally, Stroud's Judicial Dictionary defines a 'signature' as:

'Speaking generally, a signature is the writing or otherwise affixing a person's name, or a mark to represent his name, by himself or by his authority, with the intention of authenticating a document as being that of, or as binding on, the person whose name or mark is so written or affixed.'[48]

It goes on to say that 'signature does not, necessarily, mean writing a person's Christian and surname, but any mark which identifies it as the act of the party'.

4.6   Digital cash payment

4.6.1   On-line payment issues

The basic mechanism pertaining to e-money and the status of e-money has already been discussed with reference to business-to-business (B[2]B) transactions.[49] It would be appropriate to discuss briefly the issues relating to B[2]B transactions and digital cash. One of the means of facilitating business-to-consumer transactions by electronic means is to adopt a developed system of encryption, which in turn, will also develop confidence in the minds of consumers in regard to the use of on-line payments; however the issue of fraud remains important.[50] The most common payment mechanisms used in on-line purchases are credit cards, debit cards and digital cash. The crucial commercial and legal issues of these payment mechanisms are now discussed.

4.6.2   Credit cards

Section 75 of the Consumer Credit Act 1974 provides that:

'(1)   If the debtor under a debtor-creditor-supplier agreement falling within section 12(b) or (c) has, in relation to a transaction financed by the agreement, any claim against the supplier in respect of a

---

[47] op cit, at 769.

[48] London, Sweet & Maxwell (1986) at 2431.

[49] For a good discussion of the law on electronic fund transfers, see A Arora, *Electronic Banking and the Law* (1993); See also Brindle and Cox (eds), *Law of Bank Payments* (1999).

[50] Certain cards, namely, Visa and Mastercard have developed a system of protection, which is known as 'secure electronic transaction' (SET), whereby payment card details transmitted over the Internet are to be safeguarded. It is a complex system, and it attempts to ensure that a consumer's card details are not revealed. For a discussion of SET, see Chissick and Kelman, *Electronic Commercial Law and Practice* (1999) 130–131.

misrepresentation and breach of contract, he shall have a like claim against the creditor, who, with the suppliers, shall accordingly be jointly and severally liable to the debtor.

(2) Subject to any agreement between them, the creditor shall be entitled to be indemnified by the supplier for loss suffered by the creditor in satisfying his liability under subsection (1), including costs reasonably incurred by him in defending proceedings instituted by the debtor.

(3) Subsection (1) does not apply to a claim-
  (a) under a non-commercial agreement, or
  (b) so far as the claim relates to any single item to which the supplier has attached a cash price not exceeding £30 or more than £10,000.

(4) This section applies notwithstanding that the debtor, in entering into the transaction exceeded the credit limit or otherwise contravened any term of the agreement.

(5) In an action brought against the creditor under subsection (1) he shall be entitled, in accordance with rules of court, to have the supplier made a party to the proceedings.'

Where a debtor-creditor-supplier agreement subsists, section 75(1) makes the creditor and supplier subject to a heavy burden, as any claim against that supplier based on misrepresentation and breach of contract will entail the creditor whereby both of them shall be jointly and severally liable to the debtor, subject to a statutory right of indemnity against the suppliers (sub-ss 2 and 5). This liability applies even when the debtor exceeds the credit or otherwise contravenes a term of the agreement (sub-s 4).

Subsection (1) does not apply to claims of two types which have been identified in subsection (3). Where however the creditor himself is a seller or a hirer of goods under a credit sale, conditional sale or hire purchase agreement, the exceptions at subsection (3) do not apply to his liability for breach of implied terms, since such liability arises under the Sale of Goods Act 1893 (as amended) or the Supply of Goods (Implied Terms) Act 1973, or the Supply of Goods or Services Act 1982.

Section 83:

'(1) The debtor under a regulated consumer credit agreement shall not be liable to the creditor for any loss arising from use of the credit card facility by another person not acting, or to be treated acting, as the debtor's agent.

(2) This section does not apply to a non-commercial agreement, or to any loss in so far as it arises from misuse of an instrument to which section 4 of the Cheques Act 1957 applies.'

The purpose of this section is to provide protection to a debtor, under a regulated consumer credit agreement, from liability to its creditor for losses arising from the use of the credit facility by a person other than its agent or anybody who may be treated to be acting on its behalf. This section does not apply however to non-commercial agreements or to losses occasioned by or arising from misuse of an instrument to which section 4 of the Cheques Act 1957 applies, eg cheques, bankers' demand drafts, dividend and interest warrants etc and credit-token agreements as detailed in section 84.

Section 84:

'(1) Section 83 does not prevent the debtor under a credit-token agreement from being made liable to the extent of £30 (or the credit limit if lower) for loss to the creditor arising from use of the credit-token by other persons during a period beginning when the credit-token ceases to be in the possession of any authorised person and ending when the credit-token is once more in the possession of an authorised person.

(2) Section 83 does not prevent the debtor under a credit-token agreement from being made liable to any extent for loss to the creditor from use of the credit-token by a person who acquired possession of it with the debtor's consent.

(3) Subsections (1) and (2) shall not apply to any use of the credit-token after the creditor has been given oral or written notice that it is lost or stolen, or is for any other reason liable to misuse.

(4) Subsections (1) and (2) shall not apply unless there are contained in the credit-token agreement in the prescribed manner particulars of the name, address and telephone number of a person stated to be the person to whom notice is to be given under subsection (3).

(5) Notice under subsection (3) takes effect when received, but where it is given orally, and the agreement so requires, it shall be treated as not taking effect if not confirmed in writing within seven days.

(6) Any sum paid by the debtor for the issue of the credit-token, to the extent (if any) that it has not been previously offset by use made of the credit-token, shall be treated as paid towards satisfaction of any liability under subsection (1) or (2).

(7) The debtor, the creditor, and any person authorised by the debtor to use the credit-token, shall be authorised persons for the purposes of subsection (1).

(8) Where two or more credit-tokens are given under one credit-token agreement, the preceding provisions of this section apply to each credit-token separately.'

Section 84 is designed to limit the debtor's liability for losses arising from misuse of credit-tokens, eg credit cards or credit voucher, to a maximum of £30, unless a credit token is misused by virtue of a person acquiring possession of it with the debtor's consent. A debtor may not be held liable for misuse of a credit-token if he gives notice, whether oral or written to the issuer, or the person who is stated to be the person to whom notice is to be given, of its loss or any other reason whereby it may be misused. An oral notice must be confirmed in writing within seven days. Where multiple credit-tokens are issued under one credit-token agreement, eg to employees of a firm, and the agreement is presumably concluded with the firm concerned, the provisions of section 84 apply to each credit-token separately—this is because the firm cannot be held responsible for any irresponsible use of a credit-token by any of the beneficiaries.

4.6.3   Debit cards

By using a debit card the cardholder authorizes his/her bank to debit his/her account with the amount of the transaction. A common example of a debit card in the UK is SWITCH. The Consumer Credit Act 1974, in general, does not include debit cards under the protection of the Act, except where a debit card allows the consumer a credit facility. Section 83 of the Act protects overdraft-bearing debit cardholders from liability for unauthorized payments gone out of their cards, as such cards also have the characteristics of credit cards—they are mixed cards. Thus, they may also be able to take protection from section 75 of the Act.

4.6.4   Digital cash payment

Basically, the digital cash payment system stands for a system whereby digitally represented units of value, denominated (expressed) in a particular currency, and stored on an electronic device, are transferred from a buyer to a seller. Each digital coin is to be assigned a specific currency value, and its authority is verified with the help of digital cash products in the Internet payment market: Digicash's e-cash seems to be popular for use over the Internet. It is also based on a digital coin system. However, no bank in the UK, so far, is licensed to use e-cash. Its mechanism may nevertheless be explained in the following way: a customer purchases e-cash from a bank licensed to issue e-cash, and stores in on his 'hard drive', and spends it at participating merchants or transfers it to other customers. In order for such transactions to take effect, merchants must hold accounts at participating banks so that they can redeem their digital coins for real value.

The Mondex Digital Cash System has gained some ground. Mondex International, under whose auspices this scheme operates, concludes shareholder franchise agreements with selected banks. In the UK, HSBC, National Westminster Bank and the Bank of Scotland have entered shareholder franchise agreements. The Mondex digital cash is not based on digital coins, but is a stored value system based on smart cards and the stored value is expressed as units of a particular currency. The operational procedures of Mondex may be explained in the following way:

(a)   Origination—this is the process of creation and transfer of computer code in which stored value is expressed. The issuer of digital cash is known as the originator.[51] A participating bank purchases digital cash from the originator, which is transferred from the originator's master chip to the bank's purse.

(b)   The participating bank concerned makes payment to the originator by traditional methods, eg CHAPS. Such transactions take place on the basis of pre-arranged contracts between the parties.

(c)   After a consumer purchases digital cash from one of the participating banks, it is transferred from the bank to the consumer's smart card. This transfer can take effect on the smart card (loading up) even at an Automatic Teller Machine (ATM) or at a payphone.

(d)   Consumers may use digital cash to make purchases from merchants who are willing to accept this method of payment. In this instance, a consumer transfers stored value from his chip to the trader's (merchant's) chip. Once this is effected, goods/services are delivered to the consumer.

(e)   The trader (merchant) then transfers the stored value from his chip to the bank's chips; but the trader (merchant) will have to deposit the digital cash received at its participating bank.

(f)   On the basis of the digital cash received, the trader's (merchant's) bank will credit the trader's (merchant's) account with an equivalent amount (less any transaction charges).

(g)   The trader's (merchant's) bank deposits digital cash stored on its chips with the originator.

(h)   The originator makes payment to the trader's (merchant's) bank for all digital cash received.[52]

The important issue which should be considered in this connection is whether digital cash may be regarded as legal tender. What is a legal tender has already been explained in a separate section of this work.[53] In England, legal tender is defined by the Coinage Act 1971, as amended by section 1(3) of the Currency Act 1983 and section 1(2) of the Currency and Bank Notes Act 1954.

On the basis of this discussion, it may be maintained that digital cash does not qualify as legal tender in the UK. Furthermore, traders or merchants are not obliged to accept digital cash; the contract between a participating bank and a consumer does not necessarily allow the latter to compel his bank to redeem digital cash. The digital cash system will not operate if the originator and/or the participating bank becomes insolvent. Of course, the evidence of fraud in the digital cash payment system may not be ruled out. The second legal issue which should be considered is how a consumer may have any recourse against the originator, as usually, a consumer is not a party to the contract between the originator and a participating bank. This issue assumes importance when an

---

[51] In the UK, Stirling Organisation plc is the originator.
[52] Most of the states identified in this section have been based on Saul Miller's description of the Modex System; see at 65–66; see also Finlayson-Brown, 'Mondex: Structure of a New Payment System' (1997) 12 *Journal of International Banking Law* 362
[53] See 4.7.3.

originator may withdraw. Protection against such a situation many only be given to a consumer, as a third party, by incorporating a clause in the principal agreement between an originator and a participating bank, expressly allowing a third party to derive benefit from that contract.[54]

In relation to a contract between a participating bank and a merchant/trader—does the latter have any right to compel the former to redeem digital cash? The answer should be in the affirmative, however, what might happen to this contract when the originator withdraws from the scheme? The originator should be obliged to honour the payment obligations based on the contract; it also should give sufficient notice of withdrawal stating that after a stipulated date no payment will be honoured. The legal position is that in the absence of any privity between an originator and a merchant/trader the contract between an originator and a participating bank should ideally contain such a clause; this would be in the interest of participating banks from a commercial standpoint. These issues are to be governed by the relevant rules of the law of contract. The issue is not whether a party could rely on an implied term between a participating bank and a merchant/trader; the real issue is how may protection be afforded to a merchant/trader when the originator withdraws from the digital cash system—as stated earlier, either the originator gives sufficient notice to all participating banks and the latter communicate it to their merchants/traders or the participating bank protect the merchant's/trader's position by entering a clause to that effect in their contracts with originators. Of these two alternatives, the latter would be preferable.

If an originator suddenly withdraws from a digital cash payment scheme, a participating bank is still contractually bound to honour the valid commitments of a merchant/trader made to their customers. Thus, a contractual notice period for withdrawal is essential. On the other hand, the argument would be that under implied terms the participating bank concerned is obliged to settle the digital cash accounts of a merchant/trader. Although this argument may seem to be correct, in order to protect its interest, the participating bank concerned should incorporate a clause in its contract with the originator to protect the interest of merchants/traders.

As a matter of procedure, it should be pointed out that an originator does not issue digital cash to participating banks until it receives real value against it from the latter, and holds this value in what is known as a 'float' which represents the potential claims that might be made against the originator for the redemption of digital cash.[55] In this connection, so to say, between an originator, a participating bank and the merchant/trader of the latter should be borne in mind. In the absence of a privity between a merchant/trader and an originator, the originator will be left with certain funds, which actually do not

---

[54] See further Saul Miller, op cit, at 68; see also MacQueen, 'Third Party Rights in Contract: English Reform and Scottish Contracts', 1 *E.L.R.* (1997) at 488.
[55] See further Saul Miller, op cit, at 70.

belong to it. Depending upon the nature of the contract between a participating bank and a merchant/trader the same argument may apply in respect of an participating bank and its merchants/traders. This may be described as a case of 'unjust enrichment'.[56] Can a consumer or merchant bring a claim of unjust enrichment against an originator? The answer must be in the affirmative, provided of course, a causal link is established between the losses sustained by a claimant and a merchant/trader. It would be difficult to establish any direct causal link without going through the participating bank concerned because merchants/traders have direct links with participating banks in this type of transaction. This is precisely the reason why it is suggested that the contract between an originator and a participating bank should incorporate a clause which would give merchants/traders protection, and eventually in the chain consumers.

If a consumer has paid by any valid means, for example, by a charge card, and if a merchant does not receive payment from the card company, the liability of the customer is discharged.[57] There is no reason why the same principle should not apply to digital cash systems. Furthermore, in such a situation, a merchant/trader allows a customer to pay by such a method, as he is apparently certain that eventually the payment will be received by him from the participating bank. This is all the more reason that a participating bank should include a provision for the protection of third parties while contracting with an originator.

Digital cash circulated represents the amount of claims that may be made against the originator, and if the float held by the originator falls below the value of the digital cash already in circulation, then the risk is for both participating banks, merchants/traders and customers. Furthermore, excessive issue of digital cash will have a bearing upon the money supply position in the UK. However, the insolvency of an originator in England will be dealt with by a liquidator in accordance with the insolvency legislation, according to which, in general, the principle of preferred creditors will be relied upon, and a customer or a merchant may not come under that category of creditors.

On the other hand, in the event of a participating bank being insolvent, customers will remain unaffected, although the merchant concerned may have difficulty in recovering the money from the participating bank by virtue of not being a preferred creditor, unless under the Modex scheme they may be able to protect their position.

Fraudulently obtained digital cash or cash stolen from a customer subsequently transferred to an innocent third party, giving value, and accepted by the third party in goods faith, should allow the third party to have a legitimate claim or title in that money. It becomes the bona fide user of the cash.

---

[56] ibid.
[57] In *Re Charge Card Services* [1989] 1 Ch. 497.

Digital cash is incorporeal encrypted information[58]; it may not be treated as a negotiable instrument because under the Bills of Exchange Act 1882, bills of exchange and promissory notes must be in writing and signed. In other words, digital cash, currently falls outside the scope of the Bills of Exchange Act 1882.

Digital cash is a relatively cheap and speedy method of making payments. This form of payment does not entail charge-back risk,[59] and enables a merchant to receive digital cash immediately if he deposits it promptly in his bank. This method of payment requires advance payment—hence banks would prefer their customers to use this method of payment rather than the payments based on credit cards. Furthermore, this method of payment may not be governed by section 75 of the Consumer Credit Act 1974. No credit check needs to be made while making payment by digital cash, and there is no risk of losing payment by virtue of the consumer making payments by this method being insolvent. Payments under the digital cash system are instantaneous. Because of ease of payment, customers should prefer this method of payment to many others, particularly for shopping on-line.

4.7   The legal status of electronic money

Although electronic money has been in vogue for over a decade, its legal status still remains uncertain. In order to discuss this issue, it is important to explain the meanings of a 'tender' and a 'legal tender'. 'Tender' in the context of making a payment must be unconditional and in the form of money, including legally acceptable equivalents, namely, bank drafts, in satisfaction of a debt, however occasioned. It is immaterial whether a tender has been made directly or through an agent on behalf of the debtor.

A legal tender has been drafted as:

' a tender of money of such description that the person to whom it is tendered will put himself in the wrong if he refuses to accept it.'[60]

A legal tender as a recognized unit of money is guaranteed by the issuer who is usually the sovereign. However, one sovereign may not recognize a unit of money issued by another sovereign, unless exchange between currencies of sovereigns has been declared permissible and acceptable.

It is possible for a few states/sovereigns to recognize a particular unit of money as legal tender, if they so wish. Law does not prevent a joint recognition of legal

---

[58] See further Saul Miller, op cit, at 74.

[59] Payments made by credit or debit cards are subject to checks in order to avoid fraudulent transactions. This checking system prevents a merchant/trader from receiving any money from his bank based on a fraudulent transaction because of a 'charge back' clause.

[60] Perry & Ryder, *Thompson's Dictionary of Banking* (London, Pitman) at 333.

tenders. On the other hand, payment by Special Drawing Rights (SDR) is accepted since the international community has recognized such method of payment originated by the International Monetary Fund (IMF) even though it is not issued by any sovereign authority. SDRs' legitimacy is derived from the recognition accorded to it by the international community. Under the classical system, a unit of money or currency of payment was associated with sovereigns, which is no longer the case. A recognized unit of currency or legal tender thus serves as money, a medium by which goods and services may be bought and sold.

Money is a term that is used in the abstract, that is, it is a standard which is used for determining the values of commodities or services. Its value may differ from country to country. It is a medium of expressing how much of the specified currency must be paid to obtain a pre-determined quantity of goods or services. It is only a medium of payment, and it does not represent any method of payment. A method of payment stands for a way or system of making payment after the amount has been determined by reference to a recognized unit of currency (SDR is now regarded as a unit of currency, although it is not a tangible currency—SDR is an exceptional unit of currency).

E-money or electronic money is a record of monetary value registered or held in an electronic form. It is, therefore, different from the traditional monetary units, whether in metal or paper. The Committee on Legal Affairs and Citizens' Rights of the European Commission defined electronic money as a monetary value that is:

'(i)   ... stored on a electronic device such as a chip card or a computer money;
(ii)   accepted as means of payment by natural and legal person other than the issuing institution or its subsidiaries, its parent undertaking or subsidiaries of the parent company;
(iii)   generated in order to be put at the disposal of bearers to serve as an electronic surrogate for coins and banknotes.'[61]

It has the use of traditional units of payment save that it is not transacted over the counter nor does it entail any physical transfer between parties. It stands for a method of transaction by mechanical means in the monetary units recognized by the international community. As it represents merely a method of transaction in the form of monetary units, it does not require authorization by sovereign states. The international community, initially, on a de facto basis, now seems to have accepted this method as part of commercial practice and culture. In fact, like traditional methods of intra-bank transfers or transactions, that is, without moving funds, funds are accounted for by a faster means.

---

[61] Doc 598 P CO 461 (01) COM (98) 0461; See also the Commission's Report of 25 March 1999 A-4–0156/99 PE 229; 502/fin at 8.

4.7.1   Operational methods of electronic money

Two major methods are involved in e-money transactions; stored value method and digital method. In operating the stored value method, units of value are registered as a smart card, which operates like a pre-paid photocopying card or phone card. As these are used, their stored values are reduced and eventually brought to nil. Stored value methods, otherwise known as electronic purses, again seem to have developed two sub-methods: accountable and unaccountable, the latter also known as the anonymous method. This method obviously gives rise to suspicion, but it preserves privacy in transactions and does not involve intervention by any central authority. This method may be suitable, if at all, if both sides interact directly with each other.

The accountable method on the other hand, records information concerning a transaction. Under this method, on-line authorization by information may be effected or alternatively, information may be gathered which is sent to a central database after payment has been effected. Information gathering in this context means that the information supplied by the user is verified against the data held by a central database. It is very much like payment by credit or debit cards, which also entails costs for the creditor.

The digital cash method is operated on a 'coins' basis. Each coin carries its own serial number and is encrypted (signed) using digital signature by the issuer. A specific unit of value is transmitted by computer messages. Under this method, upon receipt of a request from the purchaser, the issuer supplies coins for a certain value, and debits the purchaser's account. The purchaser then remits the coins to the vendor, who then sends them to the issuer—the latter verifies their genuineness and whether they have already been sent. The issuer thereafter credits the value of the coins to the vendor's account. It is understood that the digital cash method can be used anonymously, whereby a bank may not have any means of knowing from which account the coins were withdrawn. In other words, the rogue can camouflage the method. Indeed, technology gives us benefit, but it also sometimes gives us inextricable social and legal problems. This issue has received attention in a subsequent section of this chapter.

4.7.2   Is electronic money a legal tender?

In order to answer this question, one is required to consider the most important characteristics of a legal tender. First, if one refers to cash, in view of its characteristics as a method of payment, instantaneous payment is made by it. In recent years, money as a unit of payment is concerned with its face value—the intrinsic value of money has lost its importance. In the case of payment by other methods, again, the face value of a currency is taken into account, and payment may be made, for example, by means of credit or debit cards or by drafts or by electronic means. Therefore, the intrinsic value of money is no longer a characteristic of a legal tender. Electronic money should not be confused with a legal tender's face value. It is primarily a method of sending a pre-determined price by electronic means. In this sense, electronic money is a misnomer. Electronic money is not to be perceived in terms of intrinsic value or the face value of a monetary unit. It is a method of transmitting a value only, determined by reference to a legal tender. Second, from an historical point of view, settlement of accounts by legal tenders was to be immediate and by the same token it may be maintained that, originally, the intrinsic value of money was thought to be important. Without going into the details of the reasons for abandoning the notion of the intrinsic value of money, which was largely occasioned by the shortages of appropriate metals, it may be stated that for a long period of time, the immediacy of payment, based on the face of a currency has been a common practice in the international commercial world, as has been the system of prompt payment by technological devices. Over the counter payment is the most immediate and certain method of payment, so is the method of payment by electronic means: however, the difference remains that whereas the over-the-counter payment by cash is a real money payment, all other methods of payment, including the electronic method, are simply methods of payment, representing the unit of money, but not money in itself, although in certain cases, such as payment by bank drafts or by postal orders, the legal situation becomes different. Under the electronic method, the process of authorising payments is swift, thus electronic money satisfies the condition of the immediate payment, but still does not satisfy the condition of being actual money.

Third, the units of legal tenders must be consistent. A £1 coin for example, must bear the same value for each transaction. When payment is made by electronic means a pre-determined amount is transmitted by this method, which does not accord the means of transmission the status of a legal tender. This simply implies that the means of transmitting funds (electronic) must transmit funds in accordance with the acknowledged value of each legal tender.

Fourth, durability of a legal tender; if electronic transmission were to be regarded as a method of transmitting an amount represented by legal tenders, it is not required to satisfy the criteria of a legal tender. In fact, the issue of durability is irrelevant to using an electronic means for transmitting money.

It is to be considered, therefore, whether transmission of money by a means makes the means a legal tender. The electronic means simply transfer money from one party to another (without moving any amount) in accordance with the instruction received by the transmitter. If 'directly transferable' is a quality of a legal tender, electronic means satisfies that criterion, but still it simply transfers, as a means, the money which it is contracted to transfer to the beneficiary or to the party concerned.

4.8   Conclusions

Digital signatures are signatures which are mechanically developed. Where 'personal signatures' are necessary, the courts' decisions in the cases discussed in this chapter remain valid. There is no difference between 'personal signatures' and 'digital signatures', the latter being primarily facilitating business speedily. Digital signatures are recognized by the commercial community, and thus have received a de jure recognition; indeed, in so far as e-Commerce is concerned, English law does not prevent the carrying on of business by e-Commerce on the basis of digital signatures.

In March 1997, the government published a consultation paper entitled 'Licensing of Trusted Third Parties for the Provision of Encryption Services', the salient points of which are:

(a) Certification authorities and other providers of public key certification services to the public would require a licence, and that in the UK a user would be free to choose his provider(s), although exception to the licensing requirement would be made for intra-company certification services;

(b) The definition of encryption services being broad (which included almost all cryptography-related services—key management, key storage and key generation) should be looked into; and

(c) Although the government had no intention to access private keys used solely for integrity functions, in the interest of confidentiality, it would require deposit of keys.

In April 1998, the government published a revised paper entitled 'Secure Electronic Commerce Statement', which recommended, *inter alia*, that there would be no mandatory licensing requirement, but a voluntary licensing scheme would be introduced—under which the recovery of keys would be mandatory for encryption services but not for digital signatures. These proposals culminated in the Electronic Communications Act 2000—the basic provisions of which have been examined in a separate chapter.

It is to be emphasized that the current legislation has placed sufficient stress on the issue of the security of information, but law has its own limits—criminal activities may not be prevented by legislation, it can only prescribe punishment after a criminal act has been committed. Despite its manifold advantages, business by e-Commerce is not risk-free. It is for the users of digital signatures to take fool-proof measures and actions against the abuse of digital signatures.

On-line payment method (digital cash payment) is convenient for all parties concerned: the participating bank, the merchant/trader and the consumer. Its advantages and disadvantages have been explained. The difficulties which an originator of digital cash may present to a participating bank or a merchant/trader or a consumer, deserve further consideration by the commercial community. As stated earlier, unless a sufficient mechanism is devised for providing protection to these parties, their respective position remains precarious. The digital cash system is still passing through its gestation period. Based on its use over time it should be possible to ascertain better the advantages and disadvantages associated with this system of payment.

5. Concluding contracts over the internet

5.1   Introduction

Contracts concluded over the Internet are contracts concluded impersonally by what is known as a 'remote control' method. The formalities of concluding contracts are maintained, although mechanically. The basic elements of contract under English law must be observed when contracting through the Internet: offer, acceptance, and consideration. The only difference is that whereas English law permits oral contracts, contracts through the Internet must necessarily be in written form, although not in the traditional sense of the term 'writing'—but then under English law, simple contracts need not be in writing, and when parties prefer to conclude their contracts in writing, they need not follow any form, unless a particular standard form has been accepted by the parties themselves.

One of the principal differences between ordinary contracting and contracting through the Internet is that the latter is speedier than the former and subject to more misrepresentation of facts and misrepresentation of terms than the former, unless the time-scale within which a contract is concluded allows clarification of both items. The Internet allows a speedy conclusion of a contract but at the same time speed, which is inherent in the process, may give rise to various legal problems. Inherent in the contracting process through the Internet is the risk of abuse of the technology and misrepresentation of facts, and probable misunderstanding of certain terms by parties, otherwise, the basic elements of the law of contract may be satisfied when contracting through the Internet. In this chapter an attempt is made to demonstrate whether the current English law of contract may satisfy the requirements of contracting through the Internet, and whether the English law may offer remedies to the injured party if necessary, when a contract was created through the Internet.

5.2 Do the basic elements of a contract under English law differ from contracts concluded through the Internet?

5.2.1 General

Contracts of sale are usually initiated by the description of goods or by sending samples. In the case of contracting by the Internet, sale of goods will obviously be initiated by description. This is where legal problems may arise. Misrepresentation of facts may be a cause for action. The same applies to service contracts. The ingredients of the formation of a contract under English law, without any mechanical intervention, and that with mechanical intervention, remains the same: invitation to treat, offer and acceptance with consideration, and the intention to create legal relations. The usual competition about the priority in acceptance offers (thus acceptances) applies when contracting through the Internet, and the hours shown on the messages will confirm precisely at what hours an acceptance was received by the offeror—it is immaterial at what hours an acceptor transmitted his acceptance. Of course, the fact remains that even where an agreement has been reached, it may not result to a binding contract if it is incomplete or inconclusive. The principle of *ad idem* is also applicable to contracts concluded through the Internet. Of course, in deciding whether the parties have actually reached an agreement, English courts usually apply an objective test.[1]

There is no reason why the usual principles of the law of contract under English law should not apply to contracts concluded through the Internet. Contracting through the Internet simply hastens the process, but of course, risks of misrepresentation of facts and the 'rush' about priority of acceptance and rejection of offers by mechanical means may sometimes present legal problems. In light of this, it is now considered whether contracts concluded through the Internet should be governed by any special rules that are not already covered by the law of contract under English law.

5.2.2 Invitation to treat

In this context, how a contract is usually initiated becomes relevant. A prospective seller gives publicity on his product or service to a particular person or a group of persons or to the world at large. In response to that publicity, a person may decide to contact the future supplier of goods or provider of service. Publicity may be given in various forms or by various means: publication of catalogues or by placing advertisements in magazines or by advertisement on the television or by hand bill or even by displaying products in the windows of a shop. The crucial issue is whether a statement of fact is regarded as an offer, whereas it is, in reality, a statement of a price.[2] The distinction between a

---

[1] See further Vorster (1987) 103 *Law Quarterly Review* 286; and De Moor (1990) 106 *LQR* 632.
[2] See *Harvey v Facey* [1893] A.C. 552; see also *Clifton v Palumbo* [1944] 2 All E.R. 497.

'preliminary enquiry' and an 'offer' made expressly or by conduct must be maintained. In *Gibson v Manchester City Council,*[3] in their letter the local authority stated that it 'may be prepared to sell' the property at a specified price to a tenant, which the latter regarded as an offer when it was not to be regarded as such, but merely as an invitation to make an offer.

In contracting by electronic means, care should be taken to study the description of goods or services offered, which, if not correctly described in words, might present legal difficulties in defining the act as to whether it is an invitation to treat or an offer. Under the English law of contract, a communication, by whatever means, electronically or otherwise, the purpose of which is to invite parties to make an offer is commonly called an invitation to treat, however, the problem arises when the price is shown on that communication. If a person responds to that communication, with a definite price for the goods and services offered by the offeror together with other terms and conditions attached to it, then it may be legally difficult to distinguish an invitation to treat from an actual offer.[4] The general argument has been that if the offer is not signed by the offeror, then there is no intention to be bound by it[5]; it should be treated merely as an invitation to treat. Even if the term 'offer' is contained in a statement, or the statement requests persons to make an offer,[6] or it requests persons to make an offer, it is not an offer in the sense of the law of contract. It is doubtful whether auction sales can be conducted by electronic means; in theory, it may be possible to do so, but in reality, the time gap between an offer and acceptance at a place of auction may not make it possible to do so. It has, therefore, been decided not to discuss auction sales by electronic means, however, in the event of a dispute arising in connection with an auction sale by electronic means, the judicial guidelines already developed in this regard would apply.

The distinction between an offer and an invitation to treat depends on the intention of the person who makes the statement, and how he reserves his right to maintain that his statement should not be treated as an offer, but merely as an invitation to treat.

In *Partridge v Crittenden,*[7] it was held that a newspaper advertisement that goods are for sale is not generally to be regarded as an offer. This rule, as applied to publicity on goods or services through the Internet, may present inconvenience and even a hindrance to selling goods and services speedily through the Internet. Currently, however, *Partridge* represents the applicable

---

[3] [1979] 1 W.L.R. 294.
[4] But see, *Fisher v Bell* [1961] 1 Q.B 394. The decision in this case was reversed by restriction of the Offensive Weapons Act 1961, s 1. Dicta in *Wiles v Maddison* [1943] 1 All E.R. 315 at 317 suggests that an article displayed at a shop window is an offer; see also *Esso Petroleum Ltd v Commissioners of Customs & Excise* [1976] 1 W.L.R. 1.
[5] See *Financings Ltd v Stimson* [1962] 1 W.L.R. 1184.
[6] *Harvela Investments Ltd v Royal Trust Co of Canada (CI)Ltd* [1986] A.C. 207; see also *Bigg v Boyd Gibbons Ltd* [1971] 1 W.L.R. 913.
[7] [1968] 1 W.L.R. 1204.

rule. In *Grainger & Son v Gough*[8] it was decided that the circulation of a price list was to be treated as an invitation to treat. Where unilateral advertisements may lead to further bargaining, particularly in respect of price or certain terms, there seems to be a valid reason for maintaining that advertisements of unilateral contracts should not be regarded as 'offers', but where there is no room for bargaining, there is no reason why advertisements of unilateral contracts may not be regarded as offers. The celebrated case on this point is: *Carlill v Carbolic Smoke Ball Co Ltd.*[9] One important issue in this regard which should be borne in mind is that an advertiser may be under liability when he falsely gives an advertisement, that is, without any intention to sell his goods or services. Such an advertiser may be held liable under the Trade Description Act 1968, section 14(1)(b) or the Consumer Credit Act 1974, sections 45 and 46; the Consumer Protection Act 1987, section 20; or Part II of the Fair Trading Act 1973.[10] This is a legal issue that is important in giving publicity to products and services through the Internet.

Based on *Spencer v Harding,*[11] it is an established principle that any statement made to sell goods by tender is not necessarily to be regarded as an offer to sell to the person making the highest tender—it simply indicates a readiness to receive offers. This rule applies to all tenders pertaining to the supply of goods, services or for the execution of engineering or construction works, unless the tenderer already confirms, in writing, that he will be obliged to accept the highest offer. In reality, however, the lowest offer is usually accepted by tenderers, and in that event it constitutes an offer. The situation becomes different however when a tenderer specifies a date by which tenders are to be submitted for consideration by the tenderer, although he is not required to accept any of them.[12]

Offers of shares by companies over the Internet to the public are not 'offers' to allot shares to any person, but means to ascertain how many may apply for shares, and to whom shares may have to be allocated.[13] Actual allocation of shares constitutes an offer. But, of course, if it is stated that shares will be allocated to, for example, 100 applicants, then it is an offer. Thus, the language of the communication may determine whether in certain circumstances it is an invitation to treat or an offer.

---

[8] [1896] A.C. 325.
[9] [1893] 1 Q.B. 256; see also *Bowerman v Association of British Travel Agents Ltd* 1995 N.L.J. 1815.
[10] See also *R Thomson Holidays Ltd* [1974] Q.B. 592; and *Warwickshire CC, ex. p Johnson* [1993] A.C. 583.
[11] [1870] L.R. 5 C.P. 561.
[12] *Blackpool and Fylde Acro Club Ltd v Blackpool B C* [1990] 1 W.L.R. 25; see also *Fairclough Building v Port Talbot B C* [1992] 62 B.L.R. 82.
[13] *National Westminster Bank plc v IRC* [1995] 1 A.C. 119 at 126.

5.2.3 The offer

An offer represents a willingness to contract, made with the intention of its becoming binding on the person making it as soon as it is accepted by the person to whom it is addressed.[14] The intention to become bound may be actual or apparent, so that an objective test is to be applied to confirm the position[15]; conduct which may induce a reasonable person to believe that he intends to be bound should suffice.[16] Of course, while making offers and acceptances by electronic means, the intention of a party is to be primarily determined by the correspondence exchanged between the parties concerned. In the event of any ambiguity presented by any term or word, clarification will of course be necessary. However, in case of any controversy, the genuineness of the intention to create legal relations will be determined by applying the judicial guidelines developed by the English courts.[17]

A legal problem may arise, however, where a future acceptor of an offer believes that the offeror has no real intention, or he has not correctly ascertained the offeror's intention. A conflict in judicial opinion seems to have emerged in such a situation by the development of an objective or a subjective test. The subjective test is satisfied if an offeror's conduct is such as to induce a reasonable person to believe that the offeror had the requisite intention and that the future acceptor actually held that belief.[18] On the other hand, the objective test is satisfied if an offeror's conduct or the text of the offer would induce a reasonable person to believe that the offeror had the requisite intention provided of course the future acceptor is not aware that the offeror had no such intention.[19] If parties contract impersonally, this problem is bound to arise, particularly when correspondence by email is transmitted in a rush, and in consequence, sufficient thought may not be applied in drafting correspondence. On the other hand, there may not be a satisfactory answer as to which of the two tests is legally sustainable, as parties must go by what appears on their correspondence. Of course, particularisation of offers and acceptances would be necessary after an offer has been accepted, and only then can the issue of the intention to create legal relations bilaterally become important.

---

[14] See *Storer v Manchester CC* [1974] 1 W.L.R. 1403; *First Energy (UK) Ltd v Hungarian International Bank Ltd* [1993] 2 Lloyd's Reports 195.
[15] *Ignazio Messina & Co v Polskie Linie Oceaniczne* [1995] 2 Lloyd's Reports 566.
[16] *G Percy Trentham Ltd v Architel Luxfer Ltd* [1993] 1 Lloyd's Reports 25.
[17] See, for example, *The Multibank Holsatia* [1988] 2 Lloyd's Reports 486 at 492; *Thai-Europe Tapioca Service Ltd v Seine Navigation Inc (The Martitime Winner)* [1989] 2 Lloyd's Reports 506 at 515. A dictum in *Furness Withy (Australia) Pty Ltd v Metal Distribution (UK) Ltd (The Amazonia)* [1990] 1 Lloyd's Reports 236 at 242 suggested however that there may be a contract even though neither (party) intended to make a contract.
[18] *Amherst v James Walker Goldsmith and Silversmith Ltd* [1983] Ch. 305; see also *Paal Wilson & Co A/S v Partenreederei Hannah Blumenthal (The Hannah Blumenthal)* [1983] 1 A.C. 854 at 924.
[19] See *Excomme Ltd v Guan Guan Shipping (Pte) Ltd (The Golden Bear)* [1987] 1 Lloyd's Reports 330 at 341; see also *The Multibank Holsatia*, op cit.

Any inference of an offer by reference to the conduct of an offeror will always provoke controversy, whether such a situation arises during a non-mechanical contracting procedure or otherwise; a resolution of such controversy may be achieved by relying on an objective test, including whether inactivity on the part of a party may amount to abandoning the offer made by him.[20] However, following the decision in *The Antclizo*,[21] it may be stated that one party's belief that the other party's inactivity amounted to confirming its offer may not necessarily be sufficient to confirm that offer.

In businesses conducted by electronic means (e-Commerce), the time of making an offer proves to be a crucial issue. If one follows the principle established by *Adams v Lindsell*,[22] it was held that the cause of the delay in sending the offer arose entirely from the mistake of the offerors, but there was nevertheless a valid offer. By analogy, it may be stated that delay caused by postal authorities may come under the *Adams v Lindsell* rule to accept a delayed offer as a valid offer. Until any new judicial guidelines have been developed with reference to delays in making offers effectively be electronic means, there is no reason why in controversial cases, the *Adams v Lindsell* rule may not apply. Breakdown of computer or breakdown in any form in the transmission process by electronic means may offer justification for delayed offers on the basis *of Adams v Lindsell*. The general requirement of communication has been discussed in the section entitled Acceptance.

The rule on cross-offers, that none of them may be regarded as acceptance of each other, should apply when such offers may be made by electronic means. The determination of the place of making an offer by electronic means is important for the purpose of determining the jurisdiction of a court. Under the postal rules based on *Taylor v Jones*,[23] an offer sent through the post is made where it was posted. By analogy, it may be stated that the location from which an offer is transmitted by electronic means will determine the jurisdiction of the court. But, if one maintains that the place of acceptance is equally important for the purposes of determining the jurisdiction of a court, then there is a never-ending controversy. Where statute law makes clear provision on this issue, this issue must be governed by that statute. On the other hand, parties' choice in this regard must also be respected.

5.2.4 Acceptance

Acceptance stands for an acceptance of a valid offer made by a legitimate offeror. An intention to place an order,[24] or a mere acceptance of an offer would

---

[20] *The Multibank Holsatia*, op cit; see *also Unisys International Services Ltd v Eastern Counties Newspaper Group Ltd* [1991] 1 Lloyd's Reports 538 at 553.
[21] op cit.
[22] [1818] 1 B & Ald 681.
[23] [1875] 1 C.P.D. 87.
[24] *O T M Ltd v Hudranautics* [1981] 2 Lloyd's Reports 211 at 214.

not be an acceptance. An acceptance must be conveyed to the offeror in the way the offeror may have suggested,[25] unless the offeror has agreed to accept the offer in a different way. Otherwise, acceptance must be conveyed in unequivocal terms. Of course, where a contract has begun to be performed and the offeror has not objected to it, then acceptance by the offeror must be assumed, and the existence of the contract may not be denied, but the contract will have to be given retroactive effect for the part which has already been performed.[26]

Acceptance of an offer by conduct sometimes presents problems, but this method of acceptance may be regarded as a valid form of acceptance. But conduct must be explicit, that is, it must clearly demonstrate the intention to accept the offer. Acceptance by conduct often takes place in respect of oral contracts. The offeror must, in such circumstances, adhere to the terms of the oral contract and shall not insert new terms.[27] But of course, this situation (that is, oral contracts) will not arise when communicating exclusively by electronic means (e-mail).

When intermediate correspondence takes place between an offer and acceptance and the purpose of such correspondence is to vary the original terms of the offer, then there is a case of counter offer;[28] but statements made by a party, the purpose of which is not to vary the terms of the offer, do not make the acceptance a nullity,[29] but introduction of new terms into a bargain does not amount to accepting an offer.[30] This situation should be anticipated in contracting through electronic means. Parties take advantage of making counter-offers, and add new terms in the hope that best terms may be achieved by electronic means (e-mail). It is to be borne in mind however that when conflicting communications are exchanged, each constitutes a counter-offer, and that the final document is usually relied upon for the conclusion of the contract.[31] The offeror has a discretion whether to accept or reject a counter-offer. In the process of making counter-offers, parties should ensure the extent to which the terms of the original offer are altered, and that a reference to alterations is made. In the *Butler Machine Tool* case, for example, the buyer apparently failed to take notice of a crucial clause on the seller's side whereby it was maintained that in regard to certain matters, the seller's terms would 'prevail over any terms of the buyer's counter offer'.

An intention to enter into a contract is a crucially important issue in confirming whether there was a real acceptance or not. This situation may arise when multiple opportunities/offers about similar goods or services are made by electronic

---

[25] *Financings Ltd v Stimson* [1962] 1 W.L.R. 1184.
[26] *G Perry Trentham Ltd v Archital Luxfer Ltd* [1993] 1 Lloyd's Reports 25.
[27] *Jayaar Impex Ltd v Toaken Group Ltd* [1996] 2 Lloyd's Reports 437.
[28] *Hyde v Wrench* [1840] 3 Beav. 334.
[29] *Butler Machine Tool Co Ltd v Ex-Cell-O Corporation (England) Ltd* [1979] 1 W.L.R. 401.
[30] *Global Tankers Inc v Amercoat Europa N V* [1975] 1 Lloyd's Reports 666.
[31] *Zambia Steel & Building Supplies v James Clark & Eaton LTd* [1986] 2 Lloyd's Reports 225; see also *B R S v Arthur Crutchley Ltd* [1968] All E.R. 811.

means, and a person responds to accept more than one offer with the intention to reject the others; the onus is on that person to establish that he had no intention to enter into legal relations. On the other hand, it may be difficult for such a person to reject any of the acceptances.

Computers might lure a person to make counter-offers or cross-offers to take advantage of the best deal, but he/she may find himself or herself in a legal trap. It is possible for two parties to make identical cross-offers without knowing that another person has made a cross-offer in identical terms; in such a situation there is generally no contract, unless electronic communications closely show that one offer has priority over the other as it was received by the acceptor before the other.

An 'acceptance' must satisfy the requirements of a 'communication': (a) it must be brought to the attention of the offeror; (b) or the intending acceptor does something to indicate acceptance after the stipulated time is over, if time is stipulated; (c) or, to convey an unequivocal acceptance in the form/manner stipulated by the offeror. On the other hand, the requirements of communication may be satisfied if the acceptance which is otherwise valid, somehow came to the notice or knowledge of the offeror. However, if during transmission of an acceptance, the machine/computer breaks down, then the rule in *Entroes Ltd v Miles Far East Corporation*[32] will not apply, and there will be no contract, as the originator of the message will immediately know that the message has not gone through his computer system. A legal problem may arise however if, for example, an offer is made by a subsidiary of a transnational corporation, but the acceptance has been to the headquarters of the corporation. But, in such a situation, the 'two in one principle', that is, subsidiaries and headquarters are 'one economic unit' may be applied to justify that service of an acceptance on the headquarters company should amount to serving the acceptance on the subsidiary company and vice versa. The caution should be entered that although the European Court of Justice maintains 'one economic unit' doctrine,[33] in *Adams v Cape Industrial Plc*[34] the Court of Appeal did not accept that doctrine. However, if a subsidiary or headquarters of a company makes an offer independently of the other, then logic suggests that the acceptance must be conveyed to the entity which made the offer, but this situation may be revealed only after a dispute has arisen in connection with the validity or invalidity of the acceptance. The safe rule is therefore to convey the acceptance in compliance with the form, if any, suggested to the offeror which made the offer.

In certain circumstances an acceptance may be valid even though it is not communicated to the offeror: (a) if the offeror waives the requirement of communication of acceptance, for example, where goods are sent along with the

---

[32] [1955] 2 Q.B. 327 at 332.
[33] *See*: Dyestuffs [1972] CMLR 537; and Commercial Solvents [1974] 1 CMLR 309.
[34] [1990] CL 433.

offer,[35] or in a situation such as arose in the *Carbolic Smoke Ball Co* case, in which, according to the court, the claimant was not required to notify the defendants of her acceptance of their offer. This point is particularly relevant to responding to offers made to the world at large over the computer (the Internet); (b) if the acceptance sent by electronic means is not read by anyone during the material time (office hours, for example),[36] such a message should take effect at the beginning of the next business day[37]; and (c) when communication to an authorised agent of the principal would be regarded as a proper communication of an acceptance.[38]

One of the important aspects of contracting through electronic means is that the established posting rules do not apply to acceptances made by such means, as a data message is deemed to be transmitted when it enters into the transmission system of the recipient or the anticipated recipient and the sender of the message has no control over it.[39] Two issues in this regard should be identified: (a) if the originator of a data message (e-mail) knows that the message could not be transmitted, he should make alternative attempts to notify the offeror, and communicate its acceptance by the speediest possible means, otherwise another acceptance successfully transmitted will have precedence over the first acceptor; and (b) that it is quite possible for an originator of a data message not to be aware of any failure in communication, and in that event there will be no acceptance at all for the purpose of concluding a contract.[40] There do not exist any judicial guidelines on the issue of what would be the legal effect in the event of a data message not having been properly transmitted or not transmitted at all.

In *Walford v Mills,*[41] the House of Lords held that an agreement to use 'best endeavours' would be enforceable, but Lord Ackner stated that an agreement to use one's best endeavours is relevant to the performance of a contract and not to its formation. But this decision may provoke legal controversy.[42]

On the other hand, it is to be wondered why postal rules may not apply to 'acceptance' in the formation of a contract, with certain permutations. It is appreciated that a common carrier is involved when communications are sent through the post. If delays occur or if a communication is lost in the post, the law offers the acceptor remedies: in the case of transmission of messages by

---

[35] Goods must not be 'unsolicited'—see the Unsolicited Goods and Services Act 1971, ss 1 and 6; see also *Smit International Singapore Pte Ltd v Kumari Dewi Shipping SA* [1997] 1 Lloyd's Reports 553.
[36] See *Schelde Delta Shipping BV v Astarte Shipping Ltd (The Pamela)* [1995] 2 Lloyd's Rep 249 at 252.
[37] *Schelde Delta Shipping.* op cit; see also *Galaxy Energy International Ltd v Novorossiyk Shipping Co (The Peter Schmidt)* [1998] 2 Lloyd's Rep 1.
[38] As to an agent's authority, see *Henthorn v Fraser* (1892) 2 Ch. 27 at 33.
[39] See also *UNCITRAL Model Law*, op cit.
[40] *Holwell Securities Ltd v Hughes* [1974] 1 W.L.R. 155.
[41] [1992] 2 A.C. 128.
[42] See further C Chatterjee and A Lefcovitch, *'Best Efforts may not be Good Enough'*, *'Construction Law'*, vol 11, Issue 3 at 27–29 and vol 11, Issue 4 at 14–18.

electronic means, as with the postal system, technology may contribute effectively to what may be known as 'non-transmission', which is occasioned by no fault of the acceptor.[43] Of course, if the proposed acceptor conveys his acceptance by another means, without losing his priority in the order of acceptances, the law will give him protection, but there is no reason why a transmission system may not be compared with a common carrier. *Chitty on Contracts* maintains however that the 'posting rule does not apply to acceptance made by some 'instantaneous' mode of communication, eg by telephone or by telex'.[44] The reason why the rule does not apply in such cases, according to *Chitty on Contracts* is that the acceptor will immediately know that the communication was not transmitted, and that he has had opportunities to make a proper communication. However, the problem remains that by the time the acceptor may be able to effectively transmit an acceptance he might lose his priority because other acceptances have already reached the offeror. *Chitty on Contracts*, in a subsequent passage, states however that if an offer is required to take the risk of loss or delay in the post, then there seems to be no good reason why he should not take the risk of errors in transmission of a telemessage.[45] A telemessage has the characteristics of a message sent by, for example, e-mail. By the same token it may be stated that the rule of revocation through the post should similarly apply to revocations effected through electronic means. Incidentally, the Vienna Convention on Contracts for the International Sale of Goods, clearly states that the receipt of an offer by an offeree, and the receipt of an acceptance by the offeror is crucial to satisfy the conditions of an 'offer' and 'acceptance' and that if an acceptance is lost in the post, there is no contract.[46] As the government of the UK has not ratified the Vienna Convention, English law, including case law, must prevail in regard to the issues pertaining to 'offer' and 'acceptance'.

Although users of technology are expected to communicate to all parties concerned almost instantaneously by technological means, the usual human lapses can also take place when contracting through technology. For example, a situation such as that which arose in *Felthouse v Bingley*[47] may take place, where in the circumstances the acceptances of the offer made by a nephew to his uncle as to the sale of a horse was not found necessary, and the terms of the uncle's offer were deemed to amount to a waiver of the requirement for transmitting/communicating the acceptance. But, of course, it would be unusual for parties using speedy means of communication not to take advantage of technology, but if they do not do so, relatively recent judicial guidelines suggest that silence will not amount to an acceptance,[48] unless perhaps exceptional

---

[43] See *Household Fire Insurance Co Ltd v Grant* (1879) 4 Ex. D. 216.
[44] *Chitty on Contracts* (London, Sweet & Maxwell) at 111–112.
[45] op cit, at 114.
[46] See Art 15(1) and Art 18(2). For a discussion of the Convention, see Honnold, *Uniform Law for International Sales* (1988).
[47] (1862) 11 C.B. (NS) 869; affirmed (1863) 1 N.R. 401.
[48] *Allied Marine Transport Ltd v Vall do Rio Etc (The Leonidas D)* [1985] 1 W.L.R. 925 at 927 or *Rafsanjan Pistachio Producers Co-operative v Bank Leumi (UK) plc* [1992] 1 Lloyd's Rep 513 at 542.

circumstances exist to allow a waiver,[49] or that a trade practice between the parties concerned has been developed which does not entail satisfying the legal requirements of 'offer' and 'acceptance'. However, the requirement of a formal acceptance may be waived by the offeror himself if he states that his offer would be deemed to have been accepted if he does not hear to the contrary from the acceptor without a certain period of time.[50] It is to be borne in mind that the custom of certain trades may not entail satisfying the requirement of a formal acceptance.[51] This is where legal arguments set in, and the conduct which is to be deemed as an acceptance must be established by evidence, and perhaps through examination and cross-examination of witnesses. However, silence over a long period may amount to accepting an offer, unless categorically rejected.

An offer may be withdrawn at any time before it is accepted.[52] When contracts are to be made by technological means, the offeror is better placed to confirm his position than when contracts are made through non-technological means. But the general rule of withdrawal of offers which was established by *Byrne & Co v van Tienhoven*[53] should also apply when contracts are being negotiated with the intention of concluding them by electronic means. In this context, it should be useful to state what happened in the *Byrne & Co v van Tienhoven* case: the defendants in Cardiff posted a letter to the offerors on 1 October to New York, which was received by the offeree on 11 October, on which date the offeree accepted the offer and conveyed it to the offeror by telegram on the same date, which was confirmed by a letter posted on 15 October. However, the defendants posted a letter withdrawing their offer on 8 October which letter was received by the offerees on 20 October. It was held that the withdrawal did not take effect on posting—it must reach the offeree. As the acceptance was posted before the withdrawal letter reached the offerees, there was a binding contract.[54] The *van Tienhoven* case offers two rules: one for acceptance and the other for withdrawals, but until new judicial guidelines with reference to communication by electronic means have been developed, the existing postal rules may apply save, as stated earlier, that no common carrier is involved in the process of communicating by electronic means. The *van Tienhoven* case establishes the rule that the notice of a withdrawal must actually be brought to the attention of the offeree—there is no reason why the same rule may not apply when withdrawal may be communicated by electronic means. In the case of a commercial house, 'attention of the offeree' would mean that the communication reached the organisation.[55] Communications must be effected

---

[49] But, see *The Antclizo*, op cit, at 147.
[50] This is often the case with certain life insurance policies. See also *Re Selectmove* [1995] 1 W.L.R. 474 at 478.
[51] See for example, *Minories Finance Ltd v Afrikabank Nigeria Ltd* 1995 1 Lloyd's Rep 134.
[52] See also *the Vienna Convention on Contracts for the International Sale of Goods, op cit, Art 16(2)*.
[53] (1880) 5 C.P.D. 44.
[54] See also *Art 16(1) of the Vienna Convention on Contracts for the International Sale of Goods*.
[55] *Eaglehill Ltd v J Needham (Builders) Ltd* [1973] A.C. 992 at 1011; *Schedlee Delta Shipping v Astarte Shipping Ltd (The Pamela)*, op cit.

within business hours,[56] whether they have been read or attended to by the recipient within the business hours is immaterial.

Following the argument in the *van Tienhoven* it is maintained that a communication of rejection must also reach the offeree. If an offer and an acceptance have materialised for the purpose of contracting, the formalities of contract required by the law which will govern the contract must be satisfied, and it is immaterial whether the offer and acceptance were settled by means of electronic communications.

Most of the legal problems in connection with contracting by electronic means would arise in regard to the formation of the contract: invitation to treat; offer; acceptance and intention to create legal relations. Legal problems pertaining to the performance of non-performance of a contract, whether the contract was concluded through electronic means or otherwise, may be dealt with be relying on the judicial guidelines already developed by the English courts. The legal issues concerning invitation to treat, offer and acceptance have already been dealt with. There now follows a discussion of the fourth factor—intention to create legal relations.

5.3   Intention to create legal relations

Legal controversy as to whether there existed any intention between the two parties to create legal relations usually arises when there is no express agreement, and in this latter situation, the intention is determined by applying an objective test, but this test does not apply where the parties have actually expressed their intention in a document with a view to concluding a contract. When parties are engaged in reaching an agreement with a view to contracting by electronic means, their intentions are to be ascertained by examining the texts of the messages passed between the parties.

However, an 'honour clause', that is, a promise which is expected to be honoured, in an agreement may not give rise to any contractual relations between the parties, and in that event there may not be any intention to create legal relations. *In Rose & Frank v J R Crompton & Cros Ltd*[57] the parties stated in their agency agreement, *inter alia*, that:

'This agreement is not entered into, nor is this
memorandum written, as a formal or legal agreement...
each honourably pledge themselves.'

By analogy, if such negative expressions are included in documents, when exchanging offers and acceptances, by electronic means, then there is no binding

---

[56] See *Brinkibon Ltd v Stahag Stahl und Stahlwarenhandelsgesellschaft mbH* [1983] 2 A.C. 34 at 42.
[57] [1925] A.C. 445; see also *County Ltd v Girozentrale Securities* [1966] 3 All E.R. 834.

contract. However, the expression, 'this agreement is drafted in good faith', for example, does not negative contractual intention,[58] but amounts to a 'collateral understanding'.[59]

In attempting to contract by electronic means, one should take care of whether a statement inducing a contract is, in reality, a mere puff. In the manufacturing world, it is to be considered seriously whether an offeror's offer is supported by express warranties.[60] In this connection, it should be pointed out that two decisions which have provoked legal controversy in relation to the requirement of intention to create legal relations are: *Esso Petroleum Ltd v Commissioners of Customs and Excise*[61]; and *J Evans & Son (Portsmouth) Ltd v Andrea Merzario Ltd.*[62] Whereas in the former case, the House of Lords held that there was no sale of the object (coins), the majority of the House was equally divided on the question of whether there was any contract at all; much weight seems to have been given to the customer's intention in the latter case, rather than the circumstances in which the promise was made.

5.4   Conclusions

As stated earlier, the principal issues in relation to contracting through electronic means relate to the formation of the contract, rather than its performance, because in the event on non-performance of contractual obligations, the usual rules of breach of contract and remedies thereof will apply. The other important issue is whether a contract which is being concluded by electronic means, is actually concluded. The logical answer is that when the principle of ad idem materialises in respect of any contract, the determination of ad idem may not present any problem when transactions have been successfully transacted through electronic means. It is only in exceptional circumstances, that is, when a breakdown of the system (electronic system) takes place that additional legal problems may arise; or when a third party may intervene, and frustrate the genuine attempts made by the original parties. The various difficulties that may arise in the process of contracting by electronic means have already been discussed in this chapter, nevertheless, certain special legal issues in this regard have received attention in a separate section of this work. It is to be reiterated however that the existing judicial guidelines should be adequate to deal with most of the legal issues that may arise when contracting domestically or transnationally through electronic means.

---

[58] *The Mercedes Envoy* [1995] 2 Lloyd's Rep 559.
[59] op cit, at 564.
[60] See further *Lambert v Lewis* [1913] A.C. 30; see also *IBA v EMI Electronics Ltd* 1980 14 Build B.R. 1.
[61] [1976] 1 W.L.R. 1.
[62] [1976] 1 W.L.R. 1078; see also Atiyah (1976) 39 *Modern Law Review* 335; and Adams (1977) 40 *Modern Law Review* 227.

There are two principal methods of electronic contracting: (a) by electronic mail (e-mail) which is the digital equivalent of a letter; and (b) by what may be described as the 'click method' used on the world wide web; under the second method a link is used between a server and client machines, and the contract is formed using this link which facilitates exchanging data on the web. This is the method which attracts parties who wish to conclude contracts speedily. Communications through the website become instantaneous. This does not mean however that the usual elements of contract in English law are not to be satisfied in using these methods; the only outstanding characteristic is speed, which may have its merits and disadvantages.

One of the important legal issues which should be considered when contracting by electronic means is whether electronic messages satisfy the requirements of contracts being made in the written form; in other words, whether electronic messages may be equated to 'writing', otherwise, the Interpretation Act 1978 may not apply to such contracts. This Act defines 'writing' as:

> 'typing, printing, lithography, photography and other modes of representing or reproducing words in a visible form, and expressions referring to writing are construed accordingly.'

It is true that electronic messages do not apparently satisfy the definition of writing,[63] but the commercial world, in practice, seems to have accepted 'digital messages' as documents in writing.[64] Digital messages confirm the parties' intention, which is at the heart of the formation of a contract. An electronic message (document) may be regarded as a functional equivalent of a written document.[65]

The difference between 'click method contracts' (HMTL-based contracts) and e-mail-based contracts must be maintained. Postal rules may apply to e-mail-based contracts, but not to the former category of contracts—this is because communication under the former method is instantaneous, like telephone communications. In the event of the communication process being cut off, the other party will realise this instantaneously, furthermore, there exists what is known as the 'checksum' system—an in-built self-checking mechanism. If the checksum does not arrive or is not confirmed, the client/server will immediately realise that a breakdown of communications has taken place. This method of

---

[63] See further A Murray, *Entering into Contract Electronically: The Real WWW* in L Edwards vc. Waelde (eds), *Law and the Internet: A Framework for Electronic Commerce*, Oxford, Hart Publishing (2000). pp 17–35.

[64] The analogy would be with messages sent by facsimile; during the initial period, the practice was that a message sent by facsimile would not be accepted until the hard copy of it reached the acceptor/receiver of the document; now that requirement is not rigidly followed. Messages sent by facsimile to courts are accepted and acted upon.

[65] See further A Murray, *op cit, at 20*; on the functional equivalent approach, see also *UNCITRAL Model Law on Electronic Commerce of 16 December 1996*; the *EU Directive on Electronic Commerce, No. 2000/31/EC (Recital 34)*; and the Department of Trade and Industry document entitled *Promoting Electronic Commerce (Cm 4417)* (London, The Stationery Office, 1999).

contracting does indicate that the postal rule needs to be reviewed. E-mail messages are sent in packets, therefore, there is no guarantee that all the packets will reach the other end (the other party). Thus, as stated earlier, if due to the breakdown of the system, a second offeror offers and an acceptor successfully confirms its acceptance, then the second offer and acceptance will stand.

Of the two methods of contracting by electronic means, the e-mail method seems to be a better option in that both parties have the opportunity to read all details and documents prior to their confirming that a contract may be concluded. The HTML-based contracts do not have this advantage, unless all information is sent to the prospective parties in advance, but then, that is unusual, because HMTL-based contracts are intended to be concluded primarily on the basis of advertisements, and the legal consequences of entering into contracts on the basis of mere advertisements are obvious. In other words, HMTL-based contracts may be more prone to mistake, misrepresentation and negligence on the part of parties. One of the fundamental principles of the law of contract, ad idem (the two minds meet), may not be satisfied in respect of such contracts. However, it is maintained that legal issues that may arise pertaining to contracts based on e-mail in England may still be dealt with, unless very exceptional circumstances arise, by the current rules of the English law of contract, coupled with the judicial guidelines developed by the English courts.

6. Concluding contracts over the internet and mistake

6.1 Introduction

In the context of the law of contract, mistake usually relates to two situations: (a) although the parties have agreed on the terms of their contract, they have entered into it under a mutual or what is commonly known as a 'common mistake',[1] of a fundamental nature as to the facts; and (b) in view of some mistake in the communications between the parties, the contract has lost its effectiveness.[2] Incidentally, 'mutual understanding' is different from 'mutual mistake'. In both the instances stated above, the contract will be void *ab initio*. This situation may often arise while contracting by electronic means; and the contracts will be regarded as void *ab initio*. When a mistake is mutual, and the contract cannot be performed, only equity may offer the relief by rescission. The reason for regarding such contracts as void *ab initio* is that they are not based on the principle of ad idem—the two minds have not met.[3] But, one must ensure that a mistake is 'mutual' and that the 'mutual mistake' as to the subject matter of the contract goes to the root of the contract to make it an 'unenforceable contract'. Unilateral mistake is not a ground for rescission of a contract. A mistake must be shared, and the mistake must relate to the terms of the contract. A party may not disclose a fact which it is not supposed to disclose to the other party, and in the absence of disclosure of such facts, the contract may not be invalidated; the principle of caveat emptor applies to the English law of contract.[4] A unilateral mistake as to the identity of the other party may prevent the formation of a contract, and in that event property in the goods passed to the first party will not actually pass, and can be recovered by the true owner of the goods even from a bona fide purchaser.[5] However, even if common mistake made a contract void, but the parties acted on the assumption that it was valid,

---

[1] See Cheshire, Fifoot and Furmston, *Law of Contract* (13th ed), ch 8.
[2] See *Bell v Lever Bros* [1932] A.C. 161.
[3] On 'mutual mistake', see *Anson's Law of Contract* (Beatson ed) (27th ed, 1998) at 296.
[4] *Turner v Green* (1895) 2 Ch. 203.
[5] *Cundy v Lindsay* (1878) 3 App. Cas. 459.

then neither party would be able to deny the existence of the contract. The principle of estoppel will apply.[6]

A mistake is mutual when it is shared by both parties—it is immaterial whether the mistake related to facts or law. In *Associated Japanese Bank International Ltd v Crédit du Nord SA*[7] Steyn J (as he then was) maintained that mutual mistake can make a contract void. But, on the other hand, there exists the view that when considered with implied conditions, a mutual mistake may not result in the contract being void as one of the parties should have known what the true facts were. But the actual legal position is that a mistake might render a contract void if it made the subject matter substantially different from what the parties believed it to be and that a fundamental mistake makes a contract void even though the mistake is one of law.

6.2   Certain special aspects of mistake

The general rule that a mistake as to the existence of the subject matter of the contract may render a contract void,[8] is also applicable to contracts made by electronic means. Where a contract is incapable of performance because of mutual mistake or defective construction, the very existence of the contract becomes doubtful whether it was originally concluded by electronic means or otherwise, so it must be regarded as void.[9]

Mistake as to the quality of the subject matter of the contract (goods or services) does not affect the basis of the contract unless it was a mistake of both parties, or when the quality is essentially different from what it was believed to be; the important issue is whether there was a mistake as to the substance of the subject matter for which the contract was concluded. On the other hand, implied terms offer buyers so much protection that it may be difficult to declare a contract void for mistake.

When making contracts by electronic means a party may make mistakes as to the actual nature or type of the goods or whether a product is given a generic name, that is, under this name may be included various types of the goods.[10] The crucial issue in contracting is ad idem—the minds must meet—thus, when an assumption on the part of the parties becomes the basis of a contract, and if in the course of time, that assumption proves to be untrue, then there is no basis for a contract.[11]

---

[6] *Furness Withy (Australia) Pty Ltd v Metal Distributors (UK) Ltd (The Amazonia)* [1990] 1 Lloyd's Reports 236.
[7] [1989] 1 W.L.R. 255.
[8] *Bell v Lever Brothers Ltd*, op cit, at 217. See also *Pritchard v Merchants' and Tradesmen's Life Assurance Society* (1858) 3 C.B. (NS).
[9] See also *Couturier v Hastie* (1856) 5 H.L.C. 673.
[10] See *Frederick E Rose (London) Ltd v William H Pim Junior & Co Ltd* [1953] 2 Q.B. 450.
[11] *Bell v Lever Bros*, op cit.

The climax was, of course, reached in *Galloway v Galloway*[12] in which a separation deed was declared void on the grounds that Mr and Mrs Galloway entered into it in the belief that they were married at the material time, whereas that was not the case. Again, in *Associated Japanese Bank International Ltd v Crédit du Nord SA* a guarantee of a lease of a machine was considered to be void when it was revealed that the machine did not exist, and the machine was the primary security for the guarantee, thus the guarantee was also considered to be void.

If an offeror makes an offer, and a prospective acceptor accepts it in a fundamentally different sense from that intended by the offeror, the contract may be void. The possibility of such a situation is high when contracting by electronic means. The language and the terms used in the offer may be responsible for it,[13] although courts often try to ascertain the real intention of the offeror by applying an objective test, whereby the reasonable man's understanding of the terms and language will be taken into consideration.[14]

Where parties are genuinely contracting for two different subject matters in respect of one contract, the court must hold that the contract does not exist[15]; again, the principle of ad idem applies. Non-existence of contracts based on such mistakes, may be a common phenomenon when contracting through electronic means. By the same token it may be stated that a unilateral mistake as to the terms of a contract, if known to the other party, may make the contract void. In *Hartog v Colin and Shields*[16] the defendant, by mistake, offered the goods at a price per pound (in weight) instead of so much (in price) per piece. The plaintiffs sued for damages for non-delivery. The court held that the plaintiffs must have known that the true intention of the offeror was not expressed by the offer made by him—therefore, the contract would be regarded as void.

The question arises whether in order for a mistake to be operational, it must be known to the other party, or whether the agreement that it ought to have been apparent to a reasonable man will do. In *OT Africa Line Ltd v Vickers plc*[17] this test was applied. In *Mannai Investment Co Ltd v Eagle Star Life Assurance Co Ltd,*[18] the House of Lords held that the reasonable man's test was adopted. This case was concerned with the issue whether a contractual notice to determine a lease was effective despite the fact it failed to comply with the break clause in the contract, provided the notice served to convey the lessee's intention to exercise

---

[12] (1914) T.L.R. 531.
[13] *Woodhouse AC Israel Cocoa Ltd SA v Nigerian Products Marketing Co Ltd* [1972] A.C. 741; see also *McInerny v Lloyd's Bank* [1974] 1 Lloyd's Rep 246.
[14] *Scott v Littledele* (1858) 8 E & B 815.
[15] *Raffles v Wichelhaus* (1864) 2 H. & C. 906.
[16] [1939] 3 All E.R. 566; see also *McMaster University v Wilcher Construction Ltd* [1971] 22 D.L.R. (3d) 9.
[17] [1996]1 Lloyd's Rep 700.
[18] [1997] A.C. 749; see also *Garston v Scottish Widows' Fund and Life Assurance Society* [1998] 3 All E.R. 596.

its rights would be clear to a reasonable recipient of the notice. The majority of the House of Lords held that the intention of the party serving the notice was obvious to a reasonable recipient.

Mistake must relate to the terms of the contract;[19] it is, therefore, crucial that the terms are clearly expressed, without any ambiguity in their meaning, to the other party, while transmitting them by electronic means. It is to be borne in mind that if one party knows that the other party has made a mistake but failed to point it out when a reasonable person would expect him to do so, the issue of estoppel may arise—in other words, he will be bound by the contract by acqui-escence. English law provides relief for a unilateral mistake if the mistake was known to the other party—it is a matter of evidence and proof by the party making the unilateral mistake. Disagreement as to the meaning of a term of the contract does not invalidate the contract, provided of course, there is evidence that the parties intended to make a binding contract, it is for the court to deter-mine the correct meaning of the disputed terms.[20]

The legal issues raised by *Cundy v Lindsay* as to the identity of the person with whom one is contracting remain extremely relevant to contracting by electronic means. A mistake by one party as to the identity of the person with whom he is contracting tenders the contract void. Unless the identity of the person is estab-lished by means of keys, the issue of mistaken identity may well become relevant to contracting by electronic means. Incorrect identification of the parties as happened in *Cundy v Lindsay* ('Blenkarn' and 'Blenkiron') is possible, when con-tracting by electronic means, and in that event, goods may fall into the hands of an innocent purchaser, the defendant, although property in the goods, in reality, has not passed to him. *Cundy v Lindsay* was concerned with the mistake as to the identity of a contracting party, but *King's Norton Metal & Co v Edridge, Merrett & Co Ltd*[21] presented a different legal problem. The plaintiffs dispatched goods to one Wallis who posed as a member of the firm, 'Hallam & Co'. Wallis sold the goods to the defendants who took them in good faith and for value. The Court of Appeal held that the plaintiffs had intended to contract with Wallis, and that there was no mistake as to the identity of the contracting party. Such a situation is quite possible when contracting through the Internet. The issue of the mistaken identity of the parties when contracting by electronic means is a different one. Although a situation like that which occurred in *Phillips v Brooks*[22] (the buyer impersonated another person, and the seller had an opportunity to check his identity) might not occur when contracting by electronic means, there are direct means of checking the identities of the parties when contracting by such means, and anybody can represent anybody, while even signatures may not be verified as correspondence through e-mail does not imprint signatures.[23] But

---

[19]   *Hartog v Colin and Shields* [1939] 3 All E.R. 566.
[20]   *London County Council v Henry Boot & Sons Ltd* [1959] 1 W.L.R. 1069.
[21]   (1897) 14 T.L.R. 98.
[22]   [1919] 2 K.B. 243.
[23]   See *Lake v Simmons* [1927] A.C. 487 at 500.

one may not rule out the *Ingram v Little*[24] situation, although the decision in that case was not followed *in Lewis v Averay*[25], when contracting through electronic means. The identity of an individual may be fraudulently established as Mr Hutchinson did in *Ingram v Little*. In *Lewis v Averay* the facts were very similar to those in *Ingram v Little* but the court did not follow the latter, and it pointed out that each of such cases must be decided by referring to its particular facts.

The *non est factum* doctrine is applied when the signatory to a document is successfully able to establish that it (the act of signing) is not his/her deed, or that he/she signed a document as he/she was led to believe that it was a document of an entirely different class or character,[26] and thus a fundamental mistake as to the character or effect of the document was made.[27] Apparently, this doctrine has no application to contracts concluded through e-mail as signatures will not appear on communications sent through such means, but when signed on the real contract, the doctrine, where appropriate, may be applied. Incidentally, it is also to be considered whether contracts prepared through e-mail are real contracts in the absence of any signature on them, but if nevertheless, obligations in them are performed, whether partially or otherwise, then by conduct, it is transformed into a contract, pending the real signatures of parties to them.

There does not seem to be any reason why relief in equity may not be sought when a mistake is not sufficient to avoid the contract. In that event, the court must consider whether the contract is valid or void at common law, and the court may prefer a fusion of legal and equitable principles.[28]

Relief in equity has been allowed in some cases of mutual mistake[29]—although it is to be noted that if a contract is void at common law, equity will also treat it as a nullity. If however, equity intervenes in order to provide relief to the affected party, the relief may take one of the following forms: rectification of a contract or rescission of a contract, or refusal of an order for specific performance. Specific performance is usually refused if it becomes apparent that it would cause the defendant 'a hardship amounting to injustice'.[30] It is a question of taking an objective view of what may constitute 'injustice' in a particular case. The legal rationale being that a mistake made by a party inadvertently or accidentally (which would be subject to proof) should be allowed to be corrected, otherwise, the other party is allowed to take unconscionable advantage

---

[24] [1961] 1 Q.B. 31.
[25] [1972] 1 Q.B. 198.
[26] See *Howatson v Webb* [1908] 1 Ch. 1.
[27] *Saunders v Anglia Building Society* [1971] A.C. 1004.
[28] See, for example, *Riverlate Properties Ltd v Paul* [1975] Ch. 133.
[29] *Oscar Chess Ltd v Williams* [1957] 1 W.L.R. 370; see also *Robert A Munro & Co Ltd v Meyer* [1930] 2 K.B. 312 at 333–335.
[30] *Tamplin v James* (1880) 15 Ch. D. 215 at 221.

on the defendant.[31] On the basis of the decision of the Court of Appeal in *Solle v Butcher*,[32] it may be maintained that, in general, contracts based on mistake of law, do not deserve any relief, but in *Kleinwort Benson Ltd v Lincoln City Council*,[33] the House of Lords decided that payments made under a mistake of law may be recoverable.

6.3   Conclusions

As contracts concluded by electronic means are to be treated as written contracts, the remedy of rectification may be available only if it has been otherwise vitiated by a common mistake,[34] but the real intention of the parties must be unequivocally established, by referring perhaps to an oral understanding or to some other evidence that because of incorrect use of words, the common intention was not revealed. The relief of rectification may be available only if some practical purposes of a substantive nature may be achieved by the parties concerned. It is obvious therefore that both parties to a contract must plead that there was a genuinely common mistake about the subject matter of the contract through the use of inappropriate words. Of course, the burden of proof is on the party seeking ratification, and the proof must be 'convincing',[35] which should be established primarily by documentary evidence. Confusion between the parties as to what was agreed cannot be a ground for rectification[36] as 'confusion' is different from 'mistake'. The party seeking rectification must establish that the written terms were actually contrary to their intention;[37] it is not enough to say that the written contract does not represent the true intention of the parties.[38] One of the means of establishing that the true intention of the parties was not revealed would be to refer to the inappropriate or incorrect use of language. In other words, rectification of contracts is concerned with the correction of terms and words, and not with the intention of parties. This is an important issue in concluding contracts by electronic means, when a face-to-face negotiation between the parties does not take place. In *Frederick E Rose (London) Ltd v William H Pim Junior & Co Ltd*, Denning L J (as he then was) said that:

> 'Rectification is concerned with contracts and documents, not with intentions. In order to get rectification it is necessary to show that the parties were in complete agreement on the terms of their contract, but by an error wrote them down wrongly; and in this regard, in order to ascertain the

---

[31] See further *Barrow v Scammell* (1881) 19 Ch. D. 175 at 182; see also *Stewart v Kennedy* (1890) 15 App. Cas. 75 at 105.
[32] [1950] 1 K.B. 671.
[33] [1999] 1 A.C. 153.
[34] See *Burroughs v Abbott* [1922] Ch. 86; see also *The Nile Rhapsody* [1992] 2 Lloyd's Rep 399 at 408.
[35] See *Joscelyne v Nissan* [1970] 2 Q.B. 86.
[36] See *Cambro Contractors Ltd v John Kennally Sales Ltd*, The Times, 14 April 1994.
[37] *Lloyd v Stanbury* [1971] 1 W.L.R. 535.
[38] See further *Chitty on Contracts*, op cit, at 327.

terms of the contract, you do not look into the inner minds of the parties—into their intentions—any more than you do in the formation of any other contract.'[39]

Unilateral mistake may not be a ground for rectifying or even rescinding a contract unless the other party knew of the mistake[40]—a mere suspicion of a mistake made by the other party is not enough,[41] nor would wilful or reckless failure to make enquiries as to the obvious be a justifiable ground for seeking rectification of a contract.

Rescission is an equitable remedy and may be avoided in limited situations in which equitable relief is usually allowed, such as contracts void for mistakes at common law. Such contracts are void *ab initio*. In this connection one should refer to *Salle v Butcher*[42] in which case the equitable principle of rescission was extended by the Court of Appeal. 'Mistake in equity' is a new concept which has now been developed by the Court of Appeal, on the basis of which courts, in the exercise of their discretionary power, may grant relief in the form of rescission or setting aside a contract on any other ground, which the courts may deem just.[43] It is worth pointing out that whereas the remit of common law is limited to mistake with regard to the subject matter, a wider perspective of mistake is adopted by equity.[44] When contracts are concluded by electronic means, the probability of making mistakes whether unilateral or mutual is higher than when contracts are concluded face-to-face. This is because technology necessarily prompts parties to take advantage of speed—resulting in less well anticipated and considered ideas.

The rules regarding mistakes in concluding contracts under English law are, in the main, clear. There is no reason why these rules may not be applied to contracts concluded by electronic means, be they for small businesses or large ones. It is maintained that the incidence of mistakes in concluding contracts by electronic means is higher than when contracts are concluded by non-electronic means.

---

[39] [1953] 2 Q.B. 450 at 461.
[40] *Riverlate Properties Ltd v Paul*, op cit.
[41] *Olympia Sanna Shipping Co SA v Shinwa Kaiun Kaisha Ltd (The Ypatia Halcoussi)* [1985] 2 Lloyd's Rep 364, 371.
[42] op cit.
[43] See further *Chitty on Contracts*, op cit, at 334; see also *Associated Japanese Bank International ltd v Crédit du Nord SA* [1989] 1 W.L.R. 225.
[44] See *William Sindale plc v Cambridgeshire County Council* [1994] 1 W.L.R. 1016 at 1035.

7. Concluding contracts over the Internet and misrepresentation

7.1 Introduction

In writing this chapter it has been decided to highlight the fundamental aspects of contracting by electronic means, and the legal aspects thereof. The purpose is not to write a comprehensive account of the law of contract, but to warn the reader that in negotiating and contracting a contract by electronic means, parties should take particular account of the established rules of the law of contract pertaining to offer and acceptance, mistake and misrepresentation, in addition to other statutory provisions in regard to consumer protection or terms of contract, as dictated by the Unfair Contract Terms Act 1977.

This chapter attempts to explain the law in regard to the basic issues of the law of contract, be it contracted by electronic means or otherwise. The chapter does not aim at comprehensiveness, the state of the English law in regard to contracts may be found in various established published works, namely, *Anson's Law of Contract* or *Chitty on Contract*. Incidentally, in writing this chapter reliance has been placed mostly on *Chitty on Contract* as it is regarded as a practitioner's book.

7.2 Contracting over the Internet and misrepresentation

When contracts are negotiated and concluded without any face-to-face interaction, and solely by electronic means, the incidence of misrepresentation, whether innocent, negligent or fraudulent, becomes high; thus the incidence of rescinding contracts concluded by electronic means may also become high. In so far as the English jurisdiction is concerned, in addition to other provisions, statutory or otherwise, relevant to a particular case, the governing statute is the Misrepresentation Act 1967.

There is no need to go into the details of the law of misrepresentation in this context—the discussion, therefore, primarily relates to the issue of misrepresentation of facts and its legal effect in relation to e-Commerce. In order to establish misrepresentation of facts pertaining to contracting or transacting through electronic means, the usual rules of misrepresentation under English law, including the judicial guidelines, will apply. One of the legal problems which may arise from the use of electronic means for trade and commerce is that it might prove difficult to establish that a statement of intention was or was not honestly held, especially because there is no face-to-face negotiation when contracts or transactions are negotiated by electronic means.

There may be a high incidence of what is known as 'implied representation' or representation by conduct, whether of products or offers. Furthermore, the complications about whether any clear cut distinction may be made between statements of fact and statements of opinion or implied representations[1] or statements of fact and statements of intention, and whether causal or considered or negligent misrepresentation[2] may be made, will be particularly common in conducting business through electronic commerce. However, a distinction has been drawn by courts in cases between statements of fact,[3] and statements as to the future. But it is to be stressed that under the *Hedley Byrne* principle, non-disclosure will constitute liability,[4] although it may not constitute misrepresentation. However, the general rule is that non-disclosure alone does not necessarily constitute misrepresentation. There is, generally speaking, no duty on the parties to a contract to disclose material facts to each other however dishonest the act of disclosure might be.[5]

Misrepresentation by conduct will be a common phenomenon in carrying out business by electronic means. Therefore, if payments are initially made by cheque cards, which would be the case when business is conducted by electronic means, but subsequently rejected by virtue of being unauthorized by the lender (the credit card company) it is a case of false representations[6]; by analogy, the same principle applies to uses of credit cards, when the user exceed the limits set by the credit card company.[7]

Partial non-disclosure may amount to non-misrepresentation. This issue becomes very important when parties may be contracting in haste by electronic means. Interestingly enough, total non-disclosure does not constitute a misrepresentation[8]; the difficulty about misrepresentation is that even a totally true statement may be construed as misrepresentation if certain additional facts added to the statement were untrue; again, omission of facts from a statement

---

[1] *McNally v Welltrade International Ltd* [1978] I.R.L.R. 497.
[2] *Esso Petroleum Co v Marden* [1976] Q.B. 80.
[3] See, for example, *Beckett v Cohen* [1972] 1 W.L.R. 1593; and *British Airways Board v Taylor* [1976] 1 W.L.R. 13.
[4] *Hedley Byrne & Co Ltd v Heller & Partners Ltd* [1964] A.C. 465.
[5] But, see *Hurley v Dyke* [1979] R.T.R. 265. Under certain statutes the disclosure is compulsory, for example, under insurance statutes.
[6] See further *R v Charles* [1977] A.C. 177.
[7] See further *R v Lambie* [1982] A.C. 449.
[8] *Aikwright v Newbold* (1881) 17 Ch. D. at 318; *R v Bishingiam* [1936] 1 All E.R. 586.

may amount to misleading.[9] Of course, under English law, exclusion of liability by a service renderer or a contracting party in certain circumstances may be regarded as misrepresentation. In *Curtis v Chemical Cleaning and Dyeing Co Ltd*[10] a dress owner was asked to sign a receipt by a shop assistant at a dry-cleaning shop whereby damages to beads and sequins were excluded, which was construed by the court as misrepresentation. It is to be pointed out, however, that the Misrepresentation Act applies to misrepresentations only, and not to the breach of duties of disclosure.

The principles of English law, coupled with the judicial guidelines, should be adequate to deal with the legal issues pertaining to misrepresentations of all types made in the contracting process. The following is a brief summary of the usual principles, which are applicable to all contracts, whether they are con-cluded by electronic means or otherwise.

Representations include the making of statements—if a statement which was true when made, is revealed to be untrue before the contract was concluded, it must be communicated to the other party, otherwise, the statement would be treated as misrepresentation.[11] In this context, one is required to remind oneself of the provisions of section 2(1) of the Misrepresentation Act 1967:

'Where a person has entered into a contract after a misrepresentation has been made to him by another party thereto and as a result thereof he has suffered loss, then, if the person making the misrepresentation would be liable to damages in respect thereof had the misrepresentation been made fraudulently, that person shall be so liable notwithstanding that the mis-representation was not made fraudulently, unless he proves that he had reasonable ground to believe and did believe up to the time the contract was made that the facts were true.'

In other words, any kind of misrepresentation of facts is prohibited by section 2(1) of the Act, unless the person concerned did believe up to the time the con-tract was made that the facts represented were true.

When contracts are concluded by speedy means, the incidence of misrepresen-tation, whether innocent or negligent is naturally very high. Misrepresentation made by an agent acting within the scope of his authority is also to be treated as misrepresentation by his principal; in this situation, the usual principal-agent relationship shall apply.

Only genuine representees may be entitled to relief in respect of misrepresenta-tion—representees may be of three types: (a) persons to whom representations

---

[9] *Banque Keyser Ullman S.A. v Skandia (UK) Insurance Co Ltd* [1990] 1 Q.B. 665.
[10] [1951] 1 K.B. 805.
[11] *Davies v London Provincial Marine Insurance Co* (1878) 8 Ch. D. 469.

are directly made; (b) persons to whom the representation was expected to be passed on[12]; and (c) representation addressed to members of a class.[13] In concluding contracts through electronic means, this last type of representees may seek relief, but they will be required to satisfy a difficult legal condition: if a representator acts as a promotor of a business, who issued some details of a business or prospectus, the affected parties would not be able to recover from him as the purpose of his issuing details or a prospectus could be to induce people to act on it, that is, to consider buying the product or applying for shares. Logically speaking, if a product is introduced generally to the public at large by electronic means, without any commitment, such as that in the *Carbolic Smoke Ball* case,[14] it would be difficult to maintain that the introduction was addressed to any specific individual. It is to be stated however that in the current commercial practice, issuance of a prospectus by a company to prospective purchasers of shares has far reaching legal implications. By relying on *Gross v Hillman Ltd,*[15] it may be maintained that it is not necessary that the actual representation should reach the representee—if an agent acting on behalf of the representee relies on a fraudulent inducement of a vendor to buy the vendor's property, the buyer will be entitled to relief for misrepresentation, irrespective of whether the agent passed the fraudulent statements to the buyer.

Tort actions, based on negligent misrepresentation will be a common phenomenon in commerce or business conducted by electronic means. In such actions, a defendant's liability arises from the issue whether he owed a duty of care to the claimant. Of course, in general, in negligence cases, defendants are required to discharge the burden of whether they ought to have foreseen that the claimant might act upon the statement made by the defendant in consequence of which he has sustained losses.[16] Misrepresentation is actionable if it has the effect of inducement on the mind of the other party; by the same token, if the claimant cannot prove that the was influenced by the misrepresentation, he has no sustainable claim, in that in any event, whether misrepresentation of facts took place or not, he would have entered into the contract.[17] Even if the misrepresentation was not likely to influence a reasonable person, but the claimant successfully proves that he was induced by it to enter into the contract, the contract may be rescinded.[18]

In conducting business by electronic means, an offeror in the English jurisdiction is required to be aware of the established rules of misrepresentation.

---

[12] *Yianni v Edwin Evans & Sons* [1982] Q.B. 438.
[13] *Peek v Gurney* (1873) L.R.6 H.L. 377.
[14] *Carlill v Carbolic Smoke Ball Ltd* [1893] 1 Q.B.256.
[15] [1970] Ch. 445.
[16] *Yianni v Edwin Evans & Sons,* op cit.
[17] *Industrial Properties Ltd v Associated Electrical Industries Ltd* [1977] Q.B. 580.
[18] *Museprime Properties Ltd v Adhill Properties Ltd* [1990] 2 E.G.L.R. 196.

Rescission of a contract is impermissible if the proposed claimant maintains that he could have discovered the false or negligent representation if he had exercised reasonable care.[19] It is to be pointed out however that contributory negligence is no defence to an action of dishonesty, and in such cases the Law Reform (Contributory Negligence) Act 1945 does not apply. Misrepresentation need not be the exclusive cause of inducement for the claimant to enter into a contractual arrangement; it would be sufficient for him to show that it was one of the causes that induced him to enter into a contract. In *Edgington v Fitzmaurice*[20] the plaintiff was induced to take debentures in a company partly because of a misrepresentation in the prospectus, but the plaintiff also believed that the debenture conferred a charge on the company's property. This was sufficient for him to claim rescission of the contract on the grounds that there was evidence to establish that he was effectively influenced by the misrepresentation.

Misrepresentation must be 'material' for seeking relief in law—that is, it must be such as to influence a reasonable man to decide whether to enter into the contract. The onus should be on the claimant to establish that he was directly influenced by the misrepresentation.

Intention in misrepresenting facts is important in that misrepresentation will not be effective to claim relief unless it was directed at representees or intended to be acted on by them.[21] If there existed the belief that a representee would be induced to act on the representation, and if the claimant actually acted upon this and his interest was thus adversely affected, that would be enough to make a successful claim. *Hedley Byrne & Co Ltd v Heller and Partners Ltd* was a case of negligent misrepresentation. The plaintiffs asked their bankers to obtain a reference from the defendant bankers about a client with whom the plaintiffs intended to do business. The House of Lords held, inter alia, that the fact that the defendants did not know anything about the plaintiffs directly was no defence. According to the House of Lords, any professional relationship, whether on the basis of a contract or not, will normally give rise to a duty of care provided that person making the representation knew or ought reasonably to have known that the representee (claimant) was likely to act on the representation. Thus, advice given on the basis of a 'business connection' about the credibility of a third party may give rise to a duty of care, irrespective of whether the adviser was acting in a professional capacity.[22] This issue is particularly important when advice is given impersonally by electronic means, but negligently. The judicial guidelines in this regard will be applicable in such cases. It is to be pointed out however that in *Caparo Industries plc v Dickman,*[23] it was

---

[19] See further *Nocton v Ashburton* [1914] A.C. 962; and *Laurence v Lexcourt Holdings Ltd* [1977] 1 W.L.R. 1128.

[20] (1885) 29 Ch. D. 459.

[21] See further J Beatson, *Anson's Law of Contract* (Oxford, Oxford University Press, 27th ed, 1998) at 233.

[22] *WB Anderson & Sons Ltd v Rhodes (Liverpool) Ltd* [1967] 2 All E.R. 850.

[23] [1990] 2 A.C. 605.

held that liability in tort for negligent misrepresentation will not occur unless the person making the statement knew or believed that the statement would not be communicated to the person relying on it; it is immaterial whether the information would be relied upon as an individual or as a member of a specified class.

In discussing fraudulent misrepresentation, it is to be noted that fraud is proved when a false representation has been made knowingly without belief in its truth or made recklessly.[24] But the belief of the maker of the misrepresentation that he was honest would be a defence—mere carelessness is not sufficient. In *Derry v Peek*, the prospectus issued by a company stated that it was essential to use steam power to run tram cars and this information induced the respondents to acquire shares in the company, but the information proved to be false although at the time of issuing the prospectus, the company believed that necessary permission to run tram cars by steam power would be granted by the Board of Trade, the licensing authority which permission was ultimately denied, and the company was wound up. In an action in fraud, the House of Lords held that the directors honestly[25] believed that what they stated was true. In other words, there would not be any fraudulent misrepresentation if the representator makes a statement with honest belief (which is to be substantiated by evidence) that he had no intention to mislead the claimant, and that there were sufficient reasons for making such statements. There is no reason why these principles and criteria may not be applied to representations, innocent, negligent or fraudulent, made during the course of business conducted through electronic means. It must be pointed out however that it is not necessary to prove that the defendant's motive was dishonest[26]; in other words, it is the act of the defendant that counts, and the consequential effect of it.

Legal problems may arise as to the determination of liability between a principal and an agent, and in particular, between the headquarters of a corporation and its subsidiaries and/or branches. In such a case, liability had to be particularized, that is, which unit (subsidiary or branch) has actually committed the fraudulent act, and whether on its own initiative or at the instruction of the headquarters. In connection with this matter, veil-lifting may be necessary. Generally, a principal is liable for the fraud of its agent.[27] The rigidity of the rule is maintained in that if an agent of the corporate body induces a second agent (a subsidiary or a branch) to pass fraudulent or untrue statement to a third party, and the second party does that, the principal will be liable,[28] although the grade of liability will be different for the first party and the second party. This issue is particularly important when business, by electronic means, is run by a transnational corporation through its various units.

---

[24] See *Derry v Peek* (1889) 14 App. Cas. 337.
[25] Emphasis added.
[26] *Standard Chartered Bank v Pakistan National Shipping Corporation* [1995] 2 Lloyd's Reports 365.
[27] *Briess v Woodley* [1954] A.C. 333.
[28] *London County Freehold & Leasehold Properties Ltd v Berkely Property Investment Co Ltd* [1936] 2 All E.R. 1039.

Contributory negligence is not a defence to an action in fraud, and the Law Reform (Contributory Negligence) Act 1945 does not apply. A negligent misrepresentation is one which is made carelessly, or knowing or believing that the statement made to the defendant is not true. In order to justify negligent misrepresentation, it must be established that the author of the statement owed the defendant a duty of care. *Nocton v Ashburton*[29] established that a duty of care may arise from a fiduciary relationship, but in *Hedley Byrne* it was decided that a duty of care may arise from various other types of relationship.

In considering the issue of misrepresentation under English law, one is required to consider the legal effect of section 2(1) of the Misrepresentation Act. This provision is primarily concerned with the circumstances in which a person making the misrepresentation would be liable to damages.

Misrepresentation in itself is enough to vitiate a contract; there will be no need to establish any duty of care towards the representee. Under the Act a representee has the right to bring an action for damages.[30] This section also implies that for the purpose of seeking damages the distinction between negligent misrepresentation and fraudulent misrepresentation is minimal. Inducements influencing the mind of the representee are all that matter and this is particularly so because the measure of damages under subsection 1 of section 2 (negligent misrepresentation) is the same as the measure of damages for fraud.[31]

The question remains whether a fraudulent act by one person may be imputed to another, that is, may a fraudulent act of an employee, for example, be imported to his/her employer or an act of an agent to his principal, when the employer or the principal knows that the statement made by his employee or agent is untrue. In such a case the failure of the informed person to inform others, agents or employees, may constitute a negligent act.[32] In the case of a negligent misrepresentation, the representee has the right to rescind the contract and claim damages, although the court may exercise its discretionary power to refuse to allow rescission, except in cases of fraud under section 2(2) of the Misrepresentation Act. Failure to disclose does not however give rise to liability in damages under section 2(2), even where there is a duty to disclose material facts. The issue of contributory negligence remains an important one. At common law, contributory negligence is not a defence to fraud, and the Law Reform (Contributory Negligence) Act does not seem to apply to claims under section 2(1) of the Misrepresentation Act where no concurrent liability in negligent misrepresentation (tort) exists. The burden of proof is on the representator that the representation was neither negligent nor fraudulent.

---

[29] [1914] A.C. 932.
[30] *Howard Marine and Dredging Co Ltd v A Ogden & Sons (Excavations) Ltd* [1978] Q.B. 574.
[31] In relation to calculation of damages, see *Royscot Trust Ltd v Rogerson* [1991] 2 Q.B. 297.
[32] See further *WB Anderson & Sons Ltd v Rhodes (Liverpool) Ltd* [1967] 2 All E.R. 850.

Section 2(1) applies only where the representee has already entered into a contract after a misrepresentation was made to him by the principal or by his agent (the headquarters of a multinational corporation or by a subsidiary or a branch of the corporation) acting within the remit of the agency agreement. This rule may not apply if the agent sought to enforce the contract in his own name.[33] This point is important in doing business by electronic means when a subsidiary or a branch communicates information to a third party with or without the instruction from its headquarters.

In discussing misrepresentation with reference to business by electronic commerce means, one may not disregard the issue of liability for negligence at common law. This type of liability may arise when a person is induced to enter into a contract because of misrepresentation by a third party—and liability may arise even in the absence of a formal contract being concluded. The claimant will be required to establish that the misrepresentation was the causa proxima for the losses he has sustained, and that the representator expected to benefit from his misrepresentation. Since the decision rendered by the House of Lords in *Hedley Byrne*, interpretation of the bases of liability in tort has been very broad-based; a 'duty of care' is to be considered by a representator, and whether his representation might induce the representee to act.

In *Caparo Industries plc v Dickman*[34] it was held that liability in tort for negligent misrepresentation would not arise unless the representator (the maker of the statement) knew that the statement would be communicated to the person relying on it in connection with a particular transaction or a transaction of a particular kind. The claimant will be required to establish that reliance on the representation in connection with the contract was likely; a mere disclaimer of liability by a defendant will not afford him any legal protection.[35] This is particularly so when the contract may come under the purview of the Unfair Contract Terms Act 1977. The defendant will have protection if he can prove that his disclaimer satisfies the requirements of 'reasonablene' under the Unfair Contract Terms Act.[36] The claimant will endeavour to establish that the defendant assumed liability.[37] However, misrepresentation must be made 'in the course of business', which would include negotiations for concluding contracts even though negotiations may ultimately break down.[38] The relationship between a manufacturer and a purchaser of goods is an important issue to consider in dealing with matters of misrepresentation. Unless it is a situation like that presented by the *Carbolic Smoke Ball* case, any reliance on statements made in a manufacturer's literature, however misleading, does not create a special relationship between the parties—the claimant must act on the statement

[33] *Garnac Grain Co v H M Faure & Fairlcough Ltd* [1966] 1 Q.B. 650.
[34] [1990] 2 A.C. 605.
[35] *Harris v Wyre Forest D.C.* [1990] A.C. 831.
[36] ss 2(2), 11(5) and 13.
[37] See *Henderson v Merrett Syndicates Ltd* [1955] 2 A.C. 145.
[38] See *Box v Midland Bank Ltd* [1979] 2 Lloyd's Rep 391.

to develop the basis for the special relationship. Following *Caparo*, it may be maintained that liability in tort for negligent misrepresentation will arise when the maker of the statement knew that the statement would be communicated to the person relying on it; a kind of predictable effect on a predictable party must be in the knowledge of the maker of the statement; this is the beginning of the special relationship on a de facto basis. Knowledge of the identity of the purchaser to whom the representation will be directed will give rise to what is known as 'contractual warranty'—the intent to warrant must exist.[39] However, in so far as the English jurisdiction is concerned, statutory provisions creating liability for negligent misrepresentation will apply, for example, section 150 of the Financial Services Act 1986 (although it is not clear whether the provisions of this Section have been repealed by the Financial Services and Markets Act 2000).

What is the legal position in the case of innocent misrepresentation? By 'innocent misrepresentation' is meant a misrepresentation which is neither fraudulent nor negligent, and following *Heilbert Symmonds & Co v Buckleton*[40] and *Gilchester Properties Ltd v Gomm*,[41] it may be maintained that no action for damages arise from a purely innocent misrepresentation, unless it is a contractual promise, or, for example, supported by consideration, that is, a contractual arrangement which was in the offing. If misrepresentation should become part of the contract, then liability arises, it is immaterial whether the misrepresentation was innocent, negligent or fraudulent.[42] But the situation becomes even more complex when a representee enters into a contract with a third party on the basis of the misrepresentation, as a situation of collateral contract arises. With regard to remedies, one should rely on section 2(2) of the Misrepresentation Act, which states that:

> 'Where a person has entered into a contract after a misrepresentation has been made to him otherwise than fraudulently, and he would be entitled, by reason of the misrepresentation, to rescind the contract, then, if it is claimed, in any proceedings arising out of the contract, that the contract ought to be or has been rescinded, the court or arbitrator may declare the contract subsisting and award damages in lieu of rescission, if of opinion that it would equitable to do so, having regard to the nature of the misrepresentation and the loss that would be caused by it if the contract were upheld, as well as to the loss that rescission would cause to the other party.'

The court has a discretion under section 2(2) as to the determination (calculation) of damages.

---

[39] See further *Lambert v Lewis* [1982] A.C. 225.
[40] [1913] A.C. 30.
[41] [1948] 1 All ER.. 493.
[42] *Dick Bentley Productions Ltd v Harold Smith (Motors) Ltd* [1965] 1 W.L.R. 623.

Fraudulent misrepresentation makes the contract void *ab initio*,[43] and the claimant may also rely on section 1(a) of the Misrepresentation Act 1967. By the same token it may be stated that in the event of a variation of a contractual term induced by fraud, the innocent party may rescind the variation ab initio too. It must be pointed out however that there is no absolute right to rescind for negligent or innocent misrepresentation and the court has discretion to award damages in lieu of rescission provided it is equitable to do so, having paid attention to the losses that the affected party might be subject to owing to the rescission. But, the remedy of rescission is available only to an affected party.[44] Of course, the remedy of rescission may not be available in the following circumstances:

- affirmation of the contract by the plaintiff;
- claim barred by lapse of time; and
- if a third party acquires right in the subject matter of the contract.

There is no need to go into the details of these situations, the reader may refer to any standard work on the law of contract, for instance, that by Trietel or by Anson.

Exclusion of liability for misrepresentation is governed by the revised section 3 of the Misrepresentation Act 1967 which states that:

'If a contract contains a term which would exclude or restrict:

(a)   any liability to which a party to a contract may be subject by reason of any misrepresentation made by him before the contract was made; or

(b)   any remedy available to another party to the contract by reason of such a misrepresentation,

the term shall be of no effect except in so far as is satisfied the requirement of reasonableness as stated in Section 11(1) of the Unfair Contract Terms Act 1977, and it is for those claiming that the term satisfied that requirement to show that it does.'

The exempting term must be shown to be reasonable; a very wide exempting term would be regarded as unreasonable under section 3. It is for the person relying on an exempting term to prove that it is reasonable under the Unfair Contract Terms Act. The court usually considers the reasonableness of provisions as a whole.

---

[43] *Johnson v Agnew* [1980] A.C. 367.
[44] See *Northern Bank Finance Corporation Ltd v Charlton* [1979] I.R. 149.

7.3 Conclusions

It is to be pointed out that mere non-disclosure of facts does not ordinarily amount to misrepresentation. In order to be actionable, a representation must take an active form. Of course, in relation to certain types of contract, namely, insurance contracts, full disclosure of facts must be made in good faith (*uberrimae fidei*), but even if the non-disclosure is negligent, no liability in damages arises under the Misrepresentation Act (s 2(1)). In relation to insurance contracts, an insurer is also under an obligation to disclose material facts; in other words, the duty to disclose is mutual.

In concluding this section, it is to be emphasized that the purpose of writing on misrepresentation in relation to contracts which may be concluded by electronic means is not to exhaust all aspects of misrepresentation, nor is it intended to discuss all of the intricate legal issues and judicial guidelines thereon. The purpose is to make the reader aware of the fact that the current law on misrepresentation and the judicial guidelines on misrepresentation should be able to deal with the issues of misrepresentation when the contract may be concluded by electronic means.

8. E-Commerce and negligence

8.1 Introduction

The use of e-mail and the Internet is advantageous for business and communication, but in view of technological advancement, its abuse or misuse should also be anticipated. The abuse or misuse of e-mail/the Internet may outweigh the advantages derived from their uses. It is, therefore, essential to take precautionary measures against such abuse or misuse. On the other hand, abuse or misuse might take place due to lack of information or lack of knowledge of the use of e-mail/the Internet or because of negligence, whether of the principal or of its authorized agent(s). Negligent use of the language, whether innocent or careless, might also accrue liability. Again, a user of e-mail/the Internet may be subject to abusive or defamatory messages, or his/her privacy might be encroached upon by undue access to information.

It is the purpose of this chapter to identify and examine some of the legal issues about uses and abuses of e-mail/the Internet. The intention is not to be exhaustive in identifying and examining these issues.

8.2 General discussion of negligence

A negligent act may be committed either by a user of e-mail/the Internet or even by an adviser, legal or otherwise, who may be advising over the e-mail. An example of a negligent act committed by a user of e-mail would be when it may be giving publicity to its products or services by using certain words, which were not articulate enough or even misleading or not honest enough in the description of goods or services. In order to succeed in a claim for negligence, the following conditions must be satisfied:

- there must exist a duty of care on the part of the party against whom an allegation of negligence has been brought;
- there must have been a breach of that duty of care (reasonable care) by the party against whom an allegation of negligence has been brought;

- there must exist a causal connection between the negligent act and the damage resulted thereof; and
- that the alleged negligent act has caused foreseeable damage.

The actual harm that has occurred and the foreseeability of the harm to be caused are the two most crucial factors to justify a case of negligence. Whereas a negligent act (which a professional person should not commit) in itself becomes a direct cause of harm; any failure to foresee the harm to be caused by the intended act also signifies the person's inefficiency by reference to the standards prescribed by his/her profession.

Judicial guidelines developed by the English courts in regard to negligence are identifiable, and indeed very instructive. It is now necessary to examine the judicial guidelines with reference to the principal ingredients of a negligent act. It is to be pointed out however that the modern law of negligence in England is primarily a case-based law, which has essentially developed from 1932—that is when *Donoghue v Stevenson* was decided.[1] The standards of professionalism have since then been raised and consolidated, but nevertheless, *Donoghue v Stevenson* must be regarded as the starting point for the modern law of negligence, and in particular, the basis for consumer protection. The *Donoghue v Stevenson* principle established that the person committing a negligent act owed a duty of care in relation to his profession towards the person who sought or bought his services or goods, in good faith. Thus, the standards of care and the duty of care related to a profession or occupation. Professional or occupational expertise should ensure the foreseeability of the harm, and a failure to identify it gives rise to liability. This principle also applies to users of e-mail/the Internet. Although it may be odd to think that they are professionals, they are certainly incumbents of an occupation. Thus, the principles of the law of negligence equally apply to users of e-mail/the Internet, and their consumers. There now follows a discussion of the most important principles of the law of negligence.

8.2.1   The duty of care

The principle of the duty of care is otherwise known as the 'neighbour principle'. Under English law, persons guilty of careless conduct are liable in damages to their victims.[2] The injured party must establish that the defendant owed him a duty of care (to protect him from the harm suffered) and that the defendant was in breach of that duty. Thus, the law of negligence requires more than careless conduct.[3] In every successful claim in negligence these criteria must be satisfied: duty, breach and causation. The defendant must be proved to owe a duty to the claimant to act or refrain from acting. It is not enough to show that the defendant owed a general duty of care to the particular claimant. The claimant

---

[1] [1932] A.C. 562.
[2] See Winfield, 42 *Law Quarterly Review* (1926) 184–201.
[3] See further *Lochgelly Iron & Coal, v Mcmullen* [1934] A.C. 1 *per* Lord Wright at 25.

must establish that the defendant owed him a duty in respect of the specific harm of which he complains.

The 'neighbour principle' was developed in *Donoghue v Stevenson*.

> 'The rule that you are to love your neighbour becomes in law, you must not injure your neighbour, and the lawyer's question (who is my neighbour?) receives a restricted reply. You must take reasonable care to avoid acts or omissions which you can reasonably foresee would be likely to injure your neighbour. Who, then, in law is my neighbour? The answer seems to be persons who are so closely and directly affected by my act that I ought reasonably to have them in contemplation as being so affected when I am directing my mind to the acts or omissions which are called in question.'[4]

Donoghue v Stevenson imposed on manufacturers certain minimum standards of care in favour of the consumer.[5] It was also concerned with the liabilities of manufacturers and intermediaries, and the protection that a consumer may have. The judicial guidelines offered by *Donoghue v Stevenson* may be applied to various professions on the basis of the 'neighbour principle'. There is no reason why the same principle may not be applied to e-Commerce; providers of services should be familiar with the 'neighbour principle'. Often, the existence of the 'duty of care' is evident and straightforward, for example, manufacturers of goods owe a duty of care towards their customers, doctors towards their patients, or an occupier to visitors to that land—'categories of negligence are never closed'.[6] The application of the 'neighbour principle' also depends on the profession or service and in most cases, the 'neighbour principle applies particularly when a claimant is affected by the act of a defendant. The criterion is whether the defendant has failed his 'neighbour' by not foreseeing, and by not taking preventive steps to save the claimant from the injury he/she has suffered. In *Home Office v Dorset Yacht Co Ltd*, Lord Reid stated that:

> 'The time has come when we can and should say that [the neighbour principle] ought to apply unless there is some justification or valid explanation for its exclusion.'[7]

In *Anns v Merton London Borough Council*, Lord Wilberforce proposed a two-stage test: (a) was the harm to the claimant foreseeable so as to bring him within the remit of the 'neighbour principle'; and (b) did any policy reason exist to deny the existence of a duty to the claimant?[8] In *McLoughlin v O'Brien*, Lord Scarman virtually declared that 'foreseeability' should be the sole test of the

---

[4] *Donoghue v Stevenson, op cit*, at 580 *per* Lord Atkin.
[5] ibid, at 619 *per* Lord Atkin.
[6] *Donoghue v Stevenson, op cit*, at 619 *per* Lord Macmillan.
[7] [1978] A.C. 728 at 751–752.
[8] [1983] A.C. 410 at 421.

existence of a duty. Negligence is now category-based[9] and judicial disapproval for *Anns* criteria persisted. Foreseeability of harm exclusively is not enough to create a duty of care.

> 'It has been said almost too frequently to require repetition that foreseeability of likely harm is not in itself a sufficient test of liability in negligence. Some further ingredient is invariably needed to establish the requisite proximity of relationship between the plaintiff and defendant, and all the circumstances of the case must be carefully considered and analysed in order to ascertain whether such an ingredient is present.'[10]

So, proximity of relationship is another element in the duty of care—'proximity' is not a precise criterion and it is not clear what degree of proximity would give rise to a duty of care. Nevertheless, what is to be considered is whether one person's carelessness directly caused physical damage to another, and if so, the law will impose a duty. In *Marc Rich & Co A.G. v British Rock Marine Co Ltd,*[11] the House of Lords made it clear that even in respect of claim in relation to physical damage, foreseeability alone is insufficient to give rise to a duty of care.

In relation to e-Commerce, it is important to point out that in *Caparo Industries plc v Dickman*[12] it became clear that courts are more inclined to impose responsibility to protect others from physical injury and damage to their property rather than economic loss.

In *Caparo*, Lord Bridge stated that:

> 'One of the most important distinctions always to be observed lies in the law's essentially different approach to the different kinds of damage which one party may have suffered in consequence of the acts or omissions of another. It is one thing to owe a duty to avoid causing injury to the person or property of others. It is quite another to avoid causing others to suffer purely economic loss.'[13]

The prospects of causing economic loss to consumers through service would be high in doing business through e-Commerce, although the prospect of causing physical harm to consumers by introducing harmful products to them through e-Commerce may be very low. Furthermore, the idea that the tort of negligence should be category-based needs to be taken seriously—the idea of which gained some grounds after the days of *Anns*, for there may not necessarily be any presumption that all kinds of harm consequential of negligence or the lack of the

---

[9] See further *Governors of the Peabody Donation Fund v Sir Lindsay Parkinson & Co Ltd* [1985] A.C. 210.

[10] *Hill v Chief Constable of West Yorkshire* [1988] 2 All E.R. 238 at 241.

[11] [1996] A.C. 211.

[12] [1990] 1 All E.R. 568.

[13] op cit, at 574.

duty of care take place solely because of the defendant. In *Stovin v Wise*, Lord Hoffman stated that:

> 'The trend of authorities has been to discourage the assumption that anyone who suffers loss is *prima facie* entitled to compensation from a person ... whose act or omission can be said to have caused it. The default position is that he is not.'[14]

In other words, the burden is also on the plaintiff to establish why a duty of care should arise, and why the defendant should be made responsible for the welfare of the plaintiff.

In *Marc Rich*, Lord Lloyd maintained that if any physical harm has been caused to people or property (that is, foreseeability of harm is proven), there should be strong presumption of liability.

The post-*Anns* period has also been concerned with the issue of limiting the categories of negligence (in addition to saying that negligence should be category-based, but then what would be the limits of categorization; furthermore, if categorization is allowed, then each of them may come under the broad category of general negligence. In *Leigh and Sillivan Ltd v Aliakmon Shipping Co Ltd*,[15] Lord Brandon condemned the 'neighbourhood principle'—the gist of the matter is that in order to establish negligence on the grounds of the lack of the duty of care, predictability and foreseeability of the effect of act must be proved, and the plaintiff must also discharge the burden of why a duty for the defendant should arise.

It is important to bear in mind that the defendant may be subject to a duty of care if he should have foreseen the injury when the plaintiff suffered. Where a plaintiff is outside the area of a foreseeable danger, he will not succeed on the grounds of the lack of duty of care.[16] The concept of the duty of care can also be circumstantial or relative. In *Goodwill v British Pregnancy Advisory Service*,[17] the defendants performed a vasectomy on man who later became the plaintiff's lover. The couple did not use contraception, and the plaintiff, as a result of sexual intercourse, became pregnant and gave birth to a child. In a small number of cases, vasectomy may be reversed. The plaintiff maintained that the defendant owed her a duty and was negligent in failing to warn her that he might regain his fertility. The plaintiff's claim failed because the relationship with the defendant was so tenuous that the plaintiff could not have claimed a duty of care from the defendant. The duty of care is also relative to the profession or occupation, but it must be considered by reference to the circumstance of each case.

---

[14] [1996] A.C. 923 at 949.
[15] [1986] A.C. 785.
[16] *Hay (Brownhill) v Young* [1943] A.C. 92.
[17] [1996] 1 W.L.R. 1397.

Liability may arise concurrently in tort and contract. There always exist a duty of care under a contract, and the proximity of the parties creates a duty in tort. The answer is where a defendant undertook to provide a service, and the plaintiff relied on the skills of the defendant, a duty of care should arise from the parties' relationship based on the duty implied in a contract.[18] In *Henderson v Merrett Syndications Ltd*,[19] the House of Lords held that concurrent liability in contract and tort may arise provided that a duty in tort is not contrary to the terms of the contract. According to Lord Goff:

> 'the common law is not antipathetic to concurrent liability, and there is no sound basis for a rule which automatically restricts the plaintiff to either a tortious or contractual remedy. The result may be untidy; but given that the tortious duty is imposed by the general law, and the contractual duty is attributable to the will of the parties, I do not find it objectionable that the claimant may be entitled to take advantage of the remedy which is most advantageous to him, subject only to ascertaining whether the tortious duty is so inconsistent with the applicable contract that, in accordance with ordinary principle, the parties must be taken to have agreed that the tortious remedy is to be limited or excluded.'[20]

An action in tort is also useful when a third party wishes to establish that the defendant owes him a duty in tort. Thus, liability may arise independently of any contract provided the necessary 'proximity' between the parties exists, and in such a situation the principle of 'privity' may not be invoked. But, of course, it is to be ensured that a duty in tort to a third party does not conflict with the primary duty under the relevant contract.[21]

The duty of care in tort may not be extended too far. The scope of this duty must be determined within manageable proportions. In *White v Chief Constable of South Yorkshire Police*,[22] Lord Steyn said that:

> 'The argument was that the present case can be decided on conventional employer's liability principles. And counsel relies on the undoubted duty of an employer to protect employees from harm through work. It is true that there is no contract between police officers and a chief constable. But it would be artificial to rest a judgment on this point: the relationship between the police officers and the chief constable is closely analogous to a contract of employment. And I am content to approach the problem as if there was no ordinary contract of employment between the parties. Approaching the matter in this way it became obvious that there were two separate themes to the argument. The first rested on the duty of an

---

[18] See further *Esso Petroleum Co Ltd v Mardon* [1976] Q.B. 80.
[19] [1995] 2 A.C. 145.
[20] op cit, at 193–194
[21] *White v Jones* [1995] 1 All E.R. 691.
[22] [1999] 1 All E.R. 1.

employer to care for the safety of his employees and to take reasonable steps to safeguard them from harm. When analysed this argument breaks down. It is a non sequitur to say that because an employer is under a duty to an employee not to cause him physical injury, the employer should as a necessary consequence of that (of which there is no breach) be under a duty not to cause the employee psychiatric injury: ... The rules to be applied when an employee brings an action against his employer for harm suffered at his workplace are the rule of tort. One is therefore thrown back to the ordinary rules of the law of tort which contain restrictions on the recovery of compensation for psychiatric harm. This way of putting the case does not, therefore, advance the case of the police officers. The duty of an employer to safeguard his employees from harm could also be for-mulated in contract. In that event, and absent relevant express provisions, a term is implied by law into the contract as an incident of a standardised contract: ... But such a term could not be wider in scope than the duty imposed by the law of tort. Again one is thrown back to the ordinary rules of the law of tort.'[23]

Negligence is conduct which entails taking an unreasonably great risk of caus-ing damage. It also stands for omitting to do something which a prudent and reasonable man would do. Damage must be caused by acts or omissions of the defendant[24] and it must be established that the defendant has been careless in breach of a specific legal duty to take care.

The duty of care must be considered in the light of the standard of care, and the latter must be judged in the circumstances of each case. The duty of care must also be considered by reference to 'foresight' and the latter is also relevant to determining remoteness of damage.[25] 'Foresight' or 'foreseeability' must pass the 'reasonable' test. The foresight of the reasonable man is not the necessary con-dition of liability in tort.[26] What is important is whether the defendant saw the likelihood of causing harm to the plaintiff and whether it is just and reasonable to impose an onerous duty of care.[27] This is an important issue in doing busi-ness through e-Commerce.

The common law duty to take care in order to avoid causing injury to others was restricted to physical injury to person or property and the financial losses consequent. *Hedley Byrne & Co v Heller & Partners*[28] brought economic loss within the ambit of the tort of negligence, but this progress seems to have been hindered to a significant extent by *Junior Books v Veitchi,*[29] in that this case

---

[23] op cit, at 36.
[24] See *Central Asbestos Co Ltd v Dodd* [1973] A.C. 518.
[25] See *The Wagon Mound (No. 1)* [1961] A.C. 388; and *The Wagon Mound (No. 2)* [1967[1 A.C. 617.
[26] *Muirhead* [1986] Q.B. 507 at 511.
[27] *Peabody Donation Fund*, op cit.
[28] [1964] A.C. 465.
[29] [1983] 1 A.C. 520.

established that economic losses are only recoverable in negligence in exceptional cases, rather than as a general rule. In other words, any claim for economic losses arising under business carried through e-Commerce must be exceptional and established as such.

Furthermore, it is to be remembered that within a contractual structure, a duty of care may arise (contractual negligence) provided that the imposition of the duty is not inconsistent with the relevant contract.[30] In *Henderson v Merrett Syndicates*, the House of Lords emphasized that the law of tort is the general law; even though parties can contract out of it, this does not make the law of tort 'supplementary to the law of contract'.[31]

It is important to identify the incidence and nature of economic losses that may be caused by careless acts in conducting a business by electronic means. In principle, no liability arises in tort for economic losses unless damage to the claimant's person or property is proved. In *Murphy v Brentwood District Council*[32] the claimant was not allowed to recover damages for a defect in quality which contributed to reducing the value of his house.[33] Although the general principle for disallowing economic losses in the absence of physical damage has been criticized as being a blatant departure from the 'reasonable foreseeability' principle,[34] it is primarily supported on policy grounds, in that otherwise the world of insurance would be inundated with claims arising from various types of risk giving rise to economic losses (natural catastrophes).

In so far as e-Commerce is concerned, economic losses might arise out of the breakdown, for example, of the network, but then that loss may be recovered as a breach of contract with the network organization. However, the decision of the House of Lords in *Hedley Byrne and Co Ltd* created a novel judicial principle whereby careless statements made by a person may contribute to the occasion of economic losses, provided of course, a special business relationship had existed between the claimant and the defendant. This is where economic loss becomes an important issue in e-Commerce. What is important in this relationship is that the communicator of any information must be aware that the receiver of the information shall act on it, without further independent inquiry; in other words, a degree of dependency and perhaps trust will persist between the communicator of the information and the person to whom the information is communicated. Of course, in *White v Jones*[35] it was established that liability may arise even in the absence of any reliance by the plaintiff upon the defendant. However, 'assumption of responsibility' whether directly or indirectly, by

---

[30] See further *Henderson v Merrett Syndications Ltd*, op cit.
[31] op cit, at 193 *per* Lord Goff.
[32] [1991] 1 A.C. 398.
[33] See also *Spartan Steel and Alloys Ltd v Martin and Co (Contractors) Ltd* [1973] 1 Q.B. 27; and *Elliott v Sir Robert McAlpine and Sons Ltd* [1966] 2 Lloyd's Rep 482.
[34] See the dissenting opinion of Edward-Davies CJ in *Spartan Steel*.
[35] [1995] 2 A.C. 207.

a defendant has proved to be a useful criterion or formula in this area of law.[36] Furthermore, the purposes for which and the circumstances in which information is provided must also be considered,[37] and the identity of those who are likely to suffer losses as a result of the statement being made carelessly. However, in *Galoo Ltd v Bright Grahame Murray*,[38] Evans LJ maintained that an identity test in itself would not be sufficient. *Smith v Eric S Bush*[39] however satisfied both the conditions: purposes and circumstances, and the identity test. In e-Commerce, it is possible to target information to specific persons who will eventually provide information to the whole world. Information provided carelessly to the first category of persons by electronic means may give rise to liability. Following *Caparo* one may maintain that information provided or representations made with a view to deliberately causing the conduct of or decision-making by a claimant may give rise to liability—a precautionary measure which e-Commerce business people should take. By following *McInerney v Lloyds Bank Ltd*[40] and *Hedley Byrne* one may also maintain that statements made to induce somebody to enter into a contract with the making of the statement by whatever means may also give rise to liability.

In *Smith v Littlewoods Organisation*,[41] Lord Goff maintained that in the absence of an existing duty, no liability arises for a mere omission to act.[42] But where omission to act arises liability under a statute, this statement may not be sustained. On the other hand, if a risk has arisen directly out of an act or mechanism under the control of a defendant, liability arises.[43] This point is relevant to e-Commerce. It is to be pointed out that a negligent act committed or an omission made even in the course of voluntary work by a defendant may give rise to liability.

In determining liability, in general, the rule of direct relationship applies as, in general, no liability arises from the acts or omissions of others unless there exists some special relationship between the defendant and third parties. In *Home Office v Dorset Yacht*, the House of Lords imposed liability on the Crown, when certain juvenile delinquents who escaped from a penal institution, damaged the plaintiff's yacht by careless handling of the yacht, even though there was no direct relationship between the plaintiff and the juvenile delinquents; the defendants failed to exercise control over the delinquent juveniles.

[36] See further Caparo Industries v Dickman, op cit.
[37] ibid.
[38] [1995] 1 All E.R. 14 at 43, per Evans LJ.
[39] [1990] 1 A.C. 831.
[40] [1974] 1 Lloyd's Reports 246.
[41] [1987] A.C. 241.
[42] ibid.
[43] Goldman v Hargrave [1947] 1 A.C. 645.

8.2.2   The position of the reasonable man and the standard of care

Common law invokes the standards of conduct of the reasonable man. Along with this goes the standard of foresight of the reasonable man[44] which must be determined by reference to the circumstances of each case.[45] To undertake an act, without possessing the requisite skill, and perform it without demonstrating that skill, and cause harm to the defendant arises liability.[46] Negligence does not arise from the lack of skill but for undertaking the work without skill knowing full well the consequence of so doing. This is, in fact, more an issue of undertaking risks voluntarily, rather than of foreseeability. The issue of risks should be looked at from various standpoints:

- the magnitude of the risk to which the defendant exposes third parties by his action;
- what would be attained by such risk-bearing activity;
- whether adequate precautions were taken.

These are now discussed.

8.2.2.1   The magnitude of risk

The magnitude of a risk is determined by referring to two factors: the seriousness of the injury risked; and the likelihood of the injury, which has, in fact, been caused.[47] The magnitude of risk may easily be foreseen by the risk-taker, particularly because he/she/it should have the foreseeability of the risk he/she/it is taking. But the problem is that foreseeability does not include likelihood.[48] On the other hand, in *The Wagon Mound (No. 2)*,[49] it was stated that although the incident was extremely unlikely, it was still regarded as a danger which should have been reasonably foreseen. The argument about 'foreseeability' seems to be never-ending and is often confirmed by referring to the circumstances of each case. 'Foreseeability' also emanates from the special expertise that a defendant may possess. Perhaps the best criterion to determine 'foreseeability' would be whether it was reasonable for the ordinary man or for an expert to foresee the kind of incident that has taken place; of course, in the case of an expert, the standards of his foreseeability must be higher, befitting his special knowledge and experience.[50]

8.2.2.2   What would be achieved by such risk-bearing activity?

The proportion of risks taken by the defendant in performing a task or a business should be taken into consideration. In other words, the reasonableness of the defendant's conduct must be judged by referring to the nature or proportion

---

[44] See Glasgow Corporation v Muir [1943] A.C. 448 at 457.
[45] Beckett v Newalls Insulation Co Ltd [1955] 1 W.L.R. 8 at 17.
[46] See The Lady Gwendolen [1965] P. 294.
[47] Read v J Lyons & Co [1947] A.C. 156 at 173.
[48] Chapman v Hearse (1961) C.L.R. 112, 155; see also Carmarthenshire County Council v Lewis [1955] A.C. 546, 565.
[49] op cit.
[50] See further Stewart v West African Terminals Ltd [1964] 2 Lloyd's Rep 371.

of risks he undertook to perform an act. Risks must not be disproportionate to attaining the objective. If additional safety is to be attained at too high a public cost, one may consider whether that risk-avoidance would be proportionate to the benefit to be achieved.[51] On the other hand, if an act is undertaken which would expose the public to foreseeable risks, by virtue of not taking reasonable care, the defendant may attract liability.

Again, one is, so to say, 'back to square one'; what is meant by adequate precaution, and by what standards should one measure it? Foreseeability combined with the principle of due care and skill should help determine what is an adequate precautionary measure. The burden of adequate precautions also depends upon the nature of the risks involved in an act. However, the greater the risk, the less should be the importance to be accorded to the issue of precautionary measures.[52] This principle equally applies to risks related to e-Commerce.

8.3   Conclusions

The general principles of the law of negligence are applicable to e-Commerce. People engaged in e-Commerce are to be treated as experts; thus, the principle of the care and skill becomes relevant to them as professional people. It is, therefore, expected that such people show a reasonable and competent degree of skill.[53] The generally accepted rule is that a defendant accused of negligence may clear himself if he successfully proves that he acted in accordance with the practice prevalent in the profession. However, it is to be pointed out that the existence of a statutory power may give rise to liability in negligence for those on whom the power was conferred.[54] Common law negligence must be distinguished from liability arising in tort of breach of statutory duty.

The proof of negligence is a burden that must be discharged by the claimant; in other words, he must prove causation,[55] which is an important element in bringing an action in negligence. The established rule of res ipsa loquitor, according to which the claimant must prove negligence, may prove to be onerous in that it is only the defendant who has the knowledge of the cause of the negligent act; indeed, he caused it. This is an important issue in e-Commerce. There must be reasonable evidence of negligence. In order to avoid liability, it is for a defendant to prove that the accident or incident leading to an injury or to financial loss sustained by the claimant could have happened without negligence.[56]

---

[51] Daborn v Bath Tramways Motor Co[1946] 2 All E.R. 333.
[52] Marshall v Gotham Co Ltd [1954] A.C. 360; see also Morris v Luton Corporation [1946] 1 All E.R. 1.
[53]   Smith v Eric S Bush, op cit.
[54] Home Office v Dorset Yacht Co, op cit.
[55] Kay v Ayrshire and Arran Health Board [1987] 2 All E.R. 417.
[56] *Bennett v Chemical Construction (G.B.) Ltd* [1971] 1 W.L.R. 1575. For a discussion of negligence, in general, and of the principle of res ipsa loquitor, the reader is advised to consult any standard work on negligence.

9. E-Commerce and consumer protection

9.1 Introduction

This chapter discusses the measures that have been taken to protect consumers, whether from the supply of 'unfit' or defective goods or from incorrect and/or misleading information on goods and services, particularly when the consumer may be seeking goods or services through the distance selling methods.
This topic should be discussed from various points of view:

- protection from defective product;
- protection in regard to distance sales;
- protection from misuse of computers;
- protection from abuse of data/information.

Each of these aspects has received attention in this chapter. The EU initiative in regard to protection for a consumer acquiring goods by the distant sales method was timely, and interesting. The OECD also issued Guidelines for Consumer Protection in the context of Electronic Commerce, this Guideline has been discussed in a separate section of this chapter.

It is opportune to point out that whereas e-Commerce contributes to attaining efficiency in business and makes business profitable, misuse of technology withdraws protection from the consumer—a balance should be struck whereby on the one hand, business through e-Commerce must be allowed to flourish, and on the other hand, it must not be allowed to do so at the cost of consumer protection. The extent to which these guidelines, both OECD and EU, may be implemented by the member states of these organizations remains to be seen.

9.2   OECD guidelines for consumer protection in the context of electronic commerce

9.2.1   Background to the guidelines

In order to increase consumer awareness and strengthen consumer confidence in shopping on-line by means of transparency of information and providing protection against abuse of the system of electronic commerce, on 9 December 1999, the OECD Council approved these Guidelines. These Guidelines aim at assisting governments, business and consumer representatives in developing and implementing on-line consumer protection mechanisms. Private sector initiatives, including participation of consumer representatives is thought to be crucial by the OECD in promoting consumer protection. Furthermore, the principle of fair business must be maintained in all senses of the term. In order to allow consumers appropriate redress, where necessary, the OECD Guidelines also recommend that an affordable resolution system should be provided by the member states.

Selling through the e-Commerce mechanism, is in reality, sale by description, which may entail providing fraudulent and misleading information in regard to products and services.[1] The OECD Guidelines paid much attention to this issue. Appreciating the nature of the digital networks and computer technology, the OECD, through the Guidelines, pointed out that a global approach to consumer protection should be adopted, as no individual country would be able to deal with the challenges presented by such networks. The OECD also had concerns about the disparate national policies and legislation to the operation of e-Commerce—the consequence of which is that the issue of consumer protection becomes less certain and uniform. The OECD, therefore, felt the need to promote national laws in the Member countries to accommodate the need created by the complex phenomenon of e-Commerce, and for co-operation among its member states.

The first initiative to develop a set of general guidelines to protect consumers who might be affected by e-Commerce was taken by the OECD Committee on Consumer Policy in April 1998. The purpose of the guidelines was to provide a framework and a set of principles to assist:

'(i)   Governments in reviewing, formulating and implementing consumer and law enforcement policies, practices and regulations if necessary for effective consumer protection in the context of electronic commerce;

(ii)   Business associations, consumer groups and self-regulatory bodies, by providing guidance as to the care characteristics of effective

---

[1] See further C Chatterjee, *'OECD Guidelines for Consumer Protection in the context of Electronic Commerce'* 1 *Financial Crime Review* (2000) 62–66 at 62.

consumer protection that should be considered in reviewing, formulating and implementing self-regulatory schemes in the context of electronic commerce; and

(iii)   Individual businesses and consumers engaged in electronic commerce, by providing clear guidance as to the core characteristics of information disclosure and fair business practices that business should provide and consumer should expect in the context of electronic commerce.'[2]

In developing the Guidelines, the OECD Council paid attention to the following:

(i)   Recommendation of the Council concerning Guidelines Governing the Protection of Privacy and Transborder Flows of Personal Data of 23 September 1980[3];

(ii)   Recommendation of the Council concerning Guidelines for the Security of Information Systems of 26–27 November 1992[4];

(iii) OECD Recommendation concerning Guidelines on Cryptography Policy of 27 March 1977[5];

(iv)   Ministerial Declaration on Consumer Protection in the Context of Electronic Commerce of 8–9 October 1998[6];

(v)   Ministerial Declaration on the Protection of Privacy on Global Networks of 8–9 October 1998[7]; and

(vi)   Ministerial Declaration on Authentication for Electronic Commerce of 8–9 October 1998.[8]

It was also recognized by the OECD Council that in view of the unfamiliarity of many consumers with the complex mechanism of concluding cross-border electronic commerce-based transactions, consumers' interests would be at risk. Consumers should be aware of their rights and obligations in the electronic market place, and that governments, businesses and consumers and their representatives should be involved in the development of an effective cross-border redress system.

The Guidelines were adopted in the hope that the member states would disseminate the contents to all concerned, including consumer representatives, educational institutions and public interest groups, and try to implement them as far as possible. Through the Guidelines, the OECD Council also requested that the governments invited countries to take into account the recommendations

[2] See the Guidelines, p 2.
[3] Doc C(80) 58 (Final).
[4] Doc C(42) 188/Final.
[5] Doc C(97) 62/Final.
[6] Doc C(98) 177 (Annex 2).
[7] Doc C(98) 177 (Annex 1).
[8] Doc C(98) 177 (Annex 3).

and co-operate among themselves for sharing information, resources and experiences.

9.2.2 A brief discussion of the guidelines

The Guidelines have been developed in four parts: Part I—Scope; Part II—General Principles; Part III—Implementation; and Part IV—Global Co-operation. The General Principles (Part II) have been developed under the following sub-headings:

    (i)   Transparent and Effective Protection
    (ii)   Fair Business, Advertising and Marketing Practices
        (a) On-line Disclosures:
            (i)   Information about the Business;
            (ii)   Information about the Goods or Services; and
            (iii) Information about the Transaction
        (b) Confirmation Process
        (c) Payment
        (d) Dispute Resolution and Redress:
            (i)   Applicable Law and Jurisdiction
            (ii)   Alternative Dispute Resolution and Redress
        (e) Privacy
        (f) Education and Awareness.

The OECD Council maintained that protection of consumers should be taken as an obligation in any form of business, whether electronic or otherwise. These Guidelines apply only to business-to-consumer electronic commerce and not to business-to-business transactions.

The Guidelines rightly recommend that consumers who participate in electronic commerce should be allowed transparent and effective protection which should not be any less than that to which they are entitled in other forms of commerce. Advertising and marketing practices should be fair to protect the interests of consumers. Fairness would entail avoidance of making any representation or omission that is likely to be deceptive, misleading, fraudulent or unfair. Business selling, promoting or marketing of goods or services to consumers should not cause any unreasonable risk of harm to consumers. Information should be provided in a 'clear, conspicuous, accurate and easily accessible manner'. Businesses should not hide their true identity or location or avoid compliance with consumer protection standards and/or enforcement mechanisms. Unfair contract terms should not be used by businesses. As a protection against receipt of unsolicited commercial e-mail messages, businesses should develop and implement effective, easy procedures in order to allow consumers to decide whether or not to receive such messages. As a protection against receipt of unsolicited commercial e-mail, messages should be respected. Information must be provided in clear and easy terms when provided through advertisements particularly when advertisements are targeted to children, the elderly, the seriously ill and others who might lack the capacity to fully understand information in any complex form. Businesses' identities must be clearly established and disclosed to consumers.[9]

As stated earlier, on-line disclosures have been discussed under three headings. The first heading—information about the business, provides that businesses engaged in electronic commerce should provide accurate, clear and easily accessible information as to the identification of the business; effective communication with the business; location of business and its principal, and law enforcement and regulatory officials; and where a business publicizes its membership, it should provide consumers with appropriate contact details and the relevant codes and practices of the certification body. In so far as information about the goods or services is concerned, the Guidelines recommend that in order to enable consumers to reach an informed decision about whether or not to enter into a transaction, businesses engaged in electronic commerce with consumers should provide accurate and accessible information to them in regard to the goods and services offered.

In so far as the information about the transaction is concerned, the Guidelines have provided elaborate provisions, the gist of which has been that

'businesses engaged in electronic commerce should provide sufficient information about the terms, conditions and costs associated with a transaction to enable the terms, conditions and costs associated with a transaction to enable consumers to make an informed decision about whether to enter into the transaction.'[10]

Information must be clear, accurate and easily accessible; businesses should provide consumers clear and full text of the terms and conditions of transactions in a manner that would enable consumers 'to access and maintain an adequate record of such information'.[11]

(iv) 'an itemisation of total costs collected and/or imposed by the business;
(v)   notice of the existence of other routinely applicable costs to the consumers that are not collected and/or imposed by the business;
(vi) terms of delivery or performance;
(vii) terms, conditions and methods of payment;
(viii) restrictions, limitations or conditions of purchase, such as parental/guardian approval requirements, geographic or time restrictions;
(ix) instructions for proper use including safety and health care warnings;
(x)   information relating to available after-sales services;
(xi) details of and conditions related to withdrawal, termination, return, exchange, cancellation and/or refund policy information; and

[9] See generally, Annex, pp 4–5.
[10] op cit, at 6.
[11] ibid.

(xii) available warranties and guarantees.'[12]

Consumers should be provided with an opportunity to identify precisely the goods or services he/she may wish to purchase, and the sellers or providers of services should keep a complete record of all transactions. A consumer should have the right to cancel a transaction before concluding the purchase. The payment mechanism(s) should be simple. According to the Guidelines:

> 'Limitations of liability for unauthorised or fraudulent use of payment systems, and chargeback mechanisms offer powerful tools to enhance consumer confidence and their development and use should be encouraged in the context of electronic commerce.'[13]

It is to be emphasized that the Guidelines recommend that consumers should be provided effective access to alternative dispute resolution and redress without undue cost. This facility should be provided to consumers when they may be involved in disputes arising from business-to-consumer electronic commerce, and in particular, when they may be involved in cross-border transactions. Transparent internal mechanisms should be established to address and respond to consumer complaints, in addition to establishing co-operative self-regulatory programmes to deal with consumer complaints. Alternative dispute resolution should be accorded priority in settling disputes. Thus, access to fair and speedy justice through the informal mechanism of alternative dispute resolution has been encouraged by the Guidelines.

As regards 'privacy', the Guidelines state that:

> 'Business-to-business electronic commerce should be conducted in accordance with the recognised privacy principles set out in the OECD Guidelines Governing the Protection of Privacy and Transborder Flow of Personal Data (1980), and taking into account the OECD Ministerial Declaration on the Protection of Privacy on Global Networks (1998), to provide appropriate and effective protection for consumers.'[14]

Education and awareness of consumers have received the attention of the Guidelines. Consumers should be familiar with the complexities of electronic commerce and its probable abuses that might adversely affect their interests. This should enable them to learn how to take informed decision-making and to this end, governments, media, educational institutions and consumer representatives should co-operate to adopt all effective means to educate consumers and businesses.

---

[12] op cit, at 6.
[13] op cit, at 7.
[14] op cit, at 8.

In an attempt to implement these recommendations, member states should at both the national and international levels, and in co-operation with businesses, consumers and their representatives, review, and if necessary, promote self-regulatory practices, adopt laws and practices, exchange private sector leadership in the development of technology as a means of protection and empowering consumers, and facilitate consumers' ability to gain access to information and advice and to file complaints related to electronic commerce.

The Guidelines also recommend global co-operation for electronic commerce, as it is only through such co-operation that enforcement of joint initiatives at the international level and at the level of businesses, consumer representatives and governments may take place. Use of existing international networks and entering into bilateral and/or multilateral agreements has also been recommended by the Guidelines as another means of achieving international co-operation. OECD also recommended that the Member countries should:

'Work toward building consensus, both at the national and international levels, on core consumer protections to further the goals of enhancing consumer confidence, ensuring predictability for businesses and protecting consumers.

Co-operate and work toward developing agreements or other arrangements for the mutual recognition and enforcement of judgements resulting from disputes between consumers and businesses, and judgements resulting from law enforcement actions taken to combat fraudulent, misleading or unfair commercial conduct.'[15]

The OECD Guidelines were intended to help eliminate some of the uncertainties that consumers and businesses often experience when buying and selling online and to clarify their respective rights and responsibilities.[16] The OECD provides a forum for governments to discuss economic and development issues and although its recommendations are not legally binding, its member states often voluntarily accept and implement them. The principal objectives of the Guidelines are to provide a set of principles to governments, businesses, and individual businesses and consumers. The Guidelines have clearly identified the basic issues pertaining to e-Commerce and, in particular, the means of providing protection and redress to consumers.

[15] op cit., at 9
[16] op cit, mentioned in the section of the Guidelines entitled 'Frequently Asked Questions'.

9.3   Directive of the European Parliament and of the council concerning the processing of personal data and the protection of privacy in the electronic communications Sector[17]

9.3.1   Introduction

One of the early initiatives by the European Parliament and the Council in regard to this issue was taken in 1995,[18] and the Preamble to the 2000 Directive stated that confidentiality of communications is guaranteed in accordance with the international instruments relating to human rights, in particular the European Convention for the Protection of Human Rights and Fundamental Freedoms and the constitutions of the member states. Directive 97/66/EC of the European Parliament and of the Council of 15 December 1997 pertaining to the processing of personal data and the protection of privacy in the telecommunication sector translated the principles set out in the Directive 95/46/EC. It is expected that the 1997 Directive will be

> 'adopted to developments in the markets and technologies for electronic communications services in order to provide an equal level of protection of personal data and privacy for users of publicly available electronic communication services, regardless of technologies used.'[19]

The advanced forms of digital networks have significant capacities and possibilities for processing personal data so that the issue of the protection of privacy becomes even more important. Electronic communications services over the Internet which are available to the public open new possibilities to users, but at the same time, present new risks for their personal data and privacy. Thus, the need for legal, regulatory provisions becomes important in order to protect the fundamental right of privacy of the individual. The EU, therefore, aims at harmonising legal, regulatory and technical provisions within the member states for the protection of personal data, privacy and the legitimate interests of legal persons in the electronic communications sector, but a harmonization scheme must not hinder the promotion and development of new electronic communications services and networks between the member states. Co-operation of all concerned, the member states, providers of services, and users is absolutely necessary in order to achieve these goals. Directive 95/46/EC applies, in particular, to all matters relating to the protection of fundamental rights and freedoms which are not specifically covered by the provisions of the Directive. This Directive applies to electronic communications services that are not available to the public.

---

[17] COM(2000) 385 Final; 2000/0189 (COD) dated 12 July 2000.
[18] Directive 95/46/EC of the European Parliament and of the Council of 24 October 1995.
[19] Council Directive 2000/0189 (COD), op cit at 16.

The Directive of July 2000 does not address issues of protection of fundamental rights and freedoms related to activities which are not governed by community law, as it is for the member states to take appropriate measures for the protection of public security, defence, state security, including the economic well-being of the state when the activities relate to state security matters.[20]

This Directive recommends that service providers should take appropriate measures to safeguard the security of their services, and where necessary, in conjunction with the provider of the network. Subscribers should be informed of any special risks pertaining to a breach of the security of the network. Subscribers and users of services should be fully informed by their service providers of the existing security risks over which they may not have any control, as they should notify their subscribers and users of the kind of security they may be able to provide against risks.

In regard to itemized bills, which facilitate checking the accuracy of the fees managed by service providers, it should be pointed out that they may jeopardize the privacy of the users of publicly available electronic communications services; thus the Directive encourages the member states to develop alternative payment facilities which would allow anonymous or private to electronic communications services available to the public.[21] The processing of digital mobile networks location data for value added services should only be allowed with the consent of subscribers, and not otherwise, allowing subscribers the right to refuse the processing, where necessary.

The issue of privacy of subscribers and callers has received serious attention in the Directive. It points out, *inter alia*, that subscribers of a particular nature have an interest in guaranteeing the anonymity of their callers. Subscribers should be allowed to make an informed choice about the privacy facilities they may want to use. Subscribers should also be allowed safeguards against any nuisance that may be caused by automatic call forwarding by others. Their names should not as a matter of practice be published in any directory, and if published, providers of public directories should inform the subscribers concerned. They should be safeguarded against intrusion of their privacy by means of unsolicited calls, telefaxes, electronic mails and any other form of communication for direct marketing purposes. It is to be pointed out that the Directive 95/46/EC aims at preventing any form of processing of personal data irrespective of the technology used. Manufacturers of equipment used for electronic communications services are advised to manufacture their produce in a way that would safeguard the personal data and privacy of users and subscribers.

According to the Directive, where the rights of users and subscribers are not respected, national legislation should provide for judicial remedies, and any

---

[20] op cit, at 17.
[21] For example, calling cards or payment by credit cards.

person failing to comply with the national measures taken under this Directive should be subject to penalties. The drafters of the Directive appreciated that in order to facilitate compliance with the provisions of this Directive, certain specific arrangements may be needed for processing of data. This Directive must be implemented by all member states by 31 December 2001 at the latest.

9.3.2   A brief analysis of the directive

This Directive consists of 19 Articles: Article 1 (scope and aim); Article 2 (definitions); Article 3 (services concerned); Article 4 (security); Article 5 (confidentiality of the communications); Article 6 (traffic data); Article 7 (itemised billing); Article 8 (preservation and restriction of calling and connected line identification); Article 9 (location data); Article 10 (exceptions); Article 11 (automatic all forwarding); Article 12 (directories of subscribers); Article 13 (unsolicited communications); Article 14 (technical features and standardization); Article 15 (application of certain provisions of Directive 95/46/EC); Article 16 (transitional arrangements); Article 17 (transposition); Article 18 (entry into force); and Article 19 (addresses).

The primary aim of this Directive is to harmonize the level of protection of fundamental rights and freedoms, and the right of privacy of subscribers and users in the member states with respect to the processing of personal data in the electronic communications sector, and at the same time to ensure the free movement of such data and services within the Community.[22] However, this Directive shall not apply to activities which are beyond the scope of the EC Treaty,[23] and, in particular, to activities concerning public security, defence, state security and the activities of the state in areas of criminal law.[24] There are two terms in particular, the definitions of which are important: 'traffic data', which stands for any 'any data processed in the course of or for the purpose of the transmission of a communication over an electronic communications network'[25]; and 'location data' which means 'any data processed in an electronic communication network, indicating the geographic position of the terminal equipment of a user of a publicly available electronic communications service'.[26]

The processing of personal data in relation to publicly available electronic communications services in public communications networks in the Community will be governed by this Directive.[27] It will also apply to the provisions regarding preservation and restriction of calling and connected line identification (Art 8); exceptions (Art 10); and automatic call forwarding (Art 11). Should any disproportionate economic effort be needed for fulfilling the requirements of Articles

---

[22] Art 1.
[23] The activities which are covered by Titles V and VI of the Treaty on European Union.
[24] Art 1(3).
[25] Art 2(b).
[26] Art 2(c).
[27] Art 3(1).

8, 10 and 11, the member state concerned may notify the Commission to that effect. At this point it would be appropriate to briefly refer to the exceptions (Art 10)—it is for the member state to ensure that transparent procedures exist to regulate the following circumstances for a provider of a public communications network and/or publicly available electronic communications service:

    (a)   the calling line identification requirement may be eliminated on a temporary basis upon application made by a subscriber requesting the tracing of malicious or nuisance calls[28]; and

    (b)   both calling line identification and denial of consent of a subscriber or user for the processing of location data may be eliminated on a temporary basis on a per-line basis for organizations dealing with emergency calls, and recognised as such by a Member State, namely, law enforcement agencies, ambulance services and fire brigades.[29]

Article 11 of the Directive provides that a subscriber will be provided with opportunities to use a simple means, without charge, of stopping automatic call forwarding by a third party to the subscriber's terminal. The importance of restricting calling and connected line identification, the subject matter of Article 8, has already been explained. The caller must have an opportunity to use simple means, and without any charge, of preventing the presentation of the calling-line identification on a per-call basis (Art 8(1)). A subscriber shall be entitled to the same privilege for preventing the presentation of the connected line identification to the user calling. The provisions of Article 8 shall also apply to calls to third countries whether originating in the Community or in third countries.

The provider of publicly available electronic communications must take appropriate technical and organizational measures to safeguard the security of its services and, if necessary, in co-operation with the provider of the public electronic communications network, and in the event of a breach of the security of the network taking place, the latter must inform the subscribers of such risks and probable remedies, including the costs involved.[30]

Confidentiality of communications will also include listening, tapping, storage or any other kind of interception or surveillance and the related traffic data by persons other than users, without the consent of the user concerned, unless legally authorized to do so.[31] But, this provision shall not affect:

'any legally authorised recording of communications and the related traffic data in the course of lawful business practice for the purpose of

---

[28] In such cases, the data containing the identification of the calling subscriber will be stored and made available by the provider of a public communications network and/or publicly available electronic communication service.

[29] Art 10(b).

[30] Art 4.

[31] Art 15(1).

providing evidence of a commercial transaction or of any other business communication.'[32]

Traffic data must be erased or made anonymous after completion of the transmission. Such data which may be necessary for the purpose of subscriber billing and interconnection payments may be processed only up to the end of the material period during which the relevant bill may be lawfully challenged or payment pursued. Similar provision applies to the value added services to the subscriber, that is, to the extent and for the duration necessary for such services provided the subscriber has given his consent to it. The service provider has an obligation to inform the subscriber of the types of traffic data which are to be processed. Processing of traffic data must be restricted only to authorized persons acting under the authority of providers of the public communication networks and services handling billing or traffic management, customer enquiries, detection of fraud, or providing a value added service, and to what may be necessary for the purpose of such activities.[33]

Subscribers will have the right to receive non-itemised bills. Article 7, paragraph 2 provides that:

> 'Member States shall apply national provisions in order to reconcile the rights of subscribers receiving itemised bills with the right to privacy or calling users and called-subscribers, for example, by ensuring that sufficient alternative privacy enhancing modalities for communications or payments are available to such users and subscribers.'

Location data may only be processed when they are made anonymous or made with the consent of the users or subscribers concerned only to the extent and for the period necessary for the provision of a value added service. A service provider has the obligation to inform the users or subscribers prior to its obtaining their consent of the type of location data which will be processed, in addition to disclosing the purposes and the duration of the processing, and whether the data might be transmitted to a third party for the purposes of providing the value added service.[34] Where consent of a user or a subscriber has been obtained, it must have the privilege of temporarily refusing the processing of location data (other than traffic data) for each connection to the network or for each transmission of a communication, using a simple means and without having to pay any charges. Processing of location data is to be restricted to what is necessary for the purposes of providing the value-added service.

Member states must ensure that subscribers are informed, free of charge, of the purposes of a printed or electronic directory of subscribers which would be

[32] Art 5(2).
[33] Art 6(5).
[34] Art 9.

available to the public or obtainable through directory enquiry services. Sub-scribers will have the right to withdraw their personal data from such directory. However, when personal data will be needed, member states shall ensure that the legitimate interests of subscribers other than natural persons are sufficiently protected.[35]

Unsolicited communications (that is, communications which may take place without any human intervention) through, for example, automatic calling machines, facsimile machines or electronic mail for the purposes of direct marketing may only be allowed in respect of subscribers who have given their prior consent. Unsolicited communications by any other means or method for the purposes of direct marketing are prohibited unless consent has been given by the subscriber concerned. A subscriber has the discretion not to receive these communications. Member states shall ensure that the legitimate interests of sub-scribers other than natural persons with regard to unsolicited communications are sufficiently protected,[36] and in this regard the needs for small and medium-sized firms is to be borne in mind.

Where implementation of the provisions of this Directive may require specific technical features in electronic communication networks, member states shall inform the Commission in accordance with the procedure provided for in the Directive 98/34/EC of the European Parliament and the Council Directive.[37] Article 14(3) provides that:

> 'Where required, the Commission shall adopt measures to ensure that terminal equipment incorporates the necessary safeguards to guarantee the protection of personal data and privacy of users and subscribers, in accor-dance with the Directive 1999/5/EC and Council Decision 87/95/EEC.'[38]

Article 15 allows the member states in certain circumstances to adopt legislation the effect of which may be to restrict the scope of the rights and obligations pro-vided for in Article 5 (confidentiality of the communications); Article 6 (traffic data); Article 8(1) to (4) (restriction of calling and connected line identification); and Article 9 (location data), when 'Such restriction constitutes a necessary meas-ure to safeguard national security, defence, public security, the prevention, investi-gation, detection and prosecution of criminal offences or of unauthorized use of the electronic communication system'.[39] The provisions regarding judicial reme-dies, liability and sanctions embodied in the Directive 95/46/EC shall apply. The protection of fundamental rights and freedoms and of legitimate interests in the electronic communications sector is one of the salient features of this Directive.[40]

---

[35] Art 12(3).
[36] Art 3(3).
[37] See O.J. L 204, 21 July 1998 at 37.
[38] See O.J. L 36, 7 February 1987 at 310.
[39] Art 15(1).
[40] See the Preamble to the Directive.

9.4   Directive 97/7/EC of the European Parliament and of the council of 20 May 1997 on the protection of consumers in respect of distant contracts[41]

9.4.1   Introduction

The title of this Directive is self-explanatory. This Directive is based on the assumption that cross-border distance selling may be one of the principal 'tangible results of the completion of the internal market', and that eventually consumers should be allowed to take advantage of dealings with business outside their traditional jurisdictions. The Directive pointed out that:

'some Member States have already taken different or divergent measures to protect consumers in respect of distance selling, which has a detrimental effect on competition between businesses in the internal market ... it is, therefore, necessary to introduce at Community level a minimum set of common rules in this area.'

This Directive also maintained that:

'it is important for the minimum binding rules contained in this Directive to be supplemented where appropriate by voluntary arrangements among the traders concerned, in line with Commission recommendation 92/295/EEC of 7 April 1992[42] on codes of practice for the protection of consumers in respect of contracts negotiated at a distance.'

The Directive very appropriately pointed out that:

'non-compliance with this Directive may harm not only consumers but also competitors, whereas provisions ma, therefore, be laid down enabling public bodies or their representatives or consumer organisations which, under national legislation, have a legitimate interest in consumer protection, or professional organisations which have a legitimate interest in taking action, to monitor the application thereof.'

9.4.2   An analysis of the directive

This Directive consists of 19 Articles, and two Annexes. In Article 1 the Directive confirms that its objective is to:

'approximate the laws, regulations and administrative provisions of the Member States concerning distance contracts between consumers and suppliers.'

---

[41] O.J. L 144 04/06/1997 at 0019–0027.
[42] O.J. N L 156, 10 June 1992 at 21.

Definitions of certain terms have been provided by Article 2 of the Directive. Of these terms, the definitions of the following are important to highlight:

Distant Contracts
A distant contract means 'any contract concerning goods or services concluded between a supplier and a consumer under an organised distance sales or service provisions scheme run by the supplier, who, for the purpose of the contract, makes exclusive use of one or more means of distance communication up to and including the moment at which the contract is concluded'.

Consumer
A consumer means 'any natural person who, in contracts covered by this Directive, is acting for purposes that are outside his trade, business or profession'.

Means of Distance Communication
Stands for 'any means which, without the simultaneous physical presence of the supplier and the consumer may be used for the conclusion of a contract between those parties'.

Exemptions
This Directive has no application to contracts concluded:

- for financial services;
- by means of automatic vending machines or automated commercial premises;
- with telecommunication operators through the use of public payphones;
- for the construction and sale of immovable property or other immovable property rights, except for rental; and
- at an auction.[43]

Furthermore, Article 4 (prior information); Article 5 (written confirmation of information) and Article 6 (right of withdrawal) shall not apply to contracts for the supply of foodstuffs, beverages or 'other goods intended for everyday consumption supplied to the home of the consumer, to his residence or his workplace by regular roundsmen' or contracts for the provision of accommodation, transport, catering, leisure services, generally.[44]

Article 4 provides that prior to concluding any distance contract, the consumer shall be provided, in good time, with the following information: identity of the supplier; the main characteristics of the goods or services; price of the goods or services—including taxes; delivery costs, where appropriate; the arrangements for payment, delivery or performance; the provision for right of withdrawal

---

[43] Art 3.
[44] ibid.

except in cases referred to in Article 6(3)[45]; the cost of using distance communication system; the period for which an offer or the price of goods or services may remain valid; and where appropriate, the minimum duration of the contract. The purpose of providing this information to a consumer is obviously to allow him/her to determine whether or not to obtain the goods or services.

Under Article 5 of the Directive a provider of goods or services must confirm certain information, in writing, and in good time during the performance of the contract, and at the latest at the time of delivery of goods.[46] Written information must be provided on the conditions of exercising the right of withdrawal; the geographical address of the place of business of the supplier in order to allow the consumer to address any complaint; information, if any, on after-sale services and guarantees; in the event of cancelling contracts of an unspecified duration or a duration exceeding one year, the reasons thereof.

Article 6 of the Directive deals with the right of a consumer to withdraw from a contract without penalty. In respect of any distance contract, the consumer shall have a period of at least seven working days in which to withdraw from the contract without any penalty and without giving any reason, although the consumer may be liable to meet the direct costs of returning the goods. This seven-day period will begin in one of the following way: (a) in the case of goods, this period will run from the day of receipt by the consumer provided the obligations under Article 5 (written confirmation of information) have been fulfilled; and (b) in respect of services, from the day on which the contract was concluded or from the day on which the obligations under Article 5 of the Directive were fulfilled, but this period must not exceed three months. In the event of the supplier failing to fulfil his obligations under Article 5, this period shall be three months, and the period shall begin: (i) in the case of goods, from the day of receipt by the consumer; and (ii) in the case of services, from the day on which the contract was concluded. If the information referred to in Article 5 is supplied within three months, the seven-working-day period still begins from the day on which the contract was concluded.

Where a consumer has exercised his right of withdrawal validly, the supplier will be required to reimburse the consumer the sums free of charge, except the direct cost of returning the goods, and the reimbursement must be made within 30 days of withdrawal. Unless otherwise agreed, a consumer may not exercise his right of withdrawal from (a) a contract of services if performance has already begun, with the consumer's agreement, before the end of the seven working

---

[45] The circumstances in which a consumer may not exercise his right of withdrawal is the subject matter of this paragraph.
[46] This provision shall not apply to services 'which are performed through the use of a means of distance communication where they are supplied on only one occasion and are invoiced by the operator of the means of distance communication' (Art 5(2)). However, the consumer must in all cases be able to obtain the geographical address of the place of business of the supplier to which he/she may address complaints, if any.

days; (b) for the supply of goods and services 'the price of which is dependent on fluctuations in the financial market which cannot be controlled by the supplier'; (c) where goods were to be supplied according to a consumer's specifications or where goods are personalized in consequence of which they cannot be returned or that they are liable to deterioration or becoming stale; (d) in respect of supply of audio or video recordings or computer software, if the consumer has already unsealed them; (e) in respect of the supply of newspapers, periodicals and magazines; and (f) for gaming and lottery services.

Article 7 of the Directive provides that unless the parties have agreed otherwise, a supplier is required to execute an order within a maximum of 30 days from the date of forwarding the order to the supplier; in the event of a supplier being unable to supply the goods or services owing to their unavailability, the consumer must be informed of the situation, and the money must be refunded to the consumer within 30 days.

A consumer shall be allowed to request cancellation of a payment where his credit card has been subject to a fraudulent use in connection with distance contracts, and in the event of any fraudulent use of the card, the consumer must be re-credited with the sums paid.[47]

Article 9 of the Directive is concerned with 'inertia selling'. Member states are required to take steps to prohibit the supply of goods or services to a consumer if they have not been ordered by the consumer beforehand, where such supply involves a demand for payment, and to exempt the consumer from payment of a consideration in cases of unsolicited supply where the consumer did not consent to accepting any supply of goods.

In the absence of any prior consent of the consumer, restrictions may be imposed on the following means of distant communications: (a) automated calling system without human intervention; and (b) facsimile machines.[48]

Compliance with this Directive is through (a) public bodies or their representatives; (b) consumer organizations having a legitimate interest in protecting consumers; and (c) professional organizations having a legitimate interest in acting. It is for the member states to take measures necessary for ensuring that suppliers and operators of means of communications cease practices which are contrary to the provisions of this Directive. Furthermore, member states may provide for voluntary supervision by self-regulatory bodies of compliance with the provisions of this Directive.[49]

Again, according to this Directive, member states shall take the measures required to ensure that the consumer does not lose the protection granted by

---

[47] Art 8.
[48] Art 10.
[49] Art 12.

this Directive 'by virtue of the choice of the law of a non-member country as the law applicable to the contract if the latter has close connection with the territory of one or more Member States'.[50]

Paragraph 1 of Article 13 provides that:

> 'The provisions of this Directive shall apply is so far as there are no particular provisions in rules of Community law governing certain types of distance contracts in their entirety'.

The ideal position would be where a member state maintains a standard which is higher than the standard recommended by the Directive, particularly in regard to the marketing of certain goods or services, eg medicinal products within their territory by means of distance contracts. This is known as the 'minimal clause'.[51] Member states are required to bring into force the laws, regulations and administrative provisions necessary for complying with this Directive no later than three years after it enters into force, and must notify the Commission of the effective date on which it was brought into force. Member states are also required to communicate to the Commission the text of the provision of national law which they adopt in compliance with this Directive.

This Directive certainly aims at protecting the interests of consumers when they may be engaged in distant contracts. In some respects, the Directive will have a superseding effect over national laws, as it states, for example, 'this right of withdrawal shall be without prejudice to the consumer's rights under national laws'.[52] This Directive also aims to protect consumers from certain intrusive means of communication. The Directive also provides that the minimum binding rules contained in it are to be 'supplemented where appropriate by voluntary arrangements among the traders concerned'.[53] It is to be seen whether the aspirations of the Directive will be achieved.

9.5   Defective products

Issues relating to defective products may come under the purview of the Sale of Goods Act 1979; the Fair Trading Act 1973; the Unfair Contract Terms Act 1977; the Supply of Goods and Services Act 1982; and the Consumer Protection Act 1987. This latter legislation did not replace the fault-based common law tortious liability, but preserved the existing remedies. Thus, in order to consider liability for supplying defective products, it is necessary to consider both the common law and statutory regimes. Parts II and III of the Consumer Protection Act deal respectively with the issues of consumer supply and misleading price

---

[50] Art 12.
[51] Art 14.
[52] See the Preamble to the Directive.
[53] See the Preamble to the Directive.

indications. Although actions under this Act are primarily by criminal proceedings, section 41 provides for civil action for breach of safety regulations made under the Act.

In the case of supply of goods, the nature of liability of the defendant depends upon the terms, express or implied of the contract with the claimant. In a contract of sale there is generally an implied condition that the goods are fit for the purpose for which they were bought.[54] In such cases, in addition to liability in negligence, the seller is responsible in damages for any injury caused by the supply of dangerous and/or defective goods. Furthermore, implied terms similar to those relating to contracts of sale also exist under statutes in respect of contracts for supply of goods or services,[55] or contracts of hire.

Liability arises for the defendant for supply of defective and/or dangerous goods to a third party who has sustained harm or injury from the use of such products. The issue of the liability towards third parties which in the modern period was established in its rudimentary form in *Donoghue v Stevenson* has already been addressed in the chapter entitled 'Negligence' in this work. A distinction was originally made between goods dangerous per se and goods that would be regarded as dangerous in the circumstances of a case.[56] Such a distinction between the two categories of goods, as described above, may be difficult to maintain. In *Oliver v Saddler* it was stated that an element of danger may exist in every object or product.[57] In *Read v J Lyons & Co* Sir Hartley Shawcross stated, *inter alia*, that:

> 'The true question is not whether a thing is dangerous in itself but whether by reason of some extraneous circumstances, it may become dangerous. There is really no category of dangerous things; there are only some things which require more and some which require less care'[58]

The more important legal issue is whether at the time of supply, the defendant had actual knowledge of the dangerous nature of the goods delivered to the claimant, but did not give any notice to that effect to the claimant, and the goods caused injury or harm to third parties too.[59] Sale of products and services through electronic means will be subject to these judicial guidelines too, in addition to their being governed by relevant statutory provisions. It is to be pointed out that such liability also extends to include dealers in second-had goods,[60] and also in this regard to those goods the injurious elements of which

---

[54] s 14 of the Sale of Goods Act 1979.
[55] Supply of Goods and Services Act 1982: supply of goods (ss 1–5); hire of goods (ss 6–10); and supply of services (ss 12–16).
[56] See also *Blacker v Lake and Elliott Ltd* (1912) 106 L.T. 533.
[57] [1929] A.C. 584 at 599.
[58] [1947] A.C. 156 at 161.
[59] *Barnes v Irwell Valley Water Board* [1939] 1 K.B. 21 at 44 and 46.
[60] *Andrews v Hopkinson* [1957] 1 Q.B. 229.

are an intrinsic part of, or when products should be sold with proper warning on them, but have not.[61] It is now well established that liability extends not only to second parties but also to third parties and it is immaterial how the goods passed to a third party.[62] The only caveat that may be entered in this regard is when goods have been manipulated or made defective by another party while they are in transit from the seller to the buyer or to a third party, and in that event, the seller may not be held liable. Thus the issue of maintaining control over the goods becomes important.

But, what if the buyer had an opportunity to examine the goods before use or before passing them to a third party, but did not take advantage of it? Two situations are to be considered here: (a) whether the seller asked the buyer to examine the goods before use or before passing them to a third party—if not, then the seller cannot be exonerated from liability, but if so, then the question arises; (b) whether a general examination would have revealed the inherent defects in the goods. But to exonerate a seller from liability arising from the supply of defective products would be inappropriate even though an opportunity for an examination of those products was provided by the seller, because often examination of those products was provided by the seller, because often examination of each item proves to be impossible.[63] Even if an opportunity for examination of goods is provided, the risk in the use of goods must be clearly stated.[64] Where a proper notice of risks in using the goods is given, and the buyer fails to take notice of it, the buyer will be responsible to the ultimate user.

Where, however, the examination did not reveal the defect, the manufacturer of the product may not be excused.[65] What is important to remember is whether the opportunity to inspect the goods broke the chain of causation and furthermore, whether a mere examination may reveal the defects, let alone the inherent defects in the goods.[66] The general principle of negligence will apply in such cases, because otherwise it would be difficult for the defendant to discharge the burden that he did not know of the defects in the goods. The responsibility as to the supply of goods also extends to include the container or package in which the goods are dispatched, that is, whether the package or the container was suitable for the goods.[67] What is important is to consider the incidence of liability in both contract and torts. These issues have already been discussed under the chapter entitled 'Negligence'.

---

[61] *Distillers Co (Biochemicals) Ltd v Thompson* [1971] A.C. 458.
[62] In addition to *Donoghue v Stevenson*, see also *Grant v Australian Knitting Mills* [1936] A.C. 85.
[63] *Paine v Colne Valley Electricity Co* [1938] 4 All E.R. 803.
[64] *Grant v Australian Knitting Mills*, op cit.
[65] See *Taylor v Rover Co Ltd* [1966] 1 W.L.R. 1491.
[66] *A.C. Buildings & Sons Ltd v Rider* [1858] A.C. 240.
[67] *Donoghue v Stevenson*, op cit.

9.5.1   Part I of the Consumer Protection Act, 1987

The Consumer Protection Act 1987 implemented the EC Directive on Product Liability, 1985. It is worth mentioning that since the decision in *Donghue v Stevenson*, the English law in regard to consumer protection has gone from strength to strength. Furthermore, the judicial guidelines in regard to consumer protection are extensive and creative in nature. Some of the basic features of the Act are now discussed.

One of the principal objectives of the Act is to 'make provision with respect to the liability of persons for damage caused by defective products'.[68] 'Product' under the Act means:

'any goods or electricity and (subject to subsection (3) below) includes a product which is comprised in another product, whether by virtue of being a component part of raw material or otherwise.'[69]

The meaning of 'defect', in general, under this Act has been provided in the following terms:

'there is a defect in a product for the purposes of this Part [Part I] if the safety of the product is not such as persons generally are entitled to expect; and for those purposes 'safety' in relation to a product, shall include safety with respect to products comprised in that product and safety in the context of risks of damage to property as well as in the context of risks of death or personal injury.'[70]

Under this definition the general expectation of safety by ordinary people is also required to be met, in addition to taking into consideration the risks of damage to property and/or person, including death or personal injury. In determining the general expectation of persons in relation to a product all the circumstances shall be taken into account, including:

'(a)   the manner in which, and purposes for which, the product has been marketed, its get-up, the use of any mark in relation to the product and any instructions for, or warnings with respect to, doing or refraining from doing anything with or in relation to the product;
(b)   what might reasonably be expected to be done with or in relation to the product; and
(c)   the time when the product was supplied by its producer to another.'[71]

---

[68] The Preamble to the Act.
[69] sub-s 3: 'For the purposes of this Part a person who supplies any product in which products are comprised, whether by virtue of being component parts or raw materials or otherwise, shall not be treated by reason only of his supply of that product as supplying any of the products so comprised'.
[70] s 3(1).
[71] s 3(2).

In other words, these expectations are largely created in the minds of prospective consumers by the providers of goods; thus departure from the specifications, and the purposes of and projected enjoyment arising from the use of the goods accrues liability for the provider/manufacturer of goods. Section 3(2) also implies that goods, including their use(s) must not be misrepresented and that the prospective consumers must not be misled or persuaded by false descriptions, quality and use(s) of goods to buy them.

The Act consists of the following Parts:

Part I	Product Liability
Part II	Consumer Safety
Part III	Misleading Price Indications
Part IV	Enforcement of Parts II and III
Part V	Miscellaneous and Supplemental

There are also five Schedules to the Act.

According to section 2(1) 'Where any damage is caused wholly or partly by a defect in a product every person to whom subsection (2) below applies shall be liable for the damage'. Subsection (2) applies to:

'(a) the producer of the product;
(b) any person who, by putting his name on the product or using a trade mark or other distinguishing mark in relation to the product, has held himself out to be the producer of the product;
(c) any person who has imported the product into a Member State from a place outside the Member State in order, in the course of any business of his, to supply it to another.'

Each paragraph stands for a different category of person, whether in the form of a producer, or an importer or one who has held himself out to be the producer of the product. Liability under section 2 is strict in nature. Defences are available under section 4 of the Act. Damages giving rise to liability have been identified in section 5 of the Act.

Section 7 of the Act is concerned with the prohibition on exclusions from liability:

'The liability of a person by virtue of this Part to a person who has suffered damage caused wholly or partly by a defect in a product, or to a dependant or relative of such person, shall not be limited or excluded by any contract term, by any notice or by any other provision.'

Liability under this section is not thus to be limited or excluded by any means. Section 10 (Part II—Consumer Safety) is concerned with the general safety requirements.

The Consumer Protection Act embraces not only product liability issues but also issues relating to consumer safety. The Act provides for extensive enforcement powers in relation to issues coming under Part II and III of the Act. Incidentally, section 39 provides for defence of due diligence—that is, it shall be a defence for a person to show that 'he took all reasonable steps and exercised all due diligence to avoid committing the offence'.

The duties imposed by the Act on producers and providers of goods are enforced primarily by criminal rather than civil proceedings.

9.5.2   Comments

In addition to the above, certain other issues about the responsibility of a supplier of goods should be identified. Under English law, several implied conditions exist in a contract of sale, domestic or non-domestic, namely:

(a)   that the goods must correspond with their description;
(b)   that the goods are satisfactory;
(c)   that the goods are fit for the purpose;
(d)   implied conditions in sales by sample; and
(e)   implied conditions based on trade usage.

If these conditions are satisfied then the incidence of supplying defective goods or products will be low. One of the problems with the above mentioned implied conditions is what would be the legal interpretation of 'satisfactory' (quality). The Sale of Goods Act 1979 '(which is an extension and modified version of the Sale of Goods Act 1893) as amended by the Sale and Supply of Goods Act 1994 replaced the term 'merchantability' with 'satisfactory quality' and was extensively discussed by the House of Lords in *Henry Kendall & Sons v William Lillico & Sons Ltd.*[72] Whether certain goods are of 'satisfactory quality' or not should be considered with reference to the purpose for which the goods are purchased. 'Satisfactory quality' may not be interchangeably used with 'saleable quality'. The interrelationship between the Sale and Supply of Goods Act 1994 and the Consumer Protection Act 1987 should be considered. The Consumer Protection Act does not make any direct reference to second-hand products, although the term 'goods' or 'products' may generically include second-hand goods or products. The issue of 'satisfactory quality' and 'saleability' are particularly important in respect of second-hand or used goods[73], Second-hand equipment with certain defects in it may not be called 'unmerchantable', if it is 'usable' by the buyer, who knowing the defects in the equipment bought it. The issue remains whether the test should be 'usability'. The legal point is what kind of defects may make certain goods or products of an unsatisfactory quality? Are

---

[72] 1969 2 A.C. 31; see also *Bristol Tramways Co Ltd v Fiat Motors Ltd* [1910] 2 K.B. 841 (*per* Farwell LJ) and *Rogers v Parish* [1987] Q.B. 933.
[73] See further S K Chatterjee, *Legal Aspects of Transnational Marketing and Marketing* (London, Cavendish, 1996) at 58.

unmerchantable goods necessarily of inferior quality for the purposes of uses for which they have been bought? Section 14(6) of the Sale of Goods Act 1979 defines merchantability in the following way:

> 'Goods of any kind are of merchantable quality (within the meaning of subsection 2) ... if they are fit for the purpose or purposes for which goods of the kind are commonly bought as it is reasonable to expect having regard to any description applied to them, the price (if relevant) and all the other relevant circumstances.'

But, of course, the fact remains that whatever goods may be sold, the consumer safety principle must be maintained, together with the principle of disclosure. The implied conditions under the Sale of Goods Act and the Sale and Supply of Goods Act are complementary to the Consumer Protection Act. Section 4(3) of the Sale of Goods Act provides that:

> 'Where the seller sells goods in the course of a business and the buyer, expressly or by implication, makes known ... any particular purpose for which the goods are being bought, there is an implied condition that the goods supplied under the contract are reasonably fit for the purpose, whether or not that is a purpose for which such goods are commonly supplied, except where the circumstances show that the buyer does not rely, or that it is unreasonable for him to rely on the skill or judgment of the seller or credit broker.'

Under the Sale of Goods Act, goods must be 'reasonably fit'. In fact, this conforms to the provision of section 3 of the Consumer Protection Act, because it says that 'use which might be expected to be made of it'.[74] Whatever legal controversy may surround these expressions, the fact remains that the interest of consumers must be maintained.

9.6   Data protection

9.6.1   Introduction
In e-Commerce, the need for protecting data cannot be over-emphasized. On the one hand, in the absence of a policy of free flow of data between businesses, individual businesses will suffer, yet, on the other hand, customers and consumers have to be provided with guarantees that data pertaining to their personal lives or affairs are not abused. In the context of data protection, two terms are important: (a) data controllers, that is, those who hold personal information; and (b) data subjects, that is, the people whose information is held by data controllers.

---

[74] See also *Grant v Australian Knitting Mills*, op cit.

The EU Protection Directive[75] aims at harmonising data protection laws within the EU, and to allow free flow of personal data within the Union. In the UK, this Directive has been implemented by the Data Protection Act 1998, which came into force on 1 March 2000. In discussing data protection, the impact of 'data processing' should be considered; but there does not exist any precise definition of the term. The definition of 'processing' in the EU Directive is extremely broad. It may be maintained that any use of personal data on the Internet will amount to processing. Thus, businesses have a responsibility to assure their customers that their personal data which are held by the former are secure; this is particularly important in the current climate of privacy-awareness.

9.6.2   The Data Protection Act 1998
In the context of e-Commerce, there is no need to go into the details of the provisions of the Act. It has thus been decided to highlight and analyse those provisions of the Act which are predominantly relevant to e-Commerce.

Under six parts, the Act consists of 75 sections and 16 Schedules. The following are the titles of the parts: Part I—Preliminary; Part II—Rights of Data Subjects and Others; Part III—Notification by Data Controllers; Part IV—Exemptions; Part V—Enforcement; and Part VI—Miscellaneous and General. The Preamble to the Act states its objectives as: 'An Act to make new provision for the regulation of the processing of information relating to individuals, including the obtaining, holding, use or disclosure of such information.'

The current Act repeals the Data Protection Act of 1984. One of the crucially important issues in the current legislation is to strike a balance between personal data privacy and freedom of information. Under the Act, the processing of 'sensitive personal data', that is, data relating to race, ethnic origin, religion or political beliefs, membership of trade unions etc are subject to stricter regimes than other personal data.

It would be apposite to reproduce the definitions of some of the key terms in the Act:

Data
This means information which:

   '(a) is being processed by means of equipment operating automatically in response to instructions given for that purpose,

   (b) is recorded with the intention that it should be processed by means of such equipment,

   (c) is recorded as part of a relevant filing system or with the intention that it should form part of a relevant filing system, or

---

[75] Directive 95/46/EC.

(d)   does not fall within paragraph (a), (b) or (c) but forms part of an accessible record as defined by section 68.'[76]

Processing
In relation to information or data, processing means:

obtaining, recording or holding the information or data or carrying out any operation or set of operations on the information or data, including:

'(a)   organisation, adaptation or alteration of the information or data,
(b)   retrieval, consultation or use of the information or data,
(c)   disclosure of the information or data by transmission, dissemination or otherwise making available, or
(d)   alignment, combination, blocking, erasure or destruction of the information or data.'

Relevant filing system
This means:

'any set of information relating to individuals to the extent that, although the information is not processed by means of equipment operating automatically in response to instructions given for that purpose, the set is structured, either by reference to individuals or by reference to criteria relating to individuals, in such a way that specific information relating to a particular individual is readily accessible.'

Section 4 of the Act refers to the data protection principles that have been embodied in Schedule 1 to the Act. These have been discussed in the latter part of this section of the work. These principles are to be interpreted in accordance with Part II of Schedule 1. It is opportune to note in this connection that Schedule 2[77] and Schedule 3[78] set out conditions applying for the purposes of the first principle whereas Schedule 4 set out cases in which the eighth principle does not apply. Subject to section 27(1)[79] a data controller is required to comply with the data protection principles in relation to all personal data.

Except in relation to international co-operation (s 54), this Act applies to a data controller in respect of any data only if that data controller is established in the UK and the data are processed in the context of the establishment[80], or that the

---

[76]   'Accessible record' under s 68 means, for example, a health record, or an educational record or an accessible public record etc.
[77]   Sched 2 applies to all personal data.
[78]   Sched 3 applies only to sensitive personal data.
[79]   s 27(1): 'References in any of the data protection principles or any provision of Parts II and III to personal data or to the processing of personal data do not include references to data or processing which by virtue of this Part are exempt from that principle or other provision'.
[80]   s 5(1)(a).

data controller uses equipment in the UK for processing data, without being established in the UK or any other EEA State; but in the latter event, a data controller must nominate a representative established in the UK.[81]

Section 7 of the Act deals with rights of access of data subjects and others to personal data and section 8 supplements the provision of section 7. Instead of annotating these sections, it is thought appropriate to reproduce the text:

Section 7:

'(1) Subject to the following provisions of this section and to sections 8 and 9, an individual is entitled-

    (a)   to be informed by any data controller whether personal data of which that individual is the data subject are being processed by or on behalf of that data controller,

    (b)   if that is the case, to be given by the data controller a description of-

        (i)   the personal data of which that individual is the data subject,

        (ii) the purposes for which they are being or are to be processed, and

        (iii) the recipients or classes of recipients to whom they are or may be disclosed,

    (c)   to have communicated to him in an intelligible form-

        (i)   the information constituting any personal data of which that individual is the data subject, and

        (ii) any information available to the data controller as to the source of those data, and

    (d)   where the processing by automatic means of personal data of which that individual is the data subject for the purpose of evaluating matters relating to him such as, for example, his performance at work, his creditworthiness, his reliability or his conduct, has constituted or is likely to constitute the sole basis for any decision significantly affecting him, to be informed by the data controller of the logic involved in that decision-taking.

(2) A data controller is not obliged to supply any information under subsection (1) unless he has received-

    (a)   a request in writing, and

---

[81] Examples of such representatives would be:
  (a) an individual who is ordinarily resident in the UK; or
  (b) a body corporate incorporated under the law of or of any part of the UK; or
  (c) a partnership or other unincorporated association formed under the law of or of any party of UK, or
  (d) a person who does not satisfy any of the above criteria, but maintains an office, branch or agency or a regular practice in the UK.

(b)   except in prescribed cases, such fee (not exceeding the prescribed maximum) as he may require.

(3)   A data controller is not obliged to comply with a request under this section unless he is supplied with such information as he may reasonably require in order to satisfy himself as to the identity of the person making the request and to locate the information which that person seeks.

(4)   Where a data controller cannot comply with the request without disclosing information relating to another individual who can be identified from that information, he is not obliged to comply with the request unless-

(a)   the other individual has consented to the disclosure of the information to the person making the request, or

(b)   it is reasonable in all the circumstances to comply with the request without the consent of the other individual.

(5)   In subsection (4) the reference to information relating to another individual includes a reference to information identifying that individual as the source of the information sought by the request; and that subsection is not to be construed as excusing a data controller from communicating so much of the information sought by the request as can be communicated without disclosing the identity of the other individual concerned, whether by the omission of names or other identifying particulars or otherwise.

(6)   In determining for the purposes of subsection (4)(b) whether it is reasonable in all the circumstances to comply with the request without the consent of the other individual concerned, regard shall be had, in particular, to-

(a)   any duty of confidentiality owed to the other individual,

(b)   any steps taken by the data controller with a view to seeking the consent of the other individual,

(c)   whether the other individual is capable of giving consent, and

(d)   any express refusal of consent by the other individual.

(7)   An individual making a request under this section may, in such cases as may be prescribed, specify that his request is limited to personal data of any prescribed description.

(8)   Subject to subsection (4), a data controller shall comply with a request under this section promptly and in any event before the end of the prescribed period beginning with the relevant day.

(9)   If a court is satisfied on the application of any person who has made a request under the foregoing provisions of this section that the data controller in question has failed to comply with the request in contravention of those provisions, the court may order him to comply with the request.

(10)   In this section-

'prescribed' means prescribed by the Secretary of State by regulations;

'the prescribed maximum' means such amount as may be prescribed;

'the prescribed period' means forty days or such other period as may be prescribed;

'the relevant day', in relation to a request under this section, means the day on which the data controller receives the request or, if later, the first day on which the data controller has both the required fee and the information referred to in subsection (3).

(11) Different amounts or periods may be prescribed under this section in relation to different cases.'

Section 8:

'(1) The Secretary of State may by regulations provide that, in such cases as may be prescribed, a request for information under any provision of subsection (1) of section 7 is to be treated as extending also to information under other provisions of that subsection.

(2) The obligation imposed by section 7(1)(c)(i) must be complied with by supplying the data subject with a copy of the information in permanent form unless-

(a) the supply of such a copy is not possible or would involve disproportionate effort, or

(b) the data subject agrees otherwise;

and where any of the information referred to in section 7(1)(c)(i) is expressed in terms which are not intelligible without explanation the copy must be accompanied by an explanation of those terms.

(3) Where a data controller has previously complied with a request made under section 7 by an individual, the data controller is not obliged to comply with a subsequent identical or similar request under that section by that individual unless a reasonable interval has elapsed between compliance with the previous request and the making of the current request.

(4) In determining for the purposes of subsection (3) whether requests under section 7 are made at reasonable intervals, regard shall be had to the nature of the data, the purpose for which the data are processed and the frequency with which the data are altered.

(5) Section 7(1)(d) is not to be regarded as requiring the provision of information as to the logic involved in any decision-taking if, and to the extent that, the information constitutes a trade secret.

(6) The information to be supplied pursuant to a request under section 7 must be supplied by reference to the data in question at the time when the request is received, except that it may take account of any amendment or deletion made between that time and the time when the information is supplied, being an amendment or deletion that would have been made regardless of the receipt of the request.

(7) For the purposes of section 7(4) and (5) another individual can be identified from the information being disclosed if he can be identified from that information, or from that and any other information which, in the reasonable belief of the data controller, is likely to be in, or to come into, the possession of the data subject making the request.'

An individual is entitled at any time to notify, in writing, a data controller to require the latter not to begin processing generally or processing for a specified purpose or in a specified manner any personal data on the grounds that the latter's so doing is already causing or is likely to cause substantial damage or substantial distress to him or to another or that the damage or distress is or would be unwarranted.[82] This provision does not apply in a case where any of the following conditions is met: (a) the individual concerned has given his consent; or (b) the processing is necessary for the performance of a contract to which that individual is a party; or (c) the individual concerned has requested a data controller to take steps with a view to entering into a contract; or (d) that the data controller is obliged to carry out processing in compliance with a legal obligation; or (e) that the processing is necessary in order to protect the vital interests of the individual concerned (the data subject)[83]; or (f) in such other cases as may be prescribed by the Secretary of State.

A similar right may be exercised by a data subject following the same procedure with a view to preventing processing by a data controller for purposes of direct marketing.[84] 'Direct marketing' in this context would mean 'the communication by whatever means of any advertising or marketing material which is directed to particular individuals'.[85] It is not clear how this provision (which stands for spamming) may be effectively implemented, however, this is one of the means of sending innumerable correspondence and advertising materials via e-mail.

The Act also allows an individual his rights in relation to automated decision-taking, which stands for decision-making, by the use of automatic processing to determine, for example, fitness (by psychometric testing) for employment, such as is done to determine the creditworthiness of an individual. Section 12 allows a data subject the right whereby he may require the data controller

'to ensure that no decision taken by or on behalf of the data controller which significantly affects that individual is based solely on the processing by automatic means of personal data in respect of which that individual is the data subject for the purpose of evaluating matters relating to him such, for example, his performance at work, his creditworthiness, his reliability or his conduct.'[86]

The individual concerned must serve a notice in writing to the data controller to require the latter to do what is mentioned above. Section 12 also details the procedure that a data controller is required to satisfy after receipt of such a notice.

---

[82] s 10.
[83] paras 1–4 of Sched 2.
[84] s 11.
[85] ibid.
[86] s 12.

Personal data must not be processed by any data controller unless it is included in the register maintained by the Commissioner.[87] Furthermore, processing must be 'assessable processing', and it must appear to the Secretary of State that processing of a particular description is unlikely to prejudice the rights and freedoms of data subjects.[88]'Assessable processing' means:

> 'processing which is of a description specified in an Order by the Secretary of State as appearing to him to be particularly likely:
>
> (a) to cause substantial damage or substantial distress to data subjects; or
> (b) otherwise significantly to prejudice the rights and freedoms of data subjects.'[89]

Personal data are exempt from the following:

(a) the data protection principles;
(b) Parts II, III and IV; and
(c) section 55.[90]

if exemption from any of these provisions is required for the purpose of safeguarding national security.[91]

Personal data processed for any of the following purposes are exempt from the first data protection principle unless compliance with the conditions in Schedule 2—Conditions Relevant for Purposes of the First Principle: Procuring of any Personal Data, and Schedule 3—Conditions Relevant for Purposes of the First Principle: Processing of Sensitive Personal Data and with section 7 prove to be necessary:

'(a) the prevention or detection of crime,
(b) the apprehension or prosecution of offenders, or
(c) the assessment or collection of any tax or duty or of any imposition of a similar nature.'[92]

Other exemptions have been detailed in section 29 of the Act. Exemptions are also allowed in respect of information which a data controller is obliged by or under any enactment to make available to the public (s 34) or when disclosures are required by law or made in connection with legal proceedings (s 35); 'personal data is processed by an individual only for the purposes of that

---

[87] Regarding the registration procedure, see s 19.
[88] s 17; see also s 22.
[89] s 22(1).
[90] s 55 is concerned with unlawful obtaining of personal data.
[91] s 28.
[92] s 29.

individual's personal family or household affairs (including recreational purposes) are exempt from the data protection principles and the provisions of Parts II and III' (s 36); miscellaneous exceptions are allowed by Schedule 7 (s 37); and the Secretary of State has powers to make further exemptions by Order, if it is deemed necessary to do so for safeguarding the interests of the data subject or the rights and freedoms of any other individual (s 38).

A person must not knowingly or recklessly without the consent of the data controller:

'(a) obtain or disclose personal data or the information contained in personal data, or
(b) procure the disclosure to another person of the information contained in personal data.'[93]

Obtaining, disclosure or procuring of information shall not be unlawful if the defendant can show that: (a) it was necessary for the purpose of preventing or detecting crime; or (b) it was required or authorized by or under any enactment or by the Order of a court; or (c) he acted in the reasonable belief that the data controller would have given him consent if the latter had known of the obtaining, disclosing or procuring and the circumstances of it; or (e) in the particular circumstances these acts were justified in the public interest.[94] Incidentally, 'accessible record' under the Act means:

'(a) a health record;
(b) an educational record; and
(c) an accessible public record.'[95]

9.6.3   The Data protection principles

Part I of Schedule 1 to the Act embodies eight principles, which should be read with Schedules 2, 3 and 4. These principles provide that (a) personal data must be processed fairly and lawfully, and that they shall not be processed unless at least one of the conditions in Schedule 2 is met; and in the case of sensitive data, at least one of the conditions in Schedule 3 is also met; (b) personal data shall be obtained only for specified and lawful purposes; (c) personal data shall be adequate, relevant and not excessive in relation to the purpose(s); (d) personal data shall be accurate and, where necessary, kept up to date; (e) personal data processed for any purpose(s) shall not be retained for longer than is necessary; (f) they shall be processed in accordance with the rights of data subjects under this Act; (g) appropriate technical and organizational measures must be taken 'against unauthorised or unlawful processing of personal data and against loss

---

[93] s 55.
[94] s 55(2).
[95] The meanings of these terms have been elaborated respectively in s 68(2); Sched 11 and Sched 12.

or destruction of, or damages to personal data'[96];and finally, (h) personal data shall not be transferred to a country or territory outside the EEA 'unless that country or territory ensures an adequate level of protection for the rights and freedoms of data subjects in relation to the processing of personal data'.[97]

Part II of Schedule 1 interprets these principles. In order to determine whether personal data are processed fairly, principal regard must be had to the method employed to obtain them, ensuring that they were not obtained by deception or by misleading the provider of data as to the purpose(s) for which they are to be processed. The fairness of obtaining data may be confirmed if they have been obtained from a person who is authorised by or under any enactment to supply them; or that person is 'required to supply it by or under any enactment or by any Convention or other instrument imposing an international obligation on the United Kingdom'.[98] Personal data are not to be treated as processed fairly unless the identity of the data controller concerned is disclosed; or in the event of his nominating a representative for the purpose, the identity of the representative; the purpose for which the data will be processed is disclosed; and having regard to the specific circumstances any further information which may be necessary.

In order to comply with the second principle, the data controller is required to serve on the data subject a notice specifying the purpose(s) for which personal data are to be obtained or by serving a notice on the Commission under Part III of this Act (Notification by Data Controllers). The compatibility of disclosure of data must be considered by reference to the purpose(s) of processing them and to whom they are to be disclosed.

Although the third principle has not been elaborated in the Schedule, it would be appropriate to emphasize that no attempt should be made to obtain data which would be excessive to the purpose(s) for which they are obtained.

In respect of the fourth principle, where a data subject notifies the data controller of its doubts as to the accuracy of the data provided, the data must indicate that fact. Furthermore, this principle will not be contravened by reason of any inaccuracy in personal data obtained from the data subject or a third party, if having regard to the purpose(s) for which the data were obtained and processed, the data controller took reasonable steps to ensure the accuracy of the data.

The fifth principle provides assurance to data subjects in that their data will not be retained by a data controller for a longer period than is necessary.

---

[96] Sched 1, Pt I, para 7.
[97] Sched 1, Pt II, para 8.
[98] Sched 1, para 1(2).

The sixth principle upholds the rights of data subjects by providing that personal data shall be processed in accordance with their rights. These rights have been embodies in section 7 (right of access to personal data, which section is to be read with s 8); section 10 (right to prevent processing likely to cause damage or distress); section 11 (right to prevent processing for purposes of direct marketing); and section 12 (right in relation to automated decision-taking).

As regards the seventh principle, it should be pointed out that the advent of advanced technology makes the position of a data subject vulnerable in that data might be abused unless sufficient safeguards are provided for their protection. Hence the need for data controllers to adopt measures to ensure a level of security appropriate to the harm that might result from any unauthorized or unlawful processing, of accidental loss of or destruction of or damage to any data. Data controllers are required to take reasonable steps to ensure the reliability of any of their employees who has/had access to the personal data (although it is not certain how and the extent to which a data controller may ensure that). Data controllers who may be employed by data controllers for the purpose of processing data must also provide sufficient guarantees in respect of the technical and organizational security measures governing the processing of data. In order to confirm compliance with this principle, a data controller must carry out processing of data under a contract which is made or evidenced in writing; and under which a data processor is required to act only on instructions from the data controller; and 'that the contract requires the data processor to comply with obligations equivalent to those imposed on a data controller by the seventh principle'.[99]

When personal data may have to be transferred outside the EEA, under the eight principle, the issue of adequate level of protection will have to be considered. This level of protection is to be considered having regards in particular to the following:

(a) the nature of the personal data;
(b) the origin of the information contained in the data (country or territory of origin);
(c) the country or territory of the final destination of the data;
(d) the purposes and the period for which the data are intended to be processed;
(e) the law in force in the country or territory in question;
(f) the international obligations of that country or territory;
(g) any relevant code of conduct or rules which are enforceable in that country or territory; and
(h) the security measures taken to protect that data in that country or territory.[100]

[99] Sched 1.
[100] Sched 1.

9.7   Computer misuse

Business through electronic means should take precautionary measures for avoiding offences arising out of computer misuse. The governing law of computer misuse offences may be found in the Computer Misuse Act 1990. This Act was based on a Law Commission Working Paper entitled 'Computer Misuse' published in 1988,[101] which was finalized in its Report bearing the same title in 1989.[102] The Law Commission was primarily concerned with the issue of 'hacking' (unauthorized access to computing systems), but it must be pointed out that nosey-parkering (gaining unauthorized access to correspondence or business records of another) is not an offence. Thus, in e-Commerce other forms of computer misuse offences must be avoided.

Section 1 of the Computer Misuse Act provides that:

'(1) A person is guilty of an offence if:
    (a) he causes a computer to perform any function with intent to secure access to any program or data held in any computer;
    (b) the access he intends to secure is unauthorised; and
    (c) he knows at the time when he causes the computer to perform the function that that is the case.
(2) The intent a person has to have to commit an offence under this Section need not be directed at:
    (a) any particular program or data;
    (b) a program or data of any particular kind; or
    (c) a program or data held in a particular computer.'

The basic issue is that a person will be guilty of an offence under this section if he or a company hacks a computer knowingly, and if he/it does it, then the usual criteria of a criminal offence *mens rea and actus reus* will be applied.

The phrase 'causes a computer to perform any function' has been chosen to signify that a mere physical contact with a computer will not do—the person must interact with the computer. But what if a computer hacker activates a computer by a remote control device? In that event, perhaps the law of attempt will be applied. Computer activation by an employee of a firm attracts a different legal situation altogether. By switching on a computer belonging to his firm (employer), an employee 'causes a computer to perform any function' this satisfies *actus reus*. The word 'any' signifies that the programme(s) or data held by the computer he may use at a particular point in time is not in issue only; it includes access to any programme or data on any (other) computer. The cardinal point is that the person concerned must have gained access to information

---

[101] Working Paper No. 110.
[102] Report No. 186, cmnd 819 (1989).

without any authorization from the authorizer concerned. As section 1 offences are summary offences, there can be no charge of an attempt at them.

Section 2 of the Act provides that:

> 'A person is guilty of an offence under this Section if he commits an offence under Section 1 above ('the authorised access offence') with intent:
> (a) to commit an offence to which this Section applies; or
> (b) to facilitate the commission of such an offence (whether by himself or by any other person).
> and the offence he intends to commit or facilitate is referred to below in this Section as the further notice.'

These arrestable offences are punishable on indictment. Offences under section 2 are offences of a substantive nature; the usual elements—conspiracy to commit or incitement to commit or an attempt to commit the offence are all applicable under this section.

Serious criminal intention must exist to commit section offences. There is a hierarchy between sections 1 and 2 offences; thus if no serious intention to commit an offence listed in section 2 may be proved, a conviction under section 1 may take place. Examples of committing offences with serious criminal intention under section 2 would be when unauthorized access is gained with the intention of diverting funds which were to be legitimately transferred by electronic means, to a beneficiary, to the account of the defendant or that of his accomplice.

According to section 3 of the Act:

> '(1) A person is guilty of an offence if:
> (a) he does any act which causes an unauthorised modification of the contents of any computer; and
> (b) at the time when he does the act has the requisite intent and the requisite knowledge.
> (2) For the purposes of Subsection (1)(b) above the requisite intent is an intent to cause a modification of the contents of any computer and by so doing:
> (a) to impair the operation of any computer;
> (b) to prevent or hinder access to any program or data held in any computer; or
> (c) to impair the operation of any such program or the reliability of any such data.
> (3) The intent need not be directed at:
> (a) any particular computer;
> (b) any particular program or data or a program of data of any particular kind; or
> (c) any particular modification or a modification of any particular kind.

(4) For the purposes of subsection (1)(b) above the requisite knowledge that any modification he intends to cause is unauthorised.'

Therefore, the 'requisite intent' and 'requisite knowledge' that the act will cause modification of the contents of any computer is enough to hold the person guilty of an offence (again, *mens rea and actus reus* will be satisfied). The intention of the defendant to impair a computer's operation or to hinder access to computer material by a legitimate user or to modify an already-held data without being authorized would be enough to satisfy the section 3 criteria.

In terms of e-Commerce, any contracting party or even a third party, who may be hacking the computer with a view to deliberately causing a modification of its contents will come under the purview of section 3 of the Act, and the intention of doing such an act has been identified by sub-paragraphs (a), (b) and (c) of the same section. Section 3 is primarily concerned with the sabotaging of a computer system by any of the act specified in section 3(2). This section should be read with section 17.

There is no need to go into the details of criminal damage caused by a party to a commercial contract or even by a third party when doing business through e-Commerce, as the relevant statutory provisions, including the provisions of the Criminal Damage Act 1971 will be applied, and judicial guidelines are also available on the issue of criminal damage: *Cox v Riley*[103] and *Whitley.*[104] In *Cox v Riley*, the defendant deliberately deleted the programmes from a printed circuit card that was used to operate a computerized machine. He was convicted of criminal damage because he damaged the cared, but his offence did not come under the purview of the Criminal Damage Act as the programmes themselves were intangible property; section 3 of the Computer Misuse Act covers that gap.

The offence of introducing a computer 'worm' or a 'virus' by a defendant will also come under the purview of section 3. Indeed, section 17(7) provides that:

'A modification of the contents of any computer program takes place if, by the operation of any function of the computer concerned or any other computer:

(a) any program or data held in the computer concerned is altered or erased; or
(b) any program or data is added to its contents.
(c) and any act which contributes towards causing such a modification shall be regarded as causing it.'

---

[103] (1986) 83 Cr. App. Rep. 54.
[104] 1991 Crim. L.R. 436.

For the purposes of any offences under section 1 or section 3 of this Act, it is immaterial 'whether any act or other event proof of which is required for conviction of the offence occurred in the home country concerned', or whether the accused was in the home country concerned at the time the act or event took place.[105] Generally, in order to find jurisdiction, at least one significant link with domestic jurisdiction must exist, but there is no need for any such link to exist 'for the commission of an offence under Section 1 above to be established in proof of an allegation to that effect in proceedings for an offence under Section 2'.[106]

According to this section, courts in the UK will have jurisdiction over offences of computer misuses. Section 4(3) provides however that jurisdiction to prosecute an offence under section 2 is not conditional upon the existence of a significant link for the purposes of assuming jurisdiction. It would be sufficient to prove that the accused intended to carry out further offence in the home country. Thus, an offence under section 2 will be tried in a home country where the accused committed a section 1 offence with the intent to commit an act abroad which would have amounted to committing a further offence if he had committed it in that home country; this is important in the context of e-Commerce in that an accused may hack a computer in England in order to obtain information with a view of blackmailing someone abroad.[107] The basic principle is that the location of an offence determines jurisdiction.

Section 5 lists the situations that would be regarded as significant link with a domestic jurisdiction in relation to an offence under section 1:

'(a)   that the accused was in the home country concerned at the time when he did the act which caused the computer to perform the function; or
(c)   that any computer containing any program or data to which the accused secured or intended to secure unauthorised access by doing that act was in the home country concerned at that time.'[108]

Section 5 also lists the situations which would be regarded as significant link with a domestic jurisdiction in relation to an offence under section 3:

(a)   'that the accused was in the home country concerned at the time when he did the act which caused the unauthorised modification; and
(b)   that the unauthorised modification took place in the home country concerned.'[109]

For the purposes of determining jurisdiction, in the case of section 1 offences, the accused would be in the courts (of the jurisdiction) when he illicitly accessed

---

[105] s 4(1).
[106] s 4(3).
[107] See also the commentary on the Act in *The Current Legal Statutes* (1990) at 18–7.
[108] s 5(2)(b).
[109] s 5(3).

a computer, or the computer which he so accessed or intended to access was in that country; in respect of section 3 offences, the accused was in the home country concerned when he accessed the computer in consequence of which the unauthorized modification took place or if the computer the contents of which were modified as at the material time located in that home country.

Section 6 deals with the territorial scope of inchoate offences. The important issue is where did the crime occur; the idea of a crime might originate in one jurisdiction (the conduct) but the actual crime (computer hacking in this context) be located in another jurisdiction, and then the latter jurisdiction will be deemed to be the territory on which the act took place. Section 6 does not extend to Scotland.

Section 7 of the Act deals with the territorial scope of inchoate offences related to offences under external law corresponding to offences under this Act. In other words, this section provides for the prosecution of an inchoate offence in England and Wales committed elsewhere. The provisions of section 7 are subject to section 8 of the Act. By virtue of section 16, these provisions apply to Northern Ireland, but not to Scotland.

Subsections (1) and (2), which relate to conspiracy, amend section 1 of the Criminal Law Act 1977, whereas subsection (3) which relates to attempts to commit crimes, amends section 1 of the Criminal Attempts Act 1981.

According to subsections (1) and (2) of section 7, every party to an inchoate offence which is to be performed abroad, which if performed would constitute a computer misuse offence will be triable in England and Wales provided at least one of the conspirators became a party to it in England and Wales. This provision is subject to section 8(1) of the Act. Subsection (3) which is confined to attempts, provides that every attempt in England and Wales to perform an act abroad, which, if performed in England and Wales, would be a section 3 offence will be triable in England and Wales. Again, this provision is subject to section 8(1) of the Act.

Section 8 is entitled 'Relevance of external law'. Paragraph 1 of this section provides that:

'A person is guilty of an offence triable by virtue of Section 4(4)[110] above only if what he intended to do or facilitate would involve the commission of an offence under the law where the whole or any part of it was intended to take place.' Paragraph (2) provides that:

[110] s 4(4): 'Subject to section 8 below, where:
  (a) any such link does in fact exist in the case of an offence under section 1 above; and
  (b) commission of that offence is alleged in proceedings for an offence under section 2 above;
      section 2 above shall apply as if anything the accused intended to do or facilitate in any place outside the home country concerned which would be an offence to which section 2 applies if it took place in the home country concerned were the offence in question.'

'A person is guilty of an offence triable by virtue of section 1(1A) of the Criminal Law Act 1977 only if the pursuit of the agreed course of conduct would at some time involve:

(a)   an act or omission by one or more of the parties; or
(b)   the happening of some other event;

constituting an offence under the law in force where the act, omission or other event was intended to take place.'

Paragraph (3) provides that:

'A person is guilty of an offence triable by virtue of section 1(1A) of the Criminal Attempts Act 1981 or by virtue of section 7(4)[111] above only if what he had in view would involve the commission of an offence under the law in force where the whole or in part of it was intended to take place.'

Whereas subsection (1) applies the principle of double criminality where an accused is charged with section 2 offences by virtue of section 4(4), subsections (2) and (3) apply the same principle where an accused is charged with an inchoate offence in relation to computer misuse abroad. This section is primarily concerned with the acts which are directed at committing the computer misuse offences abroad, but if these acts had been committed in a home country, that country would have jurisdiction.

Where an offence is either a section 2 or a section 7 offence, section 8 provides that any such offence may be prosecuted in the home country if, the further offence contemplated under section 2, when carried out, would be punishable in both the home country and the relevant foreign country or in respect of an inchoate offence to commit a computer misuse offence in a foreign country, then such offences may be prosecuted in the home country, if the acts contemplated when committed, would be punishable in both the home country and the relevant foreign country. The provisions of section 8 apply to the whole of the UK.

Whether the accused is a British citizen or not is immaterial under section 9 of the Act at the time of any act, omission or other even proof of which is requirement for conviction of the offence. This Section applies to the following offences:

'(a)   any offence under this Act;
(b)   conspiracy to commit an offence under this Act;
(c)   any attempt to commit an offence under Section 3 above; and
(d)   incitement to commit an offence under this Act.'[112]

---

[111] s 7(4): 'Subject to section 8 below, if any act done by a person in England and Wales would amount to the offence of incitement to commit an offence under this Act but for the fact that what he had in view would not be an offence triable in England and Wales:

(a) what he had in view shall be treated as an offence under this Act for the purposes of any charge of incitement brought in respect of that act; and

(b) any such charge shall accordingly be triable in England and Wales.'

[112] s 9.

The following sections need not be explained in the context of this work: section 10 (saving for certain law enforcement powers); section 11 (proceedings for offences under section 1); section 12 (conviction of an offence under section 11 in proceedings for an offence under section 2 or 3); section 13 (proceedings in Scotland); section 14 (search warrants for offences under section 1); section 16 (application to Northern Ireland); and section 18 (citation, commencement etc). Thus, the remaining sections, namely, section 15 (extradition where Schedule 1 to the Extradition Act 1989 applies); and section 17 (interpretation) remain to be explained.

Section 15 provides that:

'The offences to which an Order in Council under Section 2 of the Extradition Act 1870 can apply shall include:
    (a)   offences under Section 2 or 3 above;
    (b)   any conspiracy to commit such an offence; and
    (c)   any attempt to commit an offence under Section 3 above.'

Under the Extradition Act 1989 a conduct is extraditable if it is regarded as an offence in both the home country and the foreign jurisdiction concerned. The offences under section 2 or section 3 of the Computer Misuse Act are extraditable on these grounds. The reason why Schedule 1 to the Extradition Act 1989 is referred to is that by that Schedule the operation of the Extradition treaties which Britain concluded with various countries under the 1870 Act is kept intact. Section 15 of the Computer Misuse Act brings the offences under sections 2 and 3 within the remit of that Schedule.

According to section 17 of the Act, a person will be deemed to have secured access to any programme or data held in a computer if by causing a computer to perform any function he:

'(a)   alters or erases the programme or data;
(c)   copies or moves it to any storage medium other than that in which it is held;
(d)   uses it; or
(e)   has it output from the computer in which it is held.'[113]

Access is unauthorized if the person concerned is not entitled to control access of the kind he has attempted and he accessed the information without the consent from a person who is entitled to give consent. A modification of the contents of any computer takes place when any programme or data held in the computer concerned is altered or erased; or any programme or data is added to its contents. A modification is deemed to be unauthorized if the person concerned is not himself entitled to determine whether the modification should be made; and

[113] s 17(2).

that he did not have consent from any authorized person to carry out any modification. Finally, access of any kind by any person to any programme or data held in a computer is unauthorized if:

'a)   he is not himself entitled to control access of the kind in question to the program or data; and

(b)   he does not have consent to access by him of the kind in question to the program or data from any person who is entitled.'[114]

9.8   Conclusions

The Directive issued by the European Parliament and the Council on personal data also considered the impact of e-Commerce on small and medium-sized enterprises. This Directive is another element in a new regulatory framework the aim of which is to ensure that the electronic communications sector develops without any hindrance as a competitive market which would benefit all companies and individuals in the European Union using electronic communications services.

The aim of these efforts is to ensure operation and use of all electronic communications services in a technology neutral fashion; furthermore, a harmonized level of data protection in the electronic communications sector is essential for the functioning of the internal markets in electronic communications services and networks. All providers of electronic networks and providers of directory services will be affected by this Directive, but their existing legal obligations in regard to their services will remain unchanged; the Directive translates the rights of users into more details. Obviously, businesses are required to adopt good data protection practices in the design and management of the services and networks they provide. This Directive is an extension of the Directive 97/66/EC. The intention of the current Directive is, inter alia, to stimulate general consumer confidence in electronic communications services.

The Data Protection Act 1998 attempts to strike a balance between the rights of a data subject and the duties of a data controller in maintaining the free flow of information and protection for data. The Act is very clear about the circumstances in which a data subject will be required to waive his rights. The Act also makes data controllers subject to onerous obligations to protect the interests and rights of data subjects. The Act provides sanctions and enforcement measures against data controllers who may be in breach of their obligations, but a discussion of these issues would be beyond the remit of this work.

The Act requires the Commissioner to promote good practice by data controllers; he is also required, either by Order of the Secretary of State or on his

---

[114]   s 17(5).

own initiative, to consult with trade associations, data subjects and person representing data subjects 'prepare and disseminate to such persons as he considers appropriate codes of practice for guidance as to good practice'.[115] The Commissioner shall also, where he considers it appropriate to do so, encourage trade associations to prepare and disseminate to their members the code of practice. This is an admirable means of ensuring the protection of data subjects.

The data protection principles represent a novel means of protecting the position of data subjects. Whereas most of the principles are implementable, the eighth principle may prove to be problematic for e-Commerce because very few countries outside Europe have data protection regulations which may be regarded as adequate.

It is noteworthy that a regulatory body (a Commissioner) has been set up by the 1998 Act; however, advanced technology might soon overtake the current legislation. Furthermore, judicial guidelines are needed for the clarification of certain terms contained in the Act.

The Computer Misuse Act is based on the recommendation contained in the Law Commission's Report entitled 'Computer Misuse'. A similar Report was also published by the Scottish Law Commission, entitled 'Report on Computer Crime'.[116] This latter report advocated the creation of a new offence of 'obtaining unauthorised access to a computer'.[117] The current Act has created three new criminal offences:

    (a) 'unauthorised access to computer material' (triable summarily); (b) conduct sufficient to establish the first offence as at (a) coupled with an intention to commit or facilitate the commission of one of a range of more serious offences (triable summarily or on indictment—these are aggravated forms of the first offence); and (c) causing an unauthorized modification of the contents of any computer (triable summarily or on inducement). It is to be noted however that in view of the progressive advancement of science and technology, the drafters apparently decided not to provide definitions of 'computer'; 'program' or 'data' in this Act.

---

[115] s 51(3).
[116] Scot. Law Com. No. 106 (cm 174).
[117] See also *R v Gold; R v Chifreen* [1988] A.C. 1063.

10. Financial services and e-Commerce

10.1 Introduction

Banking and financial services through electronic means are most popular in the financial world. In fact, the financial world has been involved in e-Commerce for some time. However, the more advanced the technology, the more efficient and speedy these services will become. It has been pointed out in this work that business through electronic means can also present problems, particularly in the form of abuse of technology. On the positive side however, marketing of investment and financial services on the Internet is an issue which deserves special consideration for two primary reasons: (a) advertising of investments and financial services is subject to a number of restrictions; and (b) the businesses which would like to offer investment and financial services via the Internet should familiarise themselves with whether they need any authorization from any regulatory body in their own country or in the countries in which they may wish to expand their business.

This chapter briefly discusses the legal aspects of providing investment and financial services via the Internet. It is to be borne in mind that although anybody can have access to financial information available on a website, most jurisdictions have legislation restricting or prohibiting advertisements of investments and financial services. Thus, an advertiser on the Internet may be in breach of legislation in various jurisdictions.

10.2 The international position

In March 1998, the Securities and Exchange Commission (SEC) in the United States published a report ('Interpretative Release') on the use of websites which, among other issues, distinguished between ordinary website postings and targeted internet communications. According to the SEC, if a provider of services takes measures to guard against sales to US citizens, then the use of its website will not be deemed to be 'targeted' at US citizens, and in that case no registration will be necessary under the US securities registration legislation. But, when these target foreign business entities overseas, the conditions of transparency must be satisfied, that is, they must provide all information about themselves and a contact address. This is particularly to protect the position of the consumer.

In September 1998, the International Organization for Securities Commissions (IOSCO) published a report in which it was recommended that the promotion of investments and financial services should be targeted at identifiable persons.

The EU position on this matter remains unclear. Although no Directive has been issued by the EU on this matter, attention should be paid, for example, to the ethos of the distance selling Directive, and the OECD's Guidelines on consumer protection. This is a matter on which every advertiser, within the EU intending to place advertisements for investments and financial services, should familiarise itself with the laws and regulations in the country in which it would wish to target its advertisements for services of the aforesaid nature.

10.3   The UK position

The UK position on this matter may be found in section 21 of the Financial Services and Markets Act 2000, entitled 'financial promotion'. According to subsection (1) of this section, an unauthorised person must not, in the course of business, 'communicate an invitation or inducement to engage in investment activity'; and it is for the Treasury to specify the circumstances in which a person may be regarded as 'acting in the course of business'—or not acting as such. In other words, under this section an unauthorised person is prohibited from issuing financial promotions unless the subject matter of the promotion is approved by an authorised person or unless an exemption applies to the unauthorised person. If a communication originates outside the UK, the provisions of subsection (1) shall apply only if the communication is capable of producing an effect in the UK.[1] The Treasury may also by order specify circumstances in which subsection (1) does not apply (sub-s (5)). The purpose of making orders under subsection (5) is to further limit the territorial application of the financial promotion regime so that communications emanating from overseas will be subject to this provision if they are targeted at the UK. This is extremely significant in the context of internet communications.[2] 'Engaging in investment activity' means:

'(a)   entering or offering to enter into an agreement the making or performance of which by either party constitutes a controlled activity; or
(b)   exercising any rights conferred by a controlled investment to acquire, dispose of, underwrite or convert a controlled investment.'[3]

---

[1] This provision may be repealed by the Treasury at any time; see sub-s (7).
[2] sub-s (8).
[3] See also *Explanatory Notes* to the Act at 19.

According to subsection (9), an activity is a controlled activity, if:

> '(a) it is an activity of a specified kind or one which falls within a specified class of activity; and
> (b) it relates to an investment of a specified kind, or to one which falls within a specified class of investment.'

A controlled investment is an investment of a specified kind or one that falls within a specified class of investment.[4]

An order made under subsection (5) (dispensation) may provide that the restrictions under subsection (1) shall not apply in relation to the following types of communication:

- of a specified description;
- originating in a specified country outside the United Kingdom;
- originating in a country which falls within a specified description outside the United Kingdom; or
- originating outside the United Kingdom.[5]

The first two categories or types of communication would most probably be allowed exemptions for communications originating in specific groups of countries such as the EU countries.[6] Incidentally, 'investment' in this context includes any asset, right or interest, and 'communicate' will include 'causing a communication to be made'.[7] Of course, 'inducement' will have to be interpreted from a legal standpoint. It is emphasised that the prohibitions under section 21 apply to 'invitations' and/or 'inducements' to engage in investment activities, which may be made in the course of business.

According to section 25, it is an offence to breach the provisions of section 21. Subsection (2) of section 25 provides defence for an accused if he/she can show that:

> '(a) he believed on reasonable grounds that the content of the communication was prepared or approved for the purposes of section 21, by an authorised person; or
> (b) that he took all reasonable precautions and exercised all due diligence to avoid committing the offence.'

Of course, legal aspects of terms such as 'reasonable grounds' or 'reasonable precautions' will have to be considered to confirm the authenticity of the defences that may be provided by a defendant.

---

[4] s 21(10).
[5] s 21(6).
[6] See further *Explanatory Notes*, op cit, at 19.
[7] s 21(13).

Restrictions on financial promotion also exist in respect of collective investment schemes. The key provisions in this regard may be found in sections 238–241 of the Financial Services and Markets Act 2000. Section 238(1) provides that:

'An authorised person must not communicate an invitation or inducement to participate in a collective investment scheme.'

Again, this provision is subject to certain exceptions. The provision of section 238(1) applies only if a communication originates outside the UK and if it is capable of producing any effect in the UK. Section 238(1) has no application in relation to: (a) an authorised unit trust scheme; (b) a scheme constituted by an authorised open-ended investment company; or (c) a recognised scheme. The principal exemption is meant for schemes that are marketed other than the general public.[8] Under subsection (6) the Treasury may by order specify circumstances in which subsection (1) does not apply. The subsection 'enables the Treasury to adjust the scope of the restriction on promotion of collective investment schemes by authorised persons to take full account of international and technological developments'.[9] In the context of section 238, 'promotion otherwise than to the general public' includes promotion—the objective of which is to reduce as far as possible the risk of participation by persons whose participation would be unsuitable.[10] Under subsection (7) it will be possible to make exceptions in respect of promotions originating outside the UK, even if they are capable of producing effect in the UK.

Section 239 relates to single property schemes, which broadly are collective investment schemes, which relate to the management of buildings, single or in a group, but as a single enterprise. The Treasury may by regulations, make provisions for exempting single property schemes from section 238(1), that is, may make regulations exempting the promotion of participation in a single property scheme to the general public from the prohibition in section 238.[11] In the event of the Treasury making regulations under section 239, the Financial Services Authority may make rules the effect of which would be to impose duties on the operator and trustee or depository of schemes exempted under the regulations.[12]

If an authorised person is not permitted to make a communication under section 238, it cannot approve of a financial promotion under section 21.[13] If an unauthorised person contravenes a requirement imposed on him under section 238 or section 240, a private person and other persons falling within such

---

[8] See further *Explanatory Notes* to the Act, op cit, at 87.
[9] ibid.
[10] s 238(10).
[11] *Explanatory Notes*, op cit, at 88.
[12] ibid.
[13] s 240.

categories as may be prescribed by the Treasury, who suffers loss, in consequence, may claim damages.[14]

Nothing in Schedule 2 (Regulated Activities) limits the powers of the Treasury conferred by subsection (9) or (10) of section 21.[15]

10.4   Conclusions

Prohibitions against financial promotion are, in reality, a means of protecting consumer interest. Usually, promotional activities directly or indirectly tend to include expressions that would have the effect of 'inducement' to prospective customers which is contrary to the basic principles of consumer protection. Even communication of an invitation may be regarded as the beginning of 'inducement'. The Financial Services and Markets Act 2000 has therefore included very useful and appropriate provisions for the purposes of protecting the interests of consumers.

It is to be appreciated that the more powerful the investor, the higher are the chances of providing 'inducements' by sophisticated and technical means to prospective customers/consumers. The Act has, therefore, made additional provisions relating to the promotion of collective investment schemes.

Section 21 is predominantly addressed to unauthorised persons and overseas entities. Again, if consumer protection and a regulated market are the primary aims, amongst others, of the Act, then there is no reason for questioning the propriety of the provisions of section 21 in so far as unauthorised persons are concerned. The question remains whether or not communications originating overseas should be exempted in all cases, until a uniform system of restriction on financial promotion has been developed through international co-operation. It is to be pointed out however that financial promotion presents more problems in countries with sophisticated technology than in those countries that do not have such resources.

---

[14] s 241; see also *Explanatory Notes*, op cit, at 88.
[15] s 21(12).

11. Domain names and intellectual property rights and e-Commerce

11.1 Introduction

Intellectual issues are important in discussing business through electronic means in that there is a need to protect information and creative work from abuse. The law of intellectual property aims to protect ideas, innovation, information and knowledge. In e-Commerce, dissemination of information is common, hence the need to ensure that information of a nature which is fundamental to a business is not abused by unwarranted users. The most important types of intellectual property are: copyright, design and trade marks. The purpose is not to analyse all the legal issues pertaining to each of these types of intellectual property, but to provide the reader with basic information about them.[1] It must also be pointed out that the impact of intellectual property law will vary depending on the type of business carried out through electronic means. In other words, the impact of the law will depend upon the degree of originality and creativity of the business.

11.2 Intellectual co-operation for assigned names and numbers (ICANN): rules for uniform domain name dispute resolution policy adopted by ICANN on 26 August 1991[2]

The title of this Policy is self-explanatory. The Rules will have to be applied in conjunction with the Supplemental Rules of the Provider administering the

---

[1] The reader may like to consult the following texts for a broader understanding of the subject: D Bainbridge, *Intellectual Property* (London, Pitman, latest edition); W R Cornish, *Intellectual Property: Patents, Copyright, Trade Marks and Allied Rights* (London, Sweet & Maxwell, latest edition).

[2] The implementation documents were approved by ICANN on 24 October 1999. The text of this Policy has been reproduced in 39 *International Legal Materials* (2000) 952.

proceedings. These Rules have been developed under the following titles: Defin-
itions; Communications; the complainant; Notification of Complaint; the
Response; Appointment of the Panel and Timing of Decision; Impartiality and
Independence; Communication between Parties and the Panel; Transmission of
the File to the Panel; General Powers of the Panel; Language of Proceedings;
Further Statements; In-person Hearings; Default; Panel Decisions; Communi-
cation of Decision to Parties; Settlement or Other Grounds for Termination;
Effect of Court Proceedings; Fees, Exclusion of Liability; and Amendments.
These titles are now briefly discussed and analysed.

11.2.1 A brief discussion and analysis of the titles
11.2.2 Definitions

Under this title, the following have been defined: complainant; ICCAN; mutual
jurisdiction; panel; panellist, party (a complainant or a respondent); policy
(Uniform Domain Name Dispute Resolution Policy); provider (a dispute-
resolution service provider approved by ICANN)[3]; registrar; registration agreement (agreement between a registrar and a domain-name holder) respondent;
reverse domain name hijacking (using the Policy in bad faith to attempt to
deprive a registered domain-name holder of a domain name); and supplemental rules. Most of these definitions are self-explanatory, and in order to avoid
any doubts in certain cases, their meanings have been shown in brackets. Of
these definitions, 'mutual jurisdiction' and 'supplemental rules' require interpretation. 'Mutual jurisdiction' may mean jurisdiction for a court at the location of
either (a) the principal officer of the Registrar (if of course the domain-name
holder submits in its registration agreement to that jurisdiction for settlement of
disputes arising from the use of the domain name by courts in that jurisdiction);
or (b) the domain-name holder's address which has been officially shown for the
registration of the domain name and which is shown at the time the registration
of the domain name and which is shown at the time the complaint is submitted
to the Provider. Thus, opportunities are provided to the domain-name holder
also to refer to disputes to the courts in its location, if appropriate. 'Supplemental Rules' means the rules adopted by the Provider, which shall not be inconsistent with the Policy or the Rules. Supplemental Rules shall cover 'topics such
as, fees, word and page limits and guidelines, the means for communicating with
the Provider and the panel, and the form of cover sheets'.[4]

11.2.3 Communications

In forwarding a complaint to the Registrar, the provider is required to employ
reasonably available means purporting to give actual notice to a respondent. A
Provider shall discharge its responsibility in this regard by doing the following:

---

[3] A list of Providers appears at www.icann.org/udrp/approved-providers.htm.
[4] *International Legal Materials*, op cit, at 953.

(a) sending the complaint to all postal and facsimile addresses shown in the domain name's registration data for the registration of the domain name, and to the address supplied by the Registrar to the Provider for the registration's billing contract; and

(b) sending the complaint in electronic form by e-mail to:

    (i) the e-mail address if it relates to technical, administrative or billing contracts;

    (ii) the postmaster @ < the contested domain name >; and

    (iii) the e-mail address shown or e-mail links on the web page if the domain name relates to an active web page (but not a generic page which is maintained by the Registrar or ISP for parking domain names registered by multiple domain-name holders).

The Provider may also send the complaint to any address that the respondent has given to the former.

All written communications must be sent to the complainant or respondent in accordance with the means preferred by them; in the event of no means of communication being preferred by them, they shall be sent by telecopy or facsimile transmission or by postal or courier service (postage must be pre-paid and receipt requested) or electronically via the Internet.

All communications to the Provider or the panel shall be made in accordance with the relevant provisions in the Provider's Supplemental Rules, and unless otherwise agreed by the parties, the language of communications and of the administrative proceedings shall be the language of the registration agreement; however, the panel has the authority to change it if the circumstances of the administrative proceedings so requires. Where a document is prepared in a language other than the language of the administrative proceedings, the panel may order that such documents be translated into the language of the administrative proceedings. E-mail communications should, if practicable, be sent to plaintext.

Except as otherwise provided in these Rules, or decided by a panel, all communications shall be deemed to have been made if delivered by telecopy or facsimile transmission or by postal or courier service or via the Internet, but whatever means of communication may be adopted, receipt of communication will be confirmed by referring to the date transmission of the date marked on the receipt. Any communication, whether initiated by a panel or a party or a Provider must be sent to all parties concerned, preferably by keeping records of transmission or delivery. In the case of a reported non-delivery of any communication, the party concerned shall promptly notify the panel and if no panel is appointed, the Provider. In sum, all parties concerned must ensure that the recipient of a communication has actually received it, and that communications have been sent in compliance with the provisions of these Rules, and in conjunction with the Provider's Supplemental Rules, where relevant.

11.2.4 The complaint

Any person or entity may submit a complaint in accordance with the Policy and these Rules to any Provider approved by ICANN. If a Provider is not eligible for accepting a complaint, it may be submitted to another eligible Provider. A complaint must be submitted in hard copy and in electronic form, with an initial fee specified in the Provider's Supplemental Rules.[5]

A complaint must, in general, satisfy the following: it shall request a decision in accordance with the Policy and these Rules; provide the name, postal and e-mail addresses, telephone and telefax numbers of the complainant, and of its representative, if any, authorized to act on its behalf; specification of the preferred method of communication to the complainant; including the persons to be contacted and by what means; clarification of whether the complainant would like to have the dispute decided by a single or a three-member panel, and in the event of the latter, the names and contact details of three candidates to serve as one of the panellists[6]; name of the respondent (the domain-name holder) and its contact details known to the complainant including the contact details of the respondent's representative, specification of the domain name(s) which is/are registered at the time the complaint is filed; specification of the trade mark(s) or service mark(s) on which the complaint is based, and the description of the goods or services, if any, with which the mark is used; description of the grounds on which the complaint is made, including, in particular, the manner in which the domain name(s) has/have proved to be identical or confusingly similar to a trademark or service mark in which the complainant has rights; the reason why the respondent (the domain-name-holder) is not considered to have rights or legitimate interests in respect of the domain name(s) which is/are the subject of the complaint; in addition giving the reason why the domain name(s) should be considered as one registered and being used in bad faith; specification in accordance with the Policy, the remedies sought; a statement of whether any other legal proceedings have been commenced or terminated in connection with any of the domain name(s) which are subject of the complaint; a statement that a copy of the complaint, together with a cover sheet as prescribed by the Provider's Supplemental Rules, has been sent to the respondent; a statement that the complainant will submit 'with respect to any challenges to a decision in the administrative proceeding cancelling or transferring the domain name to the jurisdiction of the courts in at least one specified Mutual Jurisdiction'[7]; and conclude with the following statement with the signature thereon of the complainant or its authorized representative:

> 'Complainant agrees that its claims and remedies concerning the registration of the domain name, the dispute, or the dispute's resolution shall be solely against the domain-name holder and waives all such claims and

---

[5] In any event, if the initial fee is not received within ten days of filing the complaint, the complaint shall be deemed to have been withdrawn.
[6] These candidates may be drawn from any ICANN-approved Provider's list of panellists.
[7] r 3(xiii)

remedies against (a) the dispute-resolution provider and panellists, except in the case of deliberate wrongdoing, (b) the registrar, (c) the registry administrator, and (d) the Internet Corporation for Assigned Names and Numbers, as well as their directors, officers, employees, and agents.'

'Complainant certifies that the information contained in this Complaint is to the best of Complainant's knowledge complete and accurate, that this Complaint is not being presented for any improper purpose, such as to harass, and that the assertions in this Complaint are warranted under these Rules and under applicable law, as it now exists or as it may be extended by a good-faith and reasonable argument.'[8]

A complaint may relate to more than one domain name, provided, of course, the domain names are registered by the same domain-name holder.

11.2.5 Notification of complaint
The Provider is required to review the complaint and forward the complaint to the respondent in accordance with these Rules within three calendar days following receipt of the fees to be paid by the complainant. In the event of the Provider finding the complaint administratively deficient, it shall promptly notify the complainant and the respondent of the nature of the deficiencies identified. The complainant will have five calendar days to correct any such deficiencies, which if not corrected within this period, the administrative proceedings will be deemed withdrawn. It is for the Provider to promptly notify the complainant, the respondent, the Registrar(s) and ICANN of the date of commencement of the administrative proceedings.

11.2.6 The response
The respondent is required to submit a response to the Provider within 20 days of the date of commencement of the administrative proceedings. The response which must be submitted in hard copy and in electronic form shall contain the following: specific replies to statements and allegations contained in the complaint, and the bases for the respondent for retaining registration and the use of the disputed domain name, and the name, postal and e-mail address, telephone and telefax numbers of the respondent, and of representative, if any, authorized by the respondent; it shall specify a preferred method of communication directed to the respondent, and whether the respondent would elect for a three-member panel whereas the claimant has decided for a single-member panel. If either the complainant or the respondent elects a three-member panel, it is required to provide the names and contact details of three candidates to serve

[8] r 3(xiv): 'A Complainant is also required to submit, in the form of annexures, evidence, documentary or otherwise, including a copy of the Policy applicable to the domain name(s) in dispute and any trademark or service mark registration upon which the complaint relies, together with a schedule indexing such evidence' r 3(xv).

as one of the panellists[9]; whether any other proceedings have been commenced or terminated in connection with any of the domain name(s) that are subject to the complaint; it shall state that a copy of the response has been sent to the complainant, and conclude with the following statement with the signature of the respondent thereon:

> 'Respondent certifies that the information contained in this Response is to the best of Respondent's knowledge complete and accurate, that this Response is not being presented for any improper purpose, such as to harass, and that the assertions in this Response are warranted under these Rules and under applicable law, as it now exists or as it may be extended by a good-faith and reasonable argument.'[10]

Where a complainant chooses to have its dispute settled by a single-member panel but the respondent elects a three-member panel, the latter party will be required to pay one-half of the applicable fee for a three-member panel. In the absence of any such payment, the dispute shall be decided by a single-member panel.

Under the Rules, the time schedule for submission of response or evidence is to be rigidly followed. It is only in exceptional circumstances that at the discretion of the Provider, a request for an extension of time for filing a response may be granted. A mutually agreed extended time between the parties may be allowed provided the Provider approves it.

11.2.7 Appointment of the panel and timing of decision

The lists of panellists and their qualifications must be published by the Providers. Where parties decide to have their dispute settled by a single-member panel, the Provider shall, within five calendar days after the receipt of the response, appoint a single panellist from the list of panellists, and the fee for that panellist must be met in its entirety by the complainant. A complainant is also required to meet the expenses of a three-member panel in their entirety where a dispute is to be decided by such a panel; however, where a three-member panel is elected by the respondent, the fees for that panel shall be shared equally between the parties. Candidates for panels may be drawn from any ICANN-approved Provider's list of panellists. Where a complainant or a respondent elects a three-member panel, the Provider shall endeavour to appoint one panellist from the list of candidates provided by each of the complainant and the respondent. In the event of a Provider being unable to appoint a panel from either party's list of candidates, it will make that appointment from its list of panellists, and the third panellist shall be appointed by the Provider to form a

---

[9] These candidates may be drawn from any ICANN approved Provider's list of panellists.
[10] The respondent is required to show in an Annex, the evidence, documentary or otherwise, on which it relies, together with a schedule indexing such documents.

list of five candidates submitted by it to the parties, bearing in mind the preference made by both parties. The Provider must notify the parties of the appointment of the panellists.

The impartiality and independence of panellists must be assured. Prior to his/her accepting an appointment, each panellist is required to disclose to the Provider any circumstances which might give rise to any justifiable doubt as to his/her impartiality or independence. If during a proceedings any new circumstances may give rise to a justifiable doubt as to the impartiality or independence of a panellist, the panellist must disclose such circumstances to the Provider, and in the event of any justifiable doubt as to the impartiality or independence prevailing after consideration of the new circumstances, the Provider may appoint a substitute panellist. No party nor its representative shall communicate unilaterally to a panel. All communications between a party and the panel or the Provider shall be made to a case administrator who shall be appointed by the Provider concerned in accordance with the Provider's Supplemental Rules. The Provider must forward the file to the panel, whether it consists of one member of three members, as soon as the panel is constituted. The panel shall forward its decision on the complaint to the Provider, and the latter shall within three calendar days, after receipt of the decision, communication its full text to each party, the Registrar(s) and ICANN. The Registrar(s) concerned shall immediately communicate to each party, the Provider and ICANN the date by which the decision is to be implemented. Unless the panel determines otherwise, the Provider shall publish the full text of the decision and the date on which the decision was implemented on a website which is accessible by the public.

11.2.8 General powers of the panel

Each panel shall conduct proceedings in accordance with the Uniform Domain Name Resolution Policy and the Rules thereof. Equal treatment of parties and a fair opportunity to each party to present its case are two of the cardinal rules on which each panel must operate. Unless either at the request of a party or on its own motion, in exceptional cases, the scheduled time for the proceedings is extended, each panel must ensure that the administrative proceedings take place expeditiously. It is for each panel to determine the admissibility, relevance, materiality and credibility of evidence. Any request by a party for consolidation of multiple domain name disputes shall be considered and decided by a panel in accordance with the Policy and these Rules. Each panel has the discretionary power to require a party or parties to submit further statements or documents in addition to the complaint and the response received from the parties. In-person hearings[11] are not to take place unless, in exceptional circumstances, a panel finds it necessary to hold such a hearing; in [AQ deciding on a complaint, a documents-only basis each panel] must consider any rule or principle or law

[11] Such hearings include hearings by tele-conference, video-conference and web-conference.

which it may deem relevant. In the event of a party failing to comply with the schedules of time established by these Rules or by a panel, the latter shall proceed to consider the complaint. By the same token, if a party fails to comply with any provision of or requirement under the Rules or any request made by the panel, the latter will draw such inferences as it may deem appropriate.

Unless the time-scale is extended in exceptional circumstances, panel decisions are to be forwarded to the Provider concerned within 14 days of appointment of each panel. Decisions of a three-member panel shall be made by a majority vote. Panel decisions which are to be rendered in written form, shall provide reasons for reaching their decisions, the names of the panel members and the date on which each decision has been rendered. Dissenting opinions may be rendered, and presumably they may also be published, as they should constitute as an integral part of the full text of a panel decision. In the event of a panel reaching a finding that a complaint was brought in bad faith, for example, to harass the domain-name holder, then the panel shall so declare pointing out that the conduct of the complainant constituted an abuse of the administrative proceedings under these Rules.

Parties may agree on a settlement, and if a settlement is reached prior to a panel's rendering its decision, the panel shall be notified accordingly, and the administrative proceedings will terminate. If a panel should find it impossible or unnecessary for it to continue with an administrative proceedings for any reason, it shall terminate the proceedings unless objections are raised by a party on justifiable grounds within the period of time determined by the panel concerned.

In the event of any legal proceedings being instituted to or during an administrative proceeding pertaining to a domain-name which is also the subject matter of a complaint before a panel, the panel concerned has the discretion to either suspend or terminate or continue with the administrative proceedings. A party initiating legal proceedings during the pendency of administrative proceedings, has the obligation to notify the panel immediately to that effect.

11.2.9 Other issues
Payment to a Provider will be made according to the following formulae: (a) an initial amount fixed by the complainant; (b) where a respondent may elect to have a complaint consider by a three-member panel, as opposed to a one-member panel elected by the complainant, the respondent shall pay the Provider one-half of the fixed fee; and (c) unless an in-person hearing takes place in which case an agreed amount in additional fees[12] will be required to be paid by the parties; in all other cases, the complainant shall bear the fees for the Provider. Upon appointment of the panel, the Provider shall refund the appropriate portion of the initial fee to the complainant.

---

[12] This additional fee is to be agreed to by the parties and the panel.

Save cases of deliberate wrongdoing, neither the Provider nor a panel member shall be liable to a party for any act or omission in connection with any administrative proceedings under these Rules.[13]

Conclusions
The Rules for Uniform Domain Name Dispute Resolution Policy, which must be read with the Provider's Supplemental Rules, seem to be comprehensive, although they must go through their gestation period. Under the Rules, panels enjoy wide discretionary powers. It is interesting to note that in order to hasten the dispute settlement procedure, the Rules provide for settlement, where possible, by documents only. It is also encouraging to note that all disputes, unless exceptions are made, are to be settled within 14 days after receipt of a complaint by the Provider.

11.3   The Nominet.UK

Nominet.UK was set up as the Registry for .UK Internet domain names. It maintains the database of .UK registered Internet names; thus every organisation or individual may be identified by a numerical address. It is the central storehouse of .UK Internet Names. It is not a regulatory body—it simply provides services to the public in relation to the .UK registered Internet Names on behalf of the Internet community. The purpose of the domain name system has already been explained—Nominet.UK is the first port of call, so to say, for identifying a legal entity or an individual by a numerical address. Internet Services Providers are Nominet.UK's most active members, although its membership is drawn from a wide range of institutions, including marketing companies, local councils, intellectual property lawyers etc, but any individual or organisation interested in its membership may apply. Each member is issued with an exclusive password. Members are required to pay an initial fee, and an annual subscription.

Nominet.UK offers a dispute resolution service, and has adopted a Dispute Resolution Service Procedure, which may be reviewed from time to time. It considers whether a registration was made in bad faith, in addition to dealing with the problem of cybersquatting, that is, where a domain name is registered with a view to disputing another's business. It encourages parties to a dispute to mediate, where possible. If mediation should fail, the dispute may be referred to an independent legal expert within 14 days on payment of a fee currently between £500 and £1,000 by the complainant. The mediation service of Nominet.UK is available free.

Nominet.UK has also developed General Rules for .UK Top Level and Second Level Domains, that is, the rules for the allocation of names within the .UK

---

[13] Cl 20.

domain and its sub-domains.[14] The Rules for the .co.uk Second Level Domain is for the registration of names pertaining to commercial enterprises. Rules are also available for the .ltd.uk and .plc.UK Second Level Domains.

All domain names under Nominet.UK are registered for a period of two years, after which the holder of a domain name will have the first choice to renew that domain name. Registrations are made under Nominet's Terms and Conditions for Domain Name registration. Only one entity may use one domain name. .UK domain names are allocated by Nominet.UK on a first-come, first-served basis.

Nominet also operate a free on-line search facility, called WHOLS, which can search for domain name registrations in the UK.

Nominet has the power to suspend or cancel a domain name registration in certain specific circumstances, for example, when a legal action has been commenced, or if the basis on which a domain name was registered has change by virtue of the organisation being non-existent in law; or if a domain name is administered in a way which is likely to endanger the operation of the Domain Name System.

11.4 Intellectual property related issues

11.4.1 Introduction

11.4.2 Some basic elements of copyright, design and trade marks

11.4.2.1 Copyright

Literally speaking, 'copyright' stands for the right to copy (reproduce) certain types of creative work. The purpose of copyright law is to protect the author of the work from anyone copying his/her work. Copyright lasts for the life of the author, and another 70 years. In reality however, copyright devolves upon the publisher, and the author of the work will have what is known as 'moral right' (unless the publisher and the author are the same). In respect of e-Commerce, however, certain databases may belong to the business house concerned; thus, the copyright in those databases belongs exclusively to that business entity. Broadly speaking, the objective of copyright is to protect information from unlawful use and/or reproduction, in order to prohibit exploitation of one's work without permission. Unlike trade marks and patents, copyright is not subject to registration. Literary works, in the context of copyright law, include computer programmes and the preparatory materials used in creating the programmes. Information on the Internet of any nature, software, graphics or artwork, are works protected by copyright. When a work consists of various elements, each element may have a copyright; thus, several different copyrights may subsist in what appears to be one composite work.

---

[14] The .UK Country Code is separated into sub-categories, called Second Level Domains.

When business is carried on through an electronic means, the issue of copyright can present tricky legal problems. For example, viewing of materials on a website requires a temporary copy of the site to be made on the viewer's random access memory (RAM), of which print-outs may be made, and eventually saved in the viewer's hard drive. This process entails breaches of the owner's copyright in that the viewer has reproduced all or a substantial part of the owner's material. But the question remains—can one really prevent a viewer from viewing materials on the Internet, and if not, is this not an implied right under the licence? But, this raises the necessary follow-up question—whether this right allows a viewer to download and print out a hard copy.[15] The clear answer is that unless waivers have been allowed, viewers are not supposed to download and make print-outs. Business houses should therefore specify in the terms and conditions of sales the limits to the use of their websites along the following lines:

(a) a statement clarifying the extent of the rights in any software that the owner wishes to retain, and in what respects (texts, graphics, etc); and
(b) the extent of the right that may be allowed to a customer.

The legal issues of copyright are governed by the Copyright, Designs and Patents Act 1988, which came into force on 1 August 1989, section 1 of the Act provides that:

'(1) Copyright is a property right which subsists in accordance with this Part in the following descriptions of work—
   (a)   original literary, dramatic, musical or artistic works,
   (b)   sound recordings, films, broadcasts or cable programmes, and
   (c)   the typographical arrangement of published editions.
(2) In this Part 'copyright work' means a work of any of those descriptions in which copyright subsists.
(3) Copyright does not subsist in a work unless the requirements of this Part with respect to qualification for copyright protection are met.'[16]

---

[15] s 50A of the Copyright, Designs and Patents Act 1988, as amended, seems to acknowledge the right to make copies for archival purposes.
[16] These requirements may be found in s 153 which provides that:
   '(1) Copyright does not subsist in a work unless the qualification requirements of this Chapter are satisfied as regards—
      (a)   the author (see section 154), or
      (b)   the country in which the work was first published (see section 155), or
      (c)   in the case of a broadcast or cable programme, the country from which the broadcast was made or the cable programme was sent (see section 156).
   (2) Subsection (1) does not apply in relation to Crown copyright or Parliamentary copyright (see sections 163 to 166) or to copyright subsisting by virtue of section 168 (copyright of certain international organisations).
   (3) If the qualification requirements of this Chapter, or section 163, 165 or 168, are once satisfied in respect of a work, copyright does not cease to subsist by reason of any subsequent event.'

All of these listed above must be 'works'. The exploitation of a work may be controlled by the owner of it, unless he/she has permitted a publishing house to print and sell his/her work in return for royalty payments, and in that event, as stated earlier, the author will have moral right only over his/her work. In general, making copies of any work is impermissible, without permission from the person/entity in which copyright rests. Whereas there are certain works which are required to be original (eg literary and artistic works), other works, such as cable programmes or sound recordings or typographical arrangements need not be original; they are mere entrepreneurial works. Thus, translation of a literary work or works relating to technological developments or storing a programme or formula in a computer will be covered by copyright law. The reason for extending the copyright to include such works is that individual skill, labour and judgment are used in producing such works, which are expression of the creators intellectual ability.

Copyright law is concerned with the protection of the expression of an idea,[17] but not the idea itself; in other words, it is concerned with the final product[18] although it is often difficult to draw a dividing line between an 'idea' and an 'expression of an idea'. A work is 'original' if it originated from the author (it was not copied from another work)[19]; the work need not be even particularly meritorious. Thus, in business, production of a similar product, without using identical ingredients will be an 'original' product, and the copyright in it will rest in the manufacturer of the product; once again, skill, labour and judgment remain the three criteria for determining the originality of a work. However, insignificant changes/modifications made to an existing work do not create a new copyright in it.[20]

The definition of 'work' gives rise to a central legal problem in the copyright law. The Act defines 'copyright work', 'literary work', 'artistic work', 'graphic work', but not the term 'work'. Judicial guidelines on the definition of the term are not uniform either. In *Ladbroke (Football) Ltd v William Hill (Football) Ltd*, Lord Pearce used the expression 'work or skill or expense', whereas the expression 'knowledge, labour, judgment or literary skill or taste' was used by Lord Atkinson in *Macmillan & Co Ltd v K & J Cooper & Co Ltd*[21]; yet again, in *British Leyland Motor Corporation Ltd v Armstrong Patents co Ltd,*[22] Lord Templeman used the expression 'skill and labour'. Controversy aside, it is generally accepted that skill and judgment must be the least criteria for designating something as a piece of

---

[17] An intermediate product, as an element of a final product, may also be regarded as a final product on its own.

[18] See *University of London Press Ltd v University Tutorial Press Ltd,* 1916 2 Ch. 601 at 608–609, *per* Peterson J.

[19] See *Ladbroke (Football) Ltd v William Hill (Football) Ltd* [1964] 1 W.L.R. 273 at 291, *per* Lord Pearce. Contrast with *Bookmakers Afternoon Greyhound Services Ltd v Wilf Gilbert (Staffordshire) Ltd* (1994) F.S.R. 723.

[20] *Interlego AG v Tyco Industries Inc* [1989] 1 A.C. 217.

[21] 1923 93 L.J.P.C. 113 at 121.

[22] [1986] 2 W.L.R. 400 at 419.

'work'. Therefore, if a catalogue of goods and/or services is produced by a business house, or a description of goods and/or services are put on its website according to some idea of arrangement, the copyright vests in the owner of the website. Incidentally, Article 1(3) of the Council Directive on the Legal Protection of Computer Programmes requires copyright computer programme to be the author's own intellectual creation.[23] Under English law, in order to constitute a 'work', labour, skill and judgment must be put into it, and although the work need not be of an extremely high intellectual standard or totally original, it must stand as an expression of an idea. The work must be in some tangible form, because it must represent an expression of an idea. Tangible does not necessarily mean visible—thus, sound recordings or films satisfy the definition of copyright under English law. Copyright does not subsist in a work unless it gets a shape, whether in the form of writing or a film or recording. Section 3(2) of the 1988 Act provides that:

> 'Copyright does not subsist in a literary, dramatic or musical work unless and until it is recorded, in writing or otherwise; and references in this Part to the time at which such a work is made are to the time at which it is so recorded.'

Section 178 of the Act defines 'writing':

> 'writing' includes any form of notation or code, whether by hand or otherwise and regardless of the method by which, or medium in or on which, it is recorded, and 'written' shall be construed accordingly.'

The word 'otherwise' in section 178 would include notation by computers or by other mechanical means. Copyright cannot subsist in a work unless it has a specified description (s 1(1)). Thus, to transform ideas into identifiable expressions becomes commercially important for copyright purposes.

Copyright is a property right—to whom does this property belong? When he/she publishes his/her works through a publisher, the author will have moral rights, and the owner of the copyright possesses economic rights. The copyright in a work may be owned by the author or the author's employer (if the work is created during the course of employment) or a person to whom the copyright has been transferred. The owner of the copyright may grant licences in respect of his/her work and the licensee will have the right to exploit the licence in accordance with its terms and conditions. But, in all cases, the owner of the copyright, licensees and any other party who may be using the work, must respect the moral rights of the author.

Under the Copyright, Designs and Patents Act 1988 the following four types of right come under the broader right called the 'moral right':

---

[23] L. 122 of 14 May 1991 at 42.

(a) the paternity right (ss 77–79) (that is, the right to be identified as the author of a work);

(b) the integrity right (ss 80–83) (that is, the right to object, as the author of the work, to any derogatory treatment of the work);

(c) the right not have a work falsely attributed to a person/author (s 84); and

(d) the commissioner's right of privacy.

In England, economic rights are associated with copyright in disregard of the fact that there may often be a conflict between a moral right and an economic right (employee-authors if a work is made by an employee during the course of his employment). Under section 11(2) of the Act, the employer will be the first owner of the copyright. An author can bring an action in defamation (see s 80(2)(b)). Information created by a business house and stored in a computer belongs to that business house, it is the author and it does not engage a third party to transmit its information—in such a situation, economic right and copyright merge, and reside in the business house. The 'paternity right' of the business house must be acknowledged, but under the Act, 'paternity right' does not apply to computer programmes[24]: it applies to literary, dramatic, musical, artistic works and films. By the same token, the business house concerned may not have the right to enforce its 'integrity right'.[25] However, data bases, design material, data stored in computers may be subject to moral rights. Although section 178 is based on the assumption that in order to enforce the right to object to the derogatory treatment of work, there must be a human being as an author (because there should be a human being to be aggrieved by the derogatory treatment accorded to a work), and although a computer-generated work does not satisfy this condition—section 9(2)(a) may be an exception to this when a subsequent copyright owner or a licensee may cause distress to the creator (an individual) of a computer-generated work. Action may be brought in the case of an infringement of a moral right as a breach of statutory duty owed to the person who is entitled to that right.[26]

Infringements

Under the Copyright, Designs and Patents Act, there are certain acts that only the owner or his authorized agents can perform and a breach of these acts amounts to primary infringements. Under the Act, there are the 'acts restricted' by copyright. Other activities, which are primarily of a commercial nature, and which if done without the licence of the copyright owner, are known as 'secondary infringements'.

Unless there is a sustainable defence (permitted acts), anyone who does any act restricted by the copyright, including the secondary infringements, without the permission or licence of the owner of the copyright, infringes copyright.

---

[24] s 79(2).
[25] s 81(2).
[26] s 103(1).

Under section 16 of the Act, a copyright owner has the exclusive right over the following:

- to copy the work;
- to issue copies of the work to the public;
- to broadcast the work or to include it in a cable programme;
- to perform, show or play the work in the public; and
- to make an adaptation of the work.

Copying of a small but important or substantive part of the work amounts to an infringement[27] and infringement can be of an indirect nature too.[28] Section 51(1) states that the copyright in a design document is not infringed by making articles following the design, unless the design is itself of an artistic work. Websites equated to cable programmes may fall into the broadcasting provisions.[29] Section 17(2) provides that:

'Copying in relation to a literary, dramatic, musical or artistic work means reproducing the work in any material form. This includes storing the work in any medium by electronic means.'

Sections 22–26 deal with secondary infringement of copyright. It is thought appropriate to reproduce these sections:

Section 22:

'The copyright in a work is infringed by a person who, without the licence of the copyright owner, imports into the United Kingdom, otherwise than for his private and domestic use, an article which is, and which he knows or has reason to believe is, an infringing copy of the work.'

Section 23:

'The copyright in a work is infringed by a person who, without the licence of the copyright owner—

(a)   possesses in the course of a business,
(b)   sells or lets for hire, or offers or exposes for sale or hire,
(c)   in the course of a business exhibits in public or distributes, or
(d)   distributes otherwise than in the course of a business to such an extent as to affect prejudicially the owner of the copyright, an article which is, and which he knows or has reason to believe is, an infringing copy of the work.'

---

[27] *Ladbroke (Football) Ltd v William Hill (Football) Ltd* [1964] 1 W.L.R. 273 at 293; and *Hawkes & Sons (London) Ltd v Paramount Film Service Ltd* (1934) Ch. 593.
[28] *LB (Plastics) Ltd v Swish Products Ltd* (1979) R.P.C. 551.
[29] *Shetland Times v Willis* (1997) F.S.R. 604.

Section 24:

'(1) Copyright in a work is infringed by a person who, without the licence of the copyright owner—
  (a) makes,
  (b) imports into the United Kingdom,
  (c) possesses in the course of a business, or
  (d) sells or lets for hire, or offers or exposes for sale or hire, an article specifically designed or adapted for making copies of that work, knowing or having reason to believe that it is to be used to make infringing copies.

(2) Copyright in a work is infringed by a person who without the licence of the copyright owner transmits the work by means of a telecommunications system (otherwise than by broadcasting or inclusion in a cable programme service), knowing or having reason to believe that infringing copies of the work will be made by means of the reception of the transmission in the United Kingdom or elsewhere.'

Section 25:

'(1) Where the copyright in a literary, dramatic or musical work is infringed by a performance at a place of public entertainment, any person who gave permission for that place to be used for the performance is also liable for the infringement unless when he gave permission he believed on reasonable grounds that the performance would not infringe copyright.

(2) In this section 'place of public entertainment' includes premises which are occupied mainly for other purposes but are from time to time made available for hire for the purposes of public entertainment.'

Section 26:

'(1) Where copyright in a work is infringed by a public performance of the work, or by the playing or showing of the work in public, by means of apparatus for—
  (a) playing sound recordings,
  (b) showing films, or
  (c) receiving visual images or sounds conveyed by electronic means, the following persons are also liable for the infringement.

(2) A person who supplied the apparatus, or any substantial part of it, is liable for the infringement if when he supplied the apparatus or part—
  (a) he knew or had reason to believe that the apparatus was likely to be so used as to infringe copyright, or
  (b) in the case of apparatus whose normal use involves a public performance, playing or showing, he did not believe on reasonable grounds that it would not be so used as to infringe copyright.

(3)   An occupier of premises who gave permission for the apparatus to be brought onto the premises is liable for the infringement if when he gave permission he knew or had reason to believe that the apparatus was likely to be so used as to infringe copyright.

(4)   A person who supplied a copy of a sound recording or film used to infringe copyright is liable for the infringement if when he supplied it he knew or had reason to believe that what he supplied, or a copy made directly or indirectly from it, was likely to be so used as to infringe copyright.'

Section 27 provides the meaning and legal implications of 'infringing copies' of a work:

'(1)   In this Part 'infringing copy', in relation to a copyright work shall be construed in accordance with this section.

(2)   An article is an infringing copy if its making constituted an infringement of the copyright in the work in question.

(3)   An article is also an infringing copy if—
    (a)   it has been or is proposed to be imported into the United Kingdom, and
    (b)   its making in the United Kingdom would have constituted an infringement of the copyright in the work in question, or a breach of an exclusive licence agreement relating to that work.

(4)   Where in any proceedings the question arises whether an article is an infringing copy and it is shown—
    (a)   that the article is a copy of the work, and
    (b)   that copyright subsists in the work or has subsisted at any time,
it shall be presumed until the contrary is proved that the article was made at a time when copyright subsisted in the work.

(5)   Nothing in subsection (3) shall be construed as applying to an article which may lawfully be imported into the United Kingdom by virtue of any enforceable Community right within the meaning of section 2(1) of the [1972 c. 68.] European Communities Act 1972.

(6)   In this Part 'infringing copy' includes a copy falling to be treated as an infringing copy by virtue of any of the following provisions—
section 32(5) (copies made for purposes of instruction or examination),
section 35(3) (recordings made by educational establishments for educational purposes),
section 36(5) (reprographic copying by educational establishments for purposes of instruction),
section 37(3)(b) (copies made by librarian or archivist in reliance on false declaration),
section 56(2) (further copies, adaptations, &c. of work in electronic form retained on transfer of principal copy),
section 63(2) (copies made for purpose of advertising artistic work for sale),

section 68(4) (copies made for purpose of broadcast or cable programme), or any provision of an order under section 141 (statutory licence for certain reprographic copying by educational establishments).'

Sections 96–115 of the 1988 Act indicate the remedies for copyright infringement: they include civil remedies and criminal sanctions. Under the Copyright, Designs and Patents Act, there are certain express defences to copyright infringement known as 'permitted acts', that is, these acts do not attract liability for copyright infringement. Chapter III of the Act lists the permitted acts. The rationale behind 'permitted acts' is that although technically they infringe the copyright in a work, they do not unduly interfere with the owner's commercial exploitation of the work.

Of course, other defences may also be available, for example, if the defendant can prove that copyright does not subsist in the work in question. It is worth mentioning however that even though infringement may not be established in a case, action in breach of confidence or a passing-off action may still be instituted. Section 173 of the Act provides defences too:

'(1)   Where different persons are (whether in consequence of a partial assignment or otherwise) entitled to different aspects of copyright in a work, the copyright owner for any purpose of this Part is the person who is entitled to the aspect of copyright relevant for that purpose.

(2)   Where copyright (or any aspect of copyright) is owned by more than one person jointly, references in this Part to the copyright owner are to all the owners, so that, in particular, any requirement of the licence of the copyright owner requires the licence of all of them.'

Infringement in the public interest is also a defence. 'Fair dealing' can be a defence provided the dealing is fair; it stands for copying of works within limits (usually five per cent) for the purposes of research or private study or critical review of the works.

The five per cent limit is not an absolute one—it is the proportion of the most substantive part(s) of the work that matters. If the part copied is not substantial, then there is no infringement; thus the question of seeking defence on the grounds of 'fair dealing' would not arise. Incidentally, the Act does not define 'fair dealing'; on the basis of judicial guidelines developed by the courts it may be said that 'fair dealing' should be considered by referring to the following: (a) purpose[30]; (b) proportion[31]; (c) motive[32]; and (d) status of the work.[33] To take a

---

[30] *Hubbard v Vosper* [1972] 2 Q.B. 84.
[31] *Walter v Steinkopff* (1892) 3 Ch. 489.
[32] *Weatherby v International Horse Agency & Exchange Ltd* (1910) 2 Ch. 297.
[33] *British Oxygen Co Ltd v Liquid Air Ltd* (1925) Ch. 383; *Beloff v Pressdam Ltd* [1973] 1 All E.R. 241; see also Bainbridge.

copy of an article published in a journal for the purpose of research or private study might be fair dealing, but the proportion of the amount copied must always be taken into account. Motive is an important factor in establishing whether it was for research or for private study, or for the purpose of competing with the other work. If the work is confidential (status of the work), the question of fair dealing would not arise when such work is copied and exploited. Limited copying of published works, but not of the most substantive parts, for research and private study only may come under 'fair dealing'. In principle, 'downloading' from the Internet or from a computer programme, without the consent of the author amounts to a breach of the copyright.

The Copyright (Computer Programs) Regulation 1992[34] inserted sections 50A–50C for the purpose of making certain specific exceptions to copyright infringement of computer programmes. Section 56 which deals with work in electronic form, provides that:

'(1)   This section applies where a copy of a work in electronic form has been purchased on terms which, expressly or impliedly or by virtue of any rule of law, allow the purchaser to copy the work, or to adapt it or make copies of an adaptation, in connection with his use of it.

(2)   If there are no express terms—
   (a)   prohibiting the transfer of the copy by the purchaser, imposing obligations which continue after a transfer, prohibiting the assignment of any licence or terminating any licence on a transfer, or
   (b)   providing for the terms on which a transferee may do the things which the purchaser was permitted to do, anything which the purchaser was allowed to do may also be done without infringement of copyright by a transferee; but any copy, adaptation or copy of an adaptation made by the purchaser which is not also transferred shall be treated as an infringing copy for all purposes after the transfer.

(3)   The same applies where the original purchased copy is no longer usable and what is transferred is a further copy used in its place.

(4)   The above provisions also apply on a subsequent transfer, with the substitution for references in subsection (2) to the purchaser of references to the subsequent transferor.'

'Computer software' is an imprecise term—it is merely understood that it includes computer programmes, databases and other related materials, namely, programming languages and preparatory work, whether in printed or electronic form. Under section 3(1)(b), copyright subsists in computer programmes as a form of literary work. It is to be pointed out that the Act does not define 'computer programme'. It may be difficult to have a clear-cut distinction between

---

[34] SI 1992/3233.

'hardware' and 'software', say, where a computer programme is reduced to a 'microcode' but it is to be protected by copyright. The Computer (computer software) Amendment Act 1985 offers copyright protection to computer programmes. Thus, the copyright in a computer programme will be infringed if, a copy of the programme or of a substantial part of it, is made without the copyright owner's licence.[35]

Section 17 of the Act deals with infringement of copyright by copying. Under this section, storage by electronic means will be regarded as a 'reproduction' and by the same token, loading a computer programme amounts to copying. For the purposes of protection of copyright, each intermediate or preparatory stage to a complete programme must be regarded as a programme (specifications, layouts, flowcharts etc).

Copying of a computer programme can be literal or non-literal. Where the programme code itself is copied by means of disk to disk copying or by printing the programmes listing, the copying is literal. Where elements of a programme, namely, structure, sequence of operations, methodologies are copied (but the programme code is not directly copied), copying is non-literal.[36] In establishing infringement of literal copying, again, in addition to the general grounds, namely ownership in the programme or whether the defendant directly copied from the claimant's programme, the issue of the copy of a substantial part of the programme becomes extremely relevant.[37] Non-literal copying stands for copying of non-literal elements in a programme, such as the characters or events or a plot.

Infringements can also take place by borrowing ideas by non-literal copying.[38] What is important is whether in performing either of these two forms of copying, trade secrets are being exploited.[39]

Section 16(3)(b) and section 17(6) are concerned with 'indirect copying'. Section 16(3)(b) provides that:

'References in this Part to the doing of an act restricted by the copyright in a work are to the doing of it either directly or indirectly.'

Section 17(6) provides that:

'Copying in relation to any description of work includes the making of copies which are transient or are incidental to some other use of the work.'

---

[35] See *Total Information Processing Systems Ltd v Darnan Ltd* (1992) F.S.R. 171; see also *IBCOS Computers Ltd v Barclays Mercantile Highland Finance Ltd* (1994) F.S.R. 275.
[36] See further Bainbridge, op cit, at 180.
[37] See further *IBCOS Computer Ltd v Barclays Mercantile Highland Finance Ltd*, op cit.
[38] One of the important cases in the UK on non-literal copying is: *John Richardson Computers Ltd v Flanders* (1992) F.S.R. 497.
[39] See further *Lansing Linde Ltd v Kern* [1991] 1 W.L.R. 251.

Subject to conditions, the following are the specially permitted acts for computer programmes:

- decompilation of computer programmes;
- making back-up copies of computer programmes;
- making copies or adaptations of computer programmes.

'Decompilation right allows a lawful user of a copy of computer programme expressed in a low level language to convert it into a version expressed in a higher level language'.[40] Decompilation may be necessary for the purpose of obtaining information to create an independent programme 'which can be operated with the programme decompiled or with another programme'.[41] The 1988 Act permits the making of back-up copies for the purposes of the lawful use of a copy of a computer programme by a lawful user. Section 50A allows a lawful user who has a site licence to make his own copy for his lawful use. The permissible number of back-up copies may be mentioned in the licence agreement.

'Adaptation' means an altered version or translation of a computer programme. Section 50C, in effect, allows a lawful user of a copy of a computer programme to adapt it for lawful purposes. The distinction between a computer-generated work and the works created with the aid of a computer system is difficult to maintain. Section 178 of the Act provides definitions of various terms. The term, 'computer-generated' is defined in the following way:

'Computer-generated in relation to a work, means that the work is generated by computer in circumstances such that there is no human author of the work.'

The distinction is important to determine authorship and the ownership of the copyright in the work.

Indirect authorship seems to have been recognized by courts.[42] In view of the advancement of technology, any type of work can be made available via the Internet. But the problem is that if one decides to place materials on the Internet one intends to place them in the public domain; the risk of their being copied must be assumed. This is where the problem lies. Section 17 of the 1988 Act deals with the issues of infringement of copyright by copying:

'(1) The copying of the work is an act restricted by the copyright in every description of copyright work; and references in this Part to copying and copies shall be construed as follows.

---

[40] Bainbridge, op cit, at 193.
[41] op cit, at 194.
[42] *Express Newspapers plc v Liverpool Daily Post & Echo plc* {1985] 1 W.L.R. 1089.

(2) Copying in relation to a literary, dramatic, musical or artistic work means reproducing the work in any material form. This includes storing the work in any medium by electronic means.

(3) In relation to an artistic work copying includes the making of a copy in three dimensions of a two-dimensional work and the making of a copy in two dimensions of a three-dimensional work.

(4) Copying in relation to a film, television broadcast or cable programme includes making a photograph of the whole or any substantial part of any image forming part of the film, broadcast or cable programme.

(5) Copying in relation to the typographical arrangement of a published edition means making a facsimile copy of the arrangement.

(6) Copying in relation to any description of work includes the making of copies which are transient or are incidental to some other use of the work.'Section 1 of the Official Secrets Act 1989 refers to a number of offences arising from disclosure of confidential information to unauthorized persons. In respect of intellectual properties, it is extremely important to maintain confidentiality unless the subject matters are made public by the legitimate owner. An obligation may arise in contract or may be imposed by equity. Usually, contracts of employment incorporate terms of confidentiality between an employer and an employee. However, an obligation of confidence may be implied in many situations even in the absence of any agreement as to confidentiality. The law of confidence is not concerned with the right to privacy, generally the law of confidence is based on trust between the parties concerned, although confidentiality between two parties (eg an employer and an employee) may also protect privacy. Maintenance of confidentiality is particularly important in respect of industrial property, namely patents, trade marks and designs. In *Saltman Engineering Co Ltd v Campbell Engineering Co Ltd,*[43] Lord Greene, MR described how confidentiality may arise in a particular situation:

'The information, to be confidential, must, I apprehend, apart from the contract, have the necessary quality of confidence about it, namely, it must not be something which is public property and public knowledge. On the other hand, it is perfectly possible to have a confidential document, be it a formula, a plan, a sketch, or something of that kind, which is the result of work done by the maker on materials which may be available for the use of anybody; but what makes it confidential is the fact that the maker of the document has used his brain and thus produced a result which can only be produced by somebody who goes through the same process.'

In *Coco v A. N. Clark (Engineers) Ltd*, Megarry J identified the elements that are required by the law of confidence:

---

[43] [1963] 3 All E.R. 414 at 415.

'First, the information must be of a confidential nature.

...

The second requirement is that the information must have been communicated in circumstances importing an obligation of confidence.

...

Thirdly, there must be an authorised use of information to the detriment of the person communicating it.'[44]

In *Duchess of Argyll v Duke of Argyll*,[45] the Court pointed out the equitable nature of the law of confidence:

' that a breach of confidence or trust or faith can arise independently of any right of property or contract other, of course, than any contract which the imparting of the confidence in the relevant circumstances may itself create: (3) that the court in the exercise of its equitable jurisdiction will restrain a breach of confidence independently of any right at law.'

The law adopts an objective test whether information is confidential in nature or not—simply marking a document 'private and confidential' does not make the contents of the documents confidential, if the information is commonplace or already available in the public domain.[46] In *IBCOS Computers Ltd v Barclays Mercantile Highland Finance Ltd*[47] it was established that trade practice in a particular market or in respect of particular goods may indicate whether a form of information is to be regarded as confidential in nature. Trade secrets are certainly to be treated as confidential information.[48] One of the celebrated cases on this issue is *Faccenda Chicken Ltd v Fowler*. In this case, the Court of Appeal identified the nature of the obligation of an employee in maintaining trade secrets:

'in the absence of express terms, an employee was bound by his implied duty of good faith to his employer not to use or disclose for the duration of his employment confidential information gained in the course of the employment, and was furthermore bound by an implied term of his contract of employment not to use or disclose, either during his employment or thereafter, information which was not merely confidential but which was properly to be described as a trade secret.'[49]

PSM International plc v Whitehouse v Willenhell Automation Ltd established that:

---

[44] (1969) R.P.C. 41.
[45] [1967] Ch. 303 at 322.
[46] See further Bainbridge, op cit, at 242.
[47] op cit.
[48] *Herbert Morris Ltd v Saxelby* [1916] 1 A.C. 688.
[49] [1987] Ch. 117 at 118.

'though the courts should be wary of granting an equitable remedy which would have the effect of interfering with the rights of innocent third parties, there was no doubt that equity had the power to do so in an appropriate case.' [50]

Both *Faccenda Chicken* and *PSM International* are extremely relevant to doing business by electronic means, and when the information may be stored on computers. The consequences of disclosure of information by a person in breach of confidence were identified by the Court in *Terrapin v Builders Supply & Co (Hayes) Ltd.*[51] In the context of the case, the Court held, *inter alia,* that:

'As the works manager knew every stage of the production of the plaintiffs' original design, his mind must have been saturated with every details of its design, features, and methods of construction, which information was derived directly or indirectly from the original confidential communication made by the plaintiffs. When embarking on a new design for the defendants he could not have avoided starting his dive into the future from the spring-board of confidential information acquired by the defendants.'

If information has already been published, the question remains whether the person how owed an allegiance of confidentiality to his employee is still bound by the allegiance, if he did not himself disclose or became instrumental in disclosing the confidential information. In such a situation, use of the information by an employee would amount to a breach of contractual obligation to maintain confidentiality between himself and his employer.[52] Information disclosed in the public interest does not amount to any breach of the obligation of confidence. What is important is how the obligation of confidence arises: whether on the basis of a contract or otherwise (implied) and whether this obligation may extend beyond the termination of the contract, whether of employment or otherwise. Obligation arises for parties in a fiduciary relationship. An employer cannot unjustifiably bind an employee by the obligations of confidence, particularly after the employee has left his employment.[53] However, it is often difficult to draw a clear-cut distinction between the use of his own skill and knowledge by an employee and the use by him of his employer's trade secrets. By the same token, a too rigid covenant in restraint of trade would not be regarded as a valid covenant. On the other hand, the absolute character of the law of confidence was confirmed by Lord Denning, MR in *Fraser v Evans.*[54]

[50] [1992] F.S.R. 489 at 490.
[51] [1967] R.P.C. 375.
[52] See *Roger Bullivant Ltd v Ellis* [1987] F.S.R. 172.
[53] *Herbert Morris Ltd v Saxelby*, op cit.
[54] [1969] 1 Q.B. 349 at 350 and 261.

'although the court will grant an interim injunction to restrain publication of information which is the subject of a duty of confidence, it will do so only at the instance of the party to whom that duty is owed.'[55]

According to Lord Denning:

'The jurisdiction to restrain the publication of confidential information is based not so much on property or contract as on the duty to be of good faith.'[56]

A third party, in certain circumstances, may also be subject to the obligation of confidence, for example, when he may receive confidential information knowing it that it is confidential information, or knowledge of its confidentiality comes to him at a subsequent date. The effective date of knowledge is crucially important.[57] Cases of innocent third parties are different; equity will provide them relief.[58]

In appropriate cases of breach of confidentiality, remedies in contract and in equity may be sought. The criteria for determining damages in breach of confidentiality were provided by the court in *Seager v Copydex (No 2)*.

'that damages should be assessed by a patent judge on the basis of the market value of the information, which would depend on the nature of that information. If the plaintiff succeeded in showing that the information was about a true invention, and that it was of a special nature, he would be entitled to the capitalised value of a royalty, but if the defendants could have obtained the information from any competent consultant then the damages would be the appropriate fee in the circumstances.'[59]

11.4.2.2 Trade marks

In the UK, trade marks are governed by the Trade Marks Act, 1994, which came into force on 31 October 1994. Trade marks are important in business in that the 'marks' by which goods are identified with manufacturers deserve protection. Nobody shall be allowed to imitate a 'mark' used for trading purposes by a manufacturer; thus 'passing-off' is prohibited. Marks are an important form of intellectual property because quality is often associated with them; and consumer confidence in the product(s) develops. The proprietor of a registered trade mark enjoys a property right in the mark. Proprietorship in a trade mark stands for ownership in the mark. Trade marks serve two important purposes: (a) to protect goodwill and business reputation; and (b) protect consumers from

---

[55] op cit, at 349.
[56] op cit, at 350.
[57] *Fraser v Thames TV Ltd* [1984] 1 Q.B. 44.
[58] *Valeo Vision SA v Flexible Lamps Ltd* [1995] R.P.C. 205.
[59] [1969] R.P.C. 250 at 250–251.

being deceived by purchasing goods or products which appear to be the same as the original goods.

Section 1(1) of the Trade Marks Act, 1994 defines a trade mark as being:

'Any sign capable of being represented graphically which is capable of distinguishing goods or services of one undertaking from those of other undertakings.'

Trade marks need to be legally protected and this is achieved by publication and registration—the principal purpose of which is to allow other traders to see whether the new trade mark is very similar or identical to their marks, and if so, they will declare it unregistrable. There is no need to go into the details of the criteria of and procedure for registering a trade mark under the 1994 Act in the context of this work; suffice to say that the criteria set by section 32 must be satisfied for registration. Incidentally, serve marks are no longer treated differently to trade marks. The grounds for refusal may be found in section 3 of the Act. Sections 37–41 of the Act detail the registration procedure.

A registered trade mark is a personal property (in Scotland it is treated as an incorporated moveable property). Under section 24, trade marks may be assigned or passed by testamentary disposition. Joint proprietorship of trade marks is possible.[60]

Users of e-mail/Internet should have protection if the mark is published. They should familiarize themselves with the laws of the jurisdiction in which the mark may be registered and published, and determine who may have access to the mark. According to section 10(1) and (2) of the Act, a trade mark will be infringed if an identical or similar mark is used pertaining to identical or similar goods or services. Section 10(3) of the Act provides that:

'A person infringes a registered trade mark if he uses in the course of trade a sign which—

(a) is identical with or similar to the trade mark, and

(b) is used in relation to goods or services which are not similar to those for which the trade mark is registered, where the trade mark has a reputation in the United Kingdom and the use of the sign, being without due cause, takes unfair advantage of, or is detrimental to, the distinctive character or the repute of the trade mark.'

The following are the defences which are usually available against alleged infringements:

---

[60] ss 23(2) and 23(4) of the Act.

(a) section 38—where the owner by conduct or otherwise has acquiesced[61];
(b) honest similar or comparative advertising—the onus is on the advertiser to establish this point;
(c) honest use of a mark or descriptions—again, the onus is on the defendant[62];
(d) the passing-off was not in the course of trade;
(e) the plaintiff encouraged the defendant's act[63]; and
(f) the defendant's activities have not harmed nor are likely to cause any harm because there is no common field of activity or there is no danger of confusion to be created in the minds of users or members of the public.[64]

Under section 21, injunctive relief may be sought from the Court against unfounded restraints or prohibitions.

A domain name may be registered as a trade mark, and this should be done as soon as possible.[65] *Avnet Inc v Inoact Limited*[66] was concerned with whether a facility provided by a firm to advertise and promote services may amount to infringing trade marks. The Court held that specifications for services should be confined to the substance or core. According to the Court:

'By merely providing a facility to allow its customers to advertise on the customer's own Web page, the defendant was not in substance providing advertising and promotional services.'[67]

Use/abuse of a website or meta-tags (the list of words that describes a website) amounts to an infringements of a trade mark, as both are regarded as intellectual property.

Passing-off
Passing-off is a tort—the goodwill and reputation of a business are protected by passing-off. It is a version of misrepresentation in the law of contract. In passing-off, one trader wishes to take advantage of the established goodwill of another trader. The aim is to capture the business of the other. The essentials of passing-off have been determined differently by the Courts. In *Spalding & Bross v AW Gamage Ltd,*[68] the criteria were: (a) actual misrepresentation; (b) the misrepresentation was calculated to produce damage; and (c) the actual damage has been caused.

---

[61] *Vine Products Ltd v McKenzie & Co Ltd* [1969] R.P.C. 1.
[62] *Wright, Leyman & Umney Ltd v Wright* [1949] 66 R.P.C. 149.
[63] *Habib Bank Ltd v Habib Bank AG Zurich* [1982] R.P.C. 1.
[64] *Wombles Ltd v Wobles Skips Ltd* [1977] R.P.C. 99.
[65] *Prince plc v Prince Sports Group Inc* [1998] F.S.R. 21.
[66] [1998] F.S.R. 16.
[67] op cit, at 17.
[68] (1915) 84 L.J. Ch. 449.

In *Erven Warnink BV and Another v J Townend & Sons (Hull) Ltd and Another*[69] the Court said that:

> 'a trade name of a product can only be protected by a passing off action if it is distinctive of the goods of one particular producer, or a number of identified producers of whom the plaintiff is one, if for some reason the products of that class of producers have a character and reputation peculiar to their products; that the name 'Advocat' was a generic and *publici juris* description of a type of drink which anyone was free to make and that as such anyone was free to use the name; accordingly there was no proprietary right in the name. The plaintiff appealed.'[70]

The House of Lords allowed the appeal and held that:

> 'i) ... what was protected in a passing off action was a proprietary right, that is a right of property in a business or goodwill likely to be injured by a misrepresentation.

> (ii) ... that the characteristics for a valid cause of action in passing off were:

> (A)   per Lord Diplock
> (1)   a misrepresentation (2) made by a trader in the course of his trade (3) to prospective customers of his or ultimate consumers of goods or services supplied by him (4) which is calculated to injure the business or goodwill of another trader (in the sense that it is a reasonably foreseeable consequence) and (5) which causes actual damage to a business or goodwill of a trader by whom the action is brought or (in a *quia timet* action) will probably do so....

> (B)   per Lord Fraser of Tullybelton
> that a plaintiff must show (1) that his business consists of, or includes, selling in England a class of goods to which the particular trade name applies; (2) that the class of goods is clearly defined, and that in the minds of the public, or a section of the public, in England, the trade name distinguishes that class for other similar goods; (3) that because of the reputation of the goods, there is goodwill attached to the name; (4) that he the plaintiff, as a member of the class of those who sell the goods, is the owner of goodwill in England which is of substantial value; (5) that he has suffered, or is really likely to suffer, substantial damage to his property in the goodwill by reason of the defendant selling goods which are falsely described by the trade name to which the goodwill is attached.'[71]

---

[69] [1979] F.S.R. 397.
[70] op cit, at 397–398.
[71] op cit, at 398.

In *Reckitt & Colman Products Ltd v Borden Inc*[72] Lord Oliver identified the essence of the action for passing off. According to his Lordship:

> 'The essence of the action for passing off is a deceit practised on the public and it can be no answer, in a case where it is demonstrable that the public has been or will be deceived, that hey would not have been so deceived if they had been more careful, more literate or more perspicacious. Customers have to be taken as they are found; there is no principle of law that there must always be assumed to be a literate and careful customer.'[73]

The basic requirements for a passing-off action was very cogently stated by Lord Longdale MR in *Perry v Truefitt*: 'a man is not to sell his own goods under the pretence that they are the goods of another trade'.[74] This statement applies equally to e-Commerce. A user is not supposed to copy another person's product, and sell it giving the impression that it belongs to him. In order to succeed in a passing-off action, the following elements must be shown:

(a) that there was a misrepresentation;
(b) that the misrepresentation was made in the course of trade;
(c) that it was reasonably foreseeable that the consequences of misrepresentation would cause injury to the business or goodwill of the traders whose trade mark is misrepresented; and
(d) that the act of passing-off will cause or was likely to cause damage to the business or goodwill of the trader concerned (the future claimant).

An analysis of the above elements proves that passing-off is, generally, a deliberate act, unless the defendant is able to prove it otherwise.

Mere copying the style or name of another trader may not be sufficient for a passing-off action, although an action for breach of copyright may be brought against the person concerned. The plaintiff's goodwill and reputation must be protected. Reputation which is attained or acquired through consistent use over period of time is a crucial factor in protecting a business; and in passing-off actions reputation of the product or of the name (trade mark) is taken seriously, because nobody should by any means exploit somebody's reputation to promote his goods or business. But, goodwill may be acquired over a relatively short period of time, or even before the product or service has been made available provided a significant proportion of the public were made aware of it through publicity.[75] But it would be difficult to support an action in passing-off if reputation is without goodwill.[76] Problems may of course arise where a defendant has some goodwill with the name or mark used by the plaintiff in respect of the

---

[72] [1990] 1 All E.R. 873.
[73] op cit, at 875.
[74] (1842) 49 E.R. 74.
[75] *British Broadcasting Corporation v Talbot Motor Co Ltd* [1981] F.S.R. 228.
[76] *Calvin Klein Inc v International Apparel Syndication* [1995] F.S.R. 228.

same goods or services; such problems are to be decided by referring to facts and circumstances.

Passing-off applies equally to services. Furthermore, trade in the context of passing-off does not have the sole connotation of commercial activity, it can also be associated with professional or non-profit-making associations or organisations[77] because a non-profit-making organisation (a charity) is capable of possessing goodwill, which is different from commercial goodwill.[78] In a passing-off action one is required to establish that misrepresentation caused confusion in the minds of the users, consumers or the public and that misrepresentation is not limited to exact replicas or exact copies; similar replicas or copies sufficient to confuse users, consumers or the minds of the public.[79] In the absence of any confusion there can be no harm to goodwill.[80]

The existence of an intention to capitalize on the goodwill owned by another trader is taken seriously in passing-off actions—innocence is not defence. Where the intention is to withdraw the protection of the goodwill, and represents a calculation to injure[81] goodwill and reputation, the basis for a passing-off action exists.

A passing-off action usually arises when both parties share a common field of activity; metaphorically speaking, passing-off amounts to trespassing in another's intellectual property. This is an important issue in relation to e-Commerce. Only the use of a common or similar name along with a common field of activity may cause confusion.[82] The greater the goodwill, the greater the risk of passing-off. In passing-off cases, damage to the plaintiff's goodwill must be established in seeking monetary damage. The usual remedies in passing-off cases are: injunctive relief (injunctions) or a declaration from the defendant that he will not continue with the act complained of.

11.4.2.3 Patents
The Patents Act 1977 was passed in order to:

> 'establish a new law of patents applicable to future patents and applications for patents; to amend the law of patents applicable to existing patents and applications for patents; to give effect to certain international Conventions on patents; and for connected purposes.'

In order to protect any invention it should be patented. A 'patented product' means 'a product which is a patented invention or, in relation to a patented

---

[77] *British Medical Association v Marsh* (1931) 48 R.P.C. 565.
[78] *The British Diabetic Association v The Diabetic Society* (1992) 31 E.P.R. D-242.
[79] s 10(2) of the Trade Marks Act 1994.
[80] *Tamworth Herald Co Ltd v Thomson Free Newspapers Ltd* (1991) F.R.R. 337.
[81] *Tattinger SA v Allbev Ltd* [1993] F.S.R. 641 at 647.
[82] *Granada Group Ltd v Ford Motor Company Ltd* [1973] R.P.C. 49.

process, a product directly by means of the process or to which the process has been applied.' A 'patented invention' means 'an invention for which a patent is granted' and 'patented process' shall be construed accordingly. A patent may be granted only for an invention that satisfies the following conditions:

'(a) the invention is new;
(b) it involves an inventive step;
(c) it is capable of industrial application;
(d) the grant of a patent for it is not excluded by subsections (2) and (3) below.'[83]

Subsection (2) of section 1 provides, inter alia, that the following are not inventions:

'(a) a discovery, scientific theory or mathematical method;
(b) a literary, dramatic, musical or artistic work or any other aesthetic creation whatsoever;
(c) a rule or method for performing a mental act, playing a game or doing business or a program for a computer;
(d) the presentation of information.'

According to subsection (3) of section 1, a patent shall not be granted:

'(a) for an invention the publication or exploitation of which would be generally expected to encourage offensive, immoral or anti-social behaviour;
(b) for any variety of animal or plant or any essentially biological process for the production of animals or plants, not being a micro-biological process or the product of such a process.'

An invention shall be regarded as new if it does not form part of the state of the art. Subsection (2) of section 2 defines 'the state of the art' in the following way:

'The state of the art in the case of an invention shall be taken to comprise all matter (whether a product, a process, information about either, or anything else) which has at any time before the priority date of that invention been made available to the public (whether in the United Kingdom or elsewhere) by written or oral description, by use or in any other way.'

An invention shall be taken to entail an inventive step if it is not obvious to a person skilled in the art.[84] It must be novel in that it has not already been available to the public. In respect of patents, priority dates assume importance. On the date on which an application is made, it is judged whether it would be eligible for receiving a patent. The date on which this decision is taken, is known

[83] s 1.
[84] s 3.'

as the 'priority date'. In order to protect one's invention one should try to obtain a 'priority date' with a view to ensuring that nobody else with the same or similar invention is allocated a 'priority date'.

A patent is a form of personal property that may be assigned, licensed or charged by way of mortgage. Patenting an invention also helps the wider public to learn about the invention to enrich their knowledge. The property right in the invention is owned by the inventor. On the other hand, as stated earlier, patenting an invention is the most effective way of protecting it. But, of course, the invention will be available to the public after the expiry of patent.[85] Even if the invention relates to a process, protection should be sought by patenting it. If, on the other hand, an invention relates to a product rather than a process, some aspects of it may be registered, but the other aspects, shape of the product etc may be registered as a design. The copyright in drawings and descriptions will be intact. It is to be re-emphasized that whereas copyright protects the expression of an idea, a patent protects the ideas encapsulated in the invention from exploitation by unauthorized persons.

The owner of a patent (the proprietor) may have a tendency to demand a high price for a patented invention because of the funds and research he has put in and/or the marketing efforts made by him; thus he may also try to establish a monopoly. In *Chiron Corporation v Oreganon Tehnika Ltd (No 10),*[86] it was decided that it is in the public interest that patent monopolies are enforced. Additionally, patent law itself contains a safeguard in the form of compulsory licensing and Crown use.

Under the European Patent Convention or the Patent Co-operative Treaty, an application may be made for a UK patent, or for a European patent indicating in which of the states of the Convention and the Treaty the effect of the patented invention would be valid. It is possible however to make an application to the European Patent Office with the permission of the UK Patent Office.[87]

Old inventions are patentable if they are directed to a new use. Section 2, paragraph 6 of the Act provides that:

'In the case of an invention consisting of a substance or composition for use in a method of treatment of the human or animal body by surgery or therapy or of diagnosis practised on the human or animal body, the fact that the substance or composition forms part of the state of the art shall not prevent the invention from being taken to be new if the use of the substance or composition in any such method does not form part of the state of the art.'

---

[85] A patent subsists for a maximum of 20 years; pharmaceutical patents can be renewed up to a maximum period of 25 years.
[86] [1995] F.S.R. 325 at 333.
[87] s 23 of the Patents Act 1977.

It is to be born in mind that the Patents Act 1977 gave effect to the European Convention of 1973. Article 52(1) of that Convention provides that:

'European patents shall be granted for any new inventions which are susceptible of industrial application, which are new and which involve an inventive step.'

Returning to the British patent system, an inventor must take every precautionary measure to ensure that his invention is not disclosed to anybody—he should consider whether it would be safe to give any demonstration of his invention in private emphasising the need for its confidentiality because if the confidentiality is not maintained, the sanctity of the principle of novelty may not be maintained.[88] 'Novelty' is an important factor to satisfy in seeking a patent for an invention. If any member of the public discloses the invention without authorization, he/she can be sued in breach of confidentiality. Demonstrations of inventions in public, irrespective of whether anybody has seen them, amounts to publicity, and defeats the criterion of novelty.[89] Publication of an invention in a journal, academic or scientific or otherwise, destroys the requirement of novelty.

Old inventions may be patentable if they are meant for new uses, and sufficiently different from the old ones. It must be another inventive step (s 3), that is, when the step is not obvious to a person skilled in the art. A 'skilled worker' test is to be adopted to consider whether an invention involves an inventive step. Whether the invention is obvious is a question of fact. If an invention fulfils a 'long-felt want', non-obviousness may be evidenced[90]. However, commercial success may not be equated to 'obviousness'. An invention may be highly successful but not successful commercially, because consumers would not prefer to buy it. Therefore, commercial success may not be a measure of non-obviousness.[91] It may be difficult sometimes to draw a distinction between an old invention and a new inventive step. A slight alteration might produce a radically significant improvement upon the old invention, and may be regarded as an evidence of intellectual ingenuity.[92]

The test of obviousness was clarified first by Oliver LJ in *Windsurfing International Inc v Tabur Marine (Great Britain) Ltd,*[93] and this was confirmed by the court in *PLG Research Ltd v Arden International Ltd.*[94] The following is the test of obviousness:

'The public should not be prevented from doing anything which was merely an obvious extension of what was known at the priority date.

---

[88] *Pall Corp v Commercial Hydraulics (Bedford) Ltd* [1990] F.S.R. 329.
[89] *Lux Traffic Controls Ltd v Pike Signals Ltd* [1993] R.P.C. 107.
[90] D Bainbridge, op cit, at 301.
[91] *Mölnlycke AB v Proctor & Gamble Ltd (No 3)* [1990] R.P.C. 498.
[92] *Williams v Nye* (1890) 7 R.P.C. 62.
[93] [1985] R.P.C. 59.
[94] [1995] F.S.R. 116.

Therefore, the skilled man must be considered as sufficiently interested in each piece of prior art to consider its practical application. However, it should not be assumed that the significance of the prior art to the problem dealt with by the patent would necessarily be apparent to the skilled man. There is a danger of assessing obviousness in the light of prior art selected with the benefit of hindsight out of a range of equally plausible starting points; selection of the correct starting point for the solution of the problem may not be obvious.'[95]

Computer programmes are not generally patentable per se, because they do not stand for any 'manufacture' nor do they represent any machinery or industrial process.

Controversy as to whether computer programmes should be patentable or not still persists.[96] In fact, the proponents suggest that computer programmes deserve the protection of the law of patent. The controversy seems to centre around one idea – that is, whether one takes into account the nature of the operation of a programme or the mode of storage. In recent years, the English Courts rendered two decisions on this issue. In *Gevers' Application*,[97] the Court said that:

'That the proposed claim to a punched card having holes in it embodying information according to the claimed rules of transcription could also be properly claimed as a manner of manufacture. Such a card was analogous to a can for controlling the cutting path of a lathe or a new type of carburettor which was an accessory to a motor car for which its was intended. It differed from a card which was merely printed and which was intended to convey information to the human eye or mind but which was not intended to be ancillary to some machine by being specially shaped or constructed for that purpose.'[98]

In *Re Gale's Patent Application*,[99] the Court gave its judgment on whether instructions to be used in a computer were patentable. According to the Court:

'Instructions to be used in a computer were not patentable. Such instructions had to be recorded in a physical form which a computer could understand, typically a disc or ROM, which was no more than an established type of artefact in which the instructions were embedded. If the disc or ROM, considered as a disc or ROM, was in all respects conventional, a claim could not be made for the disc or ROM incorporating those instructions.

---

[95] op cit, at 117–118.
[96] See D Bender, 'Computer Programs: Should they be Patentable?' 68 *Columbia Law Review* (1968) 241
[97] [1970] R.P.C. 91.
[98] op cit, at 92.
[99] [1991] R.P.C. 305.

Physical differences resulting from recording instructions on a conventional disc or storing them in a ROM using conventional methods were not material, because they constituted no more than the use of the disc or ROM for its intended purpose.'[100]

Re Merril Lynch, Pierce Fenner & Smith Inc's Application[101] was concerned with patenting an invention related to an improved data processing system. The Principal Examiner of the Patent Office rejected the application on the grounds that it fell under the exceptions of section 1(2) of the Patents Act in that it did not entail any inventive step or technical effect—the operation was entirely software-based.

The European Patent Office seems to have adopted a different approach. In *Vicom Systems Inc's Patent Application,*[102] the invention related to digital image processing, the process steps of which were expressed mathematically. The application was allowed after the technical effect was amended. Thus, according to the European Patent Office, the technical effect produced by a computer programme is patentable. In *Genentech Inc's Patent*[103] the Patents Court held that the broad product claims were invalid; but the Court of Appeal held, *inter alia*, that:

'The Patents Act 1977 must be construed primarily in the context of the European Patent Convention. The authority and usage of previous patent law should be approached with caution and not applied without reserve. The Act had displaced any residual element of common law in the application for and grant of a patent, the protection of the monopoly against infringement, and the revocation of a patent.'[104]

But, in *Re The Computer Generation of Chinese Characters*[105] which was also concerned with the issue that the method claimed for the storing, processing, displaying and/or printing of Chinese characters was not of a secretive nature and was merely a method of performing usual acts. The Bundesgerichtshof held that:

'The subject-matter for which patent protection was sought had to solve a technical problem by a technical method or make a technical contribution to the state of the art. This program did neither. The organisational system set out in this application was intellectual in nature and did not use any means going beyond the use of human intellectual activity. It did not concern the functioning capacity of the computer as such, since it did not consist in enabling its elements to work together directly.'[106]

[100]   op cit, at 306.
[101]   [1998] R.P.C. 1.
[102]   [1987] 2 E.P.O.R. 74.
[103]   [1989] R.P.C. 147.
[104]   op cit, at 150.
[105]   [1993] F.S.R. 315.
[106]   op cit, at 316.

A patent is a form of personal property,[107] and it may be assigned or mortgaged. It may also be dealt with by way of licensing. If a proprietor of a patent dies, the patent vests in the proprietor's personal representatives.

Section 1(2)(c) states that a 'programme for a computer' is not an invention; thus, apparently, such programmes are not patentable. This is a point of controversy. There is a distinction between 'a programme for a computer' and 'a programme generated on a computer' which is based on inventive ideas. It is not clear why the latter may not be patented, indeed, if they are not patented, others may use them in breach of copyright. The next question that arises is whether computer programmes, which are to be regarded as inventions, may be capable of industrial application (s 4). Computer programmes are often used in industry.

- Section 60 of the Patents Act 1977 deals with infringements. A person infringes a patent if, while it is in force, he without the consent of the proprietor of the patent:
- where the invention is a product, makes, disposes of, offers or disposes of, uses or imports the product;
- where the invention is a process, he uses the process or offers it for use in the UK, knowing, or it is obvious to a reasonable person, that its use, without the consent of the proprietor, would be an infringement of the patent; and
- where the invention is a process, he disposes of , uses or imports any product 'obtained directly by means of that process or keeps any such product whether for disposal or otherwise'.

Patents are specification-based; thus a breach of a specification may amount to infringement; in fact, in cases of infringements, courts look into specifications.[108] An inventor should, therefore, ensure that he does not omit anything in his specifications, and/or his claim is not made too narrowly. In a patent infringement action, the burden of proof of infringement is on the claimant.

Where a patent is granted to two or more persons, each of them shall, unless there is any agreement to the contrary, have equal share and right.[109] Thus, in the case of a patent having joint ownership, an infringement action will have to be instituted with the consent of each proprietor. The holder of an exclusive licence under a patent shall have 'the same right as the proprietor of the patent to bring proceedings in respect of any infringement of the patent committed after the date of the licence'.[110]

Various defences against an allegation of infringement are available under the Patents Act. A defendant may question the validity of a patent in issue by way of a defence in proceedings for infringement of the patent under:

---

[107] See s 30 of the Patents Act 1977.
[108] See s 125(1) of the Patents Act 1977.
[109] s 36(1).
[110] s 67(1) of the Patents Act 1977.

(a)   section 61[111];
(b)   section 69[112];
(c)   section 70[113];
(d)   section 71[114];
(e)   section 72[115]; and section 58.[116]

Other defences to an infringement action may be found in section 60(5) of the Patents Act, 1977, which provides that:

'An act which, apart from this subsection, would constitute an infringement of a patent for an invention shall not do so if—
   (a)   it is done privately and for purposes which are not commercial;
   (b)   it is done for experimental purposes relating to the subject-matter of the invention;
   (c)   it consists of the extemporaneous preparation in a pharmacy of a medicine for an individual in accordance with a prescription given by a registered medical or dental practitioner or consists of dealing with a medicine so prepared;
   (d)   it consists of the use, exclusively for the needs of a relevant ship, of a product or process in the body of such a ship or in its machinery, tackle, apparatus or other accessories, in a case where the ship has temporarily or accidentally entered the internal or territorial waters of the United Kingdom;
   (e)   it consists of the use of a product or process in the body or operation of a relevant aircraft, hovercraft or vehicle which has temporarily or accidentally entered or is crossing the United Kingdom (including the air space above it and its territorial waters) or the use of accessories for such a relevant aircraft, hovercraft or vehicle;
   (f)   it consists of the use of an exempted aircraft which has lawfully entered or is lawfully crossing the United Kingdom as aforesaid or of the importation into the United Kingdom, or the use or storage there, of any part or accessory for such an aircraft.'

Furthermore, where a person in the UK, before the priority date of the invention, does in good faith an act or a serious preparation to do such an act, which would constitute an infringement of the patent if it were in force, but for it not being in force, it shall not amount to an infringement of the patent concerned.[117] Defence is also available under section 44(3) of the Act, which provides that:

---

[111] Proceedings for Infringement of Patents.
[112] Infringement of Rights conferred by Publication of Application.
[113] Remedy for Groundless Threats of Infringement Proceedings.
[114] Declaration of Declarator as to Non-infringement.
[115] Revocation of Patents.
[116] References to Dispute as to Crown Use.
[117] s 64.

'In proceedings against any person for infringement of a patent it shall be a defence to prove at the time of the infringement there was in force a contract relating to the patent made by or with the consent of the plaintiff or pursuer or a licence under the patent granted by him or with his consent and containing in either case a condition or term void by virtue of this Section.'

Section 62(1) also provides that:

'no order shall be made for an account of profits, against a defendant or a defender who proves that at the date of the infringement he was not aware and had no reasonable grounds for suppressing that the patent existed.'

There is a defence when a claimant's rights have been exhausted under the Community Patents Convention. Section 60(4) of the Patents Act 1977 states that:

The provisions of infringement under section 60 shall not apply

'to any act which, under any provision of the Community Patent Convention relating to the exhaustion of the rights of the proprietor of a patent, as that provision applies by virtue of that section, cannot be prevented by the proprietor of the patent.'

Defence may be available if the product or process lacks novelty or an inventive step. The usual remedies available for infringement of a patent have been detailed in section 61 of the Patents Act:

(a)   an injunction or interdict restraining the defendant from any apprehended act of infringement;
(b)   an order for the defendant to deliver up or destroy any patented product in relation to which the patent is infringed;
(c)   damages;
(d)   an account of profits derived by him from the infringement; and
(e)   a declaration by the defendant that a valid patent has been infringed by him.

But a claimant cannot claim in respect of the same infringement damages in addition to an order whereby he shall be given an account of the profits.

It is always possible for a defendant to challenge an application for an injunction, but one is required to be familiar with the judicial guidelines developed by the courts in *Chiron Corporation v Organon Teknika Ltd (No 10)*[118] and *Shelfer v City of London Electric Lighting Co.*[119] Courts usually consider whether the injury to the plaintiff's right would be small, and whether redress may be

---

[118]   [1995] F.S.R. 270.
[119]   (1895) 1 Ch. 287.

allowed at small money payment, and furthermore, whether it would be appropriate for a defendant to grant an injunction against him.

Before ending this section, perhaps a brief account should be given of the European Patent Convention.[120] All Members of the European Union belong to this Convention.[121] The Community patent system is administered by the European Patent Office. National courts may refer questions of community law, including patent law to the European Court of Justice for a preliminary ruling.[122] The manner in which a patent is being exploited may run counter to the provisions of the Competition Policy of the EU.

These issues will be considered by reference to the Competition Act, and the Competition Policy of the EU. The purpose of the European Convention is not to provide a unitary community patent system, but to offer a good and workable framework of a European Patent system. The national patents will not be replaced by a community patent. Should however a proprietor wish to obtain protection of its patent throughout the Union, it has the option to do so. The Patents Act 1977 takes account of the European Patent Convention, and give direct effect to the Convention.

11.4.2.4 Designs
Designs and matters concerned with designs, are governed by the Registered Designs Act 1949, as amended by the Copyright, Designs and Patents Act 1988. This is because there are two forms of design: one is registered design governed by the 1949 Act, and the other is the design right provided for the 1988 Act, Part III.

Under the Registered Designs Act, a 'design' means:

> 'features of shape, configuration, pattern or ornament applied to an article by any industrial process, being features which in the finished article appeal to and are judged by the eye, but does not include-
>   (a)   a method or principle of construction, or
>   (b)   features of shape or configuration of an article which-
>   (i)   are dictated solely by the function which the article has to perform, or
>   (ii) are dependent upon the appearance of another article of which the article is intended by the author of the design to form an integral part.'[123]

Section 213(2) of the 1988 Act defines a 'design' as:

---

[120] Convention on the Grant of European Patents (European Patent Convention) 5 October 1973
[121] Liechtenstein and Switzerland are also parties to this Convention.
[122] *Chiron Corp v Murex Diagnostics Ltd (No 8)* [1995] F.S.R. 309.
[123] s 1(1).

'the design of any aspect of the shape or configuration (whether internal or external) of the whole or part of an article.'

Under the 1949 Act, a design in order to be registrable must be 'new' and must have an 'eye appeal'. Whereas a registered design applies to aesthetic articles, a design right primarily applies to functional designs. A registered design is different from artistic works of copyright. However, it is often difficult to maintain a clear-cut distinction between 'artistic' works and 'aesthetic' articles. A registered design may at the same time become aesthetic and yet functional. It is to be noted however that the 1949 Act does not consider 'aesthetic' as a crucially important criterion for a design to be registered. Many functional articles may have eye-appeal. But, generally speaking, articles of a functional nature come under the purview of the design right. The problem is: whereas a functional object cannot be registered as a design, many registered designs may satisfy the requirements of a design right. The Copyright, Designs and Patents Act 1988 recognizes the existence of these rights. Section 224 provides that:

'Where a design consisting of a design in which design right subsists is registered under the [1949 c. 88.] Registered Designs Act 1949 and the proprietor of the registered design is also the design right owner, an assignment of the right in the registered design shall be taken to be also an assignment of the design right, unless a contrary intention appears.'

A design may be patentable if it satisfies the criteria of being patented: novelty, an inventive step, and industrial application. Incidentally, the creator of a registered design is known as its author. Any aspect of a shape or configuration of an article may have a design right, if it is original, and in some tangible form. A design may overlap with copyright works in certain cases, for example, when a design is incorporated/recorded in a document in which copyright subsists. Computer data will come under this category. In this connection one should refer to section 51(1) and section 236 of the Copyright, Designs and Patents Act 1988:

Section 51(1):

'It is not an infringement of any copyright in a design document or model recording or embodying a design for anything other than an artistic work or a typeface to make an article to the design or to copy an article made to the design.'

Section 236:

'Where copyright subsists in a work which consists of or includes a design in which design right subsists, it is not an infringement of design right in the design to do anything which is an infringement of the copyright in that work.'

A design recorded as computer data, and copied by somebody without permission may give rise to various legal issues: if that person after copying data on a magnetic tape prints out the data and uses them in the form of articles then he infringes both copyright and design right.

Section 213(1) deals with subsistence of right:

'Design right is a property right which subsists in accordance with this Part in an original design.'

Section 213(3) provides for exceptions to the subsistence right:

'Design right does not subsist in—
    (a)   a method or principle of construction,
    (b)   features of shape or configuration of an article which—
        (i)   enable the article to be connected to, or placed in, around or against, another article so that either article may perform its function, or
        (ii)   are dependent upon the appearance of another article of which the article is intended by the designer to form an integral part, or
    (c)   surface decoration.'

Section 213(4) which deals with the issue of 'originality' provides that:

'A design is not 'original' for the purposes of this Part if it is commonplace in the design field in question at the time of its creation.'

According to section 213(6), a design right 'does not subsist unless and until the design has been recorded in a design document or an article has been made to the design'. 'Design document' has been defined by section 263(1) of the Act: A 'design document' means 'any record of a design, whether in the form of a drawing, a written description, a photograph, data stored in a computer or otherwise'.

Section 217(1) defines 'qualifying individuals' and 'qualifying persons'. A 'qualifying individual' means 'a citizen or subject of, or an individual habitually resident in a qualifying country'; and a 'qualifying person' means a 'qualifying individual or a body corporate or other body having legal personality which- (a) is formed under the law of a part of the UK or another qualifying country, and (b) has in any qualifying country a place of business at which substantial business activity is carried on'.

The duration of a design right is determined by referring to the end of the year in which the design was either recorded in a design document or an article was created to the design. A design right subsists for 15 years from the end of its creation year. But, section 216(1)(b) provides that:

'if articles made to the design are made available for sale or hire within five years from the end of that calendar year, ten years from the end of the calendar year in which that first occurred.'

Section 215 of the Act deals with the ownership of design right:

'(1)   The designer is the first owner of any design right in a design which is not created in pursuance of a commission or in the course of employment.

(2)   Where a design is created in pursuance of a commission, the person commissioning the design is the first owner of any design right in it.

(3)   Where, in a case not falling within subsection (2) a design is created by an employee in the course of his employment, his employer is the first owner of any design right in the design.

(4)   If a design qualifies for design right protection by virtue of section 220 (qualification by reference to first marketing of articles made to the design), the above rules do not apply and the person by whom the articles in question are marketed is the first owner of the design right.'

Design rights may be assigned only in writing, whether the assignment is partial or otherwise, but assignments must be limited to the duration of the design right. Licensing of design rights is also possible. Section 225 of the Act provides that a licence must be in writing and signed by or on behalf of the owner of the design right.

Section 226 refers to the rights of a design owner and infringements:

'(1)   The owner of design right in a design has the exclusive right to reproduce the design for commercial purposes—
    (a)   by making articles to that design, or
    (b)   by making a design document recording the design for the purpose of enabling such articles to be made.

(2)   Reproduction of a design by making articles to the design means copying the design so as to produce articles exactly or substantially to that design, and references in this Part to making articles to a design shall be construed accordingly.

(3)   Design right is infringed by a person who without the licence of the design right owner does, or authorises another to do, anything which by virtue of this section is the exclusive right of the design right owner.

(4)   For the purposes of this section reproduction may be direct or indirect, and it is immaterial whether any intervening acts themselves infringe the design right.

(5)   This section has effect subject to the provisions of Chapter III (exceptions to rights of design right owner).'

Any act done in relation to a design without the permission of the owner of the design right amounts to a primary infringement. Litigation concerning infringements of design rights is not common. In determining an infringement, an objective test is applied; it is often difficult to confirm that another object has been made which is substantially similar to another design.[124]

Secondary infringements

'1)   Design right is infringed by a person who, without the licence of the design right owner—
     (a)   imports into the United Kingdom for commercial purposes, or
     (b)   has in his possession for commercial purposes, or
     (c)   sells, lets for hire, or offers or exposes for sale or hire, in the course of a business, an article which is, and which he knows or has reason to believe is, an infringing article.
(2)   This section has effect subject to the provisions of Chapter III (exceptions to rights of design right owner).'[125]

The following remedies may be made available to a party who has been a victim of infringements:

(1)   'An infringement of design right is actionable by the design right owner.
(2)   In an action for infringement of design right all such relief by way of damages, injunctions, accounts or otherwise is available to the plaintiff as is available in respect of the infringement of any other property right.
(3)   The court may in an action for infringement of design right, having regard to all the circumstances and in particular to—
     (a)   the flagrancy of the infringement, and
     (b)   any benefit accruing to the defendant by reason of the infringement,
     award such additional damages as the justice of the case may require
(4)   This section has effect subject to section 233 (innocent infringement).'[126]

11.5   Conclusions

It is to be emphasized that this chapter merely outlines the basic elements of copyright, trademarks and designs, and has attempted to relate them to computers and e-Commerce, where appropriate. It is not possible to explain exhaustively the legal issues pertaining to copyright, trademarks and designs in one chapter.

---

[124] *C & H Engineering v F Klucznik & Sons Ltd* [1952] F.S.R. 421.
[125] s 227.
[126] s 229.

As explained in this chapter, certain aspects of the law of copyright, trademarks and designs are relevant to e-Commerce. If in the course of doing business through e-Commerce, novelty and inventive steps in a programme become manifest, there should not be any reason why the relevant provisions of the copyright law should not be applied to protect it. If a product is sold through electronic means the trademark and design of the product should also be protected.

One of the means of protecting intellectual property rights is to ensure that the buyer's country has effective legislation against abuse of these rights; a clause for the protection of these rights should be included in the relevant contract, although it may not be a foolproof guarantee that these rights might be protected by the other party. In other words, instead of accusing a buyer, initially, of the breach of any intellectual property rights, one should see whether a buyer may take advantage of the rather lenient legislation in his/her country.

Finally, it should be pointed out that the copyright position of computer programmes is still uncertain in law. If advancement in science imports novelty and inventive steps in computer programmes, the current copyright law may be required to be reviewed.

12. Electronic commerce and some general tax issues[1a]

12.1 Introduction

As the title of this chapter suggests, only certain general tax issues relating to e-Commerce have been identified and discussed—the aim is not to provide a comprehensive account of all tax issues. This chapter has been developed in three parts: (1) a discussion of the OECD Technical Advisory Group (TAG) on Treaty Characterisation of Electronic Commerce Payments; (2) an analysis of the UK's Taxation Agenda, study developed by the Inland Revenue; and (3) a general discussion of the impact of e-Commerce on corporation tax and VAT.

12.2 The OECD technical advisory group (TAG) on treaty characterisation of electronic commerce payments[1]

In January 1999, the OECD Committee on Fiscal Affairs set up the Technical Advisory Group (TAG) on Treaty Characterisation Issues arising from e-Commerce. Its mandate was 'to examine the characterisation of various types of electronic commerce payments under tax Conventions with a view to providing the necessary clarifications in the commentary'. During its work, TAG examined those of the characterisation issues which would relate to alternative treaty provisions which were not found in the Model Tax Convention.

This was based on the assumption that all payments made in connection with standard e-Commerce transactions were received in the course of carrying on a business, irrespective of whether the payers were themselves carrying on business. All these payments would fall within Article 7 of the OECD Model Tax Convention, which deals with business profits.

[1a] This chapter provides an overview. For a detailed analysis the reader should see '*E-Commerce: Law, Business and Tax Planning*' J.B. Hickey, R. Mathew, C. Rose (Jordans, 1999, ISBN 0-85308-562-5).
[1] On February 2001, the OECD published its report entitled 'Tax Treaty Characterisation Issues arising from E-Commerce'. In view of the technical nature of the report, often words and statements used by it have been reproduced, without any intention to breach the copyright of the originators of the report.

According to TAG, one of the most important characterisation issues arising from e-Commerce was the distinction between 'business profits' and the part of the treaty definition of 'royalties', which 'deals with payments for the use of, or the right to use, a copyright'.[2]

As a number of issues are involved in the definition of 'royalties', TAG concluded that in any transaction the principal issue to be addressed would be 'the identification of the consideration for the payment'.[3] In certain jurisdictions downloading of computer programmes or other digital contents may amount to abuse of copyright by the customer; but where the essential consideration is for something other than the use of, or right to use, the rights in copyright and the use of copyright is limited to downloading, storage and operation on the customer's computer, performance or display device, 'such use of copyright should be disregarded in the analysis of the character of the payment for treaty purposes'.[4] The report further stated that:

> 'Whilst electronic downloading of the program may or may not constitute the use of a copyright by the user (as opposed to by the provider) depending on the relevant copyright law and contractual arrangements, the essential consideration for the payment is not the possible use of a copyright.'[5]

Where a transaction permits the customer to electronically download software and images etc (digital products), the payment is made in the form of a digital signal, and this constitutes the essential consideration for the payment. Based on the issues identified above, TAG suggested that changes be made to the commentary on Article 12 of the OECD Model Tax Convention.[6]

The OECD Report also dealt with the issue that in respect of certain transactions, it would be necessary to determine whether the consideration for a payment is the provision of services or the provision of know-how. The TAG identified the special characteristics and elements in a know-how contract:

- 'In the know-how contract, one of the parties agrees to impart to the other, so that he can use them for his own account, his special knowledge and experience which remain unrevealed to the public;
- in the know-how contract the grantor is not required to play any part himself in the application of the formula ... and ... does not guarantee the results thereof;
- the provision of know-how must be distinguished from the provision of services, in which one of the parties undertakes to use the customary skills of his calling to execute work himself for the other party.'[7]

---

[2] op cit, at 5.
[3] ibid.
[4] ibid.
[5] ibid.
[6] The suggested changes appear at paras 17.1–17.4 at p 6.
[7] op cit, at 7.

According to TAG, on-line advice, or communications with technicians would involve actual services being performed on demand rather than the provision of know-how.[8] TAG recognised that the distinction between 'payments for services rendered and payments for the supply of know-how may sometimes raise practical difficulties'.[9]

The report identified the following types of payment that should not be received as consideration for the provision of know-how:

- 'payments obtained as consideration for after-sales service;
- payments for services rendered by a seller to the purchaser under a guarantee;
- payments for pure technical assistance;
- payments for an opinion given by an engineer, an advocate or an accountant; and
- payments for advice provided electronically, for electronic communications with technicians or for accessing, through computer networks, a trouble-shooting database.'[10]

As regards business profits and payments for the use of or the right to use, industrial, commercial or scientific equipment, TAG agreed that payment for such use of digital products could not be considered as payments 'for the use of, or the right to use industrial, commercial or scientific equipment for the following reasons:

- that digital products cannot be considered as 'equipment' either because the word 'equipment' can only apply to a tangible product or in the context of the definition of royalties, the word 'equipment' does not apply to property, such as music or video or CD;
- that such products cannot be viewed as industrial, commercial or scientific when provided to the private consumer; products such as games, music or videos cannot be considered as 'industrial, commercial or scientific;' or
- that payments involved for use of digital products cannot be considered to be 'for the use, or the right to use' the product since these words do not apply to a payment made for the purpose of acquiring a property designed to have short useful life.'[11]

According to TAG, the basic distinction between a transaction resulting in the acquisition of property and a transaction in services lies in whether the consideration for the payment is the acquisition of property from the provider. In this context, a transaction which would result in the acquisition of property would include a transaction where a digital product is acquired by a customer, be it in the form of a tangible medium or in the form of a digital signal. According to

[8]   ibid.
[9]   ibid.
[10]   op cit, at 11.
[11]   op cit, at 12.

TAG, in the event of a customer owning the relevant property after the transaction (even though the property was not acquired from the provider) the transaction should be treated as a services transaction.

TAG recognised that when one party may be acquiring property from another party, the transaction may be characterised as a services transaction in that the primary nature of the transaction is the provision of services, and the acquisition of property is merely ancillary.[12]

On-line consulting is an example of an e-Commerce transaction which results in services income. In these types of transaction, the customer usually does not acquire any form of property from the other party.

TAG also discussed how various e-Commerce payments would be treated under alternative treaty provisions which allow source taxation of 'technical fees', which means 'payments of any kind to any person, other than to the employee of the person making payments in consideration for any service of a technical, managerial or consultancy nature'.[13]

TAG maintained that services would be regarded as of technical nature when special skills or knowledge would be employed; whilst techniques related to applied science or craftmanship would generally correspond to special skills or knowledge, the provision of knowledge acquired in the fields of arts or human resources would not. The use of technology in providing a service does not necessarily make a service of a technical nature; by the same token, the delivery of a service via technological means does not make the service technical. According to TAG, 'the technology underlying the Internet is often used to provide services that are not, themselves, technical'.[14]

The purpose of using special skills and knowledge is important. The fee for the provision of a service would not be regarded as a technical fee, unless that special skill or knowledge is required when the service is provided to the customer, for example, in the form of developing software and data used in a computer game which would subsequently be allowed to be used by consumers to play on the Internet for a fee.[15] The making of data and software available for a fee is not a service of a technical nature, and the service provided to a client may not be regarded as the development of that data and software.

Although TAG did not provide any definition of 'management', it considered that services of a managerial nature are services rendered in performing management functions.[16] Management is about running a business, and not about

---

[12] op cit, at 13.
[13] op cit, at 14.
[14] ibid.
[15] ibid.
[16] op cit, at 15.

performing functions involved in carrying on that business. Services provided to clients do not amount to managing their businesses; but make the software and data available to clients. According to TAG, any payment relating to the provision of access would not relate to a service of a managerial nature.[17]

As regards consultancy services, TAG recognised that this type of services 'overlapped the categories of technical and managerial services to the extent that ... [these] services could well be provided by a consultant'.[18]

TAG identified a number of e-Commerce transactions in regard to which the consideration of the payment would cover various elements (mixed payments) (eg software maintenance transactions). Some members of TAG took the view that 'in most e-Commerce transactions, the treaty classification applicable to the predominant element of the payment involved should be applied to the whole of that payment'[19] as 'an obligation to break down the payment involved would impose an unreasonable compliance burden on taxpayers, especially for consumer transactions that involve relatively small amounts of money'.[20]

TAG also suggested that certain changes be made to the commentary on Article 12 of the OECD Model Tax Convention.

12.3   Electronic commerce: the UK's taxation agenda

12.3.1 Introduction
In 1999, the Inland Revenue developed a study entitled 'Electronic Commerce: The UK's Taxation Agenda' in which it was stated, *inter alia*, that:

> 'The Government is committed to making sure that taxation is not a barrier to the growth of e-Commerce, but rather fosters a climate in which e-Commerce can grow. A package of measures has been introduced, and more are proposed, which demonstrates the strength of this commitment and ensures that enterprise, growth and investment are encouraged in the UK. These play a vital part in working towards the Government's goal.'[21]

In this study, the government recognised that international consensus was needed to give business certainty and avoid double taxation and unintentional non-taxation.[22] According to this study, the Inland Revenue and HM Customs

---

[17] ibid.
[18] ibid.
[19] op cit, at 16.
[20] ibid.
[21] HM Treasury Release 173/99 and 175/99, at p 7. It is to be pointed out that in writing this section of the work, the government paper entitled 'Electronic Commerce' has been closely followed in order to ensure that the policies and ideas of the government are not distorted. There is no intention, express or implicit, to breach the copyright of the originators of the publication.
[22] ibid.

and Excise would introduce Internet filling of customers' returns, in addition to developing a pilot partnership represented by Business in government the aim of which is to provide a 'one-stop-shop' for people setting up in business. The government further recognised however that e-Commerce poses risks to tax administration and compliance. The policy of the government is to ensure that the use of developing technology will make it easier for taxpayers to comply with their tax obligations; and that encouraging and assisting taxpayers is the most effective way of maximising voluntary compliance.[23]

The government appreciated that without multilateral action an effective application of the tax rules to international e-Commerce would not be possible. The government has been working with its international partners to provide clarification in a number of areas, in particular, to agree a clear definition for place of consumption—a key concept in the operation of VAT and to clarify the interpretation of the 'permanent establishment', another important concept in the operation of VAT.

The study entitled 'Electronic Commerce' stated that the challenge for the Inland Revenue and Customs is threefold:

- to provide confidence to those involved in e-Commerce that the tax rules are clear and fair;
- to contribute to a climate which would help e-Commerce to flourish in the UK;
- to utilise the tools and techniques of e-Commerce in order to improve the service the government offers its customers, both businesses and individuals.[24]

According to the study, taxation must not be a barrier to the growth of e-Commerce and other commercial benefits.[25] In order to achieve its aims, the government actively participates in the work programmes of the OECD and the European Union.

12.3.2   An analysis of the white paper entitled 'modernising government'

The study which is also known as the White Paper entitled 'Modernising Government', has been developed in eight chapters:

Chapter 1	Encouraging the growth of e-Commerce
Chapter 2	Shaping the Future
Chapter 3	The International Scene
Chapter 4	Harnessing the Technology: Modernising Tax Administration

---

[23] op cit, at 8.
[24] op cit, at 11.
[25] ibid.

There does not exist any internationally accepted definition of e-Commerce, but the Department of Trade and Industry proposed the following definition to the OECD:

> 'using an electronic network to simplify and speed up all stages of the business process, from design and making to buying, selling and delivery; e-Commerce is the exchange of information across electronic networks, at any stage in the supply chain, whether within an organisation, between businesses, between businesses and customers, or between the public and private sectors, whether paid or unpaid.'[26]

Growth of e-Commerce in the UK, particularly since 1998, has been rising consistently, and the White Paper predicted that the UK's e-Commerce revenue is expected to reach US$47 billion by 2002,[27] and the government is determined to reach the goal of 'creating in the UK the best environment in the world in which to trade electronically by 2000'.[28]

In order to provide incentives to smaller and new businesses, corporation tax rates for these businesses have been considerably reduced since 1997—a tax depreciation facility is allowed by entering capital allowances. A research and development (R&D) tax credit was introduced in the year 2000; in other words, an immediate deduction for capital invested in R&D will benefit businesses. Smaller employers will derive benefit from a cashflow advantage by paying over the tax deducted from employees' wages every quarter instead of monthly.[29]

The White Paper also announced its support programme for new businesses:

> 'It aims to simplify and improve the quality and coherence of all Government support for small new businesses. The Inland Revenue and Customs offer extensive guidance and support for new businesses.'[30]

In regard to investors and entrepreneurs, in 1998 the government introduced capital gains tax (CGT) taper relief to create incentives for investment in assets and 'generally sustained growth with particular support for entrepreneurial

---

[26] op cit, at 13.
[27] op cit, at 14.
[28] See further 'Benchmarking the Digital Economy'" published alongside the White Paper, 'Our Competitive Future: Building the Knowledge Driven Economy', September (1999) available at www.cabinetoffice.gov.uk/innovation.
[29] op cit, at 16.
[30] ibid.

investment'.[31] Under the broad title of Special Investment Schemes, two new schemes, the Enterprise Investment Scheme (EIS) and Venture Capital Trusts (VCTS) were set up; whereas the EIS caters for direct investment in small higher risk unquoted trading companies, the latter caters for indirect investment in them through a quoted investment fund.[32] Under the EIS scheme income tax relief is available at 20 per cent on investment up to an annual limit in new shares provided that such shares have been held for five years. The White Paper provided that:

> 'Payment of tax on a previous capital gain is deferred if it is invested in such shares. Gains when shares which qualify for income tax relief are sold are exempt and any losses can be offset against income if there are no gains that year.'[33]

Investors in a VCT which subscribers for shares in small higher risk unquoted trading companies are eligible for attract income tax relief at 20 % on investment in new shares up to an annual limit of £100,000. They are allowed to defer tax on a previous capital gain if the proceeds were invested in shares which attract income tax relief. Individuals making successive investments in EIS companies benefit from taper relief 'on a cumulative basis when they reinvest the gain arising from one EIS investment in another EIS company'.[34]

In the chapter entitled 'Shaping the Future' (ch 2) the study referred to the government's programme of delivery of electronic services by the Inland Revenue and Customs, and identified the latter's commitments and priorities:

'• to deliver public services to meet the needs of citizens, not the convenience of service providers;
• to use new technology to meet the needs of citizens and business, and not trail behind in technological development;
• development of public services that are available 24 hours a day, seven days a week where there is a demand;
• joined-up government in action – including a clear commitment for people to be able to notify different parts of government of details such as a change of address simply and electronically in one transaction; and
• development of an IT strategy which will establish cross-government co-ordination, machinery and frameworks on such issues as use of digital signatures and smart cards, web sites and call centres.'[35]

The government maintained that new technologies will not replace the traditional or existing means of communication, but will take their place alongside

---

[31] ibid.
[32] op cit, at 17.
[33] ibid.
[34] ibid.
[35] op cit, at 21.

them; the government also pledged to increase the choice for citizens and business as to how they receive services.

The following are the principles which have been identified by the government for the taxation of e-Commerce:

'• neutrality—the taxation of e-commerce should seek to be technology neutral so that no particular form of commerce is advantaged or disadvantaged;
• certainty and transparency—the rules for the taxation of e-commerce should be clear and simple so that businesses can anticipate, as far as possible, the tax consequences of transactions they enter into;
• effectiveness—the tax rules should not result in either double or unintentional non-taxation, and risks from increased evasion and avoidance should be kept to a minimum. The overriding aim should be that the right amount of tax is paid at the right time and in the right country; and
• efficiency—the tax rules should be efficient, keeping the compliance costs of business and the administration costs of government to the minimum compatible with effective tax administration. Measures to counter evasion or avoidance should be proportionate to the risks which they seek to address.'[36]

The government maintained that it would not be necessary at this stage to make any major changes to existing tax legislation and regulations or to introduce new taxes. But, as technology changes, it might be necessary to introduce some changes. This view also receives support from the Trade and Industry Select Committee.

The Performance and Innovation Unit (PIU) of the government also examined[37] the government's policy on the taxation of e-Commerce, and concluded that an internationally agreed tax framework was one of the foundations of a successful e-Commerce strategy. The PIU's recommendations, which were accepted by the government, provided inter alia, that the UK should continue to participate actively in the OECD's work to review the application of transfer pricing rules to e-Commerce and to develop rules for attributing income to permanent establishments; that the UK should identify effective mechanisms for VAT collection on consumer purchases of on-line items from outside the EU; and that the tax authorities must remain vigilant in ensuring that e-Commerce does not lead to increased tax evasion and avoidance. The PIU also recommended that the UK should work with the EU, the World Customs Organisation and other international organisations to improve the procedures for the collection of VAT and customs duties on small consignments of imports, and that the Inland Revenue and

[36] op cit, at 23.
[37] e-commerce @its.best.uk (Sept 1999) available at www.cabinet-office.gov.uk/innovation.

Customs and Excise should publish improved guidance for e-business 'targeted at small and medium-sized enterprises, explaining their tax obligations and how the tax system will treat cross-border transactions'.[38] The Inland Revenue and Customs set up an Electronic Commerce Consultation Forum in order to widen their consultation procedure with business on the taxation issues.

The study emphasized the importance of international co-operation in dealing with taxation issues pertaining to e-Commerce (ch 3). It is important that business entities are clear as to international tax rules when they are engaged in international trade. Two issues are important in this context: (a) that businesses are not overtaxed; and (b) that the government ensures that tax rules work in a way which does not lead to a loss of tax revenue. The consequences of countries' not acting in unison were identified by the study:

- double taxation or unintentional non-taxation;
- excessive compliance burdens for business; and
- opportunities for the dishonest to evade or avoid taxes.[39]

International action in relation to e-Commerce taxation was predominantly taken by the OECD, the EU, the WTO and the G8 Summit. In November 1997, at the Turku (Finland) Conference, the OECD was mandated to prepare a framework for the taxation of e-Commerce. It was agreed that the guiding criteria for the development of the tax framework would be: neutrality, fairness, certainty and the need to avoid excessive taxation.[40] At the Ottawa Conference of 1998, the following issues received attention: tax, consumer protection, authentication and privacy. A number of broad principles were adopted at this Conference: neutrality, efficiency, certainty and simplicity, effectiveness, fairness and flexibility. The commitment by the OECD countries to work with non-OECD countries proved to be vital to arriving at workable tax rules and administrative systems.

Following the Ottawa Conference, the OECD consulted with businesses to identify the priority areas:

- characterisation of income (royalties/sale of goods and services);
- permanent establishments;
- transfer pricing and attribution of profits to permanent establishments;
- consumption taxes (such as VAT); and
- tax administration and compliance.[41]

---

[38] op cit, at 25.
[39] op cit, at 27.
[40] op cit, at 28.
[41] op cit, at 29.

As part of the programme, five Technical Advisory Groups were set up, inviting participants from the member countries, non-OECD member countries, and businesses. The five advisory groups were:

- Income Characterisation
- Business Profits
- Consumption Taxes
- Technology
- Professional Data Assessment

In May 1998, the G8 Foreign and Finance Ministers met in Birmingham, England. They supported the view that taxation should be technology-neutral, and that a framework on taxation would be a priority. The G8 Summit pledged to work with international institutions and the private sector to offer the best opportunities for the future: to remove inappropriate and unnecessary legal barriers to the electronic conduct of business; taxation must be technology-neutral; public administration is to use electronic means to deliver programmes and services, governments are to involve business and consumers and to take into account the demands of the market place.

At their December 1997 Summit, the EU and the United States issued a joint declaration on e-Commerce, agreeing to work towards the development of a global market place where competition and consumer choice would drive economic activity.

The European Finance Ministers first looked at the importance of e-Commerce on VAT and customs duties in June 1997, and by 1998 issued a list of guidelines, in which it was stated that there was no need for new taxes on e-Commerce at this stage: (a) existing taxes should be adapted to meet the development of e-Commerce; (b) products supplied in digital format should be treated for VAT purposes, as supply of services; (c) services supplied for consumption within the EU should not attract tax within the EU, whereas those supplied for consumption outside the EU should do so; (d) compliance should not only be easy and simple, but also the tax system for e-Commerce must be enforceable; (e) electronic invoicing should be developed in order to facilitate tax administration; and (f) businesses should be allowed to render tax returns and payments electronically.[42]

At the second ministerial conference of the World Trade Organisation (WTO) in 1998, it was decided that all WTO members would refrain from imposing customs duties on electronic transmissions. Finally, in January 1999, a UK-US statement on e-Commerce was issued, and in relation to tax, it endorsed the following principles and policies:

---

[42] op cit, at 32.

'Any taxation of e-commerce should be clear, consistent, neutral and non- discriminatory. We shall actively participate within the OECD and work toward achieving the application of the framework principles for the taxation of electronic commerce agreed by member countries at the Ministerial Conference at Ottawa in October 1998. Close co-operation and mutual assistance between the UK and US tax authorities is necessary to ensure effective tax administration and to prevent tax evasion and avoidance.'[43]

Although e-Commerce facilitates businesses and various methods of transmitting information have been devised for efficient e-Commerce: EDI (Electronic Data Interchange), ELS (Electronic Lodgement Service), CHIEF (Customs Handling of Import & Export Freight), paperless customs declarations, provision for VAT returns and forms over the Internet, the government is aware of the fact that electronic trading provides opportunities for fraudulent activities.

Chapter 5 of the study explains the risks that e-Commerce may pose to tax administration and compliance, and the government's plans to deal with this. The study suggests that taxpayers are more likely to comply with their tax obligations if they understand and have confidence in the laws, if the laws are easy to comply with, and if taxpayers are assisted to enable them to comply with their tax obligations. The possible means of achieving these objectives would be: (a) to examine how developments in technology might be used to reduce compliance costs on business, (b) to include web site and e-mail address in tax returns, and (c) to determine, in particular, what guidance small and medium-sized enterprises which are starting to trade over the Internet for the first time, might need to help them comply with their obligations.

Collection of tax often proves to be difficult for a variety of reasons, in particular, the following:

(a) concealment of taxpayers' identity,
(b) encryption of documents and financial records or holding them in foreign jurisdictions preventing tax authorities from gaining access to them,
(c) use of record keeping systems which allow transactions to take place without leaving an audit trail, and
(d) information on growth rate and market penetration becoming out of date rapidly.[44]

In relation to risks, the study identified four areas of risk control: (a) identification; (b) access; (c) assurance; and (d) understanding. Identification of the party doing business and the party with which business is being carried out, and a

[43] ibid.
[44] op cit, at 51.

system of verification and authentication of each party to an e-Commerce transaction including encryption and decryption of data, is important particularly for the purposes of developing confidence in the mind of the purchaser. This would also help minimise tax compliance risks. Access to encryption software should not be denied to tax authorities by deliberately exploiting them, nor should non-compliant taxpayers be allowed to store their accounting records and documents on computers located outside their tax jurisdictions. Assurance should be provided to both businesses and the auditor of the security and integrity of the data. Data held in electronic form may be corrupted unintentionally or otherwise, and are capable of manipulation.

In the current business environment, it is difficult to confirm how integrity and authenticity of data for business and tax administrators may be maintained. This is not to suggest that business entities are not tax compliant, in fact, the vast majority of them are, but whereas technology provides perfection, it can also create loopholes, and the minority of unscrupulous business entities can always take advantage of them. The study stated that:

> 'Confirming the integrity and authenticity of data provides a challenge in the electronic environment both for business and tax administrations. They have traditionally relied on audit trails based on paper – with its inherent look, feel and authenticity. Data held in electronic form does not at first glance provide these comforts. It can be corrupted, unintentionally or otherwise before presentation and it is capable of manipulation.'[45]

Understanding: the Inland Revenue and Customs acknowledge that they need to understand how e-Commerce performs and the breadth of activity. Understanding will also be required to ascertain the reasons for non-compliance. The government realises that in order to keep up with development in technology and e-Commerce, in particular, it will be required to keep abreast of academic research and independent commentaries.[46] The government has adopted a policy whereby tax compliance does not appear to be a coercive matter; business entities realise that it is not difficult to comply with tax regulations. E-Commerce presents risks to tax compliance, but the government is 'actively working on the issues to ensure that a robust compliance regime can be applied to the e-Commerce environment'.[47]

The study recognised that some adaptations to the current VAT rules were needed in respect of international transactions in order to provide certainty.[48] E-Commerce transactions fall into two categories for VAT purposes:

[45] op cit, at 52.
[46] op cit, at 26.
[47] op cit, at 56.
[48] op cit, at 57.

(a)   'goods ordered over the Internet delivered to both business and private customers; and

(b)   services, including digitised products, provided on line.'[49]

The current rules ensure that tax accrues in the country to which the goods are delivered. Customs authorities will collect VAT on goods imported from outside the EU. In regard to collection of VAT on international sales of services between businesses, the place of taxation rules determine the country in which tax is due on an international transaction.[50] However, no single place of taxation rule can apply to all services. In so far as telecommunication services used in the UK are concerned, they are to be taxed in the UK. The government identified three main problems in regard to VAT collection and, in particular, collection of this tax when arising from business to private consumer transactions:

- definition of the place of consumption;
- confirmation that a transaction has taken place; and
- collecting the tax.

The current international view has been that the place of consumption for private consumers should be their usual place of business. Where businesses are required to maintain books and records, and where the government has a right to audit, identification or confirmation of a transaction does not present any problem. However, where sales take place between a party in a foreign jurisdiction and private consumers, VAT collection may present problems. Furthermore, with the advancement of technology, customers would be able to obtain and use many on-line services while on the move between countries.[51] The government believes that the 'solution may lie in harnessing the technology to provide an automated tax charging and collection mechanism'.[52]

In view of unprecedented expansion of international trade by means of e-Commerce, the taxation rules may no longer be suitable for collection of VAT. Under this rule, services are taxed in the country of the supplier, but very few services are taxed under this rule. European Ministers believe that electronic commerce should be taxed in the place of consumption. But the problem is, as the study stated, 'that the means of delivery of a service, rather than the substantive service itself, could dictate where a supply is taxed'.[53] The study therefore suggested that the rules should be redefined in such a way that taxation 'in the country of consumption becomes the basic rule for services in general, not just electronic supplies. This would preserve the principle of neutrality'.[54]

[49] op cit, at 58.
[50] ibid.
[51] op cit, at 60.
[52] ibid.
[53] op cit, at 61.
[54] ibid.

However, the government believes that no radical changes in the current legislation would be necessary; instead a degree of modernization of the current legislation and adaptation in certain instances may be required. The following represents the future framework of the government's plan in regard to VAT:

(a)   As the place of consumption principle for e-commerce is not met by the present basic rule, a new basic rule which may be applied to tax international services in the country in which they are consumed may have to be adopted. This new rule would deal with convergence[55] according to which a number of services each governed by different places of taxation rules, may be provided as a single package for a single charge.

(b)   In most cases, the place of consumption for services could be the country in which a business is established. Where consumption may occur in a different country, an additional rule would operate to ensure that tax accrued where consumption actually took place.

(c)   Overseas businesses should not be subject to the burden of registration, and UK business customers should continue to pay VAT on imported services.

(d)   Suppliers may be permitted to register, account for and pay VAT on-line. Any such system for overseas businesses may need international agreements.

(e)   Currently, services such as education and live entertainment are taxed at the location of their actual performance. When a performance takes place through the Internet, the performers and the audience may not be in one physical location. Thus, a distinction should be made between services where the participants are in the same location and those in which they are scattered. The former should be taxed in the country of performance, and the latter in the customer's country.

(f)   In order to achieve more effective collection of taxes, businesses should be encouraged 'to develop sales order procuring software that is able to cope with tax on international sales automatically. By doing so, tax collection on international sales could be automated removing the need for registering overseas suppliers'.[56]

According to the government, the VAT framework must be consistent with the commercial reality.

The UK has the largest and most highly developed bookmaking industry in Europe. E-Commerce may create opportunities to increase turnover in the betting industry. This is primarily a cash-based industry, however, credit betting, debit betting and betting by e-mail are becoming popular—money in these forms of betting is taken from customers' accounts as soon as the bets are

[55] Convergence stands for a gradual disappearance of the distinctions between telecommunications, audio visual media, the computer industry and publishing and leads to merger. Digital data from a variety of sources may be located in a 'single digital space'; op cit, at 62.

[56] op cit, at 63.

struck. Some of the UK bookmakers have opened up branches in various foreign jurisdictions which conduct internet betting. Although betting with offshore bookmakers is not illegal, if credit betting facilities are transferred offshore, the Revenue will lose in the region of £50 million. The government has therefore decided to continue the advertising ban on offshore bookmakers in order to ensure that UK betting revenue is not diverted abroad, and that the industry is fairly taxed.[57]

The study also deals with direct taxes, and the international rules in this regard. The following are the international direct tax issues: (a) place of residence of companies, (b) quantifying the business profits (transfer pricing, trading by non-residents, and attribution of profits to permanent establishments), and (c) characterisation of income.

The legal aspects of the place of residence of companies have been explained in a separate section of this chapter. Basically, a company is resident for tax purposes in the UK if its place of central management and control are often exercised in more than one jurisdiction. Vital meetings may be held by video conference links or by e-mail, thus the issue of double taxation may become relevant.

Quantifications of business profits are to be considered under three subheadings, as stated above. Transfer pricing entails a process 'whereby prices are set by enterprises which are related to or 'associated with' each other in respect of dealings between them. Such dealings may include sales or transfer of goods or assets, both tangible or intangible, and the provision of services, including finance'.[58]

In a transfer pricing process, more than one jurisdiction is involved. If both jurisdictions fail to agree on the appropriate transfer prices, and thus the sharing of taxing rights, there is a risk of double taxation.[59] According to the OECD,[60] for tax purposes, the 'arms length principle' should be used to determine transfer prices. According to the government, business and tax administrations generally maintain that an arm's length principle is still appropriate. The government modernised its own domestic transfer pricing legislation in 1998. The government is, however, mindful of the fact that the arm's length principle may have to be applied in an e-Commerce situation on a transaction by transaction basis; or when a trade is concluded among different enterprises it should be determined which enterprise, in particular, performed the relevant functions and what risks it assumed. However, because e-Commerce provides

[57] ibid.
[58] op cit, at 70.
[59] ibid.
[60] See further *Transfer Pricing Guidelines for Multinational Enterprises and Tax Administrations*, Paris, OECD (July, 1995).

cross-border trading opportunities, in particular, for small to medium-sized enterprises, transfer pricing issues will occur more frequently.

The UK taxes the profits of a trader, whether resident or non-resident, who trades here. Where a non-resident is a company trading through a branch or an agency, it will be subject to corporation tax; otherwise, non-residents are subject to income tax obligations. If a company's profits arise outside the UK by virtue of trading through a branch or an agency and the assets of the branch or agency were used, then the profits will be included for corporation tax purposes.

A non-resident will be treated as trading in the UK if the contracts out of which profits arose were concluded in the UK, or if the profits arising from the activities pertaining to contracts take place here. It has been discussed in the chapter dealing with contractual issues that Internet sales to the UK by non-residents may constitute trading in the UK if the acceptance is communicated instantaneously (by electronic means) to the acceptor, the place of contract is usually in the territory to which the acceptance is communicated. In the case of double taxation treaties, the issue of the 'permanent establishment' becomes crucially important. The territory in which a non-resident is trading, can only tax in respect of profits that arise through a 'permanent establishment' in that territory. A non-resident trading in the UK may be taxable both in the UK and in its country of residence. Likewise, a UK resident trading abroad may be taxable in the UK and abroad. There is no precise definition of 'permanent establishment'—what constitutes a 'permanent establishment' depends on the precise terms of the double taxation treaty. A fixed place from or through which business is carried on seems to be an important factor in determining a 'permanent establishment'. Places of an auxiliary character do not satisfy the criteria for being a 'permanent establishment'. However, an agency through which contracts are usually concluded may satisfy the criteria of a 'permanent establishment'.

The concept of the 'fixed place' of business provokes controversy in the context of e-Commerce. Is a website in a fixed place of business a 'permanent establishment'? On the other hand, if a website acts as an agent for concluding contracts, it may perhaps be regarded as a 'permanent establishmen'As no clear alternative to a 'permanent establishment' has emerged as yet, the government does not find any compelling reason to depart from the use of the term.[61]

In distance selling, customers may be required to pay a fee or charge before being allowed to view the images of a product or to download a copy of the product. The issue arises whether such payments should be regarded as 'royalties'. Whether a payment is for the use of, or for the right to use, a copyright depends on the copyright law of the country concerned.[62] In the UK, tax is to

[61] op cit, at 72.
[62] ibid.

be withheld from royalty payments, in some circumstances, that is, from payments for the use of, or for the right to use a copyright.[63] Payments made for viewing or downloading have a special tax implication in that if a payment made by someone in the UK to a non-resident for viewing or downloading digital information, it should be treated as a royalty because it is paid for the use of, or for the right to use copyright; in this case, the recipient may have a tax liability in the UK.[64] These issues may be covered by double taxation treaties between the UK and other countries. What constitutes 'royalty' is a difficult legal issue in the context of e-Commerce—whether payments made to view and download digitalised information constitute payments for the use of or for the right to use, a copyright, or are these to be regarded as payments for the purchase of goods or services, if payment is made for viewing copyright material, which requires a reproduction of that item, then should it be regarded as royalty? If a payment is made for downloading a product, which is protected by copyright, should that payment be regarded as a royalty?

Some of the issues explained in this part of the work may not be satisfactorily resolved without effective international co-operation both at governmental levels and at the level of inter-governmental institutions, namely, the OECD. On the other hand, it is to be pointed out that with the increasing use of the Internet, more legal problems as to taxation of profits and royalties may arise.

12.4 E-Commerce corporation tax and VAT: a general discussion

12.4.1 Introduction

In the UK, tax, in general, is chargeable on a resident in the UK, or on income derived from a business or property situated in the UK. Section 747 of the Income and Corporation Taxes Act 1988 ('ICTA') identifies certain situations in which profits created by a company registered abroad are taxable in the UK. In certain circumstances the overseas income from e-Commerce may be taxed in the UK.

The various types of taxes chargeable in the UK may broadly be divided into: (a) direct taxation; and (b) indirect taxation. Whereas under the first category come corporation tax, income tax, capital gains tax; tax on business profits based on international double taxation agreements, and tax on worldwide incomes and gains, valued added tax comes under indirect taxation. In general, income from e-Commerce is taxable under the appropriate tax regime, but the bases for imposing tax on such incomes may provoke controversy. The purpose of writing this section is not to give an exhaustive account of the tax policies

---

[63] op cit, at 73. The recipient might not have a tax liability if payment was made for physical goods or services.

[64] op cit, at 73.

and tax regimes operational in the UK but to identify some of the interesting issues arising in respect of incomes from businesses operated through e-Commerce. It is emphasized that the purpose is to familiarize the reader with some of the basic tax-related issues. For any detailed knowledge, one should consult Simon's Direct Tax Service, and Finance (No. 2) Act 1997.

12.4.2   A brief discussion of the various types of tax
12.4.2.1   Corporation tax[65]

For the purposes of corporation tax, a company or corporate body stands for 'any body corporate'[66] or unincorporated association but does not include a partnership, a local authority or a local authority association.[67] Company profits are subject to corporation tax, the rates for which tax varies depending upon the income and size of the company.[68] The following are subject to corporation tax: profits, which would include income, and chargeable gains made from the disposal of assets. Chargeable gains are calculated by reference to Taxation of Chargeable Gains Act 1992 (TCGA, s 8). Corporation tax is applicable to entities which are not strictly to be regarded as companies under the Companies Act 1985.[69]

If one follows the definition of a company for the purposes of corporation tax one would be able to conclude that if a body corporate or an unincorporated association operates e-Commerce sites for membership subscriptions let alone seeking merchandise or services by such means, it should be liable to corporation tax.

Residence of a corporate body is still the cardinal criterion for determining the tax liability of a UK resident corporation.[70] Of course, in appropriate circumstances a non-resident corporation may be subject to UK taxation if it carries on a trade through a branch or an agency in the UK. The most important condition in this respect is that such a corporation is required to establish that it is not carrying on a trade in the UK. Thus, the issue remains whether a computer server carrying on an electronic trade may be regarded as a branch or an agency for the purposes of UK tax.

The scheme of taxation applicable to individuals under the ICTA 1988 and TCGA 1992 applies to corporations too with some modifications.[71] In calculating

---

[65] See, generally, *Simon's Direct Tax Service*. Another very informative work in e-Commerce and tax is *E-Commerce: Law, Business and Tax Planning* by J. Hickey, R. Mathew and C. Rose, Bristol, Jordons (2000). Many ideas in this chapter are based on the above published work.

[66] s 832(1) of ICTA defines a 'body corporate' as 'any body politic, corporate or collegiate, and any company, fraternity, fellowship and society of persons whether corporate or not corporate.'

[67] s 832(1).

[68] See Finance (No. 2) Act 1997, s 18(1).

[69] The Companies Act 1985 defines a company as 'a company formed and registered under this Act' (s 735(1)).

[70] s 6 of ICTA 1988.

[71] See s 9 of ICTA 1988.

the tax liability of a UK resident company, profits must be measured,[72] as profit and tax accounts, and the balance sheets are required to give a 'true and fair' view of the economic performance of a company for a financial year.[73] In this regard application of the relevant accountancy rules proves to be necessary; for example, it is not for law to confirm whether expenditure should be classified as revenue or capital.[74] Taxable profits are determined by applying the recognised principles of accountancy. Reference to an accounting period of a company.[75] In *Gallagher v Jones,* the court stated, *inter alia,* that:

> 'No judge-made rule could override the application of a generally accepted rule of commercial accountancy which (a) applied to the situation in question, (b) was not one of two or more rules applicable to the situation in question and (c) was not shown to be inconsistent with the true facts or otherwise inapt to determine the true profits or losses of the business. The law did not enable or require the courts to ascertain the profits of a trade on a basis divorced from the principles of commercial accounting.'[76]

Computation of profits is done by reference to the generally acceptable accounting principles (GAAP),[77] and the GAAP principles were recognised by the court in *Odeon Associated Theatres*[78]; but the GAAP principles must be applied initially to calculate the profits of a company—profits must then be adjusted by referring to the prohibited deduction of expenditure under the legislation.[79] For tax purposes, revenue has a meaning when it is earned. By the same token, expenditure is recognised when it is incurred, and not when it is paid. There are two concepts which are extremely important in this context: 'revenue receipts' and 'revenue expenditure'. Whereas 'revenue receipts' stand for income which is generated by the day-to-day activity of a corporate entity, or any entity, the cost of earning those receipts stands for 'revenue expenditure', for example, the cost of buying materials or merchandise to sell them to customers or the cost of employing staff to earn the revenue. Incidentally, money paid for the development of business or technology, may not be taken into account in the same annual year, as the tax year of a company runs from 1 April to 31 March each year. Revenue is to be accounted for when it is earned—similarly, expenditure is recognised when it is incurred, which may not necessarily fall within a tax year.

---

[72] See *Simon's Direct Tax Service*, op cit, Pt D2; see also *Inland Revenue Guidance Manual Company Taxation*, Pt 1, para 12.

[73] s 226 of the Companies Act 1985.

[74] See *Heather v P-E Consulting Group Ltd* [1973] 1 All E.R. 8.

[75] s 12 of ICTA 1988.

[76] [1993] S.T.C. 537 CA.

[77] For a discussion of the UK GAAP policies, see Davies, Paterson and Wilson, *UK GAAP* (London, Macmillan, 1998).

[78] [1971] 48 T.C. 257; [1971] 1 W.L.R. 442.

[79] ibid at 453–454.

The source of the receipts forms the basis for calculating corporation tax. These sources are classified as Schedules and Cases.[80]

Schedule A		Annual profits or gains from land
Schedule D	Case I	Annual profits or gains from a profession
	Case II	Annual profits or gains from a profession
	Case III	(a) Annual profits or gains arising from loans
		(b) Annuity or annual payment
	Case IV	Annual profits or gains in respect of foreign possessions
	Case V	Annual profits or gains in respect of miscellaneous income
Schedule E		Emoluments from an office or employment

In all cases, tax is charged on profits less expenditures. The most appropriate scheme of taxation to e-Commerce and IT activities is Schedule D; indeed, this Schedule is the most comprehensive Schedule.

The most important foundation on which corporation tax is based is whether the corporation is resident or non-resident in the UK. A company is resident in the UK if: (a) it is incorporated in the UK[81]; and (b) the central management and control of the company is located in the UK. The factors determining the central management and control were identified by the court in the De Beers case:

'it is clearly established that the majority of directors and life governors live in England, that the directors' meetings in London are the meetings where the real contract is always exercised in practically all the important business of the company except in the mining operations. London has always controlled the negotiation of the contracts with the diamonds syndicates, has determined policy in the disposal of diamonds and other assets, the working and development of mines, the application of profits, and in appointment of directors.'[82]

The factors determining the central management and control are thus fact-based. The factors relevant to determine residence under the common law test, and the second criterion is a common law criterion, were also identified by the Inland Revenue in their Statement of Practice.[83] The most relevant factors are:

---

[80] See s 18 of ICTA 1988.
[81] The condition of residence need not be satisfied where under a double taxation agreement a company is regarded as resident outside the UK; see s 249 of the Finance Act 1994.
[82] *De Beers Consolidated Mines Ltd v Howe* [1906] A.C. 455 at 459.
[83] SP/90 (9 January 1990).

where the individual controlling the company is; and the location of directors who actively carry on the business. It is to be emphasized that where the residence of a company cannot be established under the common law test, tax cannot be charged on worldwide profits.[84]

In determining tax liability, 'trade within the UK' is referred to. This may be explained in the following way: if a non-resident company obtains business through a programme on a computer based in the UK and which accepts orders and refers them to the non-resident company, which, in turn, delivers the goods through an English distributor, it may be subject to income tax, but no corporation tax on the grounds that it was trading within the UK.

The location of the contract determines the location of trade—this is an important issue in e-Commerce—furthermore, the form of the contract prescribed by a jurisdiction or legal system has a legal implication when a contract is concluded.

However, where a foreign company engages a UK company as a branch for a website service for UK companies and thereby earns profits, the profits for tax purposes may produce liability for two entities in two different ways: (a) the profits for the foreign company will be taxable according to the tax legislation applicable to the foreign company; and (b) in so far as the UK company is concerned, its tax liability will be limited to the profits it has earned as a branch of the foreign company. In this situation, the issue of central management and control would not arise, as it is obvious that the foreign company exercises control and management over its branch.

On the other hand, where a company is incorporated in a foreign jurisdiction, but the majority of shareholders live in the UK and the financial management is carried out in the UK, in addition to holding its annual general meetings, and sending instructions to its headquarters by electronic means, the company's main tax liability will be within the UK as the main business decisions are taken in the UK, and for tax purposes the company is resident in the UK.

The position of a branch or an agency of a non-resident company in respect of its tax liability is interesting. Under section II(1) of the ICTA 1988, a non-resident company is liable to corporation tax if it carries on trade through a branch or an agency in the UK. Corporation tax is accruable on profits earned by the branch or the agency.[85] Thus the physical presence and location of an entity and its activities generating incomes would be enough for the purposes of corporation tax provided it is engaged in the activities of its parent body.[86] According to section 6(2) of ICTA 1988, a company may be subject to income

---

[84] See ss 11, 18 and 20 of the ICTA 1988.
[85] According to s 834(1) of ICTA, a branch or an agency is 'any partnership, agency, receivership branch or management'.
[86] See further *Hughes (HM Inspector of Taxes) v Bank of New Zealand* [1938] 1 All E.R. 778.

tax in the absence of a branch or an agency. In levying corporation tax, two most important factors are to be considered: chargeable income is calculated under ICTA 1988, and chargeable gains under TCGA 1992.

Computation of tax of a corporate body, including an IT company is determined by referring to 'chargeable income', 'chargeable gains', and 'expenditures'. 'Chargeable income' could relate to the following: annual profits or gains from a trade; annual profits or gains arising from a loan; annuity or annual payment, and annual profits or gains in respect of foreign possessions. But a trader, including an IT company, may be entitled to tax reliefs, known as allowances.[87] The day-to-day cost of carrying on trade, eg fixed costs—salaries of staff, rental, rates etc is otherwise known as 'revenue expenditure'. Capital expenditure is often deductible from receipts derived from a trade, and the relief (deductions) is known as 'capital allowances'.[88] The calculation of chargeable income, including revenue expenditure or allowances must be in conformity with the generally accepted principles of commercial accountancy.[89] Chargeable income is first computed; chargeable gains are calculated by reference to TCGA 1992.[90] The purpose of ascertaining 'chargeable income' and 'chargeable gains' is to determine a company's 'chargeable profits'.[91]

For the purposes of determining profits under Schedule D, income implies the deduction of expenditure from receipts in any particular accounting period. Capital expenditure is not initially allowed as a deduction,[92] as under the capital allowances system it may be allowed some relief. This deduction very much depends upon the government policy in vogue at a particular time. The percentage of deduction of the cost of plant can be high or low per tax year, according to the policy implemented by the government.[93] Section 74 of ICTA 1988 clearly states that expenditure of a revenue nature may not be deducted unless incurred entirely for the purposes of a trade. On the other hand, expenditures of a capital nature are generally not a permitted deduction, unless it is to be regarded as a capital allowance under the Capital Allowance Act 1990 (CAA), the common item of which are machinery and plant, including expenditure on copyright in computer software,[94] know-how,[95] and patents.[96]

---

[87] But a person who receives income from an investment is not entitled to deduct any expenditure.
[88] This system is governed by the Capital Allowances Act 1990.
[89] *Odeon Associated Theatres v Jones* [1971] 1 W.L.R. 422.
[90] TCGA 1992, s 8.
[91] See ICTA 1988, s 6(4)(a).
[92] ICTA, s 74(1)(f).
[93] For example, in 1997–1998, in order to encourage investment in business, the government allowed small businesses investing in machinery or plant to deduct the cost of the plant at the rate of 50 per cent of the cost per tax year; see further CAA 1990, s 22, as amended by the Finance (No. 2) Act 1997, s 42.
[94] CAA 1990, s 67A; see also CAA 2001.
[95] ICTA 1988, s 530.
[96] ICTA 1988, s 520.

In calculating tax and expenditure, deductions become crucially important. The distinction between revenue and capital expenditure also presents difficulties.[97] IT and internet business should be eligible for relief in respect of plant and machinery.[98] Currently, the relief allowance is to the extent of 25 per cent of the capital expenditure incurred. Where an expenditure is required to be reduced, usually, by virtue of an event occurring, that expenditure must be reduced prior to giving any allowance. Legal controversy persists as to the definition of a 'plant', and whether 'computer software' should be regarded as a 'plant'. In *Yarmouth v France*, the term 'plant' was described in the following way:

> 'in its ordinary sense, it includes whatever apparatus is used by a business-man for carrying on his business—not his stock-in-trade which he buys or makes for sale; but all goods and chattels fixed or moveable, live or dead, which he keeps for permanent employment in his business.'[99]

The term 'whatever apparatus' is general enough to include 'computer software'; although 'computer software' is not hardware but this popular meaning is usually attached to an 'apparatus'. In e-business, it is the 'computer software' which forms the foundation of the business; furthermore, the description goes on to say 'all goods and chattels ... which he keeps for permanent employment in business'. Certainly, 'computer software' will come under the second leg of the description; thus it may be regarded as an apparatus or a plant. For computer software to be treated as a plant, the expenditure must be incurred for the purposes of or in relation to trade. In this connection one is required to make a distinction between 'plant' and 'premises'. What is to be considered is whether an apparatus is the means which allows the business activity to be carried on, or whether it is the premises from which the activity is carried on.[100] An apparatus within the former category is a 'plant'; and in the latter, 'premises'. Of course, in the final analysis, what is a 'plant' or a 'premise' or what is an 'equipment' for the purposes of trade may be examined by the Inland Revenue on a case-by-case basis.[101] The determination of a 'plant' or an 'equipment' may provoke controversy in the IT world. In *Schofield (Inspector Taxes) v R & H Hall Ltd*,[102] the Court of Appeal upheld the decision of the Commissioner that a concrete grain silo erected at a dockside would be regarded as a plant as it was a means by which the trader ensured an efficient process for unloading grain and other related activities. Therefore, any equipment (station) built or erected (as

---

[97] See *Simon's Direct Tax Services*, Part A1.123 and A.1.2; see also *British Insulated and Helsby Cables Limited v Atherton* [1926] A.C. 205.
[98] s 24 of CAA 1990.
[99] (1887) 19 Q.B.D. 647 at 658.
[100] *Gray (Inspector of Taxes) v Seymour Garden Centre (Horticulture) (a firm)* [1995] S.T.C. 706; see also *Attwood (Inspector of Taxes) v Anduff Car Wash Ltd* [1997] S.T.C. 1167.
[101] *Bradley v London Electricity plc* [1996] S.T.C. 1054.
[102] CAA 1990, s 67A; see also Inland Revenue Guidance Manual *Capital Allowance*, para 1601 (Machinery and Plant).

stations) in carrying on trade in the IT world may be regarded as a 'plant' for corporation tax purposes.[102a]

It is to be borne in mind that the term 'computer software' is not defined in the legislation; but the Inland Revenue's Guidance Manual, *Capital Allowances* provides that all computer programmes and data should be treated as computer software; it has been stated that for a computer software to be treated as a 'plant' the expenditure must be made/incurred for the purposes of a trade.[103] Software transferred by electronic means (through the Internet) will qualify for the plant capital allowance.[104] For the determination of a corporation tax, the disposal value of an asset must be deducted from eligible expenditures incurred in acquiring that asset.[105]

Relief may be available on various grounds, for example, on short-life assets,[106] that is, assets with a life of less than five years, with a depreciation record,[107] but to qualify for this relief, an option must be made to the Inspector of Taxes within two years from the end of the accounting period in which the expenditure is incurred.[108] This provision is particularly important in respect of IT-related business because of the use of short-life assets which excludes leased plant or machinery;[109] however the relief must be utilised within four years of the expenditure being incurred. Computer software qualities for short-life asset relief.

In the case of long-life assets,[110] the rate of depreciation is limited to 6 per cent. In order to justify relief on the grounds of expenditures incurred on a long-life asset, the expenditure within a chargeable period must be over £100,000. It is unlikely that an IT company will be eligible for relief under this category because it may not use any long-life asset as described above.

Capital allowances may be available, as a relief, if capital expenditure has been incurred on industrial know-how. Section 533(7) of ICTA 1988 defines know-how as;

> 'any industrial information and technique likely to assist in the manufacture or processing of goods or materials, or in the working of a mine, oil-well or other source of mineral deposits (including the searching for, discovery or testing of deposits or the winning of access thereto) or in the carrying out of any agricultural, forestry or fishing operations.'

[102a] See further; J. Hickey, R. Math and C. Rose, *E-Commerce: Law, Business and Tax Planning*, Bristol, Jordons (2001) at 81.

[103] CAA 1990, s 67A; see also Inland Revenue Guidance Manual, *Capital Allowances*, para 1601 (Machinery and Plant); see also CAA 2001.

[104] op cit, at para 1602.

[105] For the method of accounting disposal value, see s 24(6) of CAA 1990.

[106] See *Simon's Direct Tax Services*, op cit, Part B2.326.

[107] A depreciation allowance of 25 per cent.

[108] See CAA 1990, ss 37(2) and 37(2A).

[109] CAA 1990, s 37(1); see also CAA 2001.

[110] For the purposes of corporation tax, a plant or machinery with an economic life of 25 years or more is treated as a long-life asset.

This is a relief for which many IT and e-Commerce businesses may be eligible—the expenditure on know-how must be at least £100,000 to qualify for this relief. It is to be emphasized that this definition of know-how does not apply to the know-how of a commercial nature. For the purposes of seeking relief, know-how must be used for manufacturing goods. As no proprietary right exists in know-how, incomes from the exploitation of know-how usually do not qualify as capital; nevertheless, expenditures incurred on know-how may qualify as capital.

In *Vodafone Cellular Ltd v Shaw (Inspector of Taxes)*, Millett LJ by referring to *Tucker (Inspector of Taxes) v Granada Motorway Services Ltd* [1979] S.T.C. 393 said that:

> 'In the present case the taxpayer company could obtain the necessary know-how by buying it in or by establishing its own research department. It chose to buy it in. The initial know-how was admitted by a capital asset, and the payment by which it was obtained was admittedly by a capital payment.'[111]

Under section 530(1)(a) of ICTA 1988, capital allowance may be allowed to an entity if it incurred capital expenditure on know-how for use in a trade carried on by it; this allowance may also be available to expenditures incurred prior to commencing its trade, but for the purposes of commencing its trade. Know-how is treated as goodwill, thus, in the event of a person disposing of his trade, whether in full or in part, the receipt (consideration) for the know-how is to be treated as a receipt for goodwill.[111a] However, the parties may exercise their option whereby the know-how may not be treated as goodwill, and in that event, no payment will be made.[112] Under section 531(8) of ICTA 1988, if a person disposes of its know-how in a restrictive fashion, that is, with restrictions as to its use, the receipt may nevertheless be treated as a receipt (income) received as proceeds of sale of the know-how. Tax liability on any of these items may depend on how a particular claim for relief has been submitted.

Relief may also be available for an expenditure of a capital nature incurred on scientific research,[113] but certain pre-conditions must be satisfied: (a) scientific research must relate to the trade and expenditure on it must have been incurred while carrying on that trade; and (b) that the scientific research is undertaken either by the trader itself/himself or by its authorised person on its behalf.[114] Relief may also be available on scientific research which was undertaken prior to the trade being commenced, if the research which was related to the trade was undertaken by the trader itself/himself or by his appointed agent; however, the

---

[111] [1997] S.T.C. 734 at 741.
[111a] See further Hickey et al, op. cit; at 92; See also Capital Allowances Act 2001.
[112] See further ICTA, s 531(3)(a).
[113] s 139(1)(a) of the 1990 Act defines 'scientific research' as 'any activities in the fields of natural or applied science for the extension of knowledge'.
[114] CAA 1990, s 137(1)(a).

rate of allowance is equal to 100 %of the expenditure incurred by the trader.[115] In *Gaspet Ltd v Ellis (Inspector of Taxes)*[116] it was decided that:

'In order to quality for capital allowances . . . on the basis that scientific reseach had been undertaken 'on his behalf' a claimant had to prove a close and direct link between himself and the work undertaken . . . It was not necessary however for there to be a contractual link between the claimant and the person by whom the research was directly withdrawn.'

A company may also seek what is known as a 'roll-over relief': this arises when a chargeable gain accruing on the disposal of assets is deferred by virtue of acquiring further business assets.[117] Obviously, this relief may not be available where the new assets acquired are not used for the purposes of the trade.[118]

Unless justified by a special circumstance roll-over relief may not be available when a trader/company may use only part of the proceeds arising from the disposal of assets from the acquisition of a new asset. The roll-over relief may be denied if no new asset is acquired, or no contract is in place for the acquisition of a new asset, 12 months before the disposal of the old asset or within three years of the disposal of the old asset.[119] An unconditional contract may be regarded as the basis for allowing relief on a provisional basis.[120] Satellites, space stations and launch vehicles, for example, may be eligible for roll-over relief.

Under TCGA 1992 reliefs from capital gains tax may be available for (a) schemes relating to reconstruction or amalgamation of a company's business (s 139); or (b) business assets, which, in reality, are gifts (s 165); or (c) intra-group transfers (s 171).

Chargeable gains
Chargeable gains arise from the disposal of assets.[121] In order for a chargeable gain to be determined, the following conditions must be satisfied:

(a)   existence of an asset;[122]
(b)   disposal of an asset;
(c)   disposal proceeds;
(d)   deduction of eligible costs; and
(e)   in the case of any partial disposal, apportionment of costs.

Disposal of assets by a company being one of the principal elements of chargeable gains, IT-based businesses will be very much concerned with this form of

---

[115] ibid, s 137(1).
[116] [1987] S.T.C. 362.
[117] TGGA 1992, s 152.
[118] ibid, s 152(3).
[119] ibid.
[120] ibid, s 152(4).
[121] TCGA 1992, s 1(2).
[122] 'Asset' in this context includes all forms of property (s 21(1)—TCGA 1992), and any form of property created by the company which disposes of it (s 21(1)—TCGA 1992).

corporation tax. All tangible and intangible property which may be used by IT-based companies or e-Commerce companies, generally, may be subject to this form of corporation tax.[122a] In computing chargeable gains, certain deductions are allowable, namely:

- the amount spent exclusively for the purposes of acquiring the asset;
- the amount incurred exclusively for the purposes of enhancing the value of the asset;
- the incidental costs of acquisition;
- the amount spent exclusively for preserving the asset; and
- any incidental costs incurred in the disposal of the asset.[123]

Deductions
Deduction of income tax at source is a common phenomenon. In so far as IT-related business or e-Commerce is concerned, tax deduction at source may arise when payments may be made on an annual basis; and also in regard to the payments made for the use of patent designs and copyright. The judicial guidelines on what constitutes an 'annual payment' were offered by the court in *Commissioner of Inland Revenue v Whitworth Park Coal Co Ltd et al.*[124]

This case also explained the difficulty in defining an 'annual payment'. Lord Radcliffe said that:

'The word 'annual' has not been found to admit of any significant interpretation. To the courts it means no more that 'recurrence' ... That may be so, but I think that it would be both had logic and had law to deduce that merely because a payment is in fact recurrent or capable of recurrence it is, therefore, to be treated as an annual payment.'

Any amount paid for the user of a patent may be allowed deduction of income tax at source. A payment made in relation to the use of copyright material to the owner is subject to deduction of income tax at source. Copyright in this context does not include copyright in a film or video recording or the soundtrack accompanying a film or video.[125] Deduction at source is also made in respect of payments made for computer software, but not in respect of any payment that may be made for the use of off-the-shelf computer software. It is to be borne in mind that the rates of deduction, and the items of income on which deductions may apply vary from time to time.

12.4.2.2 Taxation on computer software
Computer software is a device in which information is encoded or stored in a magnetised state (usually, a floppy disk) or recorded on a CD-ROM. A computer software thus contains information, and the intellectual property right of the owner in it is to be protected. However, the type of intellectual property

[122a] See further Hickey et al, op. cit; at 96.
[123] See s 38(2) of TCGA 1992 see also Hickey et al, op. cit; at 98.
[124] (1957) 38 T.C. 531.
[125] ICTA 1988, s 536(2).

contained in a software may vary; therefore, for tax purposes, it is important to classify softwares by referring to their constituent elements; for example, when a software is classified as goods, it will be subject to VAT as a supply of goods; but when it is classified as services, it will be subject to VAT as a supply of services.However,the problem remains as to how to classify whether a software should be classified as goods or services, or whether it may be a 'mixed software'. However, computer software is to be regarded as a literary work, thus, it is to be protected by copyright; the information in a computer software does not detail any proprietary right. Under the Copyright, Designs and Patents Act 1988, in so far as it is literary work, computer software is protected by copyright. Purchase of software from a retailer (off-the-shelf software) may give rise to two issues for tax purposes: (a) it is a payment made for the device on which the information is stored; and (b) for the licence to use the software (use of software involves the grant of a licence). The problem remains as to how to classify software in such circumstances. Should it be classified as a sale of goods or as supply of services? On the other hand, Internet-provided software may be obtained through the medium of the Internet, and again, the question remains whether the acquisition of such software amounts to supplying goods or services.

In computing tax on computer software, the two main items to be taken into account are: (a) expenditure; and (b) deductions. Under 'expenditure' will come (i) revenue expenditure; (ii) capital expenditure; and (iii) software owned outright. 'Revenue expenditure' stands for the expenditure which is incurred in earning the revenue derived from an activity. A person who has incurred such expenditure will be entitled to a deduction of the expenditure, if it is wholly and exclusively incurred[126] at the basic rate of income tax. 'Capital expenditure' stands for expenditure on capital. In the case of computer software, non-financial fixed assets do not have any physical presence, although they are identifiable. Can expenditure on this be regarded as capital expenditure? Capital expenditure has not been defined in the legislation. In its publication entitled *Revenue Interpretation* RI 56 (November 1993) and guidance note, the Inland Revenue stated that although 'computer software' remains undefined, for the purposes of CAA 1990 (see also CAA 2001), it is to be given its normal meaning which would cover both programmes and data.

Computer software is intangible other than that the information is contained in a tape or disk.[127] Under section 67A of CAA 1990, a capital allowance may be available for certain types of expenditure incurred on computer software. According to this section, capital expenditure on computer software may be entitled to relief against the profits of the trade in the following circumstances: (a) if expenditure is incurred for the purposes of a trade; and/or (b) expenditure incurred in dealing with computer software or in acquiring the right to use it. According to the Inland Revenue, the application of section 67A of CAA 1990 depends upon the nature of the payment made for a licence for the purpose of

---

[126] ICTA 1988, s 74.
[127] See further C Reed, *Computer Law* (London, Blackstone Press, 1996) at 55.

acquiring a device, namely, CD-ROM or a floppy disk. In this connection, the most important methods of payment are 'royalty' or 'lump sum'.

In the case of computer software, payments are regularly made on the use of licences; the right to use software entails taking out user licences. A company is required to pay licence fees, which is very similar to paying rental. Expenditure of this type is classified as revenue,[128] and comes under the general scheme of taxation, and is governed by the generally accepted principles of commercial accountancy. The expenditure must not be a prohibited one, that is, it must not be an expenditure which has not been incurred wholly or exclusively for the purposes of a trade carried on by the taxpayer.

The nature of the software licence is considered in determining the tax liability on lump sum payments. If the licence is regarded as a capital asset of an enduring nature, then it is classified as capital. Whether a licence is of an enduring nature or not, is determined by referring to the function of the software in the trade.[129] Where the software is of a transitory nature, expenditures on it would be of a revenue nature. A computer software licence is capable of being a capital asset[130] if it is regarded as being of an enduring nature. TCGA 1992 defines 'asset' as all 'forms of property' (s 21(1)),[131] but no property exists in pure information; thus it is not capable of being a chargeable asset.

It is quite common in the computing world to buy software and hardware as a package on a single payment. However, for tax purposes, this payment is to be divided into payment for the software and payment for the hardware, unless the expenditure is placed in the 'pool' of general machinery and plant, when apportionment will not be necessary. There is no definition of 'hardware', therefore, it becomes speculative as to what tax should be charged on what. However, the Inland Revenue Guidance, referred to above, suggests that like 'computer software', 'computer hardware' should be given its natural meaning. Usually, the expenditure on the computer hardware is treated as an expenditure on ordinary plant and machinery for the purposes of tax legislation. This seems to be an area which is full of uncertainty, and one can only hope that the tax regimes for e-Commerce-related business will be more certain in the future. The important criterion is that the licensor holds the copyright and that the corporate licensee makes annual payments, and that deduction may be allowed where payment is made to an overseas owner of copyright.[132] The amount to be deducted is determined by referring to the basic rate of income tax.[133]

---

[128] This type of revenue does not come under the purview of s 67A of CAA 1990.

[129] Enduring nature stands for a nature which is creative, for example, in the absence of using software as tools, video games may not be developed.

[130] Rights in computer software are assets for the purposes of TCGA 1992.

[131] Kirby (Inspector of Taxes) Thorn EMI plc 1987 S.T.C. 621 at 627 E Nicholls LJ said, *inter alia*, that according to s 22 of the Finance Act 165, 'property' 'bears the meaning of that which is capable of being owned, in the normal legal sense, and that it does not bear the extended meaning that would be needed if it were to include a person's freedom to trade.'

[132] ICTA 1988, s 536(1).

[133] ibid, ss 536(1), 349(1) and 4(1).

12.4.2.3 Value added tax

In the UK, value added tax (VAT) is governed by the VAT Act 1994 and the Sixth VAT Directive; the VAT Act 1994 is, of course, supplemented by statutory instruments. HM Commissioners of Customs and Excise administers VAT and VAT-related matters.

VAT is charged on the sale of goods or services. VAT is borne by the final consumer. Thus, a person who incurs VAT in supplying goods or services, is entitled to deduct it as 'input tax' from the tax charged on supplies or services made by him as 'output tax'. It is basically a sales tax, which a provider of goods and services imposes on its customers (consumers) and receives a refund on it; hence the concepts of 'input tax' and 'output tax'. Section 4 of the VAT Act identifies the scope of VAT on taxable supplies in the following way:

'(1)   VAT shall be charged on any supply of goods or services made in the United Kingdom, where it is a taxable supply made by a taxable person in the course or furtherance of any business carried on by him.

(2)   A taxable supply is supply of goods or services made in the United Kingdom other than an exempt supply.'

The rate of VAT is 17.5 per cent on standard rated supplies, but on zero-rated supplies the charge is nil. In order to clarify the basis of VAT it is necessary to briefly explain certain concepts, namely, 'supply', 'consideration', 'supply of goods', 'supply of services' and a 'taxable person'. Section 5(2)(a) of the Act defines 'supply' in the following way: 'Supply in this Act includes all forms of supply, but not anything done otherwise than for a consideration'.

VAT represents the consideration for the supply of goods or services. Therefore, it is essential that 'consideration' is justifiable, but it has not been defined either in the VAT Act or in the Sixth Directive. 'Consideration' is to be given its usual meaning, that is, money or goods or services received in exchange for a supply, whether of goods or services.[134] All consideration must be expressed in monetary terms. Gifts do not usually satisfy the criterion of consideration, and a gift the value of which is less than £15 or a gift of samples is not treated as a supply of goods.

It is a matter of controversy what constitutes 'consideration', but the simplest way to determine it might be the price which the parties concerned have agreed to put on it. In the case of fixed-price articles, the question of bargaining or agreeing to a price would not arise. Where goods are exchanged for services, there the latter becomes the consideration. In *Empire Stores Ltd v Customs and Excise Commissioners* it was shown how VAT may be charged on the exchange of goods for services. In this case, certain merchandise was sold through a catalogue, and the retailer also operated a scheme whereby customers' personal

---

[134] See further *Empire Stores Ltd v Customs and Excise Commissioners* [1994] S.T.C. 623.

information, including creditworthiness, would be collated and sold by the retailer. This information also confirmed that these customers would make purchases of its product. Against this information, a free gift was given to each provider of information. The issue arose whether VAT was chargeable on this kind of business, as the catalogue had an economic value. In this case, the 'gift' was considered to be a 'consideration', as it was in exchange of the information the retailer received and used. The 'gift' was to be regarded as 'goods' supplied in exchange for information, and the retailer also paid cost price for these gifts. VAT was chargeable because the retailer supplied goods for a consideration, which represented the cost price of the goods (the gifts).

In determining VAT, it is important to make a distinction between a physical product and the property that exists within a product. In the context of IT, the property within a product is the intellectual property entailing copyright; in this context, the tangible property is the device on which a programme is encoded, which may be sold or leased out. VAT is chargeable when the property in the goods may be or is transferred by sale, or may be transferred by means of an agreement. Transfer of property stands for supply of goods; transfer of property can take place by electronic means, thus it constitutes 'supply of goods'.

Whether software transferred by electronic means may be classified as a supply of goods—although 'goods' is not defined in the VAT Act the Sale of Goods Act 1979 defines it as 'all personal chattels other than things in action and money'. According to the Customs and Excise Guidance Manual, supply and delivery of computer software via the Internet (computer network) is to be regarded as a supply of services.[135]

The next important issue is how to determine the place of supply of goods or services. Table 14 of the Act provides guidelines as to the determination of the place of supply for both goods and services. The determination of the place of supply of goods or services is important in relation to e-Commerce in that if the location of supply of services or goods is outside the UK, then there will be no VAT liability. A business person must be aware of the territorial limits of the UK for VAT purposes. For example, whereas the Isle of Man is regarded as part of the UK for VAT purposes, the Channel Islands is not.

12.4.2.4 Trade within the european union and VAT

Trade within the European Union has two forms: (a) import trade; and (b) export trade. This section discusses how VAT liability may arise on import/export trade within the European Union. For the purposes of VAT, 'import trade' stands for 'acquisition of goods'. If an acquisition of zero-rated goods takes place, then the VAT liability is nil.[136] However, non-business entities

---

[135] Vol. 1, Appendix G. For the definition of 'supply of services' see VAT Act 1994, s 5(2)(b) and Schs 1–3.
[136] VAT Act 1994, s 30(1).

or users may be liable to VAT on 'relevant acquisitions'. According to section 1(1)(b) of the VAT Act, VAT will be charged on acquisition of goods in the UK from any other member state. The VAT on acquisition of goods is regarded as an 'input tax' which may be set-off against supplies on which 'output tax' is received.[137]

Section 10 of the Act details the scope of VAT on acquisitions from other member states:

'(1) VAT shall be charged on any acquisition from another member State of any goods where—
    (a) the acquisition is a taxable acquisition and takes place in the United Kingdom;
    (b) the acquisition is otherwise than in pursuance of a taxable supply; and
    (c) the person who makes the acquisition is a taxable person or the goods are subject to a duty of excise or consist in a new means of transport.
(2) An acquisition of goods from another member State is a taxable acquisition if—
    (a) it falls within subsection (3) below or the goods consist in a new means of transport; and
    (b) it is not an exempt acquisition.
(3) An acquisition of goods from another member State falls within this subsection if—
    (a) the goods are acquired in the course or furtherance of—
        (i) any business carried on by any person; or
        (ii) any activities carried on otherwise than by way of business by any body corporate or by any club, association, organisation or other unincorporated body;
    (b) it is the person who carries on that business or, as the case may be, those activities who acquires the goods; and
    (c) the supplier—
        (i) is taxable in another member State at the time of the transaction in pursuance of which the goods are acquired; and
        (ii) in participating in that transaction, acts in the course or furtherance of a business carried on by him.'

Section 11 of the Act defines the meaning of 'acquisition of goods' from another member state:

'(1) Subject to the following provisions of this section, references in this Act to the acquisition of goods from another member State shall be

---

[137] s 24(1)(b) and (2).

construed as references to any acquisition of goods in pursuance of a transaction in relation to which the following conditions are satisfied, that is to say—

  (a) the transaction is a supply of goods (including anything treated for the purposes of this Act as a supply of goods); and
  (b) the transaction involves the removal of the goods from another member State;

and references in this Act, in relation to such an acquisition, to the supplier shall be construed accordingly.

(2) It shall be immaterial for the purposes of subsection (1) above whether the removal of the goods from the other member State is by or under the directions of the supplier or by or under the directions of the person who acquires them or any other person.

(3) Where the person with the property in any goods does not change in consequence of anything which is treated for the purposes of this Act as a supply of goods, that supply shall be treated for the purposes of this Act as a transaction in pursuance of which there is an acquisition of goods by the person making it.

(4) (4) The Treasury may by order provide with respect to any description of transaction that the acquisition of goods in pursuance of a transaction of that description is not to be treated for the purposes of this Act as the acquisition of goods from another member State'.

The time acquisition for the purposes of VAT is defined by section 12 of the Act:

'(1) Subject to section 18 and any regulations under subsection (3) below, where goods are acquired from another member State, the acquisition shall be treated for the purposes of this Act as taking place on whichever is the earlier of—

  (a) the 15th day of the month following that in which the event occurs which, in relation to that acquisition, is the first relevant event for the purposes of taxing the acquisition; and
  (b) the day of the issue, in respect of the transaction in pursuance of which the goods are acquired, of an invoice of such a description as the Commissioners may by regulations prescribe.

(2) For the purposes of this Act the event which, in relation to any acquisition of goods from another member State, is the first relevant event for the purposes of taxing the acquisition is the first removal of the goods which is involved in the transaction in pursuance of which they are acquired.

(3) The Commissioners may by regulations make provision with respect to the time at which an acquisition is to be treated as taking place in prescribed cases where the whole or part of any consideration comprised in the transaction in pursuance of which the goods are acquired is determined or payable periodically, or from time to time, or at the end of a period; and any such regulations may provide, in

relation to any case to which they apply, for goods to be treated as separately and successively acquired at prescribed times or intervals.'

The place of acquisition is determined by section 13 of the Act:

'(1)   This section shall apply (subject to section 18) for determining for the purposes of this Act whether goods acquired from another member State are acquired in the United Kingdom.

(2)   The goods shall be treated as acquired in the United Kingdom if they are acquired in pursuance of a transaction which involves their removal to the United Kingdom and does not involve their removal from the United Kingdom, and (subject to the following provisions of this section) shall otherwise be treated as acquired outside the United Kingdom.

(3)   Subject to subsection (4) below, the goods shall be treated as acquired in the United Kingdom if they are acquired by a person who, for the purposes of their acquisition, makes use of a number assigned to him for the purposes of VAT in the United Kingdom.

(4)   Subsection (3) above shall not require any goods to be treated as acquired in the United Kingdom where it is established, in accordance with regulations made by the Commissioners for the purposes of this section that VAT—
     (a)   has been paid in another member State on the acquisition of those goods; and
     (b)   fell to be paid by virtue of provisions of the law of that member State corresponding, in relation to that member State, to the provision made by subsection (2) above.

(5)   The Commissioners may by regulations make provision for the purposes of this section—
     (a)   for the circumstances in which a person is to be treated as having been assigned a number for the purposes of VAT in the United Kingdom;
     (b)   for the circumstances in which a person is to be treated as having made use of such a number for the purposes of the acquisition of any goods; and
     (c)   for the refund, in prescribed circumstances, of VAT paid in the United Kingdom on acquisitions of goods in relation to which the conditions specified in subsection (4)(a) and (b) above are satisfied.'

The general provisions relating to goods imported from outside the member states are the subject matter of section 15 of the Act:

'(1)   For the purposes of this Act goods are imported from a place outside the member States where—
     (a)   having been removed from a place outside the member States, they enter the territory of the Community;

    (b)   they enter that territory by being removed to the United Kingdom or are removed to the United Kingdom after entering that territory; and

    (c)   the circumstances are such that it is on their removal to the United Kingdom or subsequently while they are in the United Kingdom that any Community customs debt in respect of duty on their entry into the territory of the Community would be incurred.

(2) Accordingly—

    (a)   goods shall not be treated for the purposes of this Act as imported at any time before a Community customs debt in respect of duty on their entry into the territory of the Community would be incurred, and

    (b)   the person who is to be treated for the purposes of this Act as importing any goods from a place outside the member States is the person who would be liable to discharge any such Community customs debt.

(3) Subsections (1) and (2) above shall not apply, except in so far as the context otherwise requires or provision to the contrary is contained in regulations under section 16(1), for construing any references to importation or to an importer in any enactment or subordinate legislation applied for the purposes of this Act by section 16(1).'

VAT is imposed on goods imported from the non-EU countries. When goods enter into a member state, including the UK, they are treated as 'acquisitions', but even in this situation, VAT liability is imposed upon the person 'acquiring' the goods[138] unless it is allowed dispensation on certain grounds. Import tax is governed by the Customs and Excise Management Act 1979; guidance is available from the Customs and Excise Manuals.[139] Under the Customs and Excise Management Act the obligation to pay import duty is on the importer.[140] Customs duty is payable at the entry point. Section 30 of the Act provides for relief, exemptions and repayments:

'(1) Where a taxable person supplies goods or services and the supply is zero-rated, then, whether or not VAT would be chargeable on the supply apart from this section—

    (a)   no VAT shall be charged on the supply; but

    (b)   it shall in all other respects be treated as a taxable supply;

and accordingly the rate at which VAT is treated as charged on the supply shall be nil.

(2) A supply of goods or services is zero-rated by virtue of this subsection if the goods or services are of a description for the time being

---

[138] VAT Act, s 1(3).
[139] See also Notice No. 702 'VAT Imports and Warehoused Goods'.
[140] Customs and Excise Management Act, s 43(1).

specified in Schedule 8 or the supply is of a description for the time being so specified.

(3)   Where goods of a description for the time being specified in that Schedule, or of a description forming part of a description of supply for the time being so specified, are acquired in the United Kingdom from another member State or imported from a place outside the member States, no VAT shall be chargeable on their acquisition or importation, except as otherwise provided in that Schedule.

(4)   The Treasury may by order vary Schedule 8 by adding to or deleting from it any description or by varying any description for the time being specified in it.

(5)   Where a description included in that Schedule (whether by virtue of an order under subsection (4) above or otherwise) is of a transaction which would not otherwise be a supply of goods or services, the transaction shall for the purposes of this Act be treated as a supply of goods or services in the United Kingdom.

(6)   A supply of goods is zero-rated by virtue of this subsection if the Commissioners are satisfied that the person supplying the goods—
(a)   has exported them to a place outside the member States; or
(b)   has shipped them for use as stores on a voyage or flight to an eventual destination outside the United Kingdom, or as merchandise for sale by retail to persons carried on such a voyage or flight in a ship or aircraft,
and in either case if such other conditions, if any, as may be specified in regulations or the Commissioners may impose are fulfilled.

(7)   Subsection (6)(b) above shall not apply in the case of goods shipped for use as stores on a voyage or flight to be made by the person to whom the goods were supplied and to be made for a purpose which is private.

(8)   Regulations may provide for the zero-rating of supplies of goods, or of such goods as may be specified in the regulations, in cases where—
(a)   the Commissioners are satisfied that the goods have been or are to be exported to a place outside the member States or that the supply in question involves both—
(i)   the removal of the goods from the United Kingdom; and
(ii)   their acquisition in another member State by a person who is liable for VAT on the acquisition in accordance with provisions of the law of that member State corresponding, in relation to that member State, to the provisions of section 10; and
(b)   such other conditions, if any, as may be specified in the regulations or the Commissioners may impose are fulfilled.

(9)   Regulations may provide for the zero-rating of a supply of services which is made where goods are let on hire and the Commissioners are satisfied that the goods have been or are to be removed from the United Kingdom during the period of the letting, and such other

conditions, if any, as may be specified in the regulations or the Commissioners may impose are fulfilled.

(10) Where the supply of any goods has been zero-rated by virtue of subsection (6) above or in pursuance of regulations made under subsection (8) or (9) above and—

(a) the goods are found in the United Kingdom after the date on which they were alleged to have been or were to be exported or shipped or otherwise removed from the United Kingdom; or

(b) any condition specified in the relevant regulations under subsection (6), (8) or (9) above or imposed by the Commissioners is not complied with,

and the presence of the goods in the United Kingdom after that date or the non-observance of the condition has not been authorised for the purposes of this subsection by the Commissioners, the goods shall be liable to forfeiture under the Management Act and the VAT that would have been chargeable on the supply but for the zero-rating shall become payable forthwith by the person to whom the goods were supplied or by any person in whose possession the goods are found in the United Kingdom; but the Commissioners may, if they think fit, waive payment of the whole or part of that VAT.'

According to the Value Added Tax (Imported Goods) Relief Order 1984, certain goods distributed for the purposes of promoting a trade are not subject to VAT; this relief is available to many types of traders, including business houses engaged in e-Commerce, for example, sending samples via the Internet. Various forms of printed materials relevant to e-Commerce business imported from outside the EU area are given relief; these documents are usually meant for free distribution to encourage people to attract trade, cultural and tourism events.

'Export' in this context means exportation of goods from the UK to a country outside the European Union. Transfer of goods between the EU member states is known as 'removal' or 'dispatch'. VAT for the purposes of export or removal or dispatch is usually zero-rated.[141] Of course, in order to be eligible for zero-rating, a trader is required to satisfy Customs and Excise, by evidence, that the goods have, in fact, been exported from the UK.[142] What is to be borne in mind is that the supply of electronic data is regarded as supply of services; therefore transmission of software by telephone or by the Internet will not be regarded as exportation of goods and will not qualify for zero-rating.[143]

Traders from the EU member states are required to register for VAT in the UK where the 'relevant supplies' in a year exceed £70,000 in value. Schedule 2, paragraph 10 defines a 'relevant supply' in the following way:

---

[141] VAT Act, s 30(6).
[142] VAT Act, s 30(8).
[143] See also HM Customs and Excise Notice No. 703, s 6.6.

'For the purposes of this Schedule a supply of goods is a relevant supply where—

(a)   the supply involves the removal of the goods to the United Kingdom by or under the directions of the person making the supply;

(b)   the supply does not involve the installation or assembly of the goods at a place in the United Kingdom;

(c)   the supply is a transaction in pursuance of which goods are acquired in the United Kingdom from another member State by a person who is not a taxable person;

(d)   the supply is made on or after 1st January 1993 and in the course or furtherance of a business carried on by the supplier; and

(e)   the supply is neither an exempt supply nor a supply of goods which are subject to a duty of excise or consist in a new means of transport and is not anything which is treated as a supply for the purposes of this Act by virtue only of paragraph 5(1) or 6 of Schedule 4.'

The effect of 'distance sales' should also be considered in this context. One of the features of 'distance sales' is that under this method of sales a taxable person in another EU member state may supply goods to a non-taxable person in the UK, and the governing provision will be section 7(4) of the Act, according to which:

(4) Goods whose place of supply is not determined under any of the preceding provisions of this section shall be treated as supplied in the United Kingdom where—

(a)   the supply involves the removal of the goods to the United Kingdom by or under the directions of th person who supplies them;

(b)   the supply is a transaction in pursuance of which the goods are acquired in the United Kingdom from another member State by a person who is not a taxable person;

(c)   the supplier—
   (i)   is liable to be registered under Schedule 2; or
   (ii)   would be so liable if he were not already registered under this Act or liable to be registered under Schedule 1; and

(d)   the supply is neither a supply of goods consisting in a new means of transport nor anything which is treated as a supply for the purposes of this Act by virtue only of paragraph 5(1) or 6 of Schedule 4.

If the supply exceeds £70,000 in value, the location of supply becomes the UK, and the VAT will be accounted for in the country of destination, and until this amount is met, the EU trader will charge VAT on the supply in accordance with the rate prevailing in its own jurisdiction.

Section 7(5) of the Act provides that:

'Goods whose place of supply is not determined under any of the preceding provisions of this section and which do not consist in a new means of transport shall be treated as supplied outside the United Kingdom where—

(a)   the supply involves the removal of the goods, by or under the directions of the person who supplies them, to another member State;

(b)   the person who makes the supply is taxable in another member State; and

(c)   provisions of the law of that member State corresponding, in relation to that member State, to the provisions made by subsection (4) above make that person liable to VAT on the supply;

but this subsection shall not apply in relation to any supply in a case where the liability mentioned in paragraph (c) above depends on the exercise by any person of an option in the United Kingdom corresponding to such an option as is mentioned in paragraph 1(2) of Schedule 2 unless that person has given, and has not withdrawn, a notification to the Commissioners that he wishes his supplies to be treated as taking place outside the United Kingdom where they are supplies in relation to which the other requirements of this subsection are satisfied.' In other words, in the event of a UK trader making supplies to a non-taxable person in another member state of the EU, the place of supply will not be the UK.

Section 7(7) of the Act provides that:

'Goods whose place of supply is not determined under any of the preceding provisions of this section but whose supply involves their removal to or from the United Kingdom shall be treated—

(a)   as supplied in the United Kingdom where their supply involves their removal from the United Kingdom without also involving their previous removal to the United Kingdom; and

(b)   as supplied outside the United Kingdom in any other case.'

12.4.2.5   The position of overseas traders

Certain overseas traders may be subject to VAT even in the absence of their physical presence in the UK, if the supply of goods or services takes place in the UK. Overseas traders in this context would stand for traders from non-EU countries. Section 7(6) of the Act provides that: a non-UK trader may engage an agent in the UK for the purposes of importing goods on behalf of the supplier and supplying them to UK customers. In this situation, the services of the agent will be subject to VAT at the standard rate, but the agent will be allowed to reclaim any VAT as input tax, and set-off the amount against the VAT received by virtue of goods supplied to the UK customer. The EU traders have not been treated as overseas traders in this context.

12.4.2.6 Conclusions

The system of taxation of corporate internet traders has already been discussed; this system places emphasis on 'residence' and the location of the central management and control of the company. The principal aspects of VAT have also been discussed. It is now opportune to summarise the tax issues. Although 'residence' and the location of the central management and control have been recognized as the basic criteria for levying tax, it is to be borne in mind that a non-resident internet trader may be brought within the purview of the UK corporation tax when it may be carrying on a trade through a branch or an agency or it may be subject to income tax by virtue of carrying on a trade within the UK. If a double taxation agreement exists between the UK and the non-resident, it must be proved that a trade is conducted within the UK, and the UK will be entitled to tax the business profits of a non-resident where profits are derived from a permanent place of business (establishment).[144] E-Commerce (Internet trade) may not be subject to UK taxation where a double taxation agreement based on the OECD principle exists, and that no form of presence, amounting to a permanent establishment, is capable of being established when a trade may be carried on by such means. There is a distinction between 'carrying on trade' within a country and 'trading with a country'; furthermore, whether a person is carrying on trade within a country is a question of fact;[145] and some of the factors which seem to be relevant are: (a) the place of payment; (b) the place of delivery of goods, (c) the place which issues receipts; (d) if any agent is appointed, the location of the agent; and (e) where advertisements were given for products or services by non-resident corporations or their agents in the UK for the purpose of causing contracts to be entered in the UK.[146] This last factor is extremely relevant to e-Commerce; according to this factor, there is no need to have any establishment in the UK, and profits need not be received in the UK. In *Werle & Co v Colquhoun*, it was confirmed that if contracts are made in the UK then the trade is carried on in the UK, but in *Firestone Tyre Co Ltd v Lewellin*, Lord Radcliffe stated that:

> 'the place of sale will not be the determining factor if there are other circumstances present that outweigh its importance or unless there are no other circumstances present that outweigh its importance, or unless there are no other circumstances that can.'[147]

These two cases, therefore, offered two different guidelines as to how to determine the location of contracting. Perhaps, the pragmatic way of resolving this problem would be whether the centre of operation from which profits arose[148] is

---

[144] In this connection one may refer to The Inland Revenue Guidance Manual entitled *Double Taxation Relief*.

[145] See further *Grainger & Son v William Lane Gough* (1896) A.C 325.

[146] See further *Werle & Co v Colquhoun* (1888) 20 QBD 753.

[147] [1957] 1 All E.R. 561 at 568.

[148] See further JB Hickey et al, *E-Commerce: Law, Business and Tax Planning* (Bristol, Jordans, 2000) at 213.

in the UK. It has been discussed that 'residence' of a corporation in the UK generally forms the basis for levying corporation tax on its income, but in the case of an Internet company, it need not be resident in the UK. Furthermore, the entire sales and sales promotion activities may be operated by a company from outside the UK and this may be out of reach of the UK tax authorities. When a company may be serving from a number of jurisdictions, it would be very difficult to determine its tax liability, if at all, in any jurisdiction.

The double taxation agreements based on the OECD Double Taxation Convention, offer relief on tax on profits of a non-resident who carries on a business activity within a contracting party to such agreements. This principle applies to the UK also in respect of those of the agreements to which the UK is a party. Of course, the nature of the relief that may be available under a double taxation agreement, will depend on the terms of the agreement. These agreements, in fact, assist Internet companies in seeking relief from tax; they can also trade as non-residents. In the absence of a double taxation agreement, corporation tax may be imposed only if there exists a branch through which trade is carried on in the UK. The primary aspects of the OECD Model Convention have already been discussed. However, in the final analysis, a country's domestic tax legislation is the basic instrument by reference to which the tax liability of a business enterprise is determined.

13. Jurisdiction

13.1 Introduction

The term 'jurisdiction' in the context of the law of contract or the law of torts or any other branch of law stands for the authority of a court, that is, in the event of a dispute arising under a contract or in tort, or about any other matter, which court would be the most appropriate court to consider the dispute (assumption of jurisdiction). The other issue which should be considered along with jurisdiction, is the governing law, that is, what law must that court apply in settling a dispute. In relation to e-Commerce-related disputes, this twin-issue becomes particularly important as an e-Commerce based transaction may pass through a number of separate jurisdictions/territories.

In the European Economic Area, the issue of jurisdiction is usually determined by the provisions of the Brussels Convention on Jurisdiction and the Enforcement of Judgments in Civil and Commercial Matters 1968, which was introduced into English law by the Civil Jurisdiction and Judgments Act 1982. The EU member states, the European Free Trade Area (EFTA) countries and Poland are parties either to the Brussels Convention or the Lugano Convention on Jurisdiction and Enforcement of Judgments in Civil and Commercial Matters.[1]

Why are jurisdictional issues important in relation to contracts concluded by electronic means? Unless otherwise stated by the contracting parties or if any mandatory rule of law becomes relevant, jurisdiction of a court is determined by reference to the place of performance or the residence of the defendant. Legal difficulties in relation to the determination of jurisdiction may arise pertaining to transactions effected by electronic means. Take, for example, a money

---

[1] The Lugano Convention is in respect of all substantial matters identical to the Brussels Convention. Its purpose was to apply the principles of the Brussels Convention in a wider area, namely the European Economic Area and the EFTA Area. The admission of Portugal and Spain necessitated certain changes to the Lugano Convention. After the Treaty of Amsterdam came into effect, the European Commission submitted a proposal for a Council Regulation for a further revision of the Brussels Convention.

transfer made by a British national while in Colombia from his account with an Internet bank to another person's Internet bank account set up on a website viewed in another country. Unlike transactions based on letters of credit, in respect of which the place of negotiation or the place of payment determines the jurisdiction, in relation to the transaction of the nature referred to above, it would be necessary to determine the place at which the transaction actually took place or whether it is one single transaction or a series of transactions.

Contract-related issues are often determined by the rules of private international law, which are based on the notion of territorial boundaries—e-Commerce knows no territorial boundaries—therefore, some of the underlying assumptions of private international law may not be applied in all cases of transactions based on electronic means. E-Commerce draws a distinction between business-to-business (B^2B) and business-to-consumer (B^2C).[2] It should be considered whether this distinction is still sustainable.

The use of the Internet began in the late 1960s in connection with defence-related research. Its application gradually spread from government agencies and research institutions to business entities and individuals. It is elementary that activities through the Internet deny national boundaries and national sovereignty. The Internet is a set of network protocols which have been accepted by a large number of states, and thereby commercial entities and individuals in them, allowing transfer of information on a mutual basis. Thus, the rigid territorial concept of sovereignty is necessarily compromized in using the Internet. This compromize of sovereignty is based on assumed mutual benefit, economic, political and even military.

But the problem remains that the Internet is not subject to any centralized controlling body, and if such a body had existed, it would have been a non-national body with the power to control even sovereign authorities. Thus, it is possible to conclude that the use of the Internet or electronic technology necessarily and inevitably allows encroachment upon a state's sovereignty; however, as stated earlier, in the interest of reciprocity, whether for business, politics or military advantage, a relative use rather than an absolute use of sovereignty in this regard seems to have been accepted by the participating states. In order to take advantage of its merits, not only a common language, but also draft codes of conduct and rules on the use of domain names have been developed. It is for a state to provide for regulatory/preventative and remedial legislation, in order to ensure that abuse of the Internet either does not take place or if it does take place, the injured party is provided with remedies.

---

[2] Another type of transaction, namely, business-to-government (B^2G) is currently gaining ground.

13.2 The issue of sovereignty

Sovereignty is territorial; it has already been explained in section 1 of this chapter that the territorial boundaries become meaningless when a communication system makes the world one forum in disregard of the territorial concept of sovereignty. It is an established principle of public international law that the territorial integrity of a sovereign must be maintained; the use of the Internet belies that. Exclusivity of jurisdiction over domestic matters is an integral attribute of sovereignty, and that aspect of sovereignty is not to be affected or encroached upon by any external intervention of any nature.[3] If one accepts that technological and scientific advancement will make a communication system truly international by breaking down all national boundaries, one is then required to accept the inevitability of encroachment upon sovereignty; such an encroachment upon sovereignty may have to be tolerated, but within limits, for mutual benefit; and this flexibility in a sovereign's absolute power does not subordinate its jurisdiction to any external authority in respect of its exclusively domestic matters. As internal sovereignty is to be compromised in respect of transboundary communications, the issue remains how to determine the limit beyond which an external agent or source cannot encroach upon the internal sovereignty of a state. Given the capacity of the Internet and its variety of manifestations, it is extremely difficult and perhaps an act of naivety to make an attempt to set any limit. From this standpoint, the internal sovereignty of a state may not be protected from an external interventionist. Some might look at this 'intervention' from two points of view: (a) that for the sake of globalization of the communication system, a liberal attitude towards sovereignty needs to be maintained; and (b) that states, by mutual agreement or by means of treaties, may agree to such interventionist policies, as they take place within regional economic integrations, namely, the European Union.[4] But the ramifications of intervention by electronic means and intervention by Directives and Regulations of an economic integration are entirely different; whereas the former knows no bounds, intervention by Directives and Regulations is limited by the scope of the instrument. The purpose of acquiring information by distant and electronic methods can be to threaten the security and defence of a country—unless sufficient and effective safeguards against such activity are available to a country. It has already been explained in the section entitled 'Scenario' in this work that fool-proof protective measures may not be available or guaranteed.

With the advent of electronic commerce (cyberspace) one of the tenets of sovereignty—territorial integrity, which public international law has so rigidly maintained, is not threatened.

The general policy of promoting the need for using sovereignty in a relative sense rather than in its absolute/rigid form, for international economic

---

[3] See L Oppenheim, *International Law*, vol. I.
[4] See further N MacCormick, 'Beyond Sovereign State', 56 *Modern Law Review* 1.

and commercial co-operation may not be over-emphasized; hence the need for multilateral treaties. In the case of electronic commerce, encroachment upon, not surrender of sovereignty, is inevitable, and the stronger will have the capacity to encroach in an immeasurable way upon the weaker. In order to take precautionary measures against such an onslaught on sovereignty, there only remain two means, although no guarantee as to their effectiveness may be assumed: multilateral treaties and the implementation of the Codes of Conduct adopted by international and inter-governmental organisations.

There already exists controversy as to issuance of judicial orders by courts extra-territorially[5]; extra-territorial application of electronic commerce or cyberspace power is exercised by corporate entities or even by individuals; thus corporate entities and even individuals are able to intervene in the territorial integrity of a sovereign entity, and the former may not be subject to any judicial process by the latter.

Human rights, the guardian of which is the state, may be denied, particularly in regard to privacy, by users of electronic means or cyberspace, extra-territorially, and the affected individual may not have any remedy against it, as the state to which it belongs is not a violator of human rights in such circumstances, unless, of course, the state concerned may agree to espouse its individual's case. Encroachment upon human rights or general economic and commercial rights respectively of the individual and corporate bodies by cyberspace activity extra-territorially can become a common phenomenon. The constitutional guarantees of the individual's rights are thus threatened, not by other states necessarily, but by private entities, including individuals.

The use of cyberspace may also threaten the foundations of international diplomacy by the acquisition of information from other states surreptitiously—such activities are certainly contrary to the provisions of Article 2(4) of the UN Charter, which provides that:

> 'All Members shall refrain in their international relations from the threat or use of force against the territorial integrity or political independence of any State, or in any other manner inconsistent with the Purpose of the United Nations.'

Again, in this process, the technologically advanced states will be able to overpower the technologically backward states. A cyberspace colonization process will be set in. A state's sovereignty will be at bay. The basic ethos of inter-state diplomacy based on the principle of sovereign equality, for the purpose of developing true political and economic reciprocity, will be threatened and questioned.

---

[5] See *British Nylon Spinners v. ICI* [1995] Ch. 37; *Rio Tinto Zinc v. Westinghouse Electric Corporation* [1978] AC 847; *British Airways v. Laker Airlines* [1984] AC 58; and *Wood Pulp* [1985] CMLR 474.

If diplomacy is dominated by technology, then one should reflect on the utility of creating and developing cultural, scientific and commercial diplomacy by personal interventions. The divide between the technologically developed and technologically disadvantaged states in the sphere of international diplomacy will widen, and instead of facilitating the aspirations of a global diplomacy in its true sense, grouping of states will become even more manifest, based on their technological capacity.

Cyberspace activity may also culminate in international crime in that it may promote inter-state illegal activities, whether in relation to trade, traffic in illicit commodities or conspiracy, financial or commercial crimes. In considering jurisdictional issues with regard to electronic commerce or cyberspace, one may like to bear in mind the issues which have been identified above, and in particular the all pervasiveness and ramifications of the use of technology in international commerce.

13.3 What is in issue?

As stated earlier, e-Commerce is primarily and exclusively a means of sending messages and documents by electronic means. This is done through electronic webs—the Internet. The popular perception has been that the Internet system has conquered national boundaries. E-Commerce which is carried out through the Internet is not an entirely novel means from a lawyer's perspective—it is simply a progression in the system of trans-boundary or transnational communication from say, telephone or facsimile. One of the main differences from the existing systems of trans-boundary communication and the system of transmitting information through the Internet is that the Internet makes information available simultaneously in every jurisdiction in the world, and in that event how jurisdiction is to be established.

This chapter discusses the general bases for assuming jurisdiction by courts, whether in relation to ordinary commercial contracts or intellectual property rights. It must be emphasized however that a national legal system may have its unique reasons for assuming jurisdiction, and in that event the general bases will not apply, for example, under French law, French courts may assume jurisdiction against non-EEA defendants domiciled outside the EEA area, if the plaintiff is French; in other words, the nationality principle is addressed by the French courts. This chapter is also concerned with actions in personam, that is, actions brought against a person or a corporate body to compel him/her or it to do a particular thing such as payment of damages for breach of contract or for a tortious liability or the specific performance of a contract or not to do something. Usually, the claimant will have a choice about the jurisdiction, but under the Brussels Convention, if the defendant is resident in a contracting state, the claimant, even if he is outside a contracting state will be required to be governed by the Brussels Convention, that is, he/she/it must be sued in a Brussels Convention jurisdiction.

This chapter does not discuss admiralty action in rem, as to do so would be beyond the remit of this work. Claimants and defendants outside the remit of the Brussels Convention can still decide on their jurisdiction, and even the governing law of their contract. In this context, it should be mentioned that the basic rule of 'general jurisdiction' requires that a 'link' between the defendant and the chosen court exists; this link is primarily established by referring to 'residence' or 'presence' of the defendant in the jurisdiction. There also exists the concept of 'special jurisdiction', which becomes relevant when a claimant deserves special consideration, namely, insurance cases in which a policy holder will have a claim against an insurance company in a particular jurisdiction. The 'protective jurisdiction' on the other hand, allows a claimant to sue the defendant in his home jurisdiction e0ven if the defendant is based outside the claimant's jurisdiction. Of course, English courts can always assume jurisdiction when a defendant voluntarily submits to them. Currently, jurisdiction is governed by the 'Convention' rules and the 'traditional' rules. The Convention rules are now being reviewed by the Hague Convention on Private International Law.

13.4 The convention rules

The Convention Rules were originally established by the Brussels Convention which came into force on 1 February 1973. This Convention text has been amended by four Accession Conventions: the first, signed on 10 October 1978, followed the enlargement of the Community to include Denmark, Ireland, and the UK. The 1978 text was given effect in law of the UK by the Civil Jurisdiction and Judgments Act 1982, which came into force on 1 January 1987.

In 1982, a further Accession Convention was signed because of the membership of Greece, but only minor amendments were made to the Convention. On 16 September, 1988, the Lugano Convention which was closely based on the Brussels Convention, was concluded by the Members of the European Community and of the European Free Trade Area. It is known as the 'Parallel Convention' and its purpose was to apply the principles of the Brussels Convention in a wider area; namely, the European Economic Area and the EFTA. The admission of Portugal and Spain necessitated certain changes to the Lugano Convention, but the Convention otherwise amended certain of the substantive provisions of the Brussels Convention, often with minor differences from the Brussels Convention. After the Treaty of Amsterdam came into effect, the European Commission submitted a proposal for a Council Regulation for a further revision of the Brussels Convention.

The scope of the Brussels Convention has been subject to controversy. For example, the Convention does not define the 'civil and commercial matters'. In a common law jurisdiction it may include any matter or issue other than a matter or an issue coming under the purview of criminal law. By contrast, in civil jurisdictions, specific meaning is attached to the term.[6] In *LTU GmbH v Eurocontrol*,[7] the European Court held that this term must be given a 'Convention' meaning, rather than giving a meaning with reference to any particular legal system. According to the Court:

'In the interpretation of the concept 'civil and commercial matters' for the purposes of the application of the Convention of 27 September 1978 on Jurisdiction and Enforcement of Judgments in Civil and Commercial Matters, in particular, Title III thereof, reference must not be made to the law of one of the States concerned, but, first, to the objectives and scheme of the Convention and secondly, to the general principles which stem from the corpus of the national legal systems.'[8]

This decision of the European Court has a far-reaching effect on both civil and common law systems, but the courts under both the systems are required to accept this definition when a dispute is to be governed by the provisions of the Brussels Convention, if the parties of a dispute are contracting parties and if the defendant is domiciled or present in the EU area. It would now be appropriate to discuss the concepts of 'domicile' and 'residence' which are fundamental to determining the jurisdiction of a court or tribunal.

13.5 Domicile

Over the years English courts have developed an identifiable judicial guidelines on how to determine the domicile of a defendant, be it an individual or a corporate body. The concept of domicile is now required to be considered in accordance with the provisions of the Brussels Convention.

13.5.1 Individuals

The key article under the Brussels Convention is Article 52(1), which provides that:

'In determining whether a party is domiciled in the territory of a Contracting State before whose courts action is brought, the Court shall apply its domestic law.'

According to this Article, in order to determine whether a party to a cause of action is domiciled in the contracting state with whose court an action has been filed, the court concerned is required to apply its internal law. Traditionally, English courts have placed importance on the domicile of origin or permanent

---

[6] See, for example, *Re the State of Norway's Application (Nos 1 and 2)* [1990] 1 A.C. 723.
[7] [1976] E.L.R. 1541.
[8] op cit, at 1552.

home, but the Brussels Convention seems to place most emphasis on 'habitual residence' the concept of which is not totally unknown to the English jurisprudence.[9] Section 41 of the Civil Jurisdiction and Judgments Act 1982 provides that:

'(1) Subject to Article 52 (which contains provisions for determining whether a party is domiciled in a Contracting State), the following provisions of this section determine, for the purposes of the 1968 Convention and this Act, whether an individual is domiciled in the United Kingdom or in a particular part of, or place in, the United Kingdom or in a state other than a Contracting State.

(2) An individual is domiciled in the United Kingdom if and only if-
   (a) he is resident in the United Kingdom; and
   (b) the nature and circumstances of his residence indicate that he has a substantial connection with the United Kingdom.

(3) Subject to subsection (5), an individual is domiciled in a particular part of the United Kingdom if and only if-
   (a) he is resident in that part; and
   (b) the nature and circumstances of his residence indicate that he has a substantial connection with that part.

(4) An individual is domiciled in a particular place in the United Kingdom if and only if he-
   (a) is domiciled in the part of the United Kingdom in which that place is situated; and
   (b) is resident in that place.

(5) An individual who is domiciled in the United Kingdom but in whose case the requirements of subsection (3)(b) are not satisfied in relation to any particular part of the United Kingdom shall be treated as domiciled in the part of the United Kingdom in which he is resident.

(6) In the case of an individual who-
   (a) is resident in the United Kingdom, or in a particular part of the United Kingdom; and
   (b) has been so resident for the last three months or more,
   the requirements of subsection (2)(b) or, as the case may be, subsection (3)(b) shall be presumed to be fulfilled unless the contrary is proved.

(7) An individual is domiciled in a state other than a Contracting State if and only if-
   (a) he is resident in that state; and
   (b) the nature and circumstances of his residence indicate that he has a substantial connection with that state.'

In other words, an individual is domiciled in the UK if he is resident in the UK, and has a substantial connection with the UK. The term 'residence' and

---

[9] See *Shah v Barnett London Borough Council* [1983] 2 A.C. 309; see also P M North and J J Fawcett, *Cheshire and North's Private International Law* (London, Butterworths, 1999) at 161–165.

'substantial connection' will also provoke controversy, because there does not exist any definition of these terms. In practice, however, three months' residence in the UK seems to be sufficient to satisfy the conditions of 'residence' and 'substantial connection'.[10] On the other hand, if a person is domiciled in the UK but has no substantial connection with any part of the UK, he is to be treated as domiciled in the part of the UK in which he is resident.[11] In order to determine whether a party is domiciled in another contracting state, the court must apply the law of that state.[12] In other words, domicile of a person must be determined by reference to his habitual residence and the law of the contracting state in which he is habitually resident. Finally, the issue of the 'substantial connection' may be determined by referring to the person's activities in that state and his intention to be domiciled in that area of the country.

13.5.2 Corporations and associations

The 'seat' of a corporation or an association becomes the reference point in determining the domicile of a corporation or an association.[13] Paragraphs (3) and (4) of section 42 of the Civil Jurisdiction and Judgments Act provide for the determination of the seat of corporations and associations. A corporation or an association has its seat in the UK if it was formed or incorporated under the law of a part of the UK, and has its registered office or an official address in the UK.[14] The central management and control may reside in a particular part of the country. The location of the 'seat' of the corporation is determined by reference to section 42(5) of the Act; in other words, by referring to the law of the jurisdiction in which they were formed and have their registered office or official address. Where a corporate body may have more than one seat, the effective 'seat' will be determined. In *Deichland*[15] the principal legal issues were: (a) whether the 1968 Convention had any application to Admiralty action in rem, and whether the English High Court had jurisdiction by reason of Article 57 of the Brussels Convention, section 9 of the Civil Jurisdiction and Judgments Act 1982 and the International Convention for Unification of Certain Rules relating to the Arrest of Sea-going Ships 1952; and (b) whether the Deichland could be deemed as domiciled in the Federal Republic of Germany under Article 2 of the Brussels Convention.

In a dispute concerning the quality of cargo shipped in the Deichland, the owners of the Deichland maintained that the action should have been brought in the then Federal Republic of Germany as the defendants were domiciled in

---

[10] ss 41(4) and 41(6), 1982 Act.
[11] s 41(5), 1982 Act; see also s 41(3), 1982 Act.
[12] s 52(2), 1982 Act.
[13] Art 53(1) of the Convention.
[14] See *De Beers Consolidated Mines Ltd v Howe* [1906] A.C. 455; see also *Swedish Central Railway v Thompson* [1925] A.C. 495, and *Egyptian Delta Land and Investment Co Ltd v Todd* [1929] A.C. 1. In the latter two cases the central management and control was not, in reality, located in the UK.
[15] [1990] 1 Q.B. 361.

the said jurisdiction. The relied upon Article 2 of the Brussels Convention on Jurisdiction and the Enforcement of Judgments in Civil and Commercial Matters 1968, according to which:

> 'persons domiciled in the territory of a Contracting State shall, irrespective of their nationality, be sued in the courts of that State.'

It is not necessary to discuss the matters about the admiralty jurisdiction in rem in the context of this chapter. Section 42 was the most relevant section in deciding this case, and the Court of Appeal held, *inter alia*, that:

> 'it was quite clear from s 42(3) and 42(6) that for the purpose of the 1982 Act a corporation might satisfy the statutory test in relation to more than one state; for the purpose of Article 2 Deich were domiciled in the Federal Republic of Germany because the seat of the company was in Germany by virtue of the test prescribed in s 42(6)(b) of the 1982 Act.'

Deich was incorporated in Panama, but its central management and control were exercised in the Federal Republic of Germany. The Brussels Convention has application only between contracting parties. Panama is not a contracting party to the 1968 Convention; therefore even though Deich might have multiple seats, the 'real seat' must be found between the Federal Republic of Germany and the UK. But, domicile must be determined by reference to the seat that is most effective and functional. These two criteria are to be satisfied by referring to the activities of the corporation from a seat—these activities may include but are not exclusive to, holding of annual general meetings, the maintenance of share registers, maintenance of bank account(s) or policy-making. The residence of a corporation is primarily important for purposes of taxation. Briefly, a corporation is resident in a country where its central management and control are exercised, and the country of incorporation is not important in that context, if the corporation is not resident there. Where the central management and control are divided between two or more jurisdictions, then the corporation is resident in those jurisdictions.[16]

13.6   Jurisdiction based on domicile

Article 21(1) of the Brussels Convention provides that irrespective of his/her nationality, a person domiciled in a contracting state must be sued in the courts of that state in which he/she is domiciled. In the case of a corporation or an association, the domicile (the seat) becomes important for determining the jurisdiction. For the purposes of instituting proceedings the defendant company or

---

[16] *De Beers Consolidated Mines Ltd v Howe*, [1906] AC 455; *Swedish Central Railway v Thompson* [1924] 2 K.B. 255; *Egyptian Delta Land and Investment Co Ltd v Todd* [1929] AC 1; and *Unit Construction Co Ltd v Bullock* [1960] A.C. 351.

association must be domiciled in the state concerned at the time of issuing proceedings, rather than the date on which service was effected.[17]

Under Articles 5–18 of the Convention, if a proposed defendant is domiciled in another contracting state, he may still be sued in England, but where a defendant is not domiciled in another contracting state, then the jurisdictional rules of the national law of the forum shall apply, subject to Article 16 which confers exclusive jurisdiction on the courts of particular contracting state irrespective of the domicile of the parties. This is discussed in the following section.

13.7   Exclusive jurisdiction

Article 16 provides that in view of the subject matter of the dispute, the courts of a particular contracting state shall have exclusive jurisdiction. The issue of the domicile of the defendant as a basis for jurisdiction would not arise. In such cases, the Convention rules will not apply. Thus, where a court of another contracting state has exclusive jurisdiction, other probable courts of contracting states shall declare that they lack jurisdiction.[18] The exclusive jurisdiction is determined by referring to the 'object' of the proceedings—the nature of the subject matter of the proceedings. This is to be determined in each case individually. Exclusive jurisdiction relates to the following:

(a)   immovable property;
(b)   corporations;
(c)   public registers;
(d)   intellectual property; and
(e)   enforcement of judgments.

In so far as e-Commerce related transactions are concerned, if a patent, trade mark or design is registered in England, infringement proceedings will have to be brought in England. The other items over which exclusive jurisdiction is to be exercised do not relate to transactions by electronic means.

13.8   Special jurisdiction

Article 5 of the Convention deals with cases of special jurisdiction, according to which a person who is domiciled in one contracting state may be sued in England if the subject matter of the dispute is closely connected with England. Article 5 of the Convention provides, *inter alia*, that:

---

[17] *Canada Trust Co v Stolzenberg (No. 2)* [1998] 1 W.L.R. 547.
[18] Art 19.

'A person domiciled in a Contracting State may, in another Contracting State be sued-

1   In matters relating to a contract, in the courts for the place of performance of the obligation in question; in matters relating to individual contracts of employment this place is that where the employee habitually carries out his work, or if the employee does not habitually carry out his work in any one country, the employer may also be sued in the courts for the place where the business which engaged the employee was or is not situated.

2   In matters relating to maintenance in the courts for the place where the maintenance creditors is domiciled or habitually resident or if the matter is ancillary to proceedings concerning the status of a person in the court which, according to its own law has jurisdiction to entertain those proceedings unless that jurisdiction is based solely on the nationality of one of the parties.

3   In matters relating to tort, delict or quasi-delict in the courts for the place where the harmful even occurred.

4   As regards a civil claim for damages or restitution which is based on an act giving rise to criminal proceedings in the court seised of those proceedings to the extent that that court has jurisdiction under its own law to entertain civil proceedings.

5   As regards a dispute arising out of the operation of a branch, agency, or other establishment in the courts for the place in which the branch, agency or other establishment is situated.'

In the case of an e-Commerce-related legal issue, therefore, the place of performance of the contract will have to be taken into consideration, or in the case of an employment-related issue, the jurisdiction in which the employee concerned habitually carries out his work, or where an employer is to be sued, it may be sued in the courts in the jurisdiction in which the business which engaged the employee was or is now situated. It is for each national court to determine the place of performance by referring to factual evidence.[19]

According to Article 6, a person domiciled in a contracting state may also be sued in the following circumstances: (a) if he is one of a number of defendants in the courts in the jurisdiction in which he is domiciled; (b) 'as a third party in an action on a warranty or guarantee or in any other third party proceedings in the court seised of the original proceedings unless these were instituted solely with the object of removing from the jurisdiction of the court which would be competent in his case'; (c) in the case of a counterclaim arising from the same contract or facts on which the original claim was based, the court in which the original claim is still pending.

---

[19] Case 12/76 *Industrie Tessali Italiania Como v Dunlop A.G.* [1976] E.C.R. 1473; see also Case C-440/97 *GIE Groupe Concorde v The Suhadiwarno Panjan* E.C.J. (1999); and *Viskase Ltd v Paul Kiefel GmgH* [1999] 3 All E.R. 362.

Where a claim may relate to several identifiable obligations, with different places of performance, the court is required to identify the principal obligation,[20] in accordance with the principle, accessorium sequitor. There can be cases in which the principal obligation may not be easily identifiable as several obligations may see to be of equal importance or priority.[21] In such a situation, the court can assume jurisdiction in respect of the obligation if the place of performance is within its territory; however, under Article 2, a claimant can exercise his option of bringing an action in the country of the defendant's domicile. This provision will not apply however when the parties do not belong to the contracting states of the Brussels Convention.

13.9   Other bases of jurisdiction

The other bases of jurisdiction may be found in various provisions of the Convention, for example, Article 17, Article 18, Article 21, Article 22, Article 23 and Article 24. Article 17 is concerned with the prorogation of jurisdiction—if one or more of the parties domiciled in a contracting state has or have agreed that the court or courts of a contracting state are to assume jurisdiction to settle disputes which have actually arisen or which may arise in connection with a particular legal relationship, then the court or those courts shall have exclusive jurisdiction, provided that such an agreement conferring jurisdiction is either in writing or evidenced in writing, or in a form which has been mutually agreed upon between the parties or 'in international trade or commerce, in a form which accords with a usage of which the parties are or ought to have been aware and which in such trade or commerce is widely known to, and regularly observed by the parties to contracts of the type involved in the particular trade or commerce concerned'. This latter provision is particularly important for e-Commerce related issues. In the event of such an agreement being concluded by the parties none of whom is domiciled in a contracting state, the courts of other contracting states shall have no jurisdiction over their disputes 'unless the court or courts chosen have declined jurisdiction'. Article 17 also provides that:

'If an agreement conferring jurisdiction was concluded for the benefit of only one of the parties that party shall retain the right to bring proceedings in any other court which has jurisdiction by virtue of this Convention.'

Article 18 provides that:

'Apart from jurisdiction derived from other provisions of this Convention a court of a Contracting State before whom a defendant enters an appearance shall have jurisdiction. This rule shall not apply where appearance was entered solely to contest the jurisdiction, or where another court has exclusive jurisdiction by virtue of Article 16.'

[20] *Union Transport Group plc v Continental Lines SA* [1992] 1 W.L.R. 15.
[21] Case c-420/97 *Leathertex Divisional Sintetici SpA v Bodetex B.V.B.A* E.C.J. (1999).

It is universally recognized principle that if a defendant enters on appearance before a court, that court shall have jurisdiction, provided of course, that the appearance was not entered solely to contest the jurisdiction of that court.

Articles 21, 22 and 23 are concerned with related actions—lis pendens, which need not be explained in detail. The basic principles have been stated in Article 21:

> 'Where proceedings involving the same cause of action and between the same parties are brought in the courts of different Contracting States, any court other than the court first seised of its own motion stay its proceedings until such time as the jurisdiction of the court first seised is established.
>
> Where the jurisdiction of the court first seised is established, any court other than the court first seised shall decline jurisdiction in favour of that court.'

It is important to reproduce Article 23, which provides that:

> 'Where actions come within the exclusive jurisdiction of several courts, any court other than the court first seised shall decline jurisdiction in favour of that court.'

In other words, the issue of the exclusive jurisdiction remains important. Article 16 (Exclusive Jurisdiction) will not have any overriding effect over Article 24 thatprovides for provisional, including protective measures. This Article provides that:

> 'Application may be made to the courts of a Contracting State for such provisional, including protective measures as may be available under the law of that State, even if, under this Convention, the courts of another Contracting State have jurisdiction as to the substance of the matter.'

This is because in order to facilitate provisional and protective measures, the local court concerned in the jurisdiction of which the matters to be protected or over which provisional measures need to be taken are located, should be allowed jurisdiction. Jurisdiction over provisional including protective measures and jurisdiction as to the substance of a matter are two different issues. Protective measures under Article 24 may take the form of freezing the assets of the defendant in his jurisdiction or even outside his jurisdiction, in order to ensure that he is unable to remove his assets out of the jurisdiction or that his assets are not allowed to be spent beyond the limit for which the claim has been filed by the claimant. In order to allow a claimant a freezing order, the claimant is required to establish that he has a good arguable case on the merits.[22] In *Derby v Weldon*

---

[22] The power to grant a freezing order is derived from s 37(3) of the Supreme Court Act 1981.

(No. 1) the Court of Appeal established that such orders may be granted in relation to assets abroad.[23]

13.10   Branches and agencies

In relation to e-Commerce, the issue of jurisdiction pertaining to the activities of branches and agencies assumes importance; the jurisdiction may be challenged by the parent company or the principal, as the case may be, on the grounds that the courts in the jurisdiction in which the centre of control and management is should assume jurisdiction. If the issue of the jurisdiction is not governed by the Brussels Convention, then the factors which help establish connection with a jurisdiction become important in determining the jurisdiction. The governing provision may be found in Article 5(5) of the Brussels Convention, as amended. It is important to ascertain whether a particular entity is an extension of the parent body, and is subject to its control. This issue is to be determined by referring to the commercial activities of the parent and its branches, subsidiaries or agents.[24] The place of performance should be determined by referring to the 'commercial activities' performed in that place. Indeed, Article 5(5) accords importance to the place of performance. In e-Commerce, the place from which a message is transmitted confirming that the act in whatever form it may be, has been performed, must be construed as the place of performance, and this place of performance will coincide with jurisdiction.

13.11   Jurisdiction over consumer contracts

Articles 13–15 of the Convention made provision for jurisdiction over consumer contracts. These provisions are exclusive, but they are without prejudice to the provisions of Article 4[25] and paragraph 5 of Article 5. Article 13 defines 'consumer' and 'consumer contract'. A consumer is a person who concludes a contract for 'a purpose which can be regarded as being outside his trade or profession'. A 'consumer contract', on the other hand, is 'a contract for the sale of goods on instalment credit terms'. [26] In other words, such contracts must be (a) contracts for sale of goods; and (b) they must be on credit terms. These contracts are usually sought by mail from the prospective consumers' jurisdictions. Article 14 of the Convention provides that:

---

[23] [1990] Ch. 13.

[24] Case 218/86 *S.A.R. Schotte GmbH v Parfums Rothschild* [1987] E.C.R. 4905.

[25] 'If the defendant is not domiciled in a Contracting State, the jurisdiction of the courts of each Contracting State shall, subject to the provisions of Article 16, be determined by the law of that State. As against such a defendant, any person domiciled in a Contracting State may, whatever his nationality, avail himself in that State of the rules of jurisdiction there in force, and in particular those specified in the second paragraph of Article 3, in the same way as the nationals of that State'.

[26] See Case 150/77 *Société Bertrand v Paul Ott K.G.* [1978] E.C.R. 1431.

'A consumer may bring proceedings against the other party to a contract either in the courts of the Contracting State in which that party is domiciled or in the courts of the Contracting State in which he is himself domiciled.

Proceedings may be brought against a consumer by the other party to the contract only in the courts of the Contracting State in which the consumer is domiciled.

These provisions shall not affect the right to bring a counterclaim in the court in which, in accordance with this Section, the original claim is pending.'

Thus the consumer's domicile determines the jurisdiction in the event of a dispute arising under Article 14. In the event of a consumer entering into a contract with a party who is not domiciled in a contracting state but has a branch, agency or other establishment in one of the contracting state, according to Article 13, 'that party shall, in dispute arising out of the operation of the branch, agency or establishment, be deemed to be domiciled in that State'.[27]

Article 15 offers consumers a choice to determine their jurisdiction only in certain specified circumstances:

'The provisions of this Section may be departed from only by agreement:
1. Which is entered into after the dispute has arise, or
2. Which allowed the consumer to bring proceedings in courts other than those indicated in this Section, or
3. Which is entered into by the consumer and the other party to the contract, both of whom are at the time of conclusion of the contract domiciled or habitually resident in the same Contracting State and which confers jurisdiction on the courts of that State, provided that such an agreement is not contrary to the law of that State.'

13.12 Conclusions

Whenever a defendant is an action is domiciled in England and Wales, jurisdiction shall be based on the Brussels Convention or the Lugano Convention, as the case may be. Non-parties to these Conventions have a choice to submit to the English jurisdiction, and in that event, the usual practice of dealing with foreign parties in foreign jurisdictions (service of the jurisdiction) will come into play.

Domicile based on connection with the jurisdiction still forms the foundation of jurisdiction. 'Connection' with the jurisdiction may be required to be established

---

[27] Art 13 has no application to contracts of transport.

by referring to various relevant factors, the language of the contract, the form of the contract, the currency in which payment is to be made; the place of arbitration, if mentioned etc. The Brussels Convention makes special provision for the protection of consumers. In determining jurisdiction pertaining to e-Commerce based contracts, the domicile of the transmitter (the offeror) is important; if however, the offer is transmitted from a foreign jurisdiction (through a subsidiary or a branch or an agency) at the instruction of the actual transmitter (subsidiary or a branch or an agency) will determine jurisdiction.

There is no reason why the current rules on jurisdiction, whether under the Brussels or Lugano Convention or otherwise, may not be able to settle the jurisdictional issues that may arise under e-Commerce contracts.

Conclusions

Business through e-Commerce can be simple and efficient, and yet, it may give rise to a variety of legal complexities. This work has attempted to discuss and analyse most of the important issues pertaining to e-Commerce. It is clear that with the advancement of science and technology, which seems to be unrestrained, various new dimensions to e-Commerce will emerge. This work deliberately avoids discussing illicit trade through the Internet.

In so far as contracting through e-Commerce is concerned, the current legislation and judicial guidelines seem to be adequate to deal with the issues that may emanate from e-Commerce, except in areas such as tax and intellectual property. It has been explained that the law of negligence, including the judicial guidelines developed by the English courts is adequate to deal with the issues that may arise from e-Commerce. the current law of taxation is not clear as to what kinds of income of capital gains should be taxable; this is particularly because of the intervention of technology in e-Commerce. In so far as intellectual property rights are concerned, again, the definition of computer programmes, and the issues relating to novelty and invention still remain unexplained or undetermined. It is not clear however, why certain types of computer programme containing original ideas should not have the benefit of intellectual property law universally.

It is noteworthy however, that there exists a consensus particularly among the developed states that the issue of consumer protection should be acknowledged as an important issue; indeed, this is an issue which deserves even more attention from the international community, and states should develop legislation and implement it as effectively as possible.

Finally, e-Commerce is a 'buzz word', but the buzzing will not produce any effective result unless developing countries are able to co-operate with and participate in e-Commerce in the way the developed world can. This is an important issue for the developed world because if it wishes to expand its business activities worldwide, it is essential to ensure that the developing world can effectively participate in e-Commerce. International co-operation in developing e-Commerce in the developing world is thus urgently needed.

Directive 2000/31/EC of the European Parliament and of the Council

of 8 June 2000

on certain legal aspects of information society services, in particular electronic commerce, in the Internal Market (Directive on electronic commerce)

THE EUROPEAN PARLIAMENT AND THE COUNCIL OF THE EUROPEAN UNION,

Having regard to the Treaty establishing the European Community, and in particular Articles 47(2), 55 and 95 thereof,

Having regard to the proposal from the Commission([1]),

Having regard to the opinion of the Economic and Social Committee([2]),

Acting in accordance with the procedure laid down in Article 251 of the Treaty([3]),

Whereas:

(1)   The European Union is seeking to forge ever closer links between the States and peoples of Europe, to ensure economic and social progress; in accordance with Article 14(2) of the Treaty, the internal market comprises an area without internal frontiers in which the free movements of goods, services and the freedom of establishment are ensured; the development of information society services within the area without internal frontiers is vital to eliminating the barriers which divide the European peoples.

(2)   The development of electronic commerce within the information society offers significant employment opportunities in the Community, particularly in small and medium-sized enterprises, and will stimulate economic growth and investment in innovation by European companies, and can also enhance the competitiveness of European industry, provided that everyone has access to the Internet.

(3)   Community law and the characteristics of the Community legal order are a vital asset to enable European citizens and operators to take full advantage, without consideration of borders, of the opportunities afforded by electronic commerce; this Directive therefore has the purpose of ensuring a high level of Community legal integration in order to establish a real area without internal borders for information society services.

(4)   It is important to ensure that electronic commerce could fully benefit from the internal market and therefore that, as with Council Directive 89/552/EEC of 3 October 1989 on the coordination of certain provisions laid down by law,

regulation or administrative action in Member States concerning the pursuit of television broadcasting activities([4]), a high level of Community integration is achieved.

(5) The development of information society services within the Community is hampered by a number of legal obstacles to the proper functioning of the internal market which make less attractive the exercise of the freedom of establishment and the freedom to provide services; these obstacles arise from divergences in legislation and from the legal uncertainty as to which national rules apply to such services; in the absence of coordination and adjustment of legislation in the relevant areas, obstacles might be justified in the light of the case-law of the Court of Justice of the European Communities; legal uncertainty exists with regard to the extent to which Member States may control services originating from another Member State.

(6) In the light of Community objectives, of Articles 43 and 49 of the Treaty and of secondary Community law, these obstacles should be eliminated by coordinating certain national laws and by clarifying certain legal concepts at Community level to the extent necessary for the proper functioning of the internal market; by dealing only with certain specific matters which give rise to problems for the internal market, this Directive is fully consistent with the need to respect the principle of subsidiarity as set out in Article 5 of the Treaty.

(7) In order to ensure legal certainty and consumer confidence, this Directive must lay down a clear and general framework to cover certain legal aspects of electronic commerce in the internal market.

(8) The objective of this Directive is to create a legal framework to ensure the free movement of information society services between Member States and not to harmonise the field of criminal law as such.

(9) The free movement of information society services can in many cases be a specific reflection in Community law of a more general principle, namely freedom of expression as enshrined in Article 10(1) of the Convention for the Protection of Human Rights and Fundamental Freedoms, which has been ratified by all the Member States; for this reason, directives covering the supply of information society services must ensure that this activity may be engaged in freely in the light of that Article, subject only to the restrictions laid down in paragraph 2 of that Article and in Article 46(1) of the Treaty; this Directive is not intended to affect national fundamental rules and principles relating to freedom of expression.

(10) In accordance with the principle of proportionality, the measures provided for in this Directive are strictly limited to the minimum needed to achieve the objective of the proper functioning of the internal market; where action at Community level is necessary, and in order to guarantee an area which is truly without internal frontiers as far as electronic commerce is concerned, the Directive must ensure a high level of protection of objectives of general interest, in particular the protection of minors and human dignity, consumer protection and the protection of public health; according to Article 152 of the Treaty, the protection of public health is an essential component of other Community policies.

(11) This Directive is without prejudice to the level of protection for, in particular, public health and consumer interests, as established by Community acts; amongst others, Council Directive 93/13/EEC of 5 April 1993 on unfair terms in consumer contracts([5]) and Directive 97/7/EC of the European Parliament and of the Council of 20 May 1997 on the protection of consumers in respect of distance contracts([6]) form a vital element for protecting consumers in contractual matters; those Directives also apply in their entirety to information society services; that same Community acquis, which is fully applicable to information society services, also embraces in particular Council Directive 84/450/EEC of 10 September 1984 concerning misleading and comparative advertising([7]), Council Directive 87/102/EEC of 22 December 1986 for the approximation of the laws, regulations and administrative provisions of the Member States concerning consumer credit([8]), Council Directive 93/22/EEC of 10 May 1993 on investment services in the securities field([9]), Council Directive 90/314/EEC of 13 June 1990 on package travel, package holidays and package tours([10]), Directive 98/6/EC of the European Parliament and of the Council of 16 February 1998 on consumer production in the indication of prices of products offered to consumers([11]), Council Directive 92/59/EEC of 29 June 1992 on general product safety([12]), Directive 94/47/EC of the European Parliament and of the Council of 26 October 1994 on the protection of purchasers in respect of certain aspects on contracts relating to the purchase of the right to use immovable properties on a timeshare basis([13]), Directive 98/27/EC of the European Parliament and of the Council of 19 May 1998 on injunctions for the protection of consumers' interests([14]), Council Directive 85/374/EEC of 25 July 1985 on the approximation of the laws, regulations and administrative provisions concerning liability for defective products([15]), Directive 1999/44/EC of the European Parliament and of the Council of 25 May 1999 on certain aspects of the sale of consumer goods and associated guarantees([16]), the future Directive of the European Parliament and of the Council concerning the distance marketing of consumer financial services and Council Directive 92/28/EEC of 31 March 1992 on the advertising of medicinal products([17]); this Directive should be without prejudice to Directive 98/43/EC of the European Parliament and of the Council of 6 July 1998 on the approximation of the laws, regulations and administrative provisions of the Member States relating to the advertising and sponsorship of tobacco products([18]) adopted within the framework of the internal market, or to directives on the protection of public health; this Directive complements information requirements established by the abovementioned Directives and in particular Directive 97/7/EC.

(12) It is necessary to exclude certain activities from the scope of this Directive, on the grounds that the freedom to provide services in these fields cannot, at this stage, be guaranteed under the Treaty or existing secondary legislation; excluding these activities does not preclude any instruments which might prove necessary for the proper functioning of the internal market; taxation, particularly value added tax imposed on a large number of the services covered by this Directive, must be excluded form the scope of this Directive.

(13) This Directive does not aim to establish rules on fiscal obligations nor does it pre-empt the drawing up of Community instruments concerning fiscal aspects of electronic commerce.

(14) The protection of individuals with regard to the processing of personal data is solely governed by Directive 95/46/EC of the European Parliament and of the Council of 24 October 1995 on the protection of individuals with regard to the processing of personal data and on the free movement of such data([19]) and Directive 97/66/EC of the European Parliament and of the Council of 15 December 1997 concerning the processing of personal data and the protection of privacy in the telecommunications sector([20]) which are fully applicable to information society services; these Directives already establish a Community legal framework in the field of personal data and therefore it is not necessary to cover this issue in this Directive in order to ensure the smooth functioning of the internal market, in particular the free movement of personal data between Member States; the implementation and application of this Directive should be made in full compliance with the principles relating to the protection of personal data, in particular as regards unsolicited commercial communication and the liability of intermediaries; this Directive cannot prevent the anonymous use of open networks such as the Internet.

(15) The confidentiality of communications is guaranteed by Article 5 Directive 97/66/EC; in accordance with that Directive, Member States must prohibit any kind of interception or surveillance of such communications by others than the senders and receivers, except when legally authorised.

(16) The exclusion of gambling activities from the scope of application of this Directive covers only games of chance, lotteries and betting transactions, which involve wagering a stake with monetary value; this does not cover promotional competitions or games where the purpose is to encourage the sale of goods or services and where payments, if they arise, serve only to acquire the promoted goods or services.

(17) The definition of information society services already exists in Community law in Directive 98/34/EC of the European Parliament and of the Council of 22 June 1998 laying down a procedure for the provision of information in the field of technical standards and regulations and of rules on information society services([21]) and in Directive 98/84/EC of the European Parliament and of the Council of 20 November 1998 on the legal protection of services based on, or consisting of, conditional access([22]); this definition covers any service normally provided for remuneration, at a distance, by means of electronic equipment for the processing (including digital compression) and storage of data, and at the individual request of a recipient of a service; those services referred to in the indicative list in Annex V to Directive 98/34/EC which do not imply data processing and storage are not covered by this definition.

(18) Information society services span a wide range of economic activities which take place on-line; these activities can, in particular, consist of selling goods on-line; activities such as the delivery of goods as such or the provision of services off-line are not covered; information society services are not solely restricted to services giving rise to on-line contracting but

also, in so far as they represent an economic activity, extend to services which are not remunerated by those who receive them, such as those offering on-line information or commercial communications, or those providing tools allowing for search, access and retrieval of data; information society services also include services consisting of the transmission of information via a communication network, in providing access to a communication network or in hosting information provided by a recipient of the service; television broadcasting within the meaning of Directive EEC/89/552 and radio broadcasting are not information society services because they are not provided at individual request; by contrast, services which are transmitted point to point, such as video-on-demand or the provision of commercial communications by electronic mail are information society services; the use of electronic mail or equivalent individual communications for instance by natural persons acting outside their trade, business or profession including their use for the conclusion of contracts between such persons is not an information society service; the contractual relationship between an employee and his employer is not an information society service; activities which by their very nature cannot be carried out at a distance and by electronic means, such as the statutory auditing of company accounts or medical advice requiring the physical examination of a patient are not information society services.

(19)   The place at which a service provider is established should be determined in conformity with the case-law of the Court of Justice according to which the concept of establishment involves the actual pursuit of an economic activity through a fixed establishment for an indefinite period; this requirement is also fulfilled where a company is constituted for a given period; the place of establishment of a company providing services via an Internet website is not the place at which the technology supporting its website is located or the place at which its website is accessible but the place where it pursues its economic activity; in cases where a provider has several places of establishment it is important to determine from which place of establishment the service concerned is provided; in cases where it is difficult to determine from which of several places of establishment a given service is provided, this is the place where the provider has the centre of his activities relating to this particular service.

(20)   The definition of 'recipient of a service' covers all types of usage of information society services, both by persons who provide information on open networks such as the Internet and by persons who seek information on the Internet for private or professional reasons.

(21)   The scope of the coordinated field is without prejudice to future Community harmonisation relating to information society services and to future legislation adopted at national level in accordance with Community law; the coordinated field covers only requirements relating to on-line activities such as on-line information, on-line advertising, on-line shopping, on-line contracting and does not concern Member States' legal requirements relating to goods such as safety standards, labelling obligations, or liability for goods, or Member States' requirements relating to the delivery or the transport of goods, including the distribution of medicinal products; the coordinated field does not cover the exercise of

rights of pre-emption by public authorities concerning certain goods such as works of art.

(22) Information society services should be supervised at the source of the activity, in order to ensure an effective protection of public interest objectives; to that end, it is necessary to ensure that the competent authority provides such protection not only for the citizens of its own country but for all Community citizens; in order to improve mutual trust between Member States, it is essential to state clearly this responsibility on the part of the Member State where the services originate; moreover, in order to effectively guarantee freedom to provide services and legal certainty for suppliers and recipients of services, such information society services should in principle be subject to the law of the Member State in which the service provider is established.

(23) This Directive neither aims to establish additional rules on private international law relating to conflicts of law nor does it deal with the jurisdiction of Courts; provisions of the applicable law designated by rules of private international law must not restrict the freedom to provide information society services as established in this Directive.

(24) In the context of this Directive, notwithstanding the rule on the control at source of information society services, it is legitimate under the conditions established in this Directive for Member States to take measures to restrict the free movement of information society services.

(25) National courts, including civil courts, dealing with private law disputes can take measures to derogate from the freedom to provide infor-

mation society services in conformity with conditions established in this Directive.

(26) Member States, in conformity with conditions established in this Directive, may apply their national rules on criminal law and criminal proceedings with a view to taking all investigative and other measures necessary for the detection and prosecution of criminal offences, without there being a need to notify such measures to the Commission.

(27) This Directive, together with the future Directive of the European Parliament and of the Council concerning the distance marketing of consumer financial services, contributes to the creating of a legal framework for the on-line provision of financial services; this Directive does not pre-empt future initiatives in the area of financial services in particular with regard to the harmonisation of rules of conduct in this field; the possibility for Member States, established in this Directive, under certain circumstances of restricting the freedom to provide information society services in order to protect consumers also covers measures in the area of financial services in particular measures aiming at protecting investors.

(28) The Member States' obligation not to subject access to the activity of an information society service provider to prior authorisation does not concern postal services covered by Directive 97/67/EC of the European Parliament and of the Council of 15 December 1997 on common rules for the development of the internal market of Community postal services and the improvement of quality of service[23] consisting of the physical delivery of a printed electronic mail message and does not affect

voluntary accreditation systems, in particular for providers of electronic signature certification service.

(29) Commercial communications are essential for the financing of information society services and for developing a wide variety of new, charge-free services; in the interests of consumer protection and fair trading, commercial communications, including discounts, promotional offers and promotional competitions or games, must meet a number of transparency requirements; these requirements are without prejudice to Directive 97/7/EC; this Directive should not affect existing Directives on commercial communications, in particular Directive 98/43/EC.

(30) The sending of unsolicited commercial communications by electronic mail may be undesirable for consumers and information society service providers and may disrupt the smooth functioning of interactive networks; the question of consent by recipient of certain forms of unsolicited commercial communications is not addressed by this Directive, but has already been addressed, in particular, by Directive 97/7/EC and by Directive 97/66/EC; in Member States which authorise unsolicited commercial communications by electronic mail, the setting up of appropriate industry filtering initiatives should be encouraged and facilitated; in addition it is necessary that in any event unsolicited commercial communities are clearly identifiable as such in order to improve transparency and to facilitate the functioning of such industry initiatives; unsolicited commercial communications by electronic mail should not result in additional communication costs for the recipient.

(31) Member States which allow the sending of unsolicited commercial communications by electronic mail without prior consent of the recipient by service providers established in their territory have to ensure that the service providers consult regularly and respect the opt-out registers in which natural persons not wishing to receive such commercial communications can register themselves.

(32) In order to remove barriers to the development of cross-border services within the Community which members of the regulated professions might offer on the Internet, it is necessary that compliance be guaranteed at Community level with professional rules aiming, in particular, to protect consumers or public health; codes of conduct at Community level would be the best means of determining the rules on professional ethics applicable to commercial communication; the drawing-up or, where appropriate, the adaptation of such rules should be encouraged without prejudice to the autonomy of professional bodies and associations.

(33) This Directive complements Community law and national law relating to regulated professions maintaining a coherent set of applicable rules in this field.

(34) Each Member State is to amend its legislation containing requirements, and in particular requirements as to form, which are likely to curb the use of contracts by electronic means; the examination of the legislation requiring such adjustment should be systematic and should cover all the necessary stages and acts of the contractual process, including the filing of the contract; the result of this amendment should be to make contracts concluded

electronically workable; the legal effect of electronic signatures is dealt with by Directive 1999/93/EC of the European Parliament and of the Council of 13 December 1999 on a Community framework for electronic signatures([24]); the acknowledgement of receipt by a service provider may take the form of the on-line provision of the service paid for.

(35) This Directive does not affect Member States' possibility of maintaining or establishing general or specific legal requirements for contracts which can be fulfilled by electronic means, in particular requirements concerning secure electronic signatures.

(36) Member States may maintain restrictions for the use of electronic contracts with regard to contracts requiring by law the involvement of courts, public authorities, or professions exercising public authority; this possibility also covers contracts which require the involvement of courts, public authorities, or professions exercising public authority in order to have an effect with regard to third parties as well as contracts requiring by law certification or attestation by a notary.

(37) Member States' obligation to remove obstacles to the use of electronic contracts concerns only obstacles resulting from legal requirements and not practical obstacles resulting from the impossibility of using electronic means in certain cases.

(38) Member States' obligation to remove obstacles to the use of electronic contracts is to be implemented in conformity with legal requirements for contracts enshrined in Community law.

(39) The exceptions to the provisions concerning the contracts concluded exclusively by electronic mail or by equivalent individual communications provided for by this Directive, in relation to information to be provided and the placing of orders, should not enable, as a result, the by-passing of those provisions by providers of information society services.

(40) Both existing and emerging disparities in Member States' legislation and case-law concerning liability of service providers acting as intermediaries prevent the smooth functioning of the internal market, in particular by impairing the development of cross-border services and producing distortions of competition; service providers have a duty to act, under certain circumstances, with a view to preventing or stopping illegal activities; this Directive should constitute the appropriate basis for the development of rapid and reliable procedures for removing and disabling access to illegal information; such mechanisms could be developed on the basis of voluntary agreements between all parties concerned and should be encouraged by Member States; it is in the interest of all parties involved in the provision of information society services to adopt and implement such procedures; the provisions of this Directive relating to liability should not preclude the development and effective operation, by the different interested parties, of technical systems of protection and identification and of technical surveillance instruments made possible by digital technology within the limits laid down by Directives 95/46/EC and 97/66/EC.

(41) This Directive strikes a balance between the different interests at

stake and establishes principles upon which industry agreements and standards can be based.

(42) The exemptions from liability established in this Directive cover only cases where the activity of the information society service provider is limited to the technical process of operating and giving access to a communication network over which information made available by third parties is transmitted or temporarily stored, for the sole purpose of making the transmission more efficient; this activity is of a mere technical, automatic and passive nature, which implies that the information society service provider has neither knowledge of nor control over the information which is transmitted or stored.

(43) A service provider can benefit from the exemptions for 'mere conduit' and for 'caching' when he is in no way involved with the information transmitted; this requires among other things that he does not modify the information that he transmits; this requirement does not cover manipulations of a technical nature which take place in the course of the transmission as they do not alter the integrity of the information contained in the transmission.

(44) A service provider who deliberately collaborates with one of the recipients of his service in order to undertake illegal acts goes beyond the activities of 'mere conduit' or 'caching' and as a result cannot benefit from the liability exemptions established for these activities.

(45) The limitations of the liability of intermediary service providers established in this Directive do not affect the possibility of injunctions of different kinds; such injunctions can in particular consist of orders by courts or administrative authorities requiring the termination or prevention of any infringement, including the removal of illegal information or the disabling of access to it.

(46) In order to benefit from a limitation of liability, the provider of an information society service, consisting of the storage of information, upon obtaining actual knowledge or awareness of illegal activities has to act expeditiously to remove or to disable access to the information concerned; the removal or disabling of access has to be undertaken in the observance of the principle of freedom of expression and of procedures established for this purpose at national level; this Directive does not affect Member States' possibility of establishing specific requirements which must be fulfilled expeditiously prior to the removal or disabling of information.

(47) Member States are prevented from imposing a monitoring obligation on service providers only with respect to obligations of a general nature; this does not concern monitoring obligations in a specific case and, in particular, does not affect orders by national authorities in accordance with national legislation.

(48) This Directive does not affect the possibility for Member States of requiring service providers, who host information provided by recipients of their service, to apply duties of care, which can reasonably be expected from them and which are specified by national law, in order to detect and prevent certain types of illegal activities.

(49) Member States and the Commission are to encourage the drawing-up of codes of conduct; this is not to impair the voluntary nature of such

codes and the possibility for interested parties of deciding freely whether to adhere to such codes.

(50) It is important that the proposed directive on the harmonisation of certain aspects of copyright and related rights in the information society and this Directive come into force within a similar time scale with a view to establishing a clear framework of rules relevant to the issue of liability of intermediaries for copyright and relating rights infringements at Community level.

(51) Each Member State should be required, where necessary, to amend any legislation which is liable to hamper the use of schemes for the out-of-court settlement of disputes through electronic channels; the result of this amendment must be to make the functioning of such schemes genuinely and effectively possible in law and in practice, even across borders.

(52) The effective exercise of the freedoms of the internal market makes it necessary to guarantee victims effective access to means of settling disputes; damage which may arise in connection with information society services is characterised both by its rapidity and by its geographical extent; in view of this specific character and the need to ensure that national authorities do not endanger the mutual confidence which they should have in one another, this Directive requests Member States to ensure that appropriate court actions are available; Member States should examine the need to provide access to judicial procedures by appropriate electronic means.

(53) Directive 98/27/EC, which is applicable to information society services, provides a mechanism relating to actions for an injunction aimed at the protection of the collective interests of consumers; this mechanism will contribute to the free movement of information society services by ensuring a high level of consumer protection.

(54) The sanctions provided for under this Directive are without prejudice to any other sanction or remedy provided under national law; Member States are not obliged to provide criminal sanctions for infringement of national provisions adopted pursuant to this Directive.

(55) This Directive does not affect the law applicable to contractual obligations relating to consumer contracts; accordingly, this Directive cannot have the result of depriving the consumer of the protection afforded to him by the mandatory rules relating to contractual obligations of the law of the Member State in which he has his habitual residence.

(56) As regards the derogation contained in this Directive regarding contractual obligations concerning contracts concluded by consumers, those obligations should be interpreted as including information on the essential elements of the content of the contract, including consumer rights, which have a determining influence on the decision to contract.

(57) The Court of Justice has consistently held that a Member State retains the right to take measures against a service provider that is established in another Member State but directs all or most of his activity to the territory of the first Member State if the choice of establishment was made with a view to evading the legislation that would have applied to the provider had he been established on the territory of the first Member State.

(58) This Directive should not apply to services supplied by service providers established in a third country; in view of the global dimension of electronic commerce, it is, however, appropriate to ensure that the Community rules are consistent with international rules; this Directive is without prejudice to the results of discussions within international organisations (amongst others WTO, OECD, Uncitral) on legal issues.

(59) Despite the global nature of electronic communications, coordination of national regulatory measures at European Union level is necessary in order to avoid fragmentation of the internal market, and for the establishment of an appropriate European regulatory framework; such coordination should also contribute to the establishment of a common and strong negotiating position in international forums.

(60) In order to allow the unhampered development of electronic commerce, the legal framework must be clear and simple, predictable and consistent with the rules applicable at international level so that it does not adversely affect the competitiveness of European industry or impede innovation in that sector.

(61) If the market is actually to operate by electronic means in the context of globalisation, the European Union and the major non-European areas need to consult each other with a view to making laws and procedures compatible.

(62) Cooperation with third countries should be strengthened in the area of electronic commerce, in particular with applicant countries, the developing countries and the European Union's other trading partners.

(63) The adoption of this Directive will not prevent the Member States from taking into account the various social, societal and cultural implications which are inherent in the advent of the information society; in particular it should not hinder measures which Member States might adopt in conformity with Community law to achieve social, cultural and democratic goals taking into account their linguistic diversity, national and regional specificities as well as their cultural heritage, and to ensure and maintain public access to the widest possible range of information society services; in any case, the development of the information society is to ensure that Community citizens can have access to the cultural European heritage provided in the digital environment.

(64) Electronic communication offers the Member States an excellent means of providing public services in the cultural, educational and linguistic fields.

(65) The Council, in its resolution of 19 January 1999 on the consumer dimension of the information society[25], stressed that the protection of consumers deserved special attention in this field; the Commission will examine the degree to which existing consumer protection rules provide insufficient protection in the context of the information society and will identify, where necessary, the deficiencies of this legislation and those issues which could require additional measures; if need be, the Commission should make specific additional proposals to resolve such deficiencies that will thereby have been identified,

HAVE ADOPTED THIS DIRECTIVE:

CHAPTER 1

GENERAL PROVISIONS

Article 1

Objective and scope

1. This Directive seeks to contribute to the proper functioning of the internal market by ensuring the free movement of information society services between the Member States.

2. This Directive approximates, to the extent necessary for the achievement of the objective set out in paragraph 1, certain national provisions on information society services relating to the internal market, the establishment of service providers, commercial communications, electronic contracts, the liability of intermediaries, codes of conduct, out-of-court dispute settlements, court actions and cooperation between Member States.

3. This Directive complements Community law applicable to information society services without prejudice to the level of protection for, in particular, public health and consumer interests, as established by Community acts and national legislation implementing them in so far as this does not restrict the freedom to provide information society services.

4. This Directive does not establish additional rules on private international law nor does it deal with the jurisdiction of Courts.

5. This Directive shall not apply to:

(a) the field of taxation;

(b) questions relating to information society services covered by Directives 95/46/EC and 97/66/EC;

(c) questions relating to agreements or practices governed by cartel law;

(d) the following activities of information society services:

— the activities of notaries or equivalent professions to the extent that they involve a direct and specific connection with the exercise of public authority,

— the representation of a client and defence of his interests before the courts,

— gambling activities which involve wagering a stake with monetary value in games of chance, including lotteries and betting transactions.

6. This Directive does not affect measures taken at Community or national level, in the respect of Community law, in order to promote cultural and linguistic diversity and to ensure the defence of pluralism.

Article 2

Definitions

For the purpose of this Directive, the following terms shall bear the following meanings:

(a) 'information society services': services within the meaning of Article 1(2) of Directive 98/34/EC as amended by Directive 98/48/EC;

(b) 'service provider': any natural or legal person providing an information society service;

(c) 'established service provider': a service provider who effectively pursues an economic activity using a fixed establishment for an indefinite period. The presence and use of the technical means and technologies required to provide the service do not, in themselves, constitute an establishment of the provider;

(d) 'recipient of the service': any natural or legal person who, for professional ends or otherwise, uses an information society service, in particular for the purposes of seeking information or making it accessible;

(e) 'consumer': any natural person who is acting for purposes which are outside his or her trade, business or profession;

(f) 'commercial communication': any form of communication designed to promote, directly or indirectly, the goods, services or image of a company, organisation or person pursuing a commercial, industrial or craft activity or exercising a regulated profession. The following do not in themselves constitute commercial communications:

— information allowing direct access to the activity of the company, organisation or person, in particular a domain name or an electronic-mail address,

— communications relating to the goods, services or image of the company, organisation or person compiled in an independent manner, particularly when this is without financial consideration;

(g) 'regulated profession': any profession within the meaning of either Article 1(d) of Council Directive 89/48/EEC of 21 December 1988 on a general system for the recognition of higher-education diplomas awarded on completion of professional education and training of at least three-years' duration([26]) or of Article 1(f) of Council Directive 92/51/EEC of 18 June 1992 on a second general system for the recognition of professional education and training to supplement Directive 89/48/EEC([27]);

(h) 'coordinated field': requirements laid down in Member States' legal systems applicable to information society service providers or information society services, regardless of whether they are of a general nature or specifically designed for them.

(i)   The coordinated field concerns requirements with which the service provider has to comply in respect of:

— the taking up of the activity of an information society service, such as requirements concerning qualifications, authorisation or notification,

— the pursuit of the activity of an information society service, such as requirements concerning the behaviour of the service provider, requirements regarding the quality or content of the service including those applicable to advertising and contracts, or requirements concerning the liability of the service provider;

(ii) The coordinated field does not cover requirements such as:

— requirements applicable to goods as such,

— requirements applicable to the delivery of goods,

— requirements applicable to services not provided by electronic means.

Article 3

Internal market

1.   Each Member State shall ensure that the information society services provided by a service provider established on its territory comply with the national provisions applicable in the Member State in question which fall within the coordinated field.

2.   Member States may not, for reasons falling within the coordinated field, restrict the freedom to provide information society services from another Member State.

3.   Paragraphs 1 and 2 shall not apply to the fields referred to in the Annex.

4.   Member States may take measures to derogate from paragraph 2 in respect of a given information society service if the following conditions are fulfilled:

(a) the measures shall be:

  (i)   necessary for one of the following reasons:

     — public policy, in particular the prevention, investigation, detection and prosecution of criminal offences, including the protection of minors and the fight against any incitement to hatred on grounds of race, sex, religion or nationality, and violations of human dignity concerning individual persons,

     — the protection of public health,

     — public security, including the safeguarding of national security and defence,

     — the protection of consumers, including investors;

  (ii) taken against a given information society service which prejudices the objectives referred to in point (i) or which presents a serious and grave risk of prejudice to those objectives;

  (iii) proportionate to those objectives;

(b) before taking the measures in question and without prejudice to court proceedings, including preliminary proceedings and acts carried out in the framework of a criminal investigation, the Member State has:

  — asked the Member State referred to in paragraph 1 to take measures and the latter did not take such measures, or they were inadequate,

  — notified the Commission and the Member State referred to in paragraph 1 of its intention to take such measures.

5.   Member States may, in the case of urgency, derogate from the conditions stipulated in paragraph 4(b). Where this is the case, the measures shall be notified in the shortest possible time to the Commission and to the Member State referred to in paragraph 1, indicating the reasons for which the Member State considers that there is urgency.

6.   Without prejudice to the Member State's possibility of proceeding with the measures in question, the Commission shall examine the compatibility of the notified measures with Community law in the shortest possible time; where it comes to the conclusion that the measure is incompatible with Community law, the Commission shall ask the Member State in question to refrain from taking any proposed measures or urgently to put an end to the measures in question.

CHAPTER II

PRINCIPLES

Section 1: Establishment and information requirements

Article 4

Principle excluding prior authorisation

1.   Member States shall ensure that the taking up and pursuit of the activity of

an information society service provider may not be made subject to prior authorisation or any other requirement having equivalent effect.

2. Paragraph 1 shall be without prejudice to authorisation schemes which are not specifically and exclusively targeted at information society services, or which are covered by Directive 97/13/EC of the European Parliament and of the Council of 10 April 1997 on a common framework for general authorisations and individual licences in the field of telecommunications services([28]).

Article 5

General information to be provided

1. In addition to other information requirements established by Community law, Member States shall ensure that the service provider shall render easily, directly and permanently accessible to the recipients of the service and competent authorities, at least the following information:

(a) the name of the service provider;

(b) the geographic address at which the service provider is established;

(c) the details of the service provider, including his electronic mail address, which allow him to be contacted rapidly and communicated with in a direct and effective manner;

(d) where the service provider is registered in a trade or similar public register, the trade register in which the service provider is entered and his registration number, or equivalent means of identification in that register;

(e) where the activity is subject to an authorisation scheme, the particulars of the relevant supervisory authority;

(f) as concerns the regulated professions:

— any professional body or similar institution with which the service provider is registered,

— the professional title and the Member State where it has been granted,

— a reference to the applicable professional rules in the Member State of establishment and the means to access them;

(g) where the service provider undertakes an activity that is subject to VAT, the identification number referred to in Article 22(1) of the sixth Council Directive 77/388/EEC of 17 May 1977 on the harmonisation of the laws of the Member States relating to turnover taxes — Common system of value added tax: uniform basis of assessment([29]).

2. In addition to other information requirements established by Community law, Member States shall at least ensure that, where information society services refer to prices, these are to be indicated clearly and unambiguously and, in particular, must indicate whether they are inclusive of tax and delivery costs.

Section 2: Commercial communications

Article 6

Information to be provided

In addition to other information requirements established by Community law, Member States shall ensure that commercial communications which are part of, or constitute, an information society service comply at least with the following conditions:

(a) the commercial communication shall be clearly identifiable as such;

(b) the natural or legal person on whose behalf the commercial communication is made shall be clearly identifiable;

(c) promotional offers, such as discounts, premiums and gifts, where permitted in the Member State where the service provider is established, shall be clearly identifiable as such, and the conditions which are to be met to qualify for them shall be easily accessible and be presented clearly and unambiguously;

(d) promotional competitions or games, where permitted in the Member State where the service provider is established, shall be clearly identifiable as such, and the conditions for participation shall be easily accessible and be presented clearly and unambiguously.

Article 7

Unsolicited commercial communication

1. In addition to other requirements established by Community law, Member States which permit unsolicited commercial communication by electronic mail shall ensure that such commercial communication by a service provider established in their territory shall be identifiable clearly and unambiguously as such as soon as it is received by the recipient.

2. Without prejudice to Directive 97/7/EC and Directive 97/66/EC, Member States shall take measures to ensure that service providers undertaking unsolicited commercial communications by electronic mail consult regularly and respect the opt-out registers in which natural persons not wishing to receive such commercial communications can register themselves.

Article 8

Regulated professions

1. Member States shall ensure that the use of commercial communications which are part of, or constitute, an information society service provided by a member of a regulated profession is permitted subject to compliance with the professional rules regarding, in particular, the independence, dignity and honour of the profession, professional secrecy and fairness towards clients and other members of the profession.

2. Without prejudice to the autonomy of professional bodies and associations, Member States and the Commission shall encourage professional associations and bodies to establish codes of conduct at Community level in order to determine the types of information that can be given for the purposes of commercial communication in conformity with the rules referred to in paragraph 1.

3. When drawing up proposals for Community initiatives which may become necessary to ensure the proper functioning of the Internal Market with regard to the information referred to in paragraph 2, the Commission shall take due account of codes of conduct applicable at Community level and shall act in close cooperation with the relevant professional associations and bodies.

4. This Directive shall apply in addition to Community Directives concerning access to, and the exercise of, activities of the regulated professions.

Section 3: Contracts concluded by electronic means

Article 9

Treatment of contracts

1. Member States shall ensure that their legal system allows contracts to be concluded by electronic means. Member States shall in particular ensure that the legal requirements applicable to the contractual process neither create obstacles for the use of electronic contracts nor result in such contracts being deprived of legal effectiveness and validity on account of their having been made by electronic means.

2.   Member States may lay down that paragraph 1 shall not apply to all or certain contracts falling into one of the following categories:

(a) contracts that create or transfer rights in real estate, except for rental rights;

(b) contracts requiring by law the involvement of courts, public authorities or professions exercising public authority;

(c) contracts of suretyship granted and on collateral securities furnished by persons acting for purposes outside their trade, business or profession;

(d) contracts governed by family law or by the law of succession.

3.   Member States shall indicate to the Commission the categories referred to in paragraph 2 to which they do not apply paragraph 1. Member States shall submit to the Commission every five years a report on the application of paragraph 2 explaining the reasons why they consider it necessary to maintain the category referred to in paragraph 2(b) to which they do not apply paragraph 1.

Article 10

Information to be provided

1.   In addition to other information requirements established by Community law, Member States shall ensure, except when otherwise agreed by parties who are not consumers, that at least the following information is given by the service provider clearly, comprehensibly and unambiguously and prior to the order being placed by the recipient of the service:

(a) the different technical steps to follow to conclude the contract;

(b) whether or not the concluded contract will be filed by the service provider and whether it will be accessible;

(c) the technical means for identifying and correcting input errors prior to the placing of the order;

(d) the languages offered for the conclusion of the contract.

2.   Member States shall ensure that, except when otherwise agreed by parties who are not consumers, the service provider indicates any relevant codes of conduct to which he subscribes and information on how those codes can be consulted electronically.

3.   Contract terms and general conditions provided to the recipient must be made available in a way that allows him to store and reproduce them.

4.   Paragraphs 1 and 2 shall not apply to contracts concluded exclusively by exchange of electronic mail or by equivalent individual communications.

Article 11

Placing of the order

1.   Member States shall ensure, except when otherwise agreed by parties who are not consumers, that in cases where the recipient of the service places his order through technological means, the following principles apply:

— the service provider has to acknowledge the receipt of the recipient's order without undue delay and by electronic means,

— the order and the acknowledgement of receipt are deemed to be received when the parties to whom they are addressed are able to access them.

2.   Member States shall ensure that, except when otherwise agreed by parties who are not consumers, the service provider makes available to the recipient of the service appropriate, effective and

accessible technical means allowing him to identify and correct input errors, prior to the placing of the order.

3.   Paragraph 1, first indent, and paragraph 2 shall not apply to contracts concluded exclusively by exchange of electronic mail or by equivalent individual communications.

Section 4: Liability of intermediary service providers

Article 12

'Mere conduit'

1.   Where an information society service is provided that consists of the transmission in a communication network of information provided by a recipient of the service, or the provision of access to a communication network, Member States shall ensure that the service provider is not liable for the information transmitted, on condition that the provider:

(a) does not initiate the transmission;

(b) does not select the receiver of the transmission; and

(c) does not select or modify the information contained in the transmission.

2.   The acts of transmission and of provision of access referred to in paragraph 1 include the automatic, intermediate and transient storage of the information transmitted in so far as this takes place for the sole purpose of carrying out the transmission in the communication network, and provided that the information is not stored for any period longer than is reasonably necessary for the transmission.

3.   This Article shall not affect the possibility for a court or administrative authority, in accordance with Member States' legal systems, of requiring the service

provider to terminate or prevent an infringement.

Article 13

'Caching'

1.   Where an information society service is provided that consists of the transmission in a communication network of information provided by a recipient of the service, Member States shall ensure that the service provider is not liable for the automatic, intermediate and temporary storage of that information, performed for the sole purpose of making more efficient the information's onward transmission to other recipients of the service upon their request, on condition that:

(a) the provider does not modify the information;

(b) the provider complies with conditions on access to the information;

(c) the provider complies with rules regarding the updating of the information, specified in a manner widely recognised and used by industry;

(d) the provider does not interfere with the lawful use of technology, widely recognised and used by industry, to obtain data on the use of the information; and

(e) the provider acts expeditiously to remove or to disable access to the information it has stored upon obtaining actual knowledge of the fact that the information at the initial source of the transmission has been removed from the network, or access to it has been disabled, or that a court or an administrative authority has ordered such removal or disablement.

2.   This Article shall not affect the possibility for a court or administrative authority, in accordance with Member States'

legal systems, of requiring the service provider to terminate or prevent an infringement.

Article 14

Hosting

1. Where an information society service is provided that consists of the storage of information provided by a recipient of the service, Member States shall ensure that the service provider is not liable for the information stored at the request of a recipient of the service, on condition that:

(a) the provider does not have actual knowledge of illegal activity or information and, as regards claims for damages, is not aware of facts or circumstances from which the illegal activity or information is apparent; or

(b) the provider, upon obtaining such knowledge or awareness, acts expeditiously to remove or to disable access to the information.

2. Paragraph 1 shall not apply when the recipient of the service is acting under the authority or the control of the provider.

3. This Article shall not affect the possibility for a court or administrative authority, in accordance with Member States' legal systems, of requiring the service provider to terminate or prevent an infringement, nor does it affect the possibility for Member States of establishing procedures governing the removal or disabling of access to information.

Article 15

No general obligation to monitor

1. Member States shall not impose a general obligation on providers, when providing the services covered by Articles 12, 13 and 14, to monitor the information which they transmit or store, nor a general obligation actively to seek facts or circumstances indicating illegal activity.

2. Member States may establish obligations for information society service providers promptly to inform the competent public authorities of alleged illegal activities undertaken or information provided by recipients of their service or obligations to communicate to the competent authorities, at their request, information enabling the identification of recipients of their service with whom they have storage agreements.

CHAPTER III

IMPLEMENTATION

Article 16

Codes of conduct

1. Member States and the Commission shall encourage:

(a) the drawing up of codes of conduct at Community level, by trade, professional and consumer associations or organisations, designed to contribute to the proper implementation of Articles 5 to 15;

(b) the voluntary transmission of draft codes of conduct at national or Community level to the Commission;

(c) the accessibility of these codes of conduct in the Community languages by electronic means;

(d) the communication to the Member States and the Commission, by trade, professional and consumer associations or organisations, of their assessment of the application of their codes of conduct and their impact upon practices, habits or customs relating to electronic commerce;

(e) the drawing up of codes of conduct regarding the protection of minors and human dignity.

2. Member States and the Commission shall encourage the involvement of associations or organisations representing consumers in the drafting and implementation of codes of conduct affecting their interests and drawn up in accordance with paragraph 1(a). Where appropriate, to take account of their specific needs, associations representing the visually impaired and disabled should be consulted.

Article 17

Out-of-court dispute settlement

1. Member States shall ensure that, in the event of disagreement between an information society service provider and the recipient of the service, their legislation does not hamper the use of out-of-court schemes, available under national law, for dispute settlement, including appropriate electronic means.

2. Member States shall encourage bodies responsible for the out-of-court settlement of, in particular, consumer disputes to operate in a way which provides adequate procedural guarantees for the parties concerned.

3. Member States shall encourage bodies responsible for out-of-court dispute settlement to inform the Commission of the significant decisions they take regarding information society services and to transmit any other information on the practices, usages or customs relating to electronic commerce.

Article 18

Court actions

1. Member States shall ensure that court actions available under national law concerning information society services'

activities allow for the rapid adoption of measures, including interim measures, designed to terminate any alleged infringement and to prevent any further impairment of the interests involved.

2. The Annex to Directive 98/27/EC shall be supplemented as follows:

'11. Directive 2000/31/EC of the European Parliament and of the Council of 8 June 2000 on certain legal aspects on information society services, in particular electronic commerce, in the internal market (Directive on electronic commerce) (OJ L 178, 17.7.2000, p. 1).'

Article 19

Cooperation

1. Member States shall have adequate means of supervision and investigation necessary to implement this Directive effectively and shall ensure that service providers supply them with the requisite information.

2. Member States shall cooperate with other Member States; they shall, to that end, appoint one or several contact points, whose details they shall communicate to the other Member States and to the Commission.

3. Member States shall, as quickly as possible, and in conformity with national law, provide the assistance and information requested by other Member States or by the Commission, including by appropriate electronic means.

4. Member States shall establish contact points which shall be accessible at least by electronic means and from which recipients and service providers may:

(a) obtain general information on contractual rights and obligations as well as on the complaint and redress mechanisms available in the event of disputes, including practical aspects involved in the use of such mechanisms;

(b) obtain the details of authorities, associations or organisations from which they may obtain further information or practical assistance.

5. Member States shall encourage the communication to the Commission of any significant administrative or judicial decisions taken in their territory regarding disputes relating to information society services and practices, usages and customs relating to electronic commerce. The Commission shall communicate these decisions to the other Member States.

Article 20

Sanctions

Member States shall determine the sanctions applicable to infringements of national provisions adopted pursuant to this Directive and shall take all measures necessary to ensure that they are enforced. The sanctions they provide for shall be effective, proportionate and dissuasive.

CHAPTER IV

FINAL PROVISIONS

Article 21

Re-examination

1. Before 17 July 2003, and thereafter every two years, the Commission shall submit to the European Parliament, the Council and the Economic and Social Committee a report on the application of this Directive, accompanied, where necessary, by proposals for adapting it to legal, technical and economic developments in the field of information society services, in particular with respect to crime prevention, the protection of minors, consumer protection and to the proper functioning of the internal market.

2. In examining the need for an adaptation of this Directive, the report shall in particular analyse the need for proposals concerning the liability of providers of hyperlinks and location tool services, 'notice and take down' procedures and the attribution of liability following the taking down of content. The report shall also analyse the need for additional conditions for the exemption from liability, provided for in Articles 12 and 13, in the light of technical developments, and the possibility of applying the internal market principles to unsolicited commercial communications by electronic mail.

Article 22

Transposition

1. Member States shall bring into force the laws, regulations and administrative provisions necessary to comply with this Directive before 17 January 2002. They shall forthwith inform the Commission thereof.

2. When Member States adopt the measures referred to in paragraph 1, these shall contain a reference to this Directive or shall be accompanied by such reference at the time of their official publication. The methods of making such reference shall be laid down by Member States.

Article 23

Entry into force

This Directive shall enter into force on the day of its publication in the Official Journal of the European Communities.

Article 24

Addressees

This Directive is addressed to the Member States.

Done at Luxemburg, 8 June 2000.

For the European Parliament

The President

N. FONTAINE

For the Council

The President

G. d'OLIVEIRA MARTINS

ANNEX

DEROGATIONS FROM ARTICLE 3

As provided for in Article 3(3), Article 3(1) and (2) do not apply to:

— copyright, neighbouring rights, rights referred to in Directive 87/54/EEC([30]) and Directive 96/9/EC([31]) as well as industrial property rights,

— the emission of electronic money by institutions in respect of which Member States have applied one of the derogations provided for in Article 8(1) of Directive 2000/46/EC([32]),

— Article 44(2) of Directive 85/611/EEC([33]),

— Article 30 and Title IV of Directive 92/49/EEC([34]), Title IV of Directive 92/96/EEC([35]), Articles 7 and 8 of Directive 88/357/EEC([36]) and Article 4 of Directive 90/619/EEC([37]),

— the freedom of the parties to choose the law applicable to their contract,

— contractual obligations concerning consumer contacts,

— formal validity of contracts creating or transferring rights in real estate where such contracts are subject to mandatory formal requirements of the law of the Member State where the real estate is situated,

— the permissibility of unsolicited commercial communications by electronic mail.

([1]) OJ C 30, 5.2.1999, p. 4.
([2]) OJ C 169, 16.6.1999, p. 36.
([3]) Opinion of the European Parliament of 6 May 1999 (OJ C 279, 1.10.1999, p. 389), Council common position of 28 February 2000 (OJ C 128, 8.5.2000, p. 32) and Decision of the European Parliament of 4 May 2000 (not yet published in the Official Journal).
([4]) OJ L 298, 17.10.1989, p. 23. Directive as amended by Directive 97/36/EC of the European Parliament and of the Council (OJ L 202, 30.7.1997, p. 60).
([5]) OJ L 95, 21.4.1993, p. 29.
([6]) OJ L 144, 4.6.1999, p. 19.
([7]) OJ L 250, 19.9.1984, p. 17. Directive as amended by Directive 97/55/EC of the European Parliament and of the Council (OJ L 290, 23.10.1997, p. 18).
([8]) OJ L 42, 12.2.1987, p. 48. Directive as last amended by Directive 98/7/EC of the European Parliament and of the Council (OJ L 101, 1.4.1998, p. 17).
([9]) OJ L 141, 11.6.1993, p. 27. Directive as last amended by Directive 97/9/EC of the European Parliament and of the Council (OJ L 84, 26.3.1997, p. 22).
([10]) OJ L 158, 23.6.1990, p. 59.
([11]) OJ L 80, 18.3.1998, p. 27.
([12]) OJ L 228, 11.8.1992, p. 24.
([13]) OJ L 280, 29.10.1994, p. 83.
([14]) OJ L 166, 11.6.1998, p. 51. Directive as amended by Directive 1999/44/EC (OJ L 171, 7.7.1999, p. 12).
([15]) OJ L 210, 7.8.1985, p. 29. Directive as amended by Directive 1999/34/EC (OJ L 141, 4.6.1999, p. 20).
([16]) OJ L 171, 7.7.1999, p. 12.
([17]) OJ L 113, 30.4.1992, p. 13.
([18]) OJ L 213, 30.7.1998, p. 9.
([19]) OJ L 281, 23.11.1995, p. 31.
([20]) OJ L 24, 30.1.1998, p. 1.
([21]) OJ L 204, 21.7.1998, p. 37. Directive as amended by Directive 98/48/EC (OJ L 217, 5.8.1998, p. 18).
([22]) OJ L 320, 28.11.1998, p. 54.
([23]) OJ L 15, 21.1.1998, p. 14.
([24]) OJ L 13, 19.1.2000, p. 12.
([25]) OJ C 23, 28.1.1999, p. 1.
([26]) OJ L 19, 24.1.1989, p. 16.
([27]) OJ L 209, 24.7.1992, p. 25. Directive as last amended by Commission Directive 97/38/EC (OJ L 184, 12.7.1997, p. 31).
([28]) OJ L 117, 7.5.1997, p. 15.

(^{29}) OJ L 145, 13.6.1977, p. 1. Directive as last amended by Directive 1999/85/EC (OJ L 277, 28.10.1999, p. 34).

(^{30}) OJ L 24, 27.1.1987, p. 36.

(^{31}) OJ L 77, 27.3.1996, p. 20.

(^{32}) Not yet published in the Official Journal.

(^{33}) OJ L 375, 31.12.1985, p. 3. Directive as last amended by Directive 95/26/EC (OJ L 168, 18.7.1995, p. 7).

(^{34}) OJ L 228, 11.8.1992, p. 1. Directive as last amended by Directive 95/26/EC.

(^{35}) OJ L 360, 9.12.1992, p. 2. Directive as last amended by Directive 95/26/EC.

(^{36}) OJ L 172, 4.7.1988, p. 1. Directive as last amended by Directive 92/49/EC.

(^{37}) OJ L 330, 29.11.1990, p. 50. Directive as last amended by Directive 92/96/EC.

Index

Please note that page references to footnotes are followed by an 'n' and note number.